The Science Fiction Handbook

Literature and Culture Handbooks

General Editor: Philip Tew, Brunel University, UK

Literature and Culture Handbooks are an innovative series of guides to major periods, topics and authors in British and American literature and culture. Designed to provide a comprehensive, one-stop resource for literature students, each handbook provides the essential information and guidance needed from the beginning of a course through to developing more advanced knowledge and skills.

The Eighteenth-Century Literature Handbook
Edited by Gary Day and Bridge Keegan

The Medieval British Literature Handbook
Edited by Daniel T. Kline

The Modernism Handbook
Edited by Philip Tew and Alex Murray

The Post-War British Literature Handbook
Edited by Katharine Cockin and Jago Morrison

The Renaissance Literature Handbook
Edited by Susan Bruce and Rebecca Steinberger

The Seventeenth-Century Literature Handbook
Edited by Robert C. Evans and Eric J. Sterling

The Shakespeare Handbook
Edited by Andrew Hiscock and Stephen Longstaffe

The Victorian Literature Handbook
Edited by Alexandra Warwick and Martin Willis

The Romanticism Handbook
Edited by Sue Chaplin and Joel Faflak

The Science Fiction Handbook

Edited by

Nick Hubble

and

Aris Mousoutzanis

B L O O M S B U R Y

LONDON • NEW DELHI • NEW YORK • SYDNEY

Bloomsbury Academic
An imprint of Bloomsbury Publishing Plc

50 Bedford Square	1385 Broadway
London	New York
WC1B 3DP	NY 10018
UK	USA

www.bloomsbury.com

Bloomsbury is a registered trade mark of Bloomsbury Publishing Plc

First published 2013

© Nick Hubble and Aris Mousoutzanis, 2013

British Library Cataloguing-in-Publication Data
A catalogue record for this book is available from the British Library.

ISBN: PB: 978-1-4411-7096-5
    HB: 978-1-4411-9769-6
  ePub: 978-1-4725-3896-3
  ePDF: 978-1-4725-3897-0

Library of Congress Cataloging-in-Publication Data
The Science Fiction Handbook / edited by Nick Hubble and Aris Mousoutzanis.
    pages cm. – (Literature and Culture Handbooks)
    ISBN 978-1-4411-9769-6 (hardback) – ISBN 978-1-4411-7096-5 (paperback) – ISBN 978-1-4725-3896-3 (epub) 1. Science fiction–Handbooks, manuals, etc. 2. Science fiction–Study and teaching. I. Hubble, Nick, 1965- editor of compilation. II. Mousoutzanis, Aristeidis, editor of compilation.
    PN3433.5.S326 2013
    809.3'8762–dc23
                    2013028956

Typeset by Fakenham Prepress Solutions, Fakenham, Norfolk NR21 8NN
Printed and bound in Great Britain

To Sara, Max and Alex

To Robert

Contents

Acknowledgments

Thanks to all of our contributors (especially Chris Daley for stepping in at short notice) and to Philip Tew, the series editor, and everyone at Bloomsbury including David Avital, Laura Murray and Mark Richardson.

Thanks also to Steve Bastow, Fred Botting, Mark Bould, Monica Germaná, Andrea Hammel, Emily Horton, Ewan Kirkland, Roger Luckhurst, Bill Rees, Justin Sausman, Katrina Sluis, Alex Warwick and Aybige Yilmaz.

Notes on Contributors

Andrew M. Butler is the author of *Solar Flares: Science Fiction in the1970s*, and books on Philip K. Dick, Cyberpunk, Postmodernism, Terry Pratchett and Film Studies, as well as articles on *The Man Who Fell to Earth*, Jeff Noon and Iain Banks. He is the co-editor of *The Routledge Companion to Science Fiction, Fifty Key Figures in Science Fiction, Terry Pratchett: Guilty of Literature, The True Knowledge of Ken MacLeod* and the journal *Extrapolation*. He is chair of judges for the Arthur C. Clarke Award.

Christopher Daley is a final year PhD candidate at the University of Westminster. His thesis focuses on the influence of the Cold War on British science fiction between 1945 and 1969. He was previously co-organizer of the international conference 'The Apocalypse and Discontents' held at the University of Westminster in 2010. Christopher has book chapters forthcoming on J. G. Ballard, Brian Aldiss and British disaster fiction; whilst he is also a regular contributor to the online open access journal *Alluvium*.

Roby Duncan is a student of philosophy and linguistics, focusing on philosophy of mind and the cognitive sciences at California State University at Dominguez Hills. Roby is a two-time presenter at the International Conference on the Fantastic in the Arts. He resides in Los Angeles, California, where he also works as a data curator for YouTube.

Emma Filtness teaches Creative Writing at Brunel University. She is currently studying for a PhD in Creative Writing, exploring the intersection of fiction and lived experience in contemporary women's life writing, producing a series of 'biografictions'. Her poetry recently featured in issue nine of *Popshot Magazine: The Illustrated Magazine of New Writing*. Emma is co-founder of the Brunel Faeries and Flying Saucers SF and fantasy research cluster.

David M. Higgins specializes in twentieth-century American literature and culture, and his research exposes transformations in imperial fantasy that occur within science fiction during the Cold War. His article 'Toward a Cosmopolitan Science Fiction' (published in the June 2011 issue of *American Literature*) won the 2012 SFRA Pioneer Award for excellence in scholarship, and he has also co-edited a special issue of *Science Fiction Studies* on "Science Fiction and Globalization" (November 2012). David is a Division Head for the International Association for the Fantastic in the Arts and a full time faculty member at Inver Hills Community College in Minnesota.

Nick Hubble is Head of English at Brunel University, London, UK. He is the author of *Mass-Observation and Everyday Life: Culture, History, Theory* (Palgrave Macmillan, 2006; second edition 2010) and has written articles on SF for *Extrapolation*, *Foundation*, and *Vector*. Other publications include 'Historical Psychology, Utopian Dreams and Other Fool's Errands' in *Modernist Cultures* 3: 2 (2008); 'The Intermodern Assumption of the Future: William Empson and Mass-Observation' in Kristin Bluemel (ed.), *Intermodernism* (Edinburgh University Press, 2009); and 'Naomi Mitchison: Fantasy and Intermodern Utopia' in Alice Reeve-Tucker and Nathan Waddell, eds, *Utopianism and Twentieth-Century Literary Cultures* (Palgrave Macmillan, 2013).

Jessica Langer received her PhD from Royal Holloway, University of London in 2009. She is the author of *Postcolonialism and Science Fiction* (London and New York: Palgrave, 2012) and has published widely on postcolonial theory and practice and science fiction literature, film, video games and other media. She currently lives and works in Toronto, Canada.

Aris Mousoutzanis is a Lecturer in Film and Screen Studies at the University of Brighton. He has researched and published on apocalyptic science fiction, the Gothic, *fin-de-siècle* literature and postmodern culture. His forthcoming monograph on *Fin-de-Siècle Fictions: 1890s–1990s* is due to be published by Palgrave in 2014, while he is currently co-editing a collection on *The Apocalypse and its Discontents* (2014). He has co-edited two collections on *Cybercultures* (ID-Net, 2010) and *New Media and the Politics of Online Communities* (Rodopi, 2012), whereas his next research project concentrates on the relations between trauma theory and media culture.

Joseph Norman teaches Literature and Creative Writing at Brunel University; his PhD examines Iain M. Banks's 'Culture' series. Other research interests include relations between music and literature; speculative and transgressive fiction. Co-founder of the Brunel Faeries and Flying Saucers SF and fantasy research cluster. Publications include: '"Sounds which filled me with an indefinable dread": The Cthulhu Mythopoeia of H. P. Lovecraft in Extreme Metal', in David Simmons (ed.), *New Critical Essays on H. P. Lovecraft* (Palgrave,

2013); and "Digital Souls and Virtual Afterlives in Iain M. Banks' 'Culture' Series" in Martyn Colebrook and Katharine Cox (ed.), *The Transgressive Iain Banks* (McFarland, 2013).

Adam Roberts is the author or co-editor of various critical works on Science Fiction, including *The Palgrave History of Science Fiction* (2006). He has also published a number of SF novels with Gollancz, the most recent of these being the uncanonical *By Light Alone* (2011), Jack Glass (2012) and *Twenty Trillion Leagues Under the Sea* (2013). A collection of his short stories, *Adam Robots*, was published in 2013. He is Professor of Nineteenth-century Literature at Royal Holloway, University of London.

Sherryl Vint is Professor of Science Fiction Media Studies at the University of California, Riverside, where she is co-chair of the graduate program in Science Fiction and Technoculture Studies. She is the author or editor of a number of books on science fiction, including *Bodies of Tomorrow* (2007) and *Animal Alterity* (2010). She co-edits the journals *Science Fiction Studies* and *Science Fiction Film and Television*.

Pat Wheeler is Head of English Literature and Creative Writing at the University of Hertfordshire. She has previously published on feminist science fiction, gender and sexuality in science fiction and British women's writing. Her publications include *Contemporary British and Irish Novelists: Introduction through Interview* (London: Arnold, 2004). *Sebastian Faulks's Birdsong* (New York: Continuum, 2002) and *Re-Reading Pat Barker* (Cambridge: CSP, 2011). Other publications include chapters on Carol Emshwiller's *Carmen Dog* (2002), Joanna Russ's *The Two of Them* (2008), Barker's *The Man Who Wasn't There* (2005) and *The Regeneration Trilogy* (2011).

Introduction

Nick Hubble

Science Fiction

Realist fiction sets out to describe the world; science fiction (SF) sets out to change it. For example, *2312* (2012), the most recent novel by one of the world's leading SF writers, Kim Stanley Robinson, effectively offers a blueprint for transforming the Solar System over the next 300 years. The novel begins on Mercury in a city that moves on tracks to keep always ahead of the direct glare of the Sun, which would incinerate it. Mars and the larger moons of Saturn are also the locations of major human habitation. Travel into orbit from Earth and Mars is not by rocket but by anchored 'space elevators' that are powered by planetary spin. A series of 'Extracts' interspersed throughout the novel offers step-by-step instructions for such endeavours as how to hollow out an asteroid and turn it into a self-propelled natural habitat occupied by thousands of people and animals, or how to 'terraform' (make habitable like Earth) Venus by bombarding it with ice from Saturn as part of a 200-year project to cool it and provide huge freshwater seas. The novel expresses few qualms about what might be seen from some perspectives as the rapacious development of untouched environments, with the narration stating at one point: 'for the truth is we are here to inscribe ourselves on the universe' (250). In Robinson's vision, 'spacers', those humans living off Earth, have access to a range of genetic and medical treatments that enable changes in the human condition ranging from extended longevity (up to about 200 years) to both males and females being able to have children and many opting to have two sets of sex organs.

Robinson's novel appears to contain all the features, including explosions and aliens (albeit microscopic ones living in the internal sea of a Saturnine moon), that we might expect to find in a classic space adventure written in the 'Golden Age' of American SF, a period running approximately from the late 1930s through to the 1950s, following in the aftermath of the identification of SF as a genre by Hugo Gernsback in his editorial to the first issue of the magazine *Amazing Stories* in 1926. It would be perfectly reasonable to include *2312* within the subgenre of 'space opera', a term coined by Wilson Tucker in 1941 by analogy with 'soap opera', and described here by Brian Aldiss:

Ideally, the Earth must be in peril, there must be a quest and a man to match the mighty hour. That man must confront aliens and exotic creatures. Space must flow past the ports like wine from a pitcher. Blood must run down the palace steps, and Ships launch out into the louring dark. There must be a woman fairer than the skies and a villain darker than the Black Hole. And all must come right in the end. (1974: 10)

In *2312*, however, most of the trouble appears to come from Earth and the hero, Swan Er Hong, is a 135-year-old woman, albeit with a small penis nestling in the pubic hair above her vagina. Perhaps the novel would be better described as 'Hard SF', that is SF based on accurate technical and scientific detail, and plausible extrapolation of current trends into the future (see the discussion in Chapter 6). Robinson is known for taking care with science and not just with physics and engineering or, for example, the possibilities of quantum computing which is discussed at some length in *2312*; but also with biological and environmental science. The ideas he discusses are at least plausible according to some current thinkers and there are neither mysterious ray guns nor faster-than-light intergalactic travel; the action is confined to the Solar System, all of which has been reached by man-made spacecraft over the past 50 years. Indeed, *2312* might even be described as 'Mundane SF' (see the entry on Geoff Ryman in Chapter 4) because if one accepts it as depicting plausible change, then there is no question that it also imaginatively and holistically constructs a whole series of linked social and cultural changes surrounding the representation of future science at its core. Furthermore, on these grounds, it could also be described as 'Soft SF', that is SF that envisions a future based on the extrapolation of the social, rather than the physical, sciences. Not only does Robinson include a disquisition on historical periodization, which categorizes the next 200 years as the 'long postmodern', but he also provides a sophisticated economic projection that envisages capitalism being restricted to the margins everywhere but on Earth, as libertarian and cooperative economies develop in space. On the other hand, this very description of a post-capitalist, post-scarcity (not restricted by the shortage of resources) society also qualifies *2312* as an example of 'Utopian SF'.

Science Fictionality

As the above discussion illustrates, SF can be classified by a variety of divisions and sub-genres; not all of which, it should be said, can be exemplified by *2312*. For example, it is not an 'alternate history' based on the premise that a key event in the past happened differently such as Philip K. Dick's *The Man in the High Castle* (1962), which imagines a world in which the Allies lost the Second World War. However, Robinson has written an alternate history in the past;

his *The Years of Rice and Salt* (2002), in which Europe becomes a Muslim society during the Middle Ages. Another of his novels, *Galileo's Dream* (2009), shares some of the same features as an alternate history but turns on the idea that an intervention from humans of the future changes Galileo's life on to the track that we know historically to be true; in effect the implication is that our world is both just one of many alternate histories and also inherently 'science fictional'. That is to say that the world is shaped by the same forces – ranging from the technological and scientific to the environmental and economic – that generally shape SF and, in particular, by the desire of human beings to escape from the Earth's surface. Furthermore, to claim that the world is science fictional would also be to argue that it is brought into being by the conscious imagination of SF writers. This might sound far fetched but, for example, George Orwell had no hesitation in writing in 1941 of H.G. Wells, whose status as the founder of modern SF is discussed in the next chapter of this book, that 'the minds of all of us, and therefore the physical world, would be perceptibly different if Wells had never existed' (171). Orwell goes on to add:

> A decade or so before aeroplanes were technically feasible Wells knew that within a little while men would be able to fly. He knew that because he himself *wanted* to be able to fly, and therefore felt sure that research in that direction would continue […] Up to 1914 Wells was in the main a true prophet. In physical details his vision of the new world has been fulfilled to a surprising extent. (171)

You might not be surprised to find out that Swan Er Hong is a fanatical flier and that Robinson's *2312* can also be seen as a successor to the 'scientific romances' of Wells and Olaf Stapledon (see their entries in Chapter 3). Whether all the details of his vision of the future will be fulfilled is open to question but if he is right that life expectancy will reach 200 then it will only be two or three generations before our descendents can see for themselves.

But is Science Fiction literature?

For a long time, SF was regarded mainly in relation to its association with American magazines as a form of pulp fiction, with all the attendant associations of that designation. However, today we think more favourably of pulp fiction and accord it serious academic study (see McCracken, 1998). Nevertheless, there remains hostility to SF in certain educated sections of society in particular. The leading critic and theorist, Fredric Jameson (see Chapters 5, 6 and 8) describes this 'conventional high-cultural repudiation of SF' as probably neither a manifestation of personal taste nor something that can be addressed by reference to SF writers who have attained literary status, such as J. G. Ballard (see the entry in Chapter 3). Rather, he suggests that 'we must here identify a kind of "generic revulsion", in which this form and narrative discourse is the object of psychic resistance as a whole and the target of a kind of literary "reality principle"' (xiv, footnote). The 'reality principle' is a Freudian term for explaining why people generally learn as they mature to postpone immediate gratification in favour of greater satisfactions in the long term. However, it is debateable, to say the least, whether staying in and saving up for a mortgage in the suburbs, for instance, is genuinely preferable to living to the full in the centre of town where all the nightlife is. Likewise, it is not clear that there is anything to be gained from foregoing the idea that the future might be a different place in which people can literally or metaphorically fly or live in any of the other ways that Robinson outlines in *2312*, other than not having to deal with change and the science fictionality of the world itself, which is a forlorn hope in today's world.

Considered rationally, *2312* is at least as sophisticated as any novel published in 2012. It has a complex and ambitious form that interrupts narrative progression with various 'Lists' and 'Extracts', sometimes playful in tone, which are also amusingly summarized in the Contents pages. Robinson deploys a variety of styles in the different sections, including modernist fragmentation, or, at least, a convincing pastiche of it, in order to convey the flavour of a series of 'Quantum Walks'. He also includes a number of hints that *2312* is set in the same world as some of his earlier novels, such as the *Mars Trilogy* (1993–6) and *Galileo's Dream*. However, beyond this, he includes intertextual references not only to other SF novels, including Samuel Delany's *Dhalgren* (1975) and Charles Stross's *Accelerando* (2005), but also, more than once, to Marcel Proust's *À la recherche du temps perdu* (1913–27), including the name shared between Swan Er Hong and Proust's character, Charles Swann. *2312* is also probably the only novel published in 2012 in which the main characters go surfing on the ice rings of Saturn.

Science Fiction Criticism

Despite this idea of SF not being literature turning out to be a red herring covering up some form of social neurosis, it was historically significant and has had long-term consequences. Although, following a convergence of themes between SF and ongoing critical work in the humanities over the last 20 years, SF is now fully established in the academic curriculum (which is probably why you are reading this book), this has not always been the case. In the past, its exclusion from serious literary criticism led to SF developing its own criticism out of the fan culture that surrounded it. This alternative critical structure is focused on two main areas: reviewing and awards. The best SF reviewing is very different in standard from newspaper reviews, even those in quality broadsheets, having more in common with the lengthy review articles found in periodicals such as the *London Review of Books* and the *New York Review of Books*. The leading reviewers have their articles republished in collected book editions and anybody seriously interested in the SF of recent decades should consult the work of John Clute (1988, 1996, 2003, 2009) and Gary K. Wolfe (2005, 2010, 2011). Clute is also one of the two editors, with Peter Nicholls, of the most indispensable single-volume work of reference on SF, the second edition of *The Encyclopaedia of Science Fiction* (1993); subsequently supplemented by a third, updated online edition (2011).

SF awards are taken very seriously and promote, apart from an even greater concentration of reviews, much critical commentary. The major annual awards include the following: the Hugos are awarded each year at the World Science Fiction Convention, or 'Worldcon'; the Nebulas are organized by the Science Fiction and Fantasy Writers of America; the Arthur C Clarke Award is chosen by a selected jury for the best SF novel published in Britain; the Philip K. Dick Award is given to the best original paperback published in America; and the James Tiptree Jr Award goes to works of SF and fantasy that expand notions of gender and sexuality. However, SF writers and critics are no longer content with their own awards.

Did Virginia Woolf write Science Fiction?

In 2009, Robinson was featured in press reports for publicly criticizing judges of the Booker Prize, the most prestigious literary award in Britain, and accusing them of 'ignorance' for neglecting SF in favour of historical novels, which he described as 'the best British literature of our time'. Alison Flood quoted him in the *Guardian* as saying: '[Historical novelists] tend to do the same things the modernists did in smaller ways [...] More importantly, these novels are not about now in the way science fiction is.' Robinson argued that that year's prize should go to Adam Roberts's *Yellow Blue Tibia* (2009) and went on to add that Geoff Ryman's *Air* should have won in 2005, Gwyneth Jones's *Life* in 2004 and *Signs of Life* by M. John Harrison in 1997. Flood continued:

> According to Robinson the ghettoisation of science fiction is a
> comparatively recent phenomenon. He pointed to a little known letter
> written by Virginia Woolf to the science fiction writer Olaf Stapledon,
> after he had sent her a copy of his novel *Star Maker*. 'I don't suppose
> that I have understood more than a small part – all the same I have
> understood enough to be greatly interested, and elated too, since
> sometimes it seems to me that you are grasping ideas that I have tried to

express, much more fumblingly, in fiction,' wrote Woolf. 'But you have gone much further and I can't help envying you – as one does those who reach what one has aimed at.' Robinson believes that Stapledon's 'strange novels' made a 'real impact on Woolf', changing her writing. 'Her final novel, *Between the Acts* ... ends with Stapledonian imagery, describing our species steeped in the eons. Woolf's last pages were a kind of science fiction,' he wrote in his article for the *New Scientist*. 'When it came to literature, she had no prejudices. She read widely and her judgment was superb. And so I am confident that if she were reading today, she would be reading science fiction along with everything else. And she would still be "greatly interested, and elated too" – because British science fiction is now in a golden age.'

This intriguing claim illustrates that critical battles over the status of SF are not yet a thing of the past. However, the terrain of the debate has moved on and the question is how central to the literary canon will SF eventually be considered? It is reasonable to expect that there will be an increased cultural and academic exchange over this matter as the literary heritage of the twentieth century becomes reassessed with both the benefit of hindsight and the critical distance that viewing it from its (science fictional) future provides.

Studying Science Fiction: The Contents of the Book

This book provides a framework of support for studying SF, or individual works of SF, on a university course. The first chapter, by Nick Hubble, discusses 'The Historical Context of Science Fiction' both in terms of the immediate conditions for its rise as a genre and with regards to its relationship with the future. In particular, Hubble discusses not only the difference, but also, more importantly, the similarities between the contexts for SF in Britain and America by focusing on two of the most iconic of all SF writers: Philip K. Dick and J. G. Ballard. Joseph Norman's 'An Annotated Science Fiction Timeline' charts the historical development of SF, focusing on the period from Wellsian scientific romance onwards. Key publications and films are listed chronologically, as well as pertinent historical and cultural events, in order to give students an understanding of the linear history of the genre.

In Chapter 3, 'Major Science Fiction Authors', Nick Hubble, Emma Filtness and Joseph Norman provide 21 brief critical biographies of writers who may be encountered on university courses, whether specifically focused on SF or more generally covering twentieth-century literature. There is no suggestion intended that these *are* absolutely the most significant writers in the history of SF, although a number of them would make most critics' lists of the ten most important to the genre; the claim is, rather, that these are writers who can be studied within the context of a present-day literature department. Each entry contains relevant biographical details, identifies the main themes of the writer's work and provides a brief introduction to major publications (therefore, providing a useful guide to academics seeking texts for courses as well as for students seeking subjects for dissertations). Where appropriate, readers are directed to later sections of the Handbook (for example, if the writer is the author of one of the texts discussed in more detail as a case study or in one of the other chapters). Entries conclude with references to key biographical and critical works on the author. The writers included cover a representative range of backgrounds and concerns in terms of gender, ethnicity and sexuality.

Chapter 4, 'Case Studies in Reading 1: Key Primary Literary Texts' by Christopher Daley, provides case studies discussing these five commonly studied texts: H. G. Wells's *The Time Machine* (1895), J. G. Ballard's *The Drowned World* (1962), Joanna Russ's 'When It Changed' (1972), Octavia Butler's *Kindred* (1979) and William Gibson's *Neuromancer* (1984). All are important works in the genre, which lend themselves to close study in a university context. The student is provided with exemplary close readings, critical commentaries and explanatory annotations. The texts are examined in their generic, historical and biographical contexts, with reference to contemporary critical approaches. Throughout, the aim is to show students how best to engage with primary material.

The next chapter is Jessica Langer's 'Case Studies in Reading 2: Key Theoretical and Critical Texts', which charts a course, both historical and conceptual, through the emergence and development of intersections between, and engagements of, SF and critical theory. The chapter will focus closely on four key works of SF criticism and theory: Darko Suvin's *Metamorphoses of Science Fiction* (1979), Ursula K. Le Guin's *The Language of the Night: Essays on Science Fiction and Fantasy* (1979), Donna Haraway's 'Cyborg Manifesto' (1985) and Fredric Jameson's *Archaeologies of the Future: The Desire Called Utopia and Other Science Fictions* (2005). This selection permits a variety of perspectives to be covered; authorial and academic, international and with both male and female voices. Each work is given a close reading useful for pedagogical purposes. Chapter 6, 'Key Critical Concepts, Topics and Critics' by David M. Higgins and Roby Duncan provides short alphabetical entries on key critical concepts, topics and critics in SF scholarship.

In Chapter 7, 'The Science Fiction Film', Aris Mousoutzanis discusses the strong interrelationship between fiction and film in SF. In few other genres are these two modes of narrative production so intertwined. SF literature has always served as a rich source of material for adaptation for SF films, a trend established by these first feature films that are in their majority adaptation of literary works by H. G. Wells (*Things to Come*), Jules Verne (*The Mysterious*

Island) and Camille Flammarion (*The End of the World*). Cinema, on the other hand, has encouraged a style of writing that may be seen as 'cinematic' (William Gibson's fiction would be an representative example), even as it has led to novelizations of major SF blockbuster movies, fan fictions and paperbacks that expand on the mythology of these films. Mousoutzanis illustrates his arguments with case studies of the following key SF films: *Metropolis* (1927), *The Day the Earth Stood Still* (1951), *2001: A Space Odyssey* (1968), *Star Wars* (1977), *Alien* (1979), Blade Runner (1982) and *The Matrix* (1999).

Andrew M. Butler's 'Science Fiction Criticism' (Chapter 8) describes criticism as a series of overlapping waves of dominant, emergent and residual practices, and, in effect, describes the history of a half dozen loose schools of criticism. After acknowledging the prehistory of science fiction criticism in fandom, reviews and individual champions – often from outside academia or not in literary studies – which produced much vital work, Butler focuses on a number of critical paradigms. These include Marxist criticism from the foundation of the journal *Science Fiction Studies* in the early 1970s up to special issues of journals and collections which have appeared in the twenty-first century; postmodern criticism, which despite its avowed aim of upsetting the canon – although paradoxically it ended up reducing SF to a handful of writers and a couple of films – frequently sidelined women; and feminist criticism which feeds into other approaches which reflect upon personal identity – queer theory and a range of ethnic, racial and postcolonial theories. Finally, a section on fan studies brings the chapter full circle, as the consumers of the form come under the scope of critical study.

Chapter 9, 'Changes in the Canon' by Adam Roberts, discusses the SF canon within the wider context of the politics of canon, and indicates how it is has expanded in recent years. Chapter 10, 'Issues of Sexuality, Gender and Ethnicity' by Pat Wheeler investigates the ways in which SF texts, as opposed to criticism, have engaged with the identity politics of gender, sexuality and 'race'/ethnicity and discusses the representation of these identity formations by focusing on a number of writers and texts, including Geoff Ryman's *The Child Garden* (1989), Ward Moore's *Bring the Jubilee* (1953), Samuel Delany's *The Einstein Intersection* (1967) and Carol Emschwiller's *Carmen Dog* (1988).

The final chapter is Sherryl Vint's keynote essay on 'Mapping The Current Critical Landscape', which maps out some of the main areas of emerging SF criticism in the twenty-first century, such as science studies, postcolonial theory, posthumanism, and ecocriticism. The chapter concludes with a consideration of Istvan Csicsery-Ronay Jr's *The Seven Beauties of Science Fiction* (2008) and, therefore, the volume ends, as it began, with the question of the science fictionality of the contemporary world. This leads to a discussion of to what degree the genre might be understood as a specifically twentieth-century project and whether we should continue to defend the specific nature of the genre called SF, or if we should understand it as something now proliferated out into the wider cultural formation that shapes all contemporary culture.

Works Cited

Aldiss, Brian (1974). *Space Opera*. London: Futura

Clute, John (1988). *Strokes: Essays and Reviews 1966-1986*. Seattle: Serconia Press.

—(1996). *Look at the Evidence: Essays and Reviews*. New York: Serconia Press.

—(2003). *Scores*. Harold Wood: Beccon Publications.

—(2009). *Canary Fever: Reviews*. Harold Wood: Beccon Publications.

Clute, John, and Peter Nicholls (eds) (1993). *The Encyclopaedia of Science Fiction*. London: Orbit.

Flood, Alison (2009). 'Science Fiction Author Hits Out at Booker Judges', *Guardian*, 18 September. Available online: http://www.guardian.co.uk/books/2009/sep/18/science-fiction-booker-prize [accessed 4 February 2013].

Jameson, Fredric (2005). *Archaeologies of the Future: The Desire Called Utopia and Other Science Fictions*. London, Verso.

McCracken, Scott (1998). *Pulp: Reading Popular Fiction*. Manchester and New York: Manchester University Press.

Orwell, George (1970) [1941]. 'Wells, Hitler and the World State'. *Collected Essays, Journalism and Letters*, Volume 2. Harmondsworth: Penguin.

Robinson, Kim Stanley (2012). *2312*. London: Orbit.

Wolfe, Gary K. (2005). *Soundings: Reviews 1992–1996*. Harold Wood: Beccon Publications.

—(2010). *Bearings: Reviews 1997–2001*. Harold Wood: Beccon Publications.

—(2011). *Sightings: Reviews 2002–2006*. Harold Wood: Beccon Publications.

The Historical Context of Science Fiction

1

Nick Hubble

Knowing the Future Will be Different

Science fiction has two key historical contexts: modernity and the future. This is not to deny the argument that its origins can be traced back to Ancient Greece (see Roberts 2005) but, rather, to suggest that it needed the world to become inherently science fictional (as discussed in the Introduction) for it to truly be able to express itself fully as a genre. The closing years of the nineteenth century marked a turning point in the world's history because, following the earlier developments of the industrial revolution, there now followed the first wave of globalization. In the space of a few years, from the laying in 1870 of the underwater cable from Porthcurno, Cornwall, to Darwin, Australia, via a number of key outposts of the British Empire, to the 1884 International Meridian Conference, which effectively defined time universally, all of the elements appeared that allowed the modern world to be born. One other development was of particular significance to the history of SF in Britain, which was then at the centre of this emerging modern world. The Elementary Education Act of 1870 introduced universal compulsory schooling to the age of 11; thus making a huge step towards universal literacy and generating for the first time in history a mass readership yearning for the mass-market publications that the mechanization and consolidation of printing businesses made possible. All that was needed now was someone to provide the required product.

Perhaps improbably, that someone was Herbert George Wells, the son of a shopkeeper and a domestic servant from Bromley (see entry in Chapter 3). Although other late Victorian writers imagined futuristic scenarios such as Richard Jefferies's *After England* (1885), in which a post-catastrophe England has reverted to a feudal social order, it was the sequence of novels that Wells wrote as the turn of the century approached – *The Time Machine* (1895), *The Island of Dr Moreau* (1896), *The Invisible Man* (1897) and *The War of the Worlds* (1898) among others – that established the parameters of the genre and inspired others to follow suit. As we have seen in the introduction, George Orwell argued in 'Wells, Hitler and the World State' (1941) that Wells's books shaped the modern world much more than those of any other writer because he changed the way that his readers' minds worked. Orwell explains why Wells was such a godsend to young boys at the time:

> Back in the nineteen-hundreds it was a wonderful experience for a boy to discover H. G. Wells. There you were in a world of pedants, clergymen and golfers, with your future employers exhorting you to 'get on or get out', your parents systematically warping your sexual life, and your dull-witted schoolmasters sniggering over their Latin tags; and here was this wonderful man who could tell you about the inhabitants of the planets and the bottom of the sea, and who *knew* that the future was not going to be what respectable people imagined. (1970:171)

Interestingly, Orwell is not here suggesting that Wells simply provided a blueprint for the future; indeed the implication (quite correctly) is that Wells employed a quantity of fanciful imagination. Rather, Orwell conveys that the appeal lay in a shared understanding between Wells and his readers that the future, whatever it was, was going to be completely different to the repressed and hidebound British society in place at the turn of the twentieth century.

Excavating the Future

In his 2005 book *Archaeologies of the Future* (see the later discussion in Chapter 5), Fredric Jameson makes the case that charting the complexity and totality of society requires paying as much critical attention to Utopian dreams of the future as to concrete prehistory:

Utopia is philosophically analogous to the trace, only from the other end of time. The aporia of the trace is to belong to the past and present all at once, and thus to constitute a mixture of being and not-being quite different from the traditional category of Becoming and thereby mildly scandalous for analytical Reason. Utopia which combines the not-yet-being of the future with a textual existence in the present is no less worthy of the archaeologies we are willing to grant to the trace. (xv–xvi)

Jameson's argument is complex here, littered with terms that have significance in Hegelian and Marxist philosophy, but what he is saying in essence is that in the same way that we can trace out the effect of the past in the world surrounding us, we can also locate the effect of the futures we have not yet reached. Implicit to this proposition, which comes at the beginning of a book about SF, is that imaginative fiction is one of the tools by which people uncover and understand the coming future. In the same manner that Georg Lukács, the Hungarian Marxist literary critic, wrote *The Historical Novel*, analysing examples from the genre of the historical novel in order to show what they revealed about the prehistory of society, Jameson analyses SF from its emergence in the late nineteenth century in order to reveal its Utopian dreams of the future. Both genres represent what Jameson describes as 'the emergence of a narrative form peculiarly restructured to express [a] new consciousness' (284). He goes on to note the fact that this emergence of SF in the late nineteenth century coincides with the decline of the historical novel, leading him to conclude:

We are therefore entitled to complete Lukács's account of the historical novel with the counter-panel of its opposite number, the emergence of the new genre of SF as a form which now registers some nascent sense of the future, and does so in the space on which a sense of the past had once been inscribed. (285–6)

However, a sense of the future is not the same thing as the future itself: 'the most characteristic SF does not seriously attempt to imagine the "real" future of our solar system. Rather [...] [it] transform[s] our own present into the determinate past of something yet to come' (288). Therefore, as Orwell saw, what was important about Wells was not the specifics of the future he portrayed but rather the fact that his fiction apprehended the present as history, which was soon to be bypassed. This sense that our lives are being lived in relation to the birth-struggles of a better future is a staple of Utopian literature from Wells and his British successor, Olaf Stapledon (see entry in Chapter 3), through 1970s novels such as Marge Piercy's *Woman on the Edge of Time* (1976) and Joanna Russ's *The Female Man* (1975), and

3

on to contemporary Utopias such as Kim Stanley Robinson's *Mars Trilogy* (1993–6) and *2312* (2012). However, as the fact that the 1970s and contemporary examples are by American authors attests, Britain was not to be the location of this future. With one or two notable exceptions, such as Naomi Mitchison's *Memoirs of a Spacewoman* (1962), the Utopian impulse went into abeyance in Britain as post-war stasis set in; and the Wellsian and Stapledonian influences that survived were twisted into grim scenarios that envisaged the savage destruction of most present-day society in novels such as John Wyndham's *The Day of the Triffids* (1951), J. G. Ballard's *The Drowned World* (1962) and Doris Lessing's *Shikasta* (1979). It was not until the appearance of Iain M. Banks's *Culture* series, with the publication of *Consider Phlebas* in 1987, that a fully confidant Utopian strand re-emerged in those now post-imperial islands.

Elite Engineers and Dropouts

Nevertheless, the American adoption of SF with a Wellsian sense of the future was not straightforward. While Wells's stories formed one of the staple reservoirs for the US magazine market from the publication of the first issue of Hugo Gernsback's *Amazing Stories* in 1926, the resultant 'Golden Age' bypassed his anti-colonialist tendencies and, according to Roger Luckhurst, invited readers to identify as 'the elite engineers of imperial history, who transcend the pettiness of everyday existence with uncanny scientific predictive power' (72). Such an aggressive stance to the future created a completely opposite effect to that Wells had had in late Victorian Britain. The implication of such SF was not that the present-day world would be superseded by something new and better, but that, on the contrary, the values of mid-century America would prosper, triumph and expand across the known universe: this was not a formula that left much space for subversion.

Like Wells, such subversion, when it finally arrived, turned out to come in an improbable form: a Californian university drop-out called Philip Kindred Dick. In place of the triumphalist technological determinism of 'Golden-Age' SF, Dick inserted the chaos, failure and sense of waste that had come to define small-town life in America for many in the 1950s. By so doing, he provided a motive for overcoming the present rather than prolonging it, and thereby restored the capacity of the genre to register its own content. Jameson acknowledges that Dick returns to the spirit of Wells in his technique of rendering 'our present historical by turning it into the past of a fantasised future', but further identifies the significant difference that 'his late twentieth-century object-world (unlike the gleaming technological futures of Verne or Wells) tends to disintegrate under its own momentum, disengaging films of dust over all its surfaces, growing spongy, tearing apart like rotten cloth or becoming as unreliable as a floorboard you put your foot through' (345–6). Consider Dick's 1959 novel *Time Out of Joint* in the light of this description.

The protagonist of the novel, Ragle Gumm, lives with his married sister and spends his days completing a complicated newspaper puzzle, 'Where Will the Little Man be Next?', which he always wins, flirting with the female half of their social-climbing neighbours, and generally trying to deal with the boredom of Eisenhower America:

> 'How's it going, Ragle?' Black asked, seating himself handily on the edge of the couch. Margo had gone into the kitchen with Junie. At the TV set, Vic was scowling, resentful of the interruption, trying to catch the last of a scene between [Sid] Caesar and Carl Reiner.
>
> 'Glued to the idiot box,' Ragle said to Black, meaning it as a parody of Black's utterances. But Black chose to accept it at face value.
>
> 'The great national pastime,' he murmured, sitting so that he did not have to look at the screen. (14–15)

However it transpires, as we gradually come to realize, that really this world is a false reality constructed in the future of 1997 purely to keep Gumm at the vital work, disguised as the puzzle, that he is required to do for the ongoing interstellar war effort. In *Postmodernism, or, the Cultural Logic of Late Capitalism* (1991), Jameson argues that *Time Out of Joint* has 'paradigmatic value [...] for questions of history and historicity in general' (283). He suggests that the novel solves the problem of representing 1950s America: that the everyday nature of small-town life and conformism seem to have no reality other than the mass cultural representation of themselves. High culture spurned the whole period: 'of the great writers [...] only Dick himself comes to mind as the virtual poet laureate of this material: of squabbling couples and marital dramas, of petit bourgeois shopkeepers, neighbourhoods and afternoons in front of television [...]' (280). The radical possibility that Jameson points out in connection to this situation is that the 1950s may not actually exist outside the media loop of representing themselves to themselves. An argument which taken to its logical extreme implies that 'there is no such thing as "history" either' (282). For Jameson, contemplation of this not insignificant possibility is the point at which one needs to return to the details of the text and the specific fact that the 1950s being evoked are a reproduction of themselves constructed in 1997. The situation of the hero, Ragle Gumm, is a product of both outside manipulation and his own infantile regression from anxiety in search of childhood security, which Jameson glosses as 'a certain approach to self-consciousness about the representations themselves' (283). Both Dick *and* SF, by extension, are thus shown to have a sophisticated skeptical concept of history. Rather than being like the nineteenth-century bourgeoisie, forced to bolster their alienated consciousnesses by recourse to historical novels, the readers of *Time Out of Joint* are offered the choice of rejecting imprisonment within a historical period, and given the option to construct their own periods, or environments, instead: 'reification is [...] built into the novel itself and [...] recuperated as a form of praxis [...] reification ceases to be a[n] [...] alienating process [...] and is rather transferred to the side of human possibilities and human energies' (285).

Philip K. Dick and Walter Benjamin

The proposed relationship between SF and historicity might function according to the model outlined by the German Marxist philosopher, Walter Benjamin, in his 'Theses on the Philosophy of History', with Dick's SF fulfilling the function of historical materialism in opposing all the various forms of historicism. These latter being, for Benjamin, any form of history seeking a passive empathy with the past, which can only be a cowardly retreat from the radical act of bringing the past and the future together to form the *Jetztzeit* or revolutionary now-time. As Benjamin argues, 'A historical materialist cannot do without the notion of a present which is not a transition, but in which time stands still and has come to a stop' (254). Likewise, Dick needs to represent his contemporary America of the 1950s and 1960s as a static construct so that he can bring it into contact with the notion of a radically-othered future – represented partly in the '1997' of *Time Out of Joint* by a remarkably punk-like youth culture that he imagines – in order to suggest, as Jameson notes, that 'we can build [our own constructs], just as the science fiction writer builds his own small-scale model' (285).

   Indeed, not long after the publication of *Time Out of Joint*, Dick wrote *We Can Build You*, although it was not published until 1972. Here, Benjamin's concerns are dramatized even more appropriately, albeit unknowingly (there is no suggestion that Dick knew his work), by the plot which revolves around an Abraham Lincoln simulacrum and big business' attempts to utilize it in the commercial rerunning of the US Civil War for betting purposes. As Benjamin notes, 'In every era the attempt must be made anew to wrest tradition away from a conformism that is about to overpower it' (247). However, while the Lincoln simulacrum does its considerable best, deploying all its legal and political skills, to fight its fate; Dick demonstrates exactly how conformism overpowers tradition in his next novel, *Martian Time-Slip* (1964). Here, the simulacra of famous historical personalities such as Socrates, Thomas Edison and Mark Twain, are employed as schoolteachers. As the hero of the book comes to realize, these teaching machines are 'not there to inform or educate, but to mold ... perpetuation of the culture was the goal' (63). As Benjamin argues, any such attempt to capture the past in this way without also understanding how it is affected by subsequent history can only serve to reproduce the ruling order that shaped that society and, by extension, support the present ruling order (see 247–8). Those pupils on Mars who do not respond properly to this dissemination of culture are labeled autistic and banished to institutions. The breakdown of one of the machines into a disjointed speech loop suggests the simple repetition underlying the hegemonic thrust of universal history which reaches its zenith in a manic tour of Western history as endless meaningless information: 'Gubble gubble' (153). That is why information needs to be free; otherwise it is simply shared experience reified into endless interchangeable facts that can no longer threaten alienated consciousness.

Thus, we can see that simulacral sampling of the past happens first as tragedy and secondly as farce. This state of affairs is due to the ever present threat facing whoever seeks to bring traces of the past and future into conjunction; that it will force alienated consciousness into an even more quantified retreat, driving history into farce or even pastiche by adopting a schizophrenic complete rejection of the past. For Dick, schizophrenia was the endless now (Sutin, 176), an interminable bad trip to be pitied. The answer, though, was not to drag the schizophrenic screaming and kicking back into the symbolic order, as happens in Doris Lessing's *Briefing for a Descent into Hell* (1971), but rather to let them experience the *Jetztzeit* as the schizophrenic Manfred in *Martian Time-Slip* is helped to a measure of peace by the indigenous Martian Bleekmen, with their aborigine-like sense of the here and now.

The Nearest British Equivalent

Jameson condemns Ballard's work as simultaneously rich and corrupt:

> Let the Wagnerian and Spenglerian world-dissolutions of J.G. Ballard stand as exemplary illustrations of the ways in which the imagination of a dying class – in this case the cancelled future of a vanished colonial and imperial destiny – seeks to intoxicate itself with images of death that range from the destruction of the world by fire, water and ice to lengthening sleep or the beserk orgies of high-rise buildings or superhighways reverting to barbarism. (2005: 288)

Yet it is possible to claim Ballard as the nearest British equivalent to Dick. As Dick is to the small American town, so Ballard, who spent years living as a single parent in Shepperton, is to the London suburbs. Those small towns and suburbs, of course, are also another form of historical context of SF. It might be suggested that Ballard knew the suburbs before he ever went there. As subtly fictionalized in his 1984 novel *Empire of the Sun*, which was later filmed by Spielberg, Ballard was born and grew up in Shanghai before being incarcerated with his parents in a civilian detention camp by the Japanese during the War. Here, two antithetical perspectives were abruptly superimposed upon each other – producing something similar to what Slavoj Žižek describes as a 'parallax view' (17) – so that the camp world of barter and stealing from the Japanese, where success depended on transgressing apparently fixed boundaries, was superimposed on the English values of duty, repetition and boredom, upheld by the inmates. The conceit of Jim, the adolescent protagonist of *Empire of the Sun*, is that he can bring back the dead and generally transform the world, by transgressing those English boundaries in the same manner as he transgresses the ostensible Japanese boundaries. However, on a more mundane level, it is exactly this combination of being simultaneously able to act in the two worlds while desiring the opposed ends of each, which allows Jim to save the hospital and the camp doctor from a punishment beating, while getting the dead man's shoes he wants. All Ballard's fiction is a quest for this kind of simultaneous action which generates genuine human agency (i.e. the possibility of taking conscious action which transforms the world in the manner intended). For it to function, it requires a space of repetition and boredom, like the camp or, indeed, like suburbs, to serve as the location for overtly transgressive practices.

While, as Jameson suggests, this capacity gives Ballard's work a double-edged quality so that it is not always clear whether he is seeking power from the past or the future, it is not so different from a quality that Jameson detects in Dick:

> Dick's work transcends the opposition between the subjective and the objective, and thereby confronts the dilemma which in one way or another characterises all modern literature of any consequence [...] [by] retain[ing] possession and use of both apparently contradictory, mutually exclusive subjective and objective explanation systems all at once. (2005: 350)

In other words, things in Dick's world are simultaneously objects and symbols of something else as though in a dream. Jameson takes pains to point out that this utilization of dream logic is prevented from collapsing into the fantasies and dream narratives of Symbolism and Modernism by always being given a causal attribution such as drugs or schizophrenia. However, the same qualification could equally be used for much of Ballard's deployment of dream states. For example, *The Unlimited Dream Company* (1979), depicts a radical transformation of suburban Shepperton by the regenerative activities of a crashed pilot, Blake. The repetitive nature of suburban life is used to repeat and work through a series of transgressive sexual activities which gradually change reality:

Already I was thinking of my next vision, certain now that it would not be a dream at all, but a re-ordering of reality in the service of a greater and more truthful design, where the most bizarre appetites and the most wayward impulses would find their true meaning. (106)

Blake's attempts to dream a better future for the real world are similar to those of George Orr, the protagonist of Ursula Le Guin's very Dick-like novel, *The Lathe of Heaven* (1971); although it is never entirely certain that Blake's underlying motives are quite so idealistic. However, that is not the point; what really matters in both cases is that the process fails to fulfil its direct aims but yet still, somehow, manages to secure a messily heterotopic, but nevertheless positive future. On that level, the gloss Jameson provides for *The Lathe of Heaven* could equally be applied to *The Unlimited Dream Company*, if the name of the protagonist was changed:

On the aesthetic level ... this book is 'about' its own process of production, which is recognised as impossible: George Orr cannot dream Utopia; yet in the very process of exploring the contradictions of that production, the narrative gets written, and 'Utopia' is 'produced' in the very movement by which we are shown that an 'achieved' Utopia – a full representation – is a contradiction in terms. (2005: 293–4)

Stopped Time in the Suburbs

Jameson implicitly diagnoses Ballard's condition as one of barely repressed psychosis at being denied the imperial future he was brought up to expect in Shanghai before the onset of the Second World War. However, when Ballard's autobiography, *Miracles of Life*, appeared in 2008, it soon became apparent that the motivation for his anger was more complex; aimed at both a collapse of the social agency of the middle class to which he belonged, and the retreat into a sterile and rigid hierarchy that followed from this:

The English middle class had lost its confidence [...] I think it was clear to me from the start that the English class system which I was meeting for the first time, was an instrument of political control, and not a picturesque social relic. Middle class people in the late 1940s and 1950s saw the working class as almost another species, and fenced themselves off behind a complex system of social codes [...] Everything about English middle-class life revolved around codes of behaviour that unconsciously cultivated second-rateness and low expectations. (125–6)

In his last two novels, he changed tack from the transgressive outrages of his 1970s fictions and adopted a satirical stance to the suburbs as a land of stopped time that has certain structural similarities with Dick's treatment of the small-town America of the 1950s and the 1960s. *Millennium People* (2003), despite a number of plot strands and references to events from 9/11 to the murder of British news reader Jill Dando, is essentially about 'the revolution of the middle class' (5). It begins in the deserted gated estate of Chelsea Marina from which 'eight hundred families had fled, abandoning their comfortable kitchens, herb gardens and book-lined living rooms. Without the slightest regret, they had turned their backs on themselves and all they had once believed in' (5). The Home Office is concerned in case the unrest should spread:

> Where had they gone? Many of the residents had retreated to their country cottages, or were staying with friends who supported the struggle with food parcels and cheerful emails. Others had set off on indefinite tours of the Lake District and the Scottish Highlands. Towing their trailers, they were the vanguard of an itinerant middle class, a new tribe of university-trained gypsies who knew their law and would raise hell with local councils. (7)

The story that follows is a retrospective account of the attempts of the 'leaders' of the revolution to promote it, but where they run into a metaphorical privet hedge is in the leafier suburbs: 'prosperous suburbia was one of the end states of history. Once achieved, only plague, flood or nuclear war could threaten its grip' (91). As resistant to change as Eisenhower America, leafy suburbs like Twickenham have become completely static locales of entrenched defensive middle-class values. Posing as social researchers, the revolutionaries attempt to provoke the inhabitants of by conducting a door-to-door survey:

> 'A last question.' Kay scanned her clipboard, pencil poised. 'How often would you say your lavatories are cleaned?'
> 'I've no idea. Every day, I hope'
> 'Would you consider having them cleaned every three days?'
> 'Three? Pretty risky round here.'
> 'Or once a week?'
> 'No.' The woman looked at Kay's lapel badge. 'That doesn't sound like a good idea.'
> 'You're sure? A less than snowy white bowl would worry you? How do you feel about the prevalence of toilet taboos among the professional middle class?'

'Toilet taboos? Are you working for a lavatory paper firm?'

'We're mapping social change' Kay spoke soothingly. 'Personal grooming lies at the heart of people's sense of who they are. Would your family consider washing less often?'

'Less?' The doctor reached for the door handle, shaking her head. 'It's impossible to imagine. Look –'

'And you personally?' Kay pressed. 'Would you bathe less frequently? Natural body odours are an important means of communication, especially within families. You'd have time to relax, play with your children, adopt a freer lifestyle […].' (88)

This satire at the expense of what have now become meaningless class markers, clung to not because of any inherent benefit but merely as the markers of cultural distinction, compliments Ballard's trademark sociological insight:

Twickenham is the Maginot Line of the English class system […] only here is the class system a means of political control. Its real job isn't to suppress the proles, but to keep the middle classes down, make sure they're docile and subservient.

And Twickenham is one way of doing that?'

'Absolutely. The people here are gripped by a powerful illusion, the whole middle-class dream. It's all they live for – liberal educations, civic responsibility, respect for the law. They may think they're free, but they're trapped and impoverished.'

Like the poor in a Glasgow tenement?

Exactly. (*MP* 85–6)

To be more precise, as Ballard repeatedly states, the middle class have become 'the new proletariat' (9, 64). However, the proletariat are not just the downtrodden, disempowered, labouring section of society; they are also potentially the agents of history. Therefore, Ballard's project becomes visible as one of attempting to restore social agency to the middle class, as he implicitly confirmed in the following media statement:

[…] my belief is that the middle class is the new proletariat and that in due course we will have to launch a revolution to free ourselves from the abuse we are now on the receiving end of. We are the new victims, exploited by society. We believe in virtues, charity and elitist culture and it's all-out attack on our kind. We are society's fair game – there are beaters in the woods trying to flush out the middle classes and sooner or later we will revolt. (*Guardian*, 14 March 2002)

His later work can be seen, similarly to the novels of Dick from the late 1950s and early 1960s which are discussed above, as an attempt to bring the future into conjunction with the past. The British Empire was not the only social formation damaged by the Second World War; so was the classless England that Orwell had described in *The Lion and the Unicorn* (1941) as emerging at the beginning of the 1940s and which he might have seen as the logical outcome of the Wellsian legacy of a future for the British masses:

> The place to look for the germs of the future England is in the light-industry areas and along the arterial roads. In Slough, Dagenham, Barnet, Letchworth, Hayes – everywhere, indeed, on the outskirts of great towns – the old pattern is gradually changing into something new. In those vast new wildernesses of glass and brick the sharp distinctions of the older kind of town, with its slums and mansions, or of the country, with its manor-houses and squalid cottages, no longer exist. There are wide gradations of income but it is the same kind of life that is being lived at different levels, in the labour-saving flats or Council houses, along the concrete roads and in the naked democracy of the swimming pools. (Orwell, 1970: 98)

Of course, this future never happened and the suburban frontier was left stranded by the war in the manner of the abandoned housing estate described at the beginning of Evelyn Waugh's *Brideshead Revisited* (1945). The restrictions imposed by the 1947 Town and Country Planning Act did, in effect, turn Twickenham and the other leafy suburbs surrounding London into a Maginot Line. This in turn forced the post-war estates of social housing to be built much further out from the city in isolated locations, where social distinctions could be preserved, rather than as part of a sprawl in which the social distinctions were disappearing. However, fast forward 65 years and these same germs of a future England – or possibly the past germs of a future that never was – have reappeared around the edgelands of the M25 London orbital motorway, as Ballard describes very clearly in his final novel, *Kingdom Come* (2006):

> Out around the M25, is where it's really happening. This is today's England. Consumerism rules, but people are bored. They're out on the edge, waiting for something big and strange to come along.
>   This isn't a suburb of London, it's a suburb of Heathrow and the M25.
>   We like control-tower architecture and friendships that last an afternoon. There's no civil authority telling us what to do. (101)

There is a very millennial feel to this account but, at the same time, it describes no straightforward land of promise; this would have to be built. Ballard is very conscious of the temporal disjunction by which in some way these areas are still trapped within the promise of classlessness at the end of the 1930s as a kind of stalled moment which can never be fulfilled:

> The motorway towns were built on the frontier between a tired past and a future without illusions and snobbery where the only reality was to be found in the certainties of the washing machine and the ceramic hob, as precious as an iron stove in a pioneer's shack. (266)

The Frontier Between a Tired Past and a Future Without Illusions

In *Kingdom Come*, Ballard does reveal a potential outcome for a Britain trapped in time loops. Rather as a soft fascism might have emerged in the late 1930s or 1940s – especially if the appeasers had held sway in Britain's wartime Government – the result of the return to that temporal moment could be a British fascism. But this is not the only possible outcome, and it could be that the middle-class fear Ballard dissects in *Kingdom Come* is directed at the amorphous masses gathering round what is not just a geographical frontier but, crucially, a historical one. It is not clear whether fascists or the proletariat will form the dictatorship heralded by the 'talk of a new "republic" stretching from Heathrow to Brooklands, the whole M3/M4 corridor. A new kind of dictatorship based on the Metro-Centre' (196). However, what is evident is that the historical logjam of post-war Britain is finally breaking up. The modern Utopian dream of being locked in the supermarket – with the concomitant aspect of therefore no longer be forced to provide services to the middle class – has finally expanded into a revolutionary threat. At least one radical SF version of this has already appeared in Ken Macleod's 1995 novel, *The Star Fraction*, set in a Balkanized twenty-first century Britain, which still cannot nullify the radical threat of the edgelands and their evolved mall culture:

> [Brent Cross] Mall had been hit by the war and never reclaimed, due to an obscure dispute about property rights. Norlonto [North London Town] being nothing if not an enormous tangle of private properties, the shopping centre and its surroundings had come to suffer what in a different society would be called planning blight [...] The whole area had been squatted and homesteaded until it was like a carcase occupied by an entire colony of ants, a shipwreck crusted with coral.
>   They pushed past stalls and shops selling microwaves, cast-iron cooking pots, light machine-guns, heavy-metal records, spacesuits, wedding-dresses, holodisks, oil paintings, Afro-Pak takeaways, VR snuff tapes. (146–7)

Macleod envisions the 'Greenbelt' surrounding London transformed into a sprawl of slums, shanties and skyscrapers, like those found in the novels of William Gibson; an updated version of the messy heterotopic Utopias imagined in *The Lathe of Heaven* and *The Unlimited Dream Company*. In such an environment, the middle-class proletariat of Ballard's fevered imagination would be thrown together with the dispossessed workers, street kids and aspiring small-timers who frequently make up the protagonists of SF. It seems unfortunate that Ballard did not live to write the third volume of a trilogy in which the characters of *Millennium People* and *Kingdom Come* came together in this new world, which is currently emerging in the real London. As global slums and sprawl come to Britain, a Ballardian future may well come into being in which middle-class professionals will meet the dispossessed on equal terms and perhaps together form a new proletariat; as Slavoj Žižek suggests:

> It is in fact surprising how many features of the slum-dwellers fit the good old Marxist description of the proletarian revolutionary subject […] The slum-dwellers are the counterclass to the other newly emerging class, the so-called 'symbolic class' (managers, journalists and PR people, academics, artists, and so on) which is also uprooted and perceives itself as directly universal (a New York academic has more in common with a Slovene academic than with blacks in Harlem half a mile from his campus). Is this the new axis of class struggle, or is the 'symbolic class' inherently split, so that we can make the emancipatory wager on the coalition between the slum-dwellers and the 'progressive' part of the symbolic class? What we should be looking for are the signs of the new forms of social awareness that will emerge from the slum collectives: they will be the seeds of the future. (268–9)

This future may yet be the science fictional one we have been awaiting since the late nineteenth century, when Wells first picked up his pen.

Works Cited

Ballard, J. G. (1981) [1979]. *The Unlimited Dream Company*. London: Triad Granada.
—(2006). *Kingdom Come*. London: Fourth Estate.
—(2008) [2003]. *Millennium People*. London: Harper Perennial.
—(2008). *Miracles of Life: An Autobiography*. London: Fourth Estate.
Benjamin, Walter (1992). 'Theses on the Philosophy of History'. *Illuminations*. Trans. Harry Zohn. Hammersmith: Fontana. 245–55.
Dick, Philip K. (1969) [1959]. *Time Out of Joint*. Harmondsworth: Penguin.
—(1987) [1964]. *Martian Time-Slip*. New York: Ballantine.

Jameson, Fredric (1991). *Postmodernism, or, the Cultural Logic of Late Capitalism*. London: Verso.

—(2005). *Archaeologies of the Future: The Desire Called Utopia and Other Science Fiction*. London: Verso.

Jefferies, Richard (1885). *After England*. London: Cassell.

Lukács, Georg (1981). *The Historical Novel*. Harmondsworth: Pelican.

Luckhurst, Roger (2005). *Science Fiction*. Cambridge: Polity Press.

Macleod, Ken (1998) [1995]. *The Star Fraction*. London: Orbit.

Orwell, George (1970). *Collected Essays, Journalism and Letters*. Volume 2. Harmondsworth: Penguin.

Piercy, Marge (1976). *Woman on the Edge of Time*. New York: Knopf.

Roberts, Adam (2005). *The History of Science Fiction*. Basingstoke: Palgrave Macmillan.

Robinson, Kim Stanley (1993). *Red Mars*. London: Harper Collins.

—(1994). *Green Mars*. London: Harper Collins.

—(1996). *Blue Mars*. London: Harper Collins.

—(2012). *2312*. London: Orbit.

Russ, Joanna (1975). *The Female Man*. New York: Bantam Books.

Sutin, Lawrence (ed.) (1995). *The Shifting Realities of Philip K. Dick: Selected Literary and Philosophical Writings*. New York: Pantheon Books.

Wells, H. G. (1895). *The Time Machine*. London: Heinemann.

—(1896). *The Island of Dr Moreau*. London: Heinemann.

—(1897). *The Invisible Man*. London: Pearson.

—(1898). *The War of the Worlds*. London: Heinemann.

Žižek, Slavoj (2006). *The Parallax View*. London and Cambridge, MA: The MIT Press.

2 An Annotated Science Fiction Timeline

Joseph Norman

Date	Literature, Culture, Science, History
1516	Thomas More, *Utopia*.
1543	Nicolaus Copernicus publishes *On the Revolutions of the Heavenly Spheres*, which posits a heliocentric rather than geocentric cosmology. Later known as the Copernican Revolution, this helps instigate the broader Scientific Revolution in the Early Modern period.
1620	Johannes Kepler, *Somnium*: described by Isaac Asimov and Carl Sagan as the first SF story.
1637	Cyrano de Bergerac, *The Other World*.
1638	William Goodwin, *The Men in the Moone*.
1726	Jonathan Swift, *Gulliver's Travels*
1783	Geologist, John Michell, proposes the existence of objects, now understood as 'Black Holes', to the scientist, Henry Cavendish.
1813	Willem Bilderdijk, *A Short Account of a Remarkable Aerial Voyage and Discovery of a New Planet* (trans. 1989).
1818	Mary Shelley, *Frankenstein; or The Modern Prometheus*: Brian Aldiss in *The Detached Retina* (1995) and Brian Stableford in *Essays on Science Fiction and its Precursors* (ed. David Seed, 1995), argue for Shelley's novel as the Ur-text of SF.
1830	Nikolai Lobachevsky, Russian mathematician and geometer, creates non-Euclidean geometry, instigating a paradigm shift in the history of science and subsequently influencing several generations of authors, such as Wells, Lovecraft, Heinlein and Miéville.
1844	Edgar Allan Poe, 'The Balloon Hoax'.

1848   Political theorists Karl Marx and Friedrich Engels publish *The Communist Manifesto*, widely regarded as one of the world's most influential political texts. Marxist literary criticism has played a key role in the development of SF scholarship from its inception in the late 1950s.

1856   Nikola Tesla, electrical engineer and futurist, is born in Croatia. His eccentric personality and seemingly-miraculous experiments with electricity, such as the 'Death Ray' and the 'Tesla Coil' influence the real world development of radio, wireless and X-Ray technology, as well as many works of SF, including Christopher Priest's 1995 novel *The Prestige* and *Command and Conquer: Red Alert 2* by EA Games.

1859   Charles Darwin, *The Origin of Species*.

1864   Jules Verne, *Journey to the Centre of the Earth*.

1865   Jules Verne, *From the Earth to the Moon*.
           The concept of entropy is introduced by German physicist Rudolf Clausius, which influenced SF authors, such as in the idea of 'kipple' that appears in several novels by Philip K. Dick; and featuring prominently in 'A Fall of Angels; Or, On the Possibility of Life Under Extreme Conditions' (1994) by Geoff Ryman.

1870   Jules Verne, *Twenty Thousand Leagues under the Sea*.

1872   Samuel Butler, *Erewhon*.

1886   Robert Louis Stevenson, *The Strange Case of Dr Jekyll and Mr Hyde*.

1887   H. Rider Haggard, *She*.

1888   Edward Bellamy, *Looking Backward: 2000–1887*.

1889   Sigmund Freud, *The Interpretation of Dreams*.

1890   William Morris, *News from Nowhere*.

1895   H. G. Wells, *The Time Machine*: considered by many to be the first modern SF novel.

1896   H. G. Wells, *The Island of Doctor Moreau*.

1897   Bram Stoker, *Dracula*.

1898   H. G. Wells, *The War of the Worlds*.

1902   [Film] *A Trip to the Moon*, dir. George Melies: first SF film.

1904   H. G. Wells, 'The Country of the Blind'.

1905	Albert Einstein publishes the 'Special Theory of General Relativity', suggesting that space and time be considered together as the spacetime continuum.
1912	Sir Arthur Conan Doyle, *The Lost World*.
1913	Sir Arthur Conan Doyle, *The Poison Belt*.
1914	Edgar Rice Burroughs, *The Gods of Mars*. Start of World War One: Germany invades Belgium on 4 August, prompting Britain to declare war on Germany. Gustav Holst begins composing his 32nd opera, *The Planets*; Holst composes each movement based on a planet of the solar system, giving each its own identity based upon its corresponding astrological character.
1916	[Film] *20,000 Leagues Under the Sea*, dir. Stuart Paton.
1917	The Russian Revolution leads to the fall of the Russian Empire, and the beginning of the Soviet Union. World War One: America joins the war to assist the Allied powers. Author Dorothy Scarborough, then a doctoral student at University of Chicago, publishes a chapter on 'Supernatural Science' in her thesis 'The Supernatural in Modern English Fiction', which can be considered amongst the earliest works of SF criticism.
1918	World War One: Germany instigates a major attack on the Western Front. Armistice is signed on November 11. Women over 30 years of age are authorized to vote in Britain for the first time.
1919	[Film] *The Cabinet of Dr. Caligari*, dir. Robert Wiene.
1920	Karel Čapek, *RUR (Rossum's Universal Robots)*; Yevgeny Zamayatin, *We* (translated into English 1924).
1923	*Weird Tales* magazine is first published, edited by Marvin Kaye; writers that it publishes, such as H.P. Lovecraft, Robert Bloch and Robert E. Howard, helped establish the subsequent genre of 'weird fiction'.
1924	Edwin Hubble discovers that the universe is composed of thousands of galaxies.
1926	[Film] *Metropolis*, dir. Fritz Lang. Hugo Gernsback launches *Amazing Stories*.
1927	Georges Lemaître theorizes the Big Bang.

1928   E. E. 'Doc.' Smith, *The Skylark of Space*; H.P Lovecraft, 'The Call of the Cthulhu'.

1930   Olaf Stapledon, *First and Last Men*.
[Film] *Just Imagine*, dir. David Butler.

1931   [Film] *Frankenstein*, dir. James Whale.

1932   Aldous Huxley, *Brave New World*; Olaf Stapledon, *Last Men in London*.

1933   [Film] *King Kong*, dir. Merian C. Cooper, Ernest B. Schoedsack; *The Invisible Man*, dir. James Whale.

1935   Naomi Mitchison, *We Have Been Warned*; Olaf Stapledon, *Odd John*.

1936   [Film] *Things to Come*, dir. William Cameron Menzies.

1937   Olaf Stapledon, *Starmaker*.
[Film] *Lost Horizon,* dir. Frank Capra.

1938   Lester Del Rey, 'Helen O'Loy'.
Action Comics #1 publishes the first *Superman* story.
Lysergic acid diethylamide (LSD) is first synthesized from ergotamine by Swiss scientist, Albert Hoffman.

1939   Start of World War II: Britain and France declare war on Germany on 1 September, following Germany's invasion of Poland two days previously.
The first World Science Fiction Convention (or Worldcon) is attended by 200 people in New York.

1941   [Crit.] Philip Babcock Gove, *The Imaginary Voyage in Prose Fiction*.

1944   Olaf Stapledon, *Sirius*.
D-Day landings (Operation *Neptune*): on 6 June, Allied forces invade Normandy in the largest amphibious attack in world history.

1945   World War II ends. The US drops atomic bombs on the Japanese cities Hiroshima and Nagasaki, killing between 90,000–166,000 people in the former and between 60,000–80,000 in the latter. 8 May is declared Victory In Europe Day (VE Day).

1946   *New Worlds* magazine is first published.
The Cold War begins around this time.
The world's first computer, Electronic Numerical Integrator and Computer, is announced to the public.

1947	First animal in space: fruit flies, rye, and cotton seeds are launched by the US onboard a V2 rocket. 'The Roswell Incident': Roswell, New Mexico.
1948	[Crit.] J. O. Bailey, *Pilgrims Through Space and Time*. The first Eastercon SF convention is attended by 800 people in London.
1949	George Orwell, *Nineteen Eighty-Four*. [Crit.] Marjorie Hope Nicolson, *Voyages to the Moon*.
1950	Isaac Asimov, *I, Robot*; Ray Bradbury, *The Martian Chronicles* [Film] *Destination Moon*, dir. Irving Pichel. The term 'Big Bang' is coined by Fred Hoyle, English cosmologist, mathematician and SF author, out of derision.
1951	Isaac Asimov, *Foundation*; John Wyndham, *The Day of the Triffids*; C. S. Lewis, *The Lion, the Witch and the Wardrobe*. [Film] *The Day the Earth Stood Still*, dir. Robert Wise; *The Thing From Another World*, dir. Christian Nyby; *When Worlds Collide*, dir. Rudolph Maté.
1952	Isaac Asimov, *Foundation and Empire* [Film] *The War of the Worlds*, dir. Byron Haskin. Pulp space opera author L. Ron Hubbard founds Scientology, which bases its teachings upon his previously developed self-help philosophies and his SF works. It will become the Church of Scientology in the following year when, despite attracting controversy, it is recognized as an official religion. Hubbard will employ the term 'Space Opera' to describe elements of the Church's teachings and mythical structure.
1953	Alfred Bester, *The Demolished Man* (Hugo Award for Best Novel); Ray Bradbury, *Fahrenheit 451* (Retro Hugo Award for Best Novel, 2004); Arthur C. Clarke, *Childhood's End*. The first Hugo Award is presented at the 11th World Science Fiction convention in Philadelphia, Pennsylvania. Sam Moskowitz, American SF author, fan and critic, teaches 'Science Fiction Writing', the first SF (non-credit) course in a US college.
1954	J. R. R Tolkien, *The Lord of the Rings*.
1955	James Blish, *Earthman, Come Home*. [Film] *This Island Earth*, dir. Joseph M Newman. Albert Einstein dies in New Jersey, US aged 76.

1956   James Blish, *They Shall Have Stars*; J. G. Ballard, 'Escapement'; Philip K. Dick, 'The Minority Report'.
[Film] *Forbidden Planet*, dir. Fred M. Wilcox; *Invasion of the Body Snatchers*, dir. Don Siegel.
The week-long Dartmouth Conference, widely considered to be the birth of AI, is held.

1957   Sputnik 1, the first artificial Earth satellite, is launched by the Soviet Union on 4 October, triggering the Space Race, and instigating further significant technological, political and scientific developments.
Sputnik 2, launched on 3 November, makes the dog Laika the first mammal placed in space orbit.

1958   Robert A. Heinlein, *Methuselah's Children*.

1959   William S. Burroughs, *Naked Lunch*; Robert A. Heinlein, *Starship Troopers* (Hugo Award for Best Novel), 1960; Philip K. Dick, *Time Out of Joint*; Joanna Russ, 'Nor Custom Stale'.
[Film] *Journey To The Centre Of The Earth*, dir. Henry Levin.
Extrapolation, established by Thomas D. Clareson, becomes the first academic journal focused exclusively on speculative fiction.

1960   Walter M. Miller Jr, *A Canticle for Leibowitz* (Hugo Award for Best Novel, 1961).
[Crit.] Kingsley Amis, *New Maps of Hell: A Survey of Science Fiction*.
Sputnik 5 launches two dogs, Bella and Strelka, into orbit; they become the first animals to survive space travel.
Series of two unmanned spacecraft, Mars 1M, is launched by Soviet Union to explore Mars.

1961   Robert Heinlein. *Stranger in a Strange Land* (Hugo Award for Best Novel, 1962).
The first for-credit SF modules in a US college are taught by Mark Hillegas at Colgate and H. Bruce Franklyn at Stamford.

1962   J. G. Ballard, *The Drowned World*; James Blish, *A Life for the Stars*; Naomi Mitchison, *Memoirs of a Space Woman*; Samuel Delany, *The Jewels of Aptor*; Philip K. Dick, *The Man in the High Castle* (Hugo Award for Best Novel, 1963)
The Cuban Missile Crisis occurs between 16 and 28 October; it marks a major conflict in the Cold War, and is generally understood as the occasion when nuclear war appeared to be most likely to occur.

1963   Valentine Tereshlova becomes the first woman in space.

[TV] First season of BBC TV show Dr Who airs on 23 November, which will later be described as the longest running, and the most successful, SF TV show of all time.

1964   William S. Burroughs, *Nova Express*; Brian Aldiss, *Greybeard*; Philip K. Dick, *Martian Time-Slip*; Robert A. Heinlein, *Farnham's Freehold*. Michael Moorcock becomes editor of *New Worlds*.
Mariner 4, a US spacecraft, completes the first successful flyby of Mars, returning the first photographs of the planet's surface.
Peter Higgs, a British theoretical physicist, alongside several colleagues at the University of Edinburgh propose the existence of the Higgs Boson: the last unobserved particle in the Standard Model of particle physics, which is referenced in several SF works, including *Solaris* by Stephen Soderbergh and *White Mars* by Brian Aldiss.
The Moog synthesizer is commercially available for the first time, already achieving fame for its use in the 1955 SF film *Forbidden Planet*.

1965   Frank Herbert, *Dune* (Hugo Award for Best Novel, 1966); Michael Moorcock, *Stormbringer*; J. G. Ballard, *The Drought*.
[Film] *Alphaville*, dir. Jean-Luc Godard.
First Mars flyby achieved by Mariner 4 on 14 July.

1966   Robert Heinlein, *The Moon is a Harsh Mistress*, (Hugo Award for Best Novel, 1967); Samuel Delany, *Babel-17*; Ursula le Guin, *Rocannon's World, Planet of Exile*.
[Film] *Fahrenheit 451*, dir. François Truffaut.
First soft landing of an unmanned craft (Luna 9) on the Moon.

1967   Samuel Delany, *The Einstein Intersection*, 'Aye, and Gomorrah ...'; Ursula le Guin, *City of Illusions*.
L. Ron Hubbard announces previously restricted information about Scientology's founding mythopoeia to his followers, including: 'Operating Thetan III', the highest spiritual state in his Gnostic system; and 'Xenu', a pre-historic, genocidal, extra-terrestrial overlord upon whom many of the world's problems can be blamed – both later denied by key figures in Scientology.

1968   Samuel Delany, *Nova*; Philip K. Dick, *Do Androids Dream of Electric Sheep?*; Ursula le Guin, *A Wizard of Earthsea*; Joanna Russ, *Picnic on Paradise*, 'The Birth of a Salesman'.
[Film] *Planet Of The Apes*, dir. Franklyn K. Schaffner; *Barberella*, dir. Roger Vadim.
Ivan Sutherland creates first virtual reality headset.

1969   Philip K. Dick, *Ubik*; John Brunner, *Stand on Zanzibar* (Hugo Award for Best Novel); Ursula Le Guin, *The Left Hand of Darkness* (Hugo Award for Best Novel, 1970); Samuel Delany, 'Time Considered as a Helix of Semi-Precious Stones'; Doris Lessing, *The Four-Gated City*; James Tiptree Jr, 'The Last Flight of Dr Ain'.
[TV] Gene Roddenbury, *Star Trek* (original series).
Apollo 11 is the first manned mission to land on the moon.
David Bowie's eponymous album includes 'Space Oddity', which recounts the story of a fictional astronaut, Major Tom, on a failed mission – later used in BBC coverage of the Apollo 11 moon landing.

1970   Larry Niven, *Ringworld* (Hugo Award for Best Novel, 1971); J. G. Ballard, *The Atrocity Exhibition*; Philip K. Dick, *Maze of Death*; Robert A. Heinlein, *I Will Fear No Evil*; Joanna Russ, *And Chaos Died*.
Lunukhord 1, launched by the Soviet Union, is the first (unmanned) rover to land on the Moon.

1971   Ursula le Guin, *The Lathe of Heaven*; Doris Lessing, *Briefing for a Descent into Hell*.
[Film] *THX-1138*, dir. George Lucas; *A Clockwork Orange*, dir. Stanley Kubrick.
On 23 April, Salyut 1 becomes the first space station of any kind to be established. Mariner 9, a US spacecraft, becomes the first to orbit another planet (Mars).
E-mail developed by Ray Tomlinson.
The University of Aston organizes the first Novacom SF convention.

1972   Joanna Russ 'When It Changed' (Nebula Award, 1972); Arthur C. Clarke, *Rendezvous with Rama* (Hugo Award for Best Novel, 1974); Philip K. Dick, *We Can Build You*; Ursula le Guin, *The Word for World is Forest*, *The Tombs of Atuan*; James Tiptree Jr, 'And I Awoke and Found Me here on the Cold Hill's Side'.
[Film] *Solaris*, dir. Andrei Tarkovsky; *Flight Of The Navigator*, dir. Randal Kleiser.
Foundation: The International Review of Science Fiction, a peer reviewed journal, is founded.
Space Invaders, an SF-influenced arcade game, is released, later becoming a pop culture phenomenon.
Pioneer 10 performs the first Jupiter flyby on 3 December; communication is lost in January 2003.

1973   J. G. Ballard, *Crash*; Samuel Delany, 'The Tides of Lust'; Robert A. Heinlein, *Time Enough for Love*; Ursula le Guin, *The Farthest Shore*; James Tiptree Jr, 'The Girl Who Was Plugged In'.
The peer-reviewed journal *Science Fiction Studies* is founded by R. D Mullen: published three times yearly to the present day and described by the *Times Literary Supplement* as the most academic, theoretical and daring of SF journals.

1974   Ursula K. le Guin, *The Dispossessed*; J. G. Ballard, *Concrete Island*; Christopher Priest, *Inverted World*.

1975   J. G. Ballard, *High Rise*; Samuel Delany, *Dhalgren*; Naomi Mitchison, *Solution Three*; Joanna Russ, *The Female Man*; James Tiptree Jr, 'A Momentary Taste of Being'.
[Crit.] Robert Scholes, *Structural Fabulation: An Essay on Fiction of the Future*.
Hawkwind, English progenitors of the 'space rock' sub-genre, release the *Warrior On the Edge of Time* concept album, a collaboration with influential SF author Michael Moorcock.
Apollo-Soyuz link-up. Mariner 10 performs both the first flyby of Venus on 5 February, and the first flyby of Mercury on 29 of March. Venera 9 performs the first orbit around Venus, making it the first planet to be photographed successfully.

1976   Octavia Butler, *Patternmaster*; Samuel Delany, *Triton*; Joanna Russ, *The Adventures of Alyx*; Geoff Ryman, 'The Death of a Translator'.
[Crit.] Eric S. Rabkin, *The Fantastic in Literature*.

1977   Octavia Butler, *Mind of my Mind*; Doris Lessing, *Memoirs of a Survivor*; Christopher Priest, *A Dream of Wessex*; Joanna Russ, *We Who Are About To*.
[Crit.] Samuel Delany, *The Jewel-Hinged Jaw: Notes on the Language of Science Fiction*.

1978   Octavia Butler, *Survivor*; Joanna Russ, *The Two of Them*, *Kittatinny: A Tale of Magic*.

1979   Octavia Butler *Kindred*; Douglas Adams, *The Hitchhiker's Guide to the Galaxy*; J. G. Ballard, *The Unlimited Dream Company*; Samuel Delany, *Tales of Nevèrÿon*; Doris Lessing, *Shikasta*.
[Film] *Star Trek: The Motion Picture*, dir. Robert Wise; *Alien*, dir. Ridley Scott; *Dune*, dir. David Lynch.
[Crit.] Darko Suvin, *Metamorphoses of Science Fiction: On the Poetics and History of a Literary Genre*.
Apple Computer, Inc introduces the Macintosh Personal Computer.

1980   Octavia Butler, *Wild Seed*; Robert A. Heinlein, *The Number of the Beast*; Doris Lessing, *The Marriages Between Zones Three, Four and Five*.
[Crit.] Ursula K. le Guin, *The Language of the Night: Essays on Fantasy and Science Fiction*; H. Bruce Franklin, *Robert A. Heinlein: America as Science Fiction*.
Iconic Japanese arcade game *Pacman* is first released; it depicts a conflict in space, between an alien and various monsters; it will go on to become the highest-grossing video game of all time.

1981   Philip K. Dick, *VALIS, The Divine Invasion*; Christopher Priest, *The Affirmation*.
IBM announces its first Personal Computer.
Microsoft creates DOS.

1982   Joanna Russ, 'The Mystery of the Young Gentleman'; Philip K. Dick, *The Transmigration of Timothy Archer*.
[Film] *Blade Runner*, dir. Ridley Scott; *E.T: The Extra-Terrestrial*, dir. Stephen Spielberg; *Tron*, dir. Stephen Lisberger.
Interzone magazine first published.
Jarvik-7, an artificial heart designed by American scientists Robert Jarvik, is successfully implanted into patients Barney Clarke and Robert Schroeder, extending their lives for 112 and 620 days respectively following surgery.

1983   Naomi Mitchison, *Not By Bread Alone*.
[Crit.] Joanna Russ, *How to Suppress Women's Writing*.
Pioneer 10 is the first craft to fly beyond the orbit of Neptune and thus the boundaries of our Solar System.

1984   William Gibson, *Neuromancer* (Hugo Award for Best Novel, 1985); J. G. Ballard, *Empire of the Sun*; Octavia Butler, *Clay's Ark*, 'Bloodchild' (Winner of the Nebula and Hugo awards); Samuel Delany, *Stars in My Pocket Like Grains of Sand*; Gwyneth Jones, *Divine Endurance*; Kim Stanley Robinson, *Icehenge, The Wild Shore*; Geoff Ryman, 'The Unconquered Country'; Neal Stephenson, *The Big U*.

1985   Margaret Atwood, *The Handmaid's Tale*; Don Delillo, *White Noise*; Ursula le Guin, *Always Coming Home*; Geoff Ryman, *The Warrior Who Carried Life*.
[Film] *Back To The Future*, dir. Robert Zemeckis.
[Crit.] Donna Haraway, 'A Cyborg Manifesto: Science, Technology, and Socialist-Feminism in the Late Twentieth Century'.

1986   William Gibson, *Count Zero*.
[Film] *Aliens*, dir. James Cameron; *Short Circuit*, dir. John Badham.

[Crit.] Tom Moylan, *Demand the Impossible: Science Fiction and the Utopian Imagination.*
After O-ring failure on 28 January, Space Shuttle Challenger breaks apart during launch over the Atlantic Ocean killing all seven crew members; media coverage of the disaster is extensive.

1987   Iain M. Banks, *Consider Phlebas.*
[Film] *RoboCop*, dir. Paul Verhoeven.
[Crit.] Leon Stover's *Robert Heinlein.*
The first Arthur C. Clarke Award is presented to Margaret Atwood.

1988   Carol Emschwiller, *Carmen Dog*; William Gibson, *Mona Lisa Overdrive*; Gwyneth Jones, *Kairos*; Kim Stanley Robinson, *The Gold Coast.*
[Film] *Akira*, dir. Katsuhiro Otomo.
[Crit.] Sarah Lefanu, *In the Chinks of the World Machine: Feminism and Science Fiction.*
Stephen Hawking publishes his best-selling *A Brief History of Time*; it remains on the New York Times bestsellers list for over four years.

1989   Geoff Ryman, *The Child Garden*; Dan Simmons, *Hyperion* (Hugo Award for Best Novel, 1990).
Human Genome Project begins.
Demolition of the Berlin wall begins.

1990   Bruce Sterling and William Gibson, *The Difference Engine*; Iain M. Banks, *Use of Weapons*; Kim Stanley Robinson, *Pacific Edge.*
The first photograph of the entire solar system is taken by Voyager 1 on Valentine's Day.

1991   Gwyneth Jones, *White Queen* (Winner of the James Tiptree Jr Award); Martin Amis, *Time's Arrow; or The Nature of the Offence.*
[Film] *Terminator 2*, dir. James Cameron.
[Crit.] Fredric Jameson, *Postmodernism, or, the Cultural Logic of Late Capitalism.*
World Wide Web launched by CERN.

1992   William Gibson, *Virtual Light*; Geoff Ryman, *Was.*
[Film] *The Lawnmower Man*, dir. Brett Leonard.

1993   Octavia Butler, *Parable of the Sower*; Kim Stanley Robinson, *Red Mars*; Neal Stephenson, *Snow Crash.*
[Film] *Jurassic Park*, dir. Stephen Spielberg.
[TV] *The X-Files.*
[Crit.] John Clute and Peter Nicholls (eds), *The Encyclopedia of Science Fiction* (2nd edn).

Billy Idol releases *Neuromancer*-influenced concept album, *Cyberpunk*.

1994   Kim Stanley Robinson, *Green Mars*.

1995   Christopher Priest, *The Prestige*; Philip Pullman, *Northern Lights*; Gwyneth Jones, *Phoenix Café*; Neal Stephenson, *The Diamond Age*.

1996   Melissa Scott, *Shadow Man*; William Gibson, *Idoru*; Kim Stanley Robinson, *Blue Mars*; Geoff Ryman, *253*.
        [Film] *Independence Day*, dir. Roland Emmerich.
        [Crit.] Gary Westfahl, *Cosmic Engineers: A Study of Hard Science Fiction*.
        The search engine *Google* begins as a research project by two students, Larry Page and Sergey Brin, at Stanford University, California.
        'Spaceman', the debut single by Wolverhampton alternative rock band Babylon Zoo, enters the chart at number one, becoming the fastest selling UK single at the time.

1997   Philip Pullman, *The Subtle Knife*.
        [Film] *Gattaca*, dir. Andrew Niccol.
        [Crit.] Roger Luckhurst, *The Angle Between Two Walls: The Fiction of J. G. Ballard*.
        Dolly the Sheep becomes the first animal to be cloned from an adult cell, using the process of somatic cell nuclear transfer, at the Roslin Institute, Edinburgh, but dies at the age of six from a progressive lung disease.

1998   Tricia Sullivan, *Dreaming in Smoke*; Carolyn Ives Gilman, *Halfway Human*; Octavia Butler, *Parable of the Talents* (Winner of the Nebula Award).
        [Film] *Armageddon*, dir. Michael Bay; *Deep Impact*, dir. Mimi Leder.
        The first hybrid human embryo clone was produced from a man's leg cell, and a cow's egg with removed DNA, by Advanced Cell Technologies.

1999   Naola Hopkinson, *Brown Girl in the Ring*; Neal Stephenson, *Cryptonomicon*; William Gibson, *All Tomorrow's Parties*.
        [Film] *The Matrix*, dir. Larry and Andy Wachowski.
        [Crit.] Gwyneth Jones, *Deconstructing the Starships: Science Fiction and Reality*; Jeanne Cortiel, *Demand My Writing: Joanna Russ/ Feminism/ Science Fiction*.

2000   Mary Gentle, *Ash*; China Miéville, *Perdido Street Station*; Octavia Butler, *Lilith's Breed*; Ursula le Guin, *The Telling*.

[Film] *The Hitchhiker's Guide to the Galaxy*, dir. Garth Jenkins.

[Crit.] Adam Roberts, *Science Fiction: the New Critical Idiom*; Dani Cavallaro, *Cyberpunk and Cyberculture: Science Fiction and the Work of William Gibson*.

Radar data uncovers large quantities of ice in Mars's poles; if melted, this water could cover the surface of the planet to a depth of 11 metres.

2001 Gwyneth Jones, *Bold as Love*; Geoff Ryman, *Lust*.

On September 11, the Islamist terrorist group Al-Qaeda co-ordinates a series of attacks on the New York City and Washington D.C. areas of the United States, profoundly changing worldwide socio-political relations.

The Human Genome Project produces a first draft of the complete set of human genetic information, known simply as the human genome.

2002 Gwyneth Jones, *Castles Made of Sand*; Christopher Priest, *The Separation*; Kim Stanley Robinson, *The Years of Rice and Salt*.

2003 Neal Stephenson, *Quicksilver*; Tricia Sullivan, *Maul*; J. G. Ballard, *Millennium People*; William Gibson, *Pattern Recognition*; Gwyneth Jones, *Midnight Lamp*.

On 1 February Space Shuttle *Columbia* disintegrated over Texas and Louisiana killing all seven crew members during re-entry, which disaster was caused by damage after debris struck the craft's heat shield during take-off.

2004 Geoff Ryman, *Air*; Neal Stephenson, *The Confusion*, *The System of the World*; David Mitchell, *Cloud Atlas*; Iain M. Banks, *The Algebraist*; Gwyneth Jones, *Life*; Kim Stanley Robinson, *Forty Signs of Rain*.

2005 Octavia Butler, *Fledgling*; Gwyneth Jones, *Band of Gypsies*; Doris Lessing, *The Story of General Dann and Mara's Daughter, Griot, and the Snow Dog*; Kim Stanley Robinson, *Fifty Degrees Below*; Charles Stross, *Accelerando*,

[Crit.] Frederic Jameson, *Archaeologies of the Future: The Desire Called Utopia and Other Science Fictions*; Andrzej Gasiorek, *J. G. Ballard*; Andrew M. Butler (ed.), *Christopher Priest: The Interaction*.

Frequently dubbed the '7/7 bombings', three Islamic terrorists targeted the London public transport network with suicide attacks, killing 52 people and injuring over 700 others.

2006 Cormac McCarthy, *The Road*; Ken MacLeod, *Learning the World*; J. G. Ballard, *Kingdom Come*; Geoff Ryman, *The King's Last Song*.

[Film] *A Scanner Darkly*, dir. Richard Linklater; *V for Vendetta*, dir. James McTeigue.

[Crit.] Adam Roberts, *The History of Science Fiction*.

2007 Sarah Hall, *The Carhullan Army*; Ken MacLeod, *The Execution Channel*; Richard Morgan, *Black Man*; Charles Stross, *Glasshouse*; William Gibson, *Spook Country*; Kim Stanley Robinson, *Sixty Days and Counting*.

[Film] *I Am Legend*, dir. Francis Laurence; *Sunshine*, dir. Danny Boyle.

2008 Ken MacLeod, *The Night Sessions*; Gwyneth Jones, *Spirit*; Ursula le Guin, *Lavinia*; Neal Stephenson, *Anathem*.

[Film] *Cloverfield*, dir. Matt Reeves; *Iron Man*, dir. Jon Favreau.

[Crit.] Istran Csicsery-Ronay Jr, *The Seven Beauties of Science Fiction*. Construction of the Large Hadron Collider (LHC) – the world's largest and highest energy particle accelerator – underneath the Franco-Swiss border is completed, uniquely allowing physicists to test their theories.

2009 Margaret Atwood, *The Year of the Flood*; Neil Gaiman, *The Graveyard Book*; China Miéville, *The City and the City* (Hugo Award for Best Novel, 2010); Adam Roberts, *Yellow Blue Tibia*; Kim Stanley Robinson, *Galileo's Dream*; Iain Banks, *Transition*.

[Film] *Avatar*, dir. James Cameron; *Moon*, dir. Duncan Jones; *Splice*, dir. Vincenzo Natali; *Pandorum*, dir. Christian Alvert.

[Crit.] Gwyneth Jones, *Imagination/Space: Essays and Talks on Fiction, Feminism, Technology and Politics*.

2010 Lauren Beukes, *Zoo City*; William Gibson, *Zero History*.

[Film] *Inception*, dir. Christopher Nolan; *The Book of Eli*, dir. Allen and Albert Hughes; *Tron: Legacy*, dir. Joseph Kosinski.

[Crit.] Ingrid Thaler, *Black Atlantic Speculative Fictions: Octavia E. Butler, Jewelle Gomez and Nalo Hopkinson*.

Large Hadron Collider sets world record for highest-energy man-made particle collisions.

2011 China Miéville, *Embassytown*; Jane Rogers, *The Testament of Jessie Lamb*; Christopher Priest, *The Islanders*; Neal Stephenson, *Reamde*.

[Film] *Attack the Block*, dir. Joe Cornish.

[Crit.] Margaret Atwood, *In Other Worlds: Science Fiction and the Human Imagination*.

In September, whilst attempting to prove the existence of tau neutrinos, the OPERA experiment mistakenly reports neutrinos travelling faster-than-light, challenging the theory of special relativity that underpins contemporary understanding of physics, leading to short-lived excitement and speculation in the press about the possibility of SF-esque scenarios.

2012   Iain M. Banks, *The Hydrogen Sonata*; Ken MacLeod, *Intrusion*; Kim Stanley Robinson, *2312*; Samuel Delany, *Through the Valley of the Nest of Spiders*.
[Film] *Prometheus*, dir. Ridley Scott; *The Hunger Games*, dir. Gary Ross.
The NASA Curiosity Rover lands on Mars investigating climate, geology, microbial life and the role of water on the planet.

3 Major Science Fiction Authors

Nick Hubble, Emma Filtness and Joseph Norman

Chapter Overview

Margaret Atwood (1939–) was born in Ottawa, Canada, and is a prolific novelist, poet, short story writer, essayist and critic. Her father was a field entomologist, so her early childhood was spent moving around the forests and small settlements of Ontario and Quebec. The family settled in Toronto at the end of the Second World War, where Atwood admits to experiencing a culture shock in response to city life. She has lived briefly in Britain and France, and now lives in Toronto with her husband. In 1961, she received an Arts degree from the University of Toronto and then went to Radcliffe College, Harvard University, on a graduate fellowship, where she again mentions culture shock, this time from being a Canadian woman in an America where Canadians were invisible. She never completed her PhD thesis on English Metaphysical Romance preferring instead to write her first novel, *The Edible Woman*, the story of a woman experiencing a separation between body and mind that anticipates the concerns of second-wave feminism, subsequently published in 1969. Since then, Atwood has become noted as a feminist and activist, concerned with addressing contemporary social and political issues. She is also known for her Canadian nationalism, manifested in her early works such as in her second novel, *Surfacing* (1972), and her Canadian literary history, *Survival* (1972).

Atwood first became linked, controversially, to SF with the publication of *The Handmaid's Tale* (1985). A dystopia set in the Republic of Gilead, it depicts a Christian fundamentalist dictatorship occupying the territory of the former USA. Women's rights have been removed and the narrator of the main part of the novel, the eponymous handmaid, is known only as Offred; a name which makes clear her relationship as the possession of the powerful official in whose household she lives. The novel finishes with a transcript from a Symposium on Gileadean Studies taking place in 2195, thus implying that Gilead no longer exists and that more egalitarian gender relationships have been restored. One interesting aspect of the novel is the implication that radical feminism was somehow complicit in the establishment of Gilead. The novel won the inaugural Arthur C. Clarke Award for Best Science Fiction published in Britain, which award triggered controversy as it led to Atwood repeatedly denying, sometimes in intemperate terms, that she wrote science fiction as opposed to speculative fiction, a term she was happy to accept.

The Blind Assassin (2000), winner of the Booker Prize, is a complex narrative of a novel within a novel, in which there is a further layer created by a story embedded within the fictional novel. Given that this embedded story is openly acknowledged as pulp SF, it might be assumed that Atwood had become more at ease with the label. However, she still took pains to label her next novel, the futuristic dystopia *Oryx and Crake* (2003), as specu-lative fiction. This novel begins after the collapse of civilization, in a world containing apparently only one human and a group of creatures who turn out to be genetically-modified beings, reminiscent of the Eloi in Wells's *The Time Machine* (1895). However, the story of what has happened gradually emerges in flashback; presenting a strong critique both of science and masculinity, as well as consumerism in general. *The Year of the Flood* (2009) is set in the same world and covers the same time period from the perspective of a different group of characters. A third novel in the series, *Maddaddam*, is due to be published in the autumn of 2013.

Atwood's most recent publication is a book of SF criticism entitled *In Other Worlds: SF and the Human Imagination* (2011), which elaborates on the differences as she sees them between 'science fiction' proper and 'speculative fiction', as well as discussing other related genres such as fantasy and Utopias and dystopias, including her own fictions. Atwood is the most written about Canadian writer ever, with much academic criticism produced particularly in North America and Britain and increasingly in Europe, Australia and India. Biographical and critical works on Atwood include *The Cambridge Companion to Margaret Atwood* (2005) edited by Coral Ann Howells and Nathalie Cooke's *Margaret Atwood* (1998). However, with her continued publication of novels that can clearly be considered SF, not to mention her critical work on the genre, it seems certain she will eventually be fully integrated into the SF canon.

Works Cited

Atwood, Margaret (1969). *The Edible Woman*. Toronto: McClelland & Stewart.
—(1972). *Surfacing*. Toronto: McClelland & Stewart.
—(1972). *Survival*. Toronto: Anansi.
—(1985). *The Handmaid's Tale*. Toronto: McClelland & Stewart.
—(2000). *The Blind Assassin*. Toronto: McClelland & Stewart.
—(2003). *Oryx and Crake*. Toronto: McClelland & Stewart.
—(2009). *The Year of the Flood*. Toronto: McClelland & Stewart.
—(2011). *In Other Worlds: SF and the Human Imagination*. Toronto: McClelland & Stewart.
—(2013). *Maddaddam*. Toronto: McClelland & Stewart.
Cooke, Nathalie (1998). *Margaret Atwood: A Biography*. Toronto: ECW Press.
Howells, Coral Ann (ed.) (2006). *The Cambridge Companion to Margaret Atwood*. Cambridge: Cambridge University Press.
Wells, H. G. (1895). *The Time Machine*. London: Heinemann.

J. G. Ballard (1930–2009) was an award-winning novelist and short-story writer, particularly influential during the British 'New Wave' of SF. Born into a wealthy expatriate family in Shanghai, Ballard's early exposure to death and violence while interned in Lunghua Camp by the Japanese from 1943–5 inevitably shaped the apocalyptic tone of much of his fiction, even though he admitted being 'largely happy' in this environment. These experiences are documented in his autobiography, *Miracles of Life* (2008), but were earlier fictionalized in the semi-autobiographical novel, *Empire of the Sun* (1984), which won Ballard the *Guardian* fiction prize and the James Tate Black Memorial prize, and was also shortlisted for the Booker prize, establishing him as a successful mainstream author.

After the War, Ballard arrived in Britain in 1946 and completed his schooling before brief periods spent studying medicine at King's College and English at Queen Mary College, where he began writing avant-garde stories influenced by psychoanalysis and Surrealism. In 1954, Ballard joined the RAF and was posted to Canada, where he was introduced to American SF magazines. After returning to Britain, he worked as an assistant editor for a science journal, married and fathered his first child. In 1960, he moved to the London suburb of Shepperton, where he was to remain in residence for the rest of his life. Following the death of his wife, Mary, in 1964 he was left to bring up their three children as a single parent; eventually settling into a pattern of writing during the day while the children were at school. The suburbs might seem a surprising location for a writer whose work so consistently challenged social norms, but Ballard clearly viewed them as a prime location for millennial transformation and depicted them as such unforgettably in *The Unlimited Dream Company* (1979), *Millennium People* (2003) and *Kingdom Come* (2006).

Ballard's first stories appeared in 1956; the publication of 'Escapement' by *New Worlds* magazine instigated a long and fruitful relationship first under the editorship of Ted Carnell and later under Michael Moorcock. His work helped transform the SF genre, using self-reflexive, interdisciplinary and experimental literary approaches to depict, not the politics of outer space environments familiar from 1930s pulp SF, but the inner space of psychological trauma and urban psychosis. In this way Ballard was often unsympathetic towards the SF genre, displaying little appreciation for its history or the pioneering authors that preceded him. Therefore, although his first novel was a Wyndhamesque disaster fiction, *The Winds from Nowhere* (1962), in subsequent books, such as *The Drowned World* (1962) [see Chapter 4 of this book] and *The Burning World* (1965), now more commonly known by its UK title *The Drought*, he inverted the whole model by having his anti-hero protagonists reject any idea of escape to form a better world in favour of seeking out the centre of the crisis in order to experience the destruction and disintegration at first hand.

In writing stories such as 'The Assassination of John Fitzgerald Kennedy Considered as a Downhill Motor Race' (1966), later collected as part of his 'condensed novel' experiment, *The Atrocity Exhibition* (1970), Ballard unveiled the hidden relationships between sex, consumerism and the death drive that underpinned the liberalization of social attitudes at the time. Publishers' readers doubted his sanity and questions were asked in Parliament about his work, but, viewed in hindsight, it becomes clear that Ballard was actually a moralist who dissected the public façade of a culture that appeared to be in its death throes.

Ballard's novel *Crash* (1973) provoked controversy with its depiction of explicitly sexualized car crashes; it was successfully filmed by David Cronenberg in 1996, and inspired theoretical interest among postmodernists such as Jean Baudrillard. Alongside *Concrete Island* (1974) and *High-Rise* (1975), *Crash* forms a trilogy focused around the changing London landscape in an era of high-Capitalism and new technology. The adjective 'Ballardian' has entered the Collins English Dictionary, referring to conditions that resemble the bleak, entropic urbanity that characterizes many of his works. In his later work, he turned his attention to wider outposts of capitalism: both *Cocaine Nights* (1996) and *Super Cannes* (2000), which won the Commonwealth Writers Prize, rely upon a loose crime narrative to explore apparently close-knit and closed ex-patriot Mediterranean resort communities, where consumerism, class conflict and the *ennui* experienced by the ultra-rich lead to violence.

However, any assessment of Ballard's legacy also needs to take account of his *Complete Short Stories*, first published in 2001, and reprinted in several different formats since. Important critical works on Ballard include Roger Luckhurst's *The Angle Between Two Walls: The Fiction of J. G. Ballard* (1997), Andrzej Gasiorek's *J. G. Ballard* (2005), and Jeanette Baxter's edited collection, *J. G. Ballard* (2008).

Works Cited

Ballard, J. G. (1956). 'Escapement'. *New Worlds Science Fiction*. 54 (December). 27–39.

—(1962). *The Drowned World*. New York: Berkley Medallion.

—(1962). *The Winds from Nowhere*. New York: Berkley Medallion.

—(1964). *The Burning World*. New York: Berkley Medallion.

—(1966). 'The Assassination of John Fitzgerald Kennedy Considered as a Downhill Motor Race'. *New Worlds and SF Impulse*. 50. 171 (March). 119–21.

—(1970). *The Atrocity Exhibition*. London: Jonathan Cape.

—(1973). *Crash*. London: Jonathan Cape.

—(1974). *Concrete Island*. London: Jonathan Cape.

—(1975). *High-Rise*. London: Jonathan Cape.

—(1979). *The Unlimited Dream Company*. London: Jonathan Cape.

—(1984). *Empire of the Sun*. London: Gollancz.

—(1996). *Cocaine Nights*. London: Flamingo.

—(2000). *Super Cannes*. London: Flamingo.

—(2001). *Complete Short Stories*. London: Flamingo.

—(2003). *Millennium People*. London: Flamingo.

—(2006). *Kingdom Come*. London: Fourth Estate.

—(2008). *Miracles of Life: An Autobiography*. London: Fourth Estate.

Baxter, Jeanette (ed.) (2008). *J. G. Ballard*. London: Continuum.

Luckhurst, Roger (1997). *The Angle Between Two Walls: The Fiction of J. G. Ballard*. Liverpool: Liverpool University Press.

Gasiorek, Andrzej (2005). *J. G. Ballard*. Manchester: Manchester University Press.

Iain (M.) Banks (1954–2013) was a prolific Scottish author whose SF, which mostly features the pan-galactic civilization called the Culture, is distinguished by the use of a middle initial. However, a number of his 'mainstream' works blur genre boundaries, incorporating elements of SF, gothic, fantasy and crime fiction. For example, despite being published as by Iain Banks in the UK, *Transition* (2009) is clearly SF and was published in the US as being by Iain M. Banks. Banks spent his early years in Fife before moving with his family to Gourock on the Firth of Clyde at the age of nine. He attended Greenock High School, where he became friends with fellow SF writer Ken MacLeod, before going on to study English, Philosophy and Psychology at the University of Stirling, where he began writing more seriously (he had already written one novel while at school), influenced by Jorges Luis Borges, Hunter S. Thompson, Robert A. Heinlein and Alasdair Gray, amongst others. After University, he took a variety of jobs, travelled a bit and continued with his writing – the idea of the Culture and the first drafts of novels such as *Use of Weapons* (1990) and the non-Culture *Against a Dark Background* (1993) date from the 1970s – before eventually drifting down to London. Here he met up with MacLeod again and was politically involved on the fringes of the International Marxist Group, before starting work for a law firm, meeting his future wife, Annie, and getting published. Banks's politics, as reflected in his fiction, continued to remain firmly to the left and militantly atheistic. He regularly wrote provocative letters to prominent national newspapers, campaigned on issues such as state funding for faith schools, and was notable for his idiosyncratic acts of political protest, such as plastering his Land Rover with anti-war slogans and posting his shredded passport to then-Prime Minister Tony Blair in 2003, following the invasion of Iraq.

Banks's debut novel *The Wasp Factory* (1984), whilst initially causing moral outrage in the press for its portrayal of a disturbed, deformed child Frank and his ritualistic practices, is now considered a classic of contemporary gothic fiction. It established reoccurring features of Banks's writing, including symbolic descriptions of Scotland's various bridges, rivers, castles and mountains, and themes of complex inter-familial relationship, the individual and the State, the fluidity of personal identity and the nature of borders and boundaries. Banks's most significant contribution to SF is his 'personal Utopia' the Culture, an egalitarian inter-species federation with limitless resources, explored in ten works over 25 years. In *Consider Phlebas* (1987), Banks depicts a war between the secular Culture and a society of ideologically-opposed, religious zealots, which was influenced by the Soviet Union's war in Afghanistan. Alongside subsequent texts like *The Player of Games* (1988) and *Excession* (1996), *Consider Phlebas* played a crucial role in the re-invigoration of space opera, using its expansive scope in a Stapledonian manner to explore historical and philosophical themes, such as postcolonial military intervention and posthuman subjectivity, whilst subtly deconstructing the Culture from an outsider's perspective. Recent Culture novels, such as *Matter* (2008), *Surface Detail* (2010) and *The Hydrogen Sonata* (2012), focus on the relationship between physical and virtual space in order to explore metaphysical questions of materialism, simulation and identity. His work is notable for its treatment of all forms of artificial intelligence as living beings with rights, which is a particularly strong theme in the non-Culture SF novel, *The Algebraist* (2004).

Despite rejecting postmodern experimentation in favour of a more traditional approach to narrative, many of Banks's works are formally complex: for example, *Use of Weapons* innovatively alternates forward and reverse chronology and the non-SF *Complicity* (1993) varies first- and second-person perspectives. The themes of play and gaming reoccur often in his work, both in the form and content of his narratives. The non-Culture *Feersum Endjinn* (1994) is notable for its linguistic playfulness, featuring a bizarre phonetic language that recalls modern Scottish dialect, in an attempt to convey extra-terrestrial otherness. *Walking on Glass* (1985), *The Bridge* (1986) and *Transition* – all published in the UK as by Iain Banks – turn on the protagonists' everyday lives becoming confused with co-existing alternative realities, located either elsewhere in the universe, in their unconscious mind or in a drug-induced parallel plane of existence. In conclusion, it becomes clear that Banks is determined both to be widely read and to challenge convention and provoke thought. This commitment to reaching a large audience has perhaps played a role in the lack of critical attention to his work beyond a handful of essays and book chapters. However, Martyn Colebrooke and Katherine Cox's collected volume of essays, *Border Crossing: Critical Perspectives on the Writing of Iain Banks* is due to appear later in 2013.

Works Cited

Banks, Iain (1984). *The Wasp Factory*. London: Macmillan.
—(1985). *Walking on Glass*. London: Macmillan.
—(1986). *The Bridge*. London: Macmillan.
—(1993). *Complicity*. London: Little, Brown.
—(2009). *Transition*. London: Little, Brown.
Banks, Iain M. (1987). *Consider Phlebas*. London: Macmillan.
—(1988). *The Player of Games*. London: Macmillan.
—(1990). *Use of Weapons*. London: Orbit.
—(1993). *Against a Dark Background*. London: Orbit.
—(1994). *Feersum Endjinn*. London: Orbit.
—(1996). *Excession*. London: Orbit.
—(2004). *The Algebraist*. London: Orbit.
—(2008). *Matter*. London: Orbit.
—(2009). *Transition*. New York: Orbit.
—(2010). *Surface Detail*. London: Orbit.
—(2012). *The Hydrogen Sonata*. London: Orbit.
Colebrook, Martyn and Katherine Cox (2013). *Border Crossing: Critical Perspectives on the Writing of Iain Banks*. Jefferson, NC: McFarland.

Octavia Butler (1947–2006) was the first significant African American female SF author and was born and raised in California by her Baptist mother and grandmother, after her father died when she was a baby. Butler was dyslexic, yet began writing at the age of ten. She received an associate's degree from Pasadena City College in 1968 then enrolled at California State University, Los

Angeles. Following her time at California State she took a number of writing classes and workshops.

She published 12 novels and one short story collection in total, beginning with the publication of the short story 'Crossover' in 1971, but it was her *Patternist* novels – *Patternmaster* (1976), *Mind of My Mind* (1977), *Survivor* (1978), *Wild Seed* (1980) and *Clay's Ark* (1984) – that drew significant attention. *Patternmaster* is set in a future America in which Patternists – humans with psychic abilities – fight against Clayarks, who are alien descendants of humans who were infected by a virus brought to Earth following the first interstellar expedition. The *Patternist* series explores teleportation, immortality, shape-shifting, the establishment of space colonies, the theme of power and control, the struggle against oppression and racial differences.

Kindred (1979) is perhaps Butler's best-known novel and is responsible for securing her place as one of the most well-respected African-American writers of the time. The novel features the protagonist Dana, a Black American woman, who is regularly torn from her modern-day surroundings and placed into the antebellum South to save the life of her ancestor, Rufus, the white son of a plantation owner (see discussion in Chapter 4 of this book). *Kindred's* narrative was undoubtedly influenced by autobiographical accounts of former slaves, such as Frederick Douglass.

Dawn (1987) was the first in Butler's *Xenogenesis* trilogy, later collected as *Lilith's Brood* (2000), which begins with protagonist Lilith awakening on a starship after a spell of suspended animation while the Earth was repaired by aliens following nuclear war. What follows involves human-alien sexual collaboration, often not consensual, followed by human-alien offspring. Explorations of the collapse of civilization and its various possible consequences form a recurring theme in Butler's work, along with slave narratives, race-relations and other power struggles, such as in *Parable of the Sower* (1993) in which protagonist Lauren, fearful that the world is on the brink of economic, environmental and ethical disaster, creates her own religion and multi-racial Utopian community. Butler also published a vampire novel, *Fledgling* (2005), favouring science-fictional rather than supernatural explanations for the vampire 'species'.

She won the Nebula and the Hugo for 'Bloodchild' (1984), a Hugo for 'Speech Sounds' (1983) and a Nebula for *Parable of the Talents* (1998), as well as various nominations and a MacArthur Foundation 'Genius' Grant in 1995 and a PEN West lifetime achievement award in 2000. Biographies of Butler can be found in *The Norton Anthology of African American Literature* (2004) edited by Henry Louis Gates and *Postmodern American Fiction: A Norton Anthology* (1997) edited by Paula Geyh. Recent critical works about Butler include *Changing Bodies in the Fiction of Octavia Butler: Slaves, Aliens and Vampires* (2010) by Gregory Jerome Hampton and *Black Atlantic Speculative Fictions: Octavia E. Butler, Jewelle Gomez and Nalo Hopkinson* (2010) by Ingrid Thaler.

Works Cited

Butler, Octavia (1971). 'Crossover'. *Clarion*. Robert Scott Wilson (ed.). New York: Signet.

—(1976). *Patternmaster*. New York: Doubleday.

—(1977). *Mind of My Mind*. New York: Doubleday.

—(1978). *Survivor*. New York: Doubleday.

—(1979). *Kindred*. New York: Doubleday.

—(1980). *Wild Seed*. New York: Doubleday.

—(1983). 'Speech Sounds'. *Isaac Asimov's Science Fiction Magazine* (Mid-December).

—(1984). 'Bloodchild'. *Isaac Asimov's Science Fiction Magazine* (June).

—(1984). *Clay's Ark*. New York: St. Martin's Press.

—(1987). *Dawn*. New York: Warner Books.

—(1993). *Parable of the Sower*. New York: Four Walls Eight Windows

—(1998). *Parable of the Talents*. New York: Seven Stories Press.

—(2000). *Lilith's Brood*. New York: Grand Central Publishing.

—(2005). *The Fledgling*. New York: Seven Stories Press.

Gates, Henry Louis (ed.) (2004). *The Norton Anthology of African American Literature*. New York: W. W. Norton.

Geyh, Paula (ed.) (1997). *Postmodern American Fiction: A Norton Anthology*. New York: W. W. Norton.

Hampton, Gregory Jerome (2010). *Changing Bodies in the Fiction of Octavia Butler: Slaves, Aliens and Vampires*. Lanham, MD: Lexington Books.

Thaler, Ingrid (2010). *Black Atlantic Speculative Fictions: Octavia E. Butler, Jewelle Gomez and Nalo Hopkinson*. New York: Routledge.

Samuel Delany (1942–) grew up in Harlem, New York; the son of a library clerk and an undertaker. He attended the Bronx High School of Science, where he met the future poet, Marilyn Hacker, whom he would marry in 1961 in Detroit, Michigan, one of the few states in which it was then legal for a black man to wed a white woman. Before he was 20, Delany dropped out of the City College of New York and finished writing his first novel, *The Jewels of Aptor* (1962), which was published by Ace Books, where Hacker was working as an assistant editor. The marriage was complicated – Delany primarily identified as gay and Hacker as lesbian – and involved various living arrangements and periods of separation before a final split in 1975. Delany has written autobiographically about the 1960s in *Heavenly Breakfast* (1979) and *The Motion of Light in Water: Sex and Science Fiction Writing in the East Village 1957–1965* (1988), which won a Hugo for Best Non-Fiction. Another memoir, *Bread and Wine: An Erotic Tale of New York* (2000), charts the origins of his relationship with his current partner, Dennis Rickett.

The *Jewels of Aptor* was the first of the nine novels that he wrote in the 1960s and which established him as a major SF author. These included *Babel-17* (1966), which mixes space opera with speculation on the role of language in the construction of reality, *The Einstein Intersection* (1967), a post-disaster novel in which aliens try to make sense of the human cultural space they have come to inhabit, and *Nova* (1968), a thirty-first century grail quest that requires its protagonists to seek out the heart of an exploding nova. Delany also began to publish short stories in the later half of the decade; including 'Aye, and Gomorrah ...,' (1967), about the sexual attraction of 'frelks' to neutered 'spacers', and 'Time Considered as a Helix of Semi-Precious Stones' (1969), a longer story about a small-time crook rising through the ranks.

After a hiatus that included two years living in London and also writing the pornographic novels, *The Tides of Lust* (1973), later re-titled *Equinox*, and *Hogg* (not published until 1995), *Dhalgren* (1975) marked a best-selling return to SF. This sprawling novel investigates the urban experience of America as represented by the apparently cut-off city of Bellona. It develops concerns with race and gender present in Delany's earlier fiction and includes the first overt treatment of homosexuality in his SF. This novel was quickly followed by *Triton* (1976), which is set on Neptune's moon of that name, featuring a sexually-conservative man, unsettled by the extremely emancipated environment he finds himself within, who eventually becomes a woman. As with much of Delany's work, brief summary cannot do the novel justice because it is impossible for it to capture the metafictional playfulness with which, even as it narrates its story, it simultaneously deconstructs itself as both a work of SF and a linguistic construct. Fittingly, Delany's next book, *The Jewel-Hinged Jaw: Notes on the Language of Science Fiction* (1977), was a critical study focusing on the specific linguistic and stylistic practices of SF as manifest in its distinctive syntax. Subsequent publication has confirmed Delany's status as a major SF theorist and, despite his lack of a degree, he was eventually to progress from several visiting fellowships in the late 1970s and become a full-time academic from 1988. Delany, himself, has also become the subject of a critical corpus including George Edgar Slusser's *The Delany Intersection* (1977), Seth McEvoy's *Samuel R. Delany* (1984), and Jeffrey A. Tucker's *A Sense of Wonder: Samuel R. Delany, Race, Identity and Difference* (2004).

Tales of Nevèrÿon (1979) marked the beginning of the *Nevèrÿon* series (1979–87), which is technically more fantasy than SF but concerned with the same themes of sexuality and race that animate Delany's oeuvre as a whole. The series was punctuated in 1984 by *Stars in My Pocket Like Grains of Sand*, arguably the zenith of Delany's SF output, featuring thousands of planets of equivalent diversity to Earth. This monumental attempt to embrace and encompass almost unimaginable difference foregrounds, as Carl Freedman notes in his foreword to the twentieth anniversary edition of the novel, the importance for peaceful egalitarian living of 'not mere liberal toleration but rather *desire*. In *Stars in My Pocket*, differences among "women" (the text's generic and gender-neutral term for all intelligent life-forms) exist not to be treated with leniency and forbearance but to be actively embraced' (xiii). Apart from the futuristic content of *Through the Valley of the Nest of Spiders* (2011), Delany has not written anything that can be considered SF since the 1980s, although his subsequent fiction often treats similar themes. Nonetheless, he remains one of the most important living SF writers and his work still represents the frontier of the genre's interaction with difference.

Works Cited

Delany, Samuel (1962). *The Jewels of Aptor*. New York: Ace Books.

—(1966). *Babel-17*. New York: Ace Books.

—(1967). 'Aye, and Gomorrah …,'. *Dangerous Visions*. Harlan Ellison (ed.). New York: Doubleday. 508–20.

—(1967). *The Einstein Intersection*. New York: Ace Books.

—(1968). *Nova*. New York: Doubleday.

—(1969). 'Time Considered as a Helix of Semi-Precious Stones'. *New Worlds* 185 (December). 40–64.

—(1973). *The Tides of Lust*. New York: Lancer Books.

—(1975). *Dhalgren*. New York: Bantam Books.

—(1976). *Triton*. New York: Bantam Books.

—(1977). *The Jewel-Hinged Jaw: Notes on the Language of Science Fiction*. Elizabethtown, NY: Dragon Press.

—(1979). *Heavenly Breakfast*. New York: Bantam Books.

—(1979). *Tales of Nevèrÿon*. New York: Bantam Books.

—(1984). *Stars in My Pocket Like Grains of Sand*. New York: Bantam Books.

—(1988). *The Motion of Light in Water: Sex and Science Fiction Writing in the East Village 1957–1965*. New York: Arbor House/William Morrow.

—(1995). *Hogg*. Salt Lake City: Black Ice Books/Fiction Collective Two.

—(2000). *Bread and Wine: An Erotic Tale of New York*. New York: Powerhouse Books.

—(2011). *Through the Valley of the Nest of Spiders*. New York: Alyson Books.

McEvoy, Seth (1984). *Samuel R. Delany*. New York: Frederick Ungar.

Freeman, Carl (2004). 'Foreword'. Samuel Delany. *Stars in My Pocket Like Grains of Sand*. Middletown, CT: Wesleyan University Press. xi–xiv.

Slusser, George Edgar (1977). *The Delany Intersection*. San Francisco: The Borgo Press.

Tucker, Jeffrey A. (2004). *A Sense of Wonder: Samuel R. Delany, Race, Identity and Difference*. Middletown, CT: Wesleyan University Press.

Philip K. Dick (1928–82) was described by Fredric Jameson as 'the Shakespeare of Science Fiction' (345) for his productivity; yet Dick regarded many of his 44 novels and 121 short stories as disposable 'potboilers'. Nevertheless, retrospectively, they number amongst the most widely admired and consistently influential works in the genre. He was born in Chicago as one of a pair of twins but his sister Jane died six weeks later, leaving him with a permanent sense of loss and a fascination for doubling and alternate selves. The family soon moved to San Francisco. Following his parents' separation, Dick and his mother spent two years in Washington D.C. before moving back to Berkeley, where he completed high school and briefly attended the University of California. Although he dropped his formal studies in History, Zoology, Philosophy and Psychology, he pursued a life-long interest in the latter two disciplines and they greatly informed his writing.

Dick published his first short story in 1951, and his first novel in 1955; he initially intended to be a 'serious', literary writer but only one of his mainstream novels written in the 1950s, *Confessions of a Crap Artist* (1975), was published during his lifetime. Arguably, it was the rejection of such work by publishers that contributed to Dick's development of the distinctive style and content for which his fiction is celebrated, because he was forced to include his ideas within ostensibly pulp science fiction. This led to a series of hybrid books such as *Time Out of Joint* (1959), *The Man in the High Castle* (1962), *Martian Time-Slip* (1964) and *We Can Build You* (1972), which disrupted readers' expectations by adopting an elegant naturalistic tone in order to strip it away outrageously. For example, when the protagonist of *Time Out of Joint* walks up to a soft-drink stand in a park to see if it has any beer, everything suddenly goes eerily quiet and the stand dissolves into molecules leaving only a fluttering slip of paper, on which is printed 'SOFT-DRINK STAND' (40). In this manner, Dick pioneered what might be described as pulp postmodernism, as acknowledged by the consideration of his work in Jameson's *Postmodernism, or, the Cultural Logic of Late Capitalism* (1991). While it is precisely the combination of quirky wit and offbeat characters with serious engagement with philosophical ideas that makes him unique, the ideas have caused him to be analysed as a philosopher in his own right. Erik Davis, a key scholar on Dick's work, identifies five main themes in his work: false realities: *A Maze of Death* (1970); human vs. machine: *Do Androids Dream of Electric Sheep?* (1968); entropy: various; the nature of God: *VALIS* (1981); and social control: 'The Minority Report' (1956).

From 2 December 1974, Dick began experiencing a series of visions or hallucinations, which he interpreted variously as signs from deities, extra-terrestrials and glimpses of past lives. From herein, for the rest of his life, Dick's work was almost exclusively dedicated to exploring these experi-ences through Gnosticism and Spirituality, as manifested in the thematic trilogy of *VALIS*, *The Divine Invasion* (1981) and *The Transmigration of Timothy Archer* (1982). Short extracts from Dick's *Exegesis*, the notebooks in which he recorded his philosophical investigations into his 1974 experiences, along with most of his essays on SF, various autobiographical writings and other miscellaneous material, were collected in *The Shifting Realities of Philip K. Dick: Selected Literary and Philosophical Writings* (1995), edited by Lawrence Sutin. By 2011, scholarly and public interest had grown to the extent that it was possible to publish over 900 pages of *The Exegesis of Philip K. Dick*, edited by Pamela Jackson and Jonathan Lethem.

Since his death, Dick's work has had a huge influence upon both popular and literary culture. Philosophers such as Slavoj Žižek and Jean Baudrillard recognize a nascent awareness of postmodernism in his visions. Several generations of rock and pop musicians have referenced his works in their songs and film directors have adapted his novels to screen, most notably Ridley Scott's *Blade Runner* (1982), a version of *Do Androids Dream of Electric Sheep?*. His enduring importance for the genre was acknowledged by the launch of the Philip K. Dick Award in his honour. Critical and biographical works on Dick include the March 1975 special issue of *Science Fiction Studies* on 'The Science Fiction of Philip K. Dick', Kim Stanley Robinson's *The Novels of Philip K. Dick* (1984), Lawrence Sutin's *Divine Invasions: A Life of Philip K. Dick* (1989), Emmanuel Carrère's *I am Alive and You are Dead: A Journey into the Mind of Philip K. Dick* (1993), and Lejla Kucakalic's *Philip K. Dick: Canonical Writer of the Digital Age* (2008).

Works Cited

Carrère, Emmanuel [1993] (2005). *I am Alive and You are Dead: A Journey into the Mind of Philip K. Dick*. London: Bloomsbury.

Dick, Philip K. (1956). 'The Minority Report'. *Fantastic Universe* (January).

—(1959). *Time Out of Joint*. Philadelphia, PA: J. B. Lippincott.

—(1962). *The Man in the High Castle*. New York: Putnam.

—(1964). *Martian Time-Slip*. New York: Ballantine

—(1968). *Do Androids Dream of Electric Sheep?* New York: Doubleday.

—(1970). *A Maze of Death*. New York: Doubleday.

—(1972). *We Can Build You*. New York: Daw Books.

—(1975). *Confessions of a Crap Artist*. New York: Entwhistle Books.

—(1981). *The Divine Invasion*. New York: Timescape Books.

—(1981). *VALIS*. New York: Bantam Books.

—(1982). *The Transmigration of Timothy Archer*. New York: Timescape Books.

Jackson, Pamela and Jonathan Lethem (eds) (2011). *The Exegesis of Philip K. Dick*. Boston, MA: Houghton Mifflin Harcourt.

Jameson, Fredric (1991). *Postmodernism, or, the Cultural Logic of Late Capitalism*. London: Verso.

Kucakalic, Lejla (2008). *Philip K. Dick: Canonical Writer of the Digital Age*. London: Routledge.

Robinson, Kim Stanley (1984). *The Novels of Philip K. Dick*. Ann Arbor, MI: UMI Research Press.

Scott, Ridley (dir.) (1982). *Blade Runner*.

Sutin, Lawrence [1989] (1994). *Divine Invasions: A Life of Philip K. Dick*. Hammersmith: Harper Collins.

—(ed.). (1995). *The Shifting Realities of Philip K. Dick: Selected Literary and Philosophical Writings*. New York: Pantheon Books.

Various (1975). 'The Science Fiction of Philip K. Dick'. *Science Fiction Studies* 5 (March).

William Gibson (1948–) is an American-Canadian author, poet, screenwriter and performance art contributor, most famous as the 'father of cyberpunk' due to his extensive influence in this sub-genre, and the associated sub-genre of 'steampunk'. Born in Conway, South Carolina, Gibson yearned to write science fiction professionally from the age of 12, but would not start writing seriously until he was 29. Gibson's father died when was six, and following the death of his mother when he was 18, he travelled around California and Europe, immersing himself in the 1960s counterculture before avoiding being drafted into the Vietnam War by moving to Canada, where he eventually settled down with his future-wife, Deborah Thompson, in Vancouver at the beginning of the 1970s. He received his BA in English at the University of British Columbia in 1977, where he attended an SF module that inspired him to write his first short story, 'Fragments of a Hologram Rose' (1977). Impending parenthood compelled him to begin writing seriously and he quickly produced a number of impressive short stories, including 'Burning Chrome' (1982), which introduced the term 'cyberspace' to the world.

Inspired by classic SF texts, 'Beat' authors such as William Burroughs and Henry Miller and also punk music, Gibson's work interrogates humanity's uneasy relationships with new technologies; speculating about how future developments and nascent technology might change behaviour. His first and still perhaps most famous novel is *Neuromancer* (1984), which together with *Count Zero* (1986) and *Mona Lisa Overdrive* (1988) forms the *Sprawl* trilogy. Close in feel to, if not necessarily influenced by, the film *Blade Runner* (1982), *Neuromancer*, the archetypal 'cyberpunk' novel, depicts a near-future post-Third World War dystopia, where street-smart hackers challenge the artificial intelligences that control global corporations (see Chapter 4 of this book). The novel has won three major SF awards; the Philip K. Dick, the Nebula, and the Hugo.

Gibson's next book was *The Difference Engine* (1990), co-written with Bruce Sterling, an alternate history exploring the mid-nineteenth century as it might have been if Charles Babbage had been able to develop successfully the steam-powered mechanical computer he designed; the novel did much to popularize the nascent genre of steampunk. After this came the *Bridge* series: *Virtual Light* (1993), *Idoru* (1996) and *All Tomorrow's Parties* (1999). These were set nearer into the future than the *Sprawl* trilogy and, at least the first and the third of them, partly located in a neighbourhood that has grown up on the San Francisco-Oakland Bay Bridge. While similar themes to those of the earlier works occur concerning, for example, the interaction of humans with technology, the tone is both more understated and less despairing. Even as his protagonists are involved in various class struggles thrown up by late capitalism, there is nonetheless a sense of the possibilities of everyday resistance that allows them to maintain belief in themselves and thus continue to live as human beings.

Gibson's most recent novels, *Pattern Recognition* (2003), *Spook Country* (2007) and *Zero History* (2010), which are sometimes collectively referred to as the *Bigend* trilogy after a shared character, are less easily identifiable as science fiction or cyberpunk, being set in the contemporary world and focusing on themes of consumerism, marketing and globalization. Notably, Gibson was in the middle of writing *Pattern Recognition* when the September 2011 attacks happened and was forced to revise his manuscript precisely because he did not want to end up writing an alternate history. Considering Gibson's oeuvre overall, therefore, it is possible to see the steady progression by which his work is converging on the present from the future and this tells us how much the world we live in has become like science fiction. Key critical works on Gibson include Lance Olsen's *William Gibson* (1992), Dani Cavallaro's *Cyberpunk and Cyberculture: Science Fiction and the Work of William Gibson* (2000), Tatiana G. Rapatzikou's *Gothic Motifs in the Fiction of William Gibson* (2004) and Carl B. Yoke and Carol L. Robinson's edited collection, *The Cultural Influences of William Gibson, The 'Father' of Cyberpunk Science Fiction: Critical and Interpretive Essays* (2007).

Works Cited

Cavallaro, Dani (2000). *Cyberpunk and Cyberculture: Science Fiction and the Work of William Gibson*. London and New Brunswick, NJ: The Athlone Press.
Gibson, William (1977). 'Fragments of a Hologram Rose'. *Unearth* (Summer).
—(1982). 'Burning Chrome'. *Omni* (July).
—(1984). *Neuromancer*. New York: Ace Books.
—(1986). *Count Zero*. London: Gollancz.
—(1988). *Mona Lisa Overdrive*. London: Gollancz.
—(1993). *Virtual Light*. New York: Bantam Spectra.
—(1996). *Idoru*. New York: Putnam.
—(1999). *All Tomorrow's Parties*. New York: Putnam.
—(2003). *Pattern Recognition*. New York: Putnam.
—(2007). *Spook Country*. New York: Putnam.
—(2010). *Zero History*. New York: Putnam.
Gibson, William and Bruce Sterling (1990). *The Difference Engine*. New York: Bantam Spectra.

Olsen, Lance (1992). *William Gibson*. San Francisco: The Borgo Press.
Rapatzikou, Tatiana G. (2004). *Gothic Motifs in the Fiction of William Gibson*. Amsterdam/New York: Rodopi.
Scott, Ridley (dir.) (1982). *Blade Runner*.
Yoke, Carl B. and Carol L. Robinson (eds) (2007) *The Cultural Influences of William Gibson, The 'Father' of Cyberpunk Science Fiction: Critical and Interpretive Essays*. Lewiston, NY: Edwin Mellen Press.

Robert A. Heinlein (1907–88), was a prolific and bestselling American author who published 32 novels, 59 stories and 16 collections in his lifetime. He is most notable for raising the literary standard of SF, and for his effective combination of 'hard' scientific plausibility with an astute 'soft' social awareness. Key themes of his work include: individual liberty, self-reliance and (non-) conformism. Heinlein's penchant for creating memorable neologisms introduced several phrases into common usage, if mainly in the US: 'waldo', a mechanical grip powered by a human arm; 'No Such Thing as a Free Lunch'; and 'grok', to understand intuitively. The son of an accountant, he was born in Butler, Missouri, and grew up in Kansas City. He graduated from the United States Naval Academy in Annapolis in 1929 and spent the next five years serving as an officer in the US Navy, an experience which profoundly influenced his fiction, before being discharged with tuberculosis.

Heinlein was first published in *Astounding Science-Fiction* magazine in 1939; his early work mostly consists of short stories, which follow fairly common pulp formulas. His works from 1947 until the early 1960s are often known collectively as Heinlein's 'juveniles': adventure stories aimed at young adults that extol the virtues of science and technology. His military SF novel *Starship Troopers* (1959), initially intended for younger readers, marked the point of transition to a more mature phase in his writing, winning the Hugo Award for Best Novel in 1960. Despite being well-written and highly readable, as is the case with much of Heinlein's work, the book has proven highly controversial over the years, even to the point of being labelled 'fascist' for its overzealous lauding of military virtues, evident approval of violence and didactic presentation of politically conservative opinion. However, similar combinations of outrageous behaviour and unrestricted social theorizing could produce different results when tied to a different storyline and presented in a different context. For example, *Starship Troopers* was followed by the equally iconoclastic *Stranger in a Strange Land* (1961), which also won a Hugo for Best Novel. In this case, though, the novel's themes of free love and communal living struck a chord with the burdening 1960s counter culture and radical Left and its depiction of the foundation of a Martian Church continue to influence real world Neopagans.

The contradictions characteristic of Heinlein, not least his ability to combine fiercely independent female characters with a firmly patriarchal world view, characterize most of this mature work, written during the 1960s and early 1970s, for which he is now chiefly famous. While *Farnham's Freehold* (1964) is a post-apocalyptic tale involving time travel, race war, white slavery and cannibalism, *The Moon is a Harsh Mistress* (1966), another Hugo winner, has a very different feel as it depicts a lunar colony's revolution against Earth. Both articulate right-wing libertarian individualism but while the former reads in places like a crazed survivalist manifesto, the latter evokes parallels with the American War of Independence and sets its stall against tyranny, bureaucracy and big corporations in the name of liberty. *I Will Fear No Evil* (1970) extends the sexual liberation theme of *Stranger in a Strange Land* in its tale of a rich old man who takes on the body of his young secretary; neatly demonstrating, but not necessarily criticizing, the gender inequality inherent in free love that sees men freed to beget children on women. *Time Enough for Love* (1973) preceded an extended break in his writing due to illness, but by reviving the character Lazarus Long, from the earlier *Methuselah's Children* (1958), who was to go on to be Heinlein's *alter ego* in his final novels such as *The Number of the Beast* (1980), it links disparate strands from his career. That through time travel, the immensely old Long manages to meet and sleep with his mother seems a fitting coda to Heinlein's contradictions. Critical and biographical works include H. Bruce Franklin's *Robert A. Heinlein: America as Science Fiction* (1980), Leon Stover's *Robert Heinlein* (1987), James Gifford's *Robert A. Heinlein: A Reader's Companion* (2000) and William H. Patterson, Jr's *Robert A. Heinlein: Volume 1 (1907–1948): Learning Curve* (2011). The second volume of the Patterson biography is scheduled to be published late in 2013.

Works Cited

Franklin, H. Bruce (1980). *Robert A. Heinlein: America as Science Fiction*. Oxford: Oxford University Press.

Gifford, James (2000). *Robert A. Heinlein: A Reader's Companion*. Sacramento: Nitrosyncretic Press.

Heinlein, Robert (1958). *Methuselah's Children*. New York: Gnome Press

—(1959). *Starship Troopers*. New York: Putnam.

—(1961). *Stranger in a Strange Land*. New York: Putnam.

—(1964). *Farnham's Freehold*. New York: Putnam.

—(1966). *The Moon is a Harsh Mistress*. New York: Putnam.

—(1970). *I Will Fear No Evil*. New York: Putnam.

—(1973). *Time Enough for Love*. New York: Putnam.

—(1980). *The Number of the Beast*. London: NEL.

Patterson, Jr, William H. (2011). *Robert A. Heinlein: Volume 1 (1907–1948): Learning Curve*. New York: Tor Books.

Stover, Leon (1987). *Robert Heinlein*. Boston: Twayne.

Gwyneth Jones (1952–) was born and raised in Manchester and was educated at a convent school. She received a BA in European History of Ideas from the University of Sussex. Her first publications, beginning with *Water in the Air* (1977), were directed at younger readers; but, beginning with *Ally Ally Aster* (1981), she adopted the pseudonym Ann Halam for this purpose and has now written over 20 novels under that name. These works generally fall within the fantasy spectrum, although some contain science fictional content, such as *Dr Franklin's Island* (2001) in which three survivors of a plane crash become test subjects for the doctor's experiments in genetic engineering. Jones's first adult SF novel was *Divine Endurance* (1984), which features a post-holocaust matriarchal society in Southeast Asia. *Kairos* (1988) imagines a dystopic early twenty-first-century Britain, although much of the feel of the novel is a projection of the Thatcherite experience of the 1980s, in which the female protagonist is involved in a drug-influenced struggle to control reality.

Jones came to prominence with her *Aleutian* trilogy: *White Queen* (1991), which won the James Tiptree Jr Award, *North Wind* (1994) and *Phoenix Café* (1997). On the one hand, this is an almost satirical take on first-contact stories as aliens crash land on the Aleutian Islands and henceforth claim to come from the planet Aleutia. On the other hand, it allows Jones to inter-rogate themes of colonial occupation, gender and sexuality. In particular, the Aleutians' difficulty with grasping human gender roles beyond a division between 'childbearers' and 'parasites' enables a sophisticated critique of patriarchal society which is linked to the trilogy's wider investigation of the relationship between self, language, reality and the world.

Her *Bold As Love* series – *Bold As Love* (2001), which won the Arthur C. Clarke Award, *Castles Made of Sand* (2002), *Midnight Lamp* (2003), *Band of Gypsies* (2005) and *Rainbow Bridge* (2006) – begins with the collapse of the neoliberal ideology that has held sway in Britain since 1979 and its consequent division into its constituent nations and, eventually, ends with occupation by the Chinese and the establishment of a world government. The series, which has a very fine set of frontispieces by Bryan Talbot, blends SF and fantasy by reworking Arthurian motifs into the events that befall the central countercultural triumvirate of rock musicians, Ax, Fiorinda and Sage, who are also mutually sexually involved. On one level, even as contemporary political events moved in the opposite direction to those Jones describes, the novels exuberantly hold open the power of story, itself, as a resource for hope.

During the same period as she was writing the *Bold As Love* series, Jones also published *Life* (2004), which won the Philip K. Dick Award, the near-future tale of a geneticist, Anna, who detects a chromosomal change in humans that she calls 'Transferred Y syndrome'. This sets up a complex exploration of gender values in areas ranging from institutional sexism and the supposed neutrality of science itself, to marriage and economic relationships generally.

Spirit (2008) is set in a universe that appears to link elements from the *Aleutian* trilogy and the *Bold As Love* series, but, more generally, it is a fast-paced space opera reworking the theme of Alexandre Dumas's *The Count of Monte Cristo*. Nonetheless, as with most of Jones's work, *Spirit* explores themes of gender and its relation to societies in transition.

Jones has published two major works of SF criticism, *Deconstructing the Starships: Science Fiction and Reality* (1999) and *Imagination/Space: Essays and Talks on Fiction, Feminism, Technology and Politics* (2009), as well as chapters such as 'True Life Science Fiction: Sexual Politics and the Lab Procedural' in *Tactical Biopolitics: Art, Activism and Technoscience* (2008). A special Gwyneth Jones issue of the journal *FemSpec* in 2004 was devoted to critical analysis of her work.

Works Cited

Halam, Ann (1981). *Ally Ally Aster*. London: Allen & Unwin.
—(2001). *Dr Franklin's Island*. London: Dolphin.
Jones, Gwyneth. (1977). *Water in the Air*. London: Macmillan.
—(1984). *Divine Endurance*. London: Allen & Unwin.
—(1988). *Kairos*. London: Unwin Hyman.
—(1991). *White Queen*. London: Gollancz.
—(1994). *North Wind*. London: Gollancz.
—(1997). *Phoenix Café*. London: Gollancz.
—(1999). *Deconstructing the Starships: Science Fiction and Reality*. Liverpool: Liverpool University Press.
—(2001). *Bold As Love*. London: Gollancz.
—(2002). *Castles Made of Sand*. London: Gollancz.
—(2003). *Midnight Lamp*. London: Gollancz.
—(2004). *Life*. Seattle, WA: Aqueduct Press.
—(2005). *Band of Gypsies*. London: Gollancz.
—(2006). *Rainbow Bridge*. London: Gollancz.
—(2008). *Spirit*. London: Gollancz.
—(2008). 'True Life Science Fiction: Sexual Politics and the Lab Procedural'. *Tactical Biopolitics: Art, Activism and Technoscience*. Beatriz da Costa and Kavita Philip (eds). Cambridge, MA: The MIT Press. 289–306.
—(2009). *Imagination/Space: Essays and Talks on Fiction, Feminism, Technology and Politics*. Seattle, WA: Aqueduct Press.
Various (2004). *Femspec* 5 (1).

Ursula Le Guin (1929–), the daughter of an anthropologist and a writer, was born in Berkeley, California, and grew up in various contrasting locations, on both the west and east coasts of the United States, as well as in Europe. She received a BA from Radcliffe College in 1951 and an MA in 1952 from Columbia. Her publishing career began in 1958 with a book review and poetry in small magazines. She published her first SF story in 1962 and her first SF novel, *Rocannon's World*, in 1966. Over the next eight years, she produced both the *Hainish* and *Earthsea* sequence of novels, respectively SF and fantasy, for which she is chiefly famous, as well as other novels and numerous shorter and longer stories.

Rocannon's World, together with *Planet of Exile* (1966) and *City of Illusions* (1967), forms a trilogy set in a common universe in which widespread human life originates from the planet Hain. *The Left Hand of Darkness* (1969), which won both Hugo and Nebula Awards, occupies an earlier point of time in Hainish history and develops themes concerning balance and mutuality present in the preceding trilogy by foregrounding gender and sexuality (see discussions later in this book). The novella, 'The Word for World is Forest' (1972), presented a critical allegory of the American role in the Vietnam War. The fifth Hainish novel, *The Dispossessed* (1974), actually comes first in terms of the internal chronology because it tells of the invention of the 'ansible', an interstellar communication device, which features in the earlier books. However, the novel is most significant for the examination of the nature of Utopia created by its setting on twin worlds, one anarchist and one capitalist. A very different examination of Utopia is provided by her non-Hainish SF novel of the period, *The Lathe of Heaven* (1971), in which the idealistic (and evocatively named) George Orr dreams of changes for the better and wakes up each time to a world infinitely worse. Fredric Jameson critically discusses this novel, as well as the last two Hainish novels, in essays collected in his *Archaeologies of the Future* (2005).

Concurrently with the Hainish novels, Le Guin wrote what was initially the *Earthsea* trilogy: *A Wizard of Earthsea* (1968), *The Tombs of Atuan* (1971) and *The Farthest Shore* (1972). This story of the life of the wizard Ged from apprenticeship to full maturity, when he becomes Archmage, turns on the same underlying principle of the need to maintain balance as the Hainish novels. The trilogy subsequently received criticism for an alleged privileging of male agency and *Tehanu* (1990), Le Guin's explicitly feminist addition to the series, has been seen by some as an act of restitution although arguably it draws on ideas and tendencies implicitly present throughout the original trilogy. The series has subsequently been further extended by *The Other Wind* (2001) and a volume of stories, *Tales from Earthsea* (2001).

As well as the *Earthsea* novels, Le Guin has continued to produce other significant fiction since the 1970s, such as *Always Coming Home* (1985), a collage of extracts and stories which build up a picture of a future matriarchal society, *The Telling* (2000), a return to the Hainish universe, and *Lavinia* (2008), a prose reworking of the last six books of Vergil's *Aeneid*. However, it is fair to say that her status rests largely on what she had written by the mid-1970s and that this forms the subject of most of the extensive secondary criticism focusing on her work; including the special issue of *Science Fiction Studies* devoted to her in November 1975, and books such as Harold Bloom's edited collection *Ursula K. Le Guin: Modern Critical Views* (1985), Elizabeth Cummins's *Understanding Ursula K. Le Guin* (1990), and Mike Cadden's *Ursula K. Le Guin Beyond Genre: Fiction for Children and Adults* (2004). Le Guin's own critical writings and reviews were collected in 1979 in *The Language of the Night: Essays on Science Fiction and Fantasy* (discussed in Chapter 5 of this book) a later collection, *Dancing at the Edge of the World*, appeared in 1989.

Works Cited

Bloom, Harold (ed.) (1985). *Ursula K. Le Guin: Modern Critical Views*. New York: Chelsea House.

Cadden, Mike (2004). *Ursula K. Le Guin Beyond Genre: Fiction for Children and Adults*. New York: Routledge.

Cummins, Elizabeth (1990). *Understanding Ursula K. Le Guin*. Columbia, SC: University of South Carolina Press.

Jameson, Fredric (2005). *Archaeologies of the Future: The Desire Called Utopia and Other Science Fictions*. London, Verso.

Le Guin, Ursula. (1966). *Rocannon's World*. New York: Ace Books.

—(1966). *Planet of Exile*. New York: Ace Books.

—(1967). *City of Illusions*. New York: Ace Books.

—(1968). *A Wizard of Earthsea*. Berkeley, CA: Parnassus Press.

—(1969). *The Left Hand of Darkness*. New York: Ace Books.

—(1971). *Lathe of Heaven*. New York: Charles Scribner's Sons.

—(1971). *The Tombs of Atuan*. New York: Atheneum.

—(1972). *The Farthest Shore*. New York: Atheneum.

—(1972). 'The Word for World is Forest'. *Again Dangerous Visions*. Harlan Ellison (ed.). New York: Doubleday. 26–108.

—(1974). *The Dispossessed*. New York: Harper & Row.

—(1979). *The Language of the Night: Essays on Science Fiction and Fantasy*. New York: Putnam.

—(1985). *Always Coming Home*. New York: Harper & Row.

—(1989). *Dancing at the Edge of the World*. New York: Grove Press.

—(1990). *Tehanu*. New York: Atheneum.

—(2000). *The Telling*. San Diego: Harcourt.

—(2001). *The Other Wind*. San Diego: Harcourt.

—(2001). *Tales from Earthsea*. San Diego: Harcourt.

—(2008). *Lavinia*. San Diego: Harcourt.

Various (1975). *Science Fiction Studies*.

Doris Lessing (1919–) was born in Persia (now Iran) to British parents but grew up in Rhodesia (now Zimbabwe) after her parents moved there to run a farm. She left her convent school at the age of 14 and her home soon after to become a nursemaid. In 1937, she moved to Salisbury (now Harare) to become a telephone operator and subsequently married and had two children. After her first marriage ended in divorce in 1943, she became involved with the communist politics of the Left Book Club and there met Gottfried Lessing, with whom she got married and had a son, Peter. When that marriage ended in 1949, she moved to Britain with Peter, where she joined the Communist Party Writers' Group. During this period she toured the Soviet Union as part of a group including Naomi Mitchison and subsequently visited Mitchison several times at her Scottish home. Lessing's first novel, *The Grass is Singing* (1950) dealt with racial politics in Rhodesia and had an immediate impact, but the book which made her famous was *The Golden Notebook* (1962). The novel marks an important moment in the post-war rise of feminist consciousness and, although not itself a work of SF, prefigures her later SF stylistically and thematically, especially in terms of its exploration of inner consciousness. The five volume *Children of Violence* series, beginning with *Martha Quest* (1952), includes speculative, fantastic elements in its fifth volume, *The Four-Gated City* (1969).

Between 1970 and 1983, Lessing's work was almost exclusively SF. Similarly to J. G. Ballard, but probably more influenced by R. D. Laing's critique of conventional psychiatry, she chose to focus on 'inner space' in her fiction; exploring the apparent break-up of Britain that was occurring in the 1970s from within the psyche. *Briefing for a Descent into Hell* (1971) employs a collage of fragmented narratives and doctors' reports to tell the story of a man found 'wandering on the Embankment near Waterloo Bridge' in London who is gradually restored to his 'normal' life as a married Professor of Classics. The irony is that through this process of curing him, the doctors destroy the quest that he has been pursuing in his inner space, seeking meaning beyond the hell which is everyday life in the twentieth century. Her next novel but one and, arguably, her finest, *Memoirs of a Survivor* (1977), details the breakdown of society in an unnamed city from the perspective of a female narrator who lives in a tower block that undergoes a transformation that is quite as extreme as anything found in the work of Ballard. This irreversible decline is interweaved with both the narrator's descriptions of a series of transcendental experiences she undergoes in which she passes through the wall of her flat and an account of the development through puberty of a girl, Emily, who (along with her sentient pet dog, Hugo) is entrusted to her mysteriously. The cumulative effect is extremely unsettling as Emily's typically early teenage oscillation between childhood and adulthood, in which, torn between the street life of her peer group and her loyalty to her dog and the narrator, she experiments with smoking, drinking and sex, is contrasted with the increasingly psycho-sexual scenes that take place behind the wall. Lessing is not calling for the return to moral values that would later underwrite the electoral appeal of the British Conservative Party, but utterly condemning and rejecting Western society.

Shikasta (1979), the first of five books in the *Canopus of Argos* series (1979–83), was prefaced with 'Some Remarks' in which she cited Stapledon's *First and Last Men* as a precedent and argued that, with the inadequacy of social norms now widely apparent, 'space fiction, with science fiction, makes up the most original branch of literature now'. Despite its framework of good and evil galactic empires, *Shikasta* is as much about the decline of post-war Britain as her previous two novels. The second half of the twentieth century is described as 'a time of near total debasement and falseness' (78) and related to the complicity of the West in general with the crimes of colonialism and the two World Wars. Lessing's indictment reaches its zenith with a memorable 70 page series of 'case studies' and 'Illustrations' that depicts this decay at a personal level, as manifested in individuals ranging from a workers' leader to various revolutionaries. The second book in the series, *The Marriages Between Zones Three, Four and Five* (1980), has a narrower focus; narrating the relationship of a man and a woman in the form of 'a fable, or myth'. While the Utopian Zone Three is initially contrasted positively with the patriarchal and militaristic Zone Four, the novel subverts readers' expectations by using the demonstrated inadequacies of Zone Four to critique the complacency of Zone Three. Lessing is not, of course, extolling the virtues of patriarchy but making the point that overcoming it is not an end in itself but merely the point of departure for achieving a genuine existence of full consciousness.

The series as a whole gave Lessing a status in the genre at the time that saw her appear as Guest of Honour at the Brighton Worldcon in 1987. Since then, interest by SF fans and critics in Lessing has waned although she has continued to publish in the genre, as Adam Roberts notes in 'Doris Lessing and SF' (2008). *The Story of General Dann and Mara's Daughter, Griot, and the Snow Dog* (2005) is set in a post-apocalyptic world; *The Cleft* (2007) is another myth-like tale of the relationship between men and women; and *Alfred and Emily* (2008) is an alternate history which tells her parents' story first as it was and then as it might have been. This lack of interest from within the genre is particularly mystifying because when Lessing won the Nobel Prize for Literature in 2007, it was because of her SF, and *Canopus in Argos* in particular, rather than in spite of it.

Works Cited

Lessing, Doris (1950). *The Grass is Singing*. London: Michael Joseph.
—(1952). *Martha Quest*. London: Michael Joseph.
—(1962). *The Golden Notebook*. London: Michael Joseph.

—(1969). *The Four-Gated City*. London: MacGibbon & Kee.

—(1971). *Briefing for a Descent into Hell*. London: Jonathan Cape.

—(1977). *Memoirs of a Survivor*. London: Octagon.

—(1979). *Shikasta*. London: Jonathan Cape.

—(1980). *The Marriages Between Zones Three, Four and Five*. London: Jonathan Cape.

—(2005). *The Story of General Dann and Mara's Daughter, Griot, and the Snow Dog*. London: Fourth Estate.

—(2007). *The Cleft*. London: Fourth Estate.

—(2008). *Alfred and Emily*. London: Fourth Estate.

Roberts, Adam (2008). 'Doris Lessing and SF'. *Vector* 257. 6–8.

Naomi Mitchison (1897–1999) was the author of over 70 books published across eight decades and a central figure in British, especially Scottish, literary circles of the twentieth century. Initially raised and schooled with boys, she was educated at home by governesses from the age of 12, but the fact that the family lived in Oxford and were connected to the intellectual elite meant that she still gained an unusually good education for her gender at that time. In particular, a love for the classics informed a range of early historical novels from her first, *The Conquered* (1923), set in Roman Gaul, through *The Corn King and the Spring Queen* (1931), set in and around ancient Greece, and up to *The Blood of the Martyrs* (1939) set in Nero's Rome. While her work of this period often contained fantastic elements – the protagonist of *The Conquered* turns into a wolf, for example – Mitchison did not go on to write SF novels until many years later with the notable exception of *We Have Been Warned* (1935). This dystopian account of the failure of the leftist politics of the decade to address the reality of class and gender oppression in Britain, climaxed with a violent fascist counter-revolution. The novel was critically excoriated and used by the Conservative Party as propaganda against her husband Dick (himself the author of *The First Worker's Government*, a politically-themed SF novel published in 1934), when he stood as a Labour Party candidate in the 1935 General Election.

From 1939, Mitchison lived at Carradale, a Scottish country estate she bought with Dick. The years of the Second World War are copiously recorded in the diary she kept for Mass-Observation (published in 1985 as *Among You Taking Notes …*). Notable post-war works included a Scottish historical novel, *The Bull Calves* (1947), and a fantasy, *Travel Light* (1952), before the publication in 1962 of a book destined to become an SF classic, *Memoirs of a Spacewoman*. Mary, the novel's protagonist, is a female inter-cultural communications expert who spends most of her time investigating the reproductive cycles of alien societies from close quarters in what amounts to a playful, but telling, corrective to the male-centric American 'Golden-Age' SF that still persisted residually. However, Mitchison still took the trouble to display hard-science knowledge – as befitted the sister of the eminent geneticist, J. B. S. Haldane, and the dedicatee of James Watson's account of his own role in the discovery of the structure of DNA, *The Double Helix* (1968) – in her explanation that the daughter Mary conceives after sex with a Martian is no inter-species hybrid but a haploid child (i.e. the mother's chromosomes in the egg double to make up the full complement). In its critiques of dualism and patriarchy, *Memoirs of a Spacewoman* paved the way for the subsequent feminist SF of writers such as Doris Lessing and Ursula Le Guin.

Mitchison's 1982 story 'Remember Me' is a gloomy tale of the survivors of a nuclear strike in north Scotland and her last two SF novels, *Solution Three* (1975) and *Not By Bread Alone* (1983), are both genetics-informed complex investigations of the pursuit of new ways of living in a world threatened by environmental disaster. However, the essential seriousness of the plots does not completely preclude the expression of desires such as that of the latter's Australian aboriginal character, Naburdja: 'One day, she said to herself, I will pilot a space ship.' The idea that romance is necessarily an element of the good life remained central to Mitchison's oeuvre throughout her career.

Works Cited

Mitchison, Naomi (1923). *The Conquered*. London: Jonathan Cape.
—(1931). *The Corn King and the Spring Queen*. London: Jonathan Cape.
—(1935). *We Have Been Warned*. London: Constable.
—(1939). *The Blood of the Martyrs*. London: Constable.
—(1947). *The Bull Calves*. London: Jonathan Cape.
—(1952). *Travel Light*. London: Faber and Faber.
—(1962). *Memoirs of a Spacewoman*. London: Gollancz.
—(1975). *Solution Three*. London: Dobson.
—(1982). 'Remember Me'. *What Do You Think Yourself?* Edinburgh: Paul Harris.
—(1983). *Not By Bread Alone*. London and New York: Marion Boyars.
—(1985). *Among You Taking Notes … .* Dorothy Sheridan (ed.). London: Gollancz.
Mitchison, Richard (1934). *The First Worker's Government*. London: Gollancz.
Watson, James (1968). *The Double Helix*. New York: Atheneum.

Christopher Priest (1943–) grew up in Cheshire; leaving school at 16 when his family relocated to Essex. For the next seven years, he worked unhappily with a firm of chartered accountants in central London, but found consolation when a colleague introduced him to SF. After becoming involved in organized fandom with the British Science Fiction Association (BSFA) and attending its conventions from 1964 onwards, Priest also began writing his own stories. Influenced by H. G. Wells, John Wyndham, Brian Aldiss and, particularly, J. G. Ballard, he became briefly associated with the British 'New Wave'. However, the independence of mind, evident throughout his career, manifested itself in a 1968 article for the BSFA journal, *Vector*, 'The Tankless Task of Thinking', which argued that the philosophical SF 'idea' underpinning a story or novel was more important than the SF 'notion' – the futuristic devices and gadgets furnishing the text. Given the centrality of the 'notion', or 'novum' as it is more commonly known within the genre following the work of Darko Suvin (1979: 63–4), to critical definitions of SF it is not surprising that this commitment to intellectual integrity was to eventually take Priest not only beyond the New Wave but, in the opinions of some, beyond SF itself, as reflected by Nicholas Ruddick's 1986 article in *Modern Fiction Studies*, 'Priest's Abandonment of Science Fiction'. This apparent deviation, as well as rancorous public disputes with leading US authors such as Norman Spinrad and Harlan Ellison, has led to Priest's work gaining less attention than it deserves in America.

Of Priest's early novels, published by Faber and Faber, *Inverted World* (1974), set in a reversed world consisting of a flat disk with the poles heading off into infinity, was an instant success. It won the 1975 BSFA Award, was shortlisted for a Hugo, and is now considered a classic of the genre. Translated as *Le Monde inverti*, it was also very popular in France, where it has remained constantly in print and has been taught widely in schools. *A Dream of Wessex* (1977), an exploration of 'inner space' comparable to Doris Lessing's novels of the same period, explores the uncertainty of late 1970s Britain caught between the Thatcherite future that shortly emerged and the more Utopian alternatives that seemed tantalisingly in reach. The drowned English landscape that features in the novel's future scenes presages the island location of the Dream Archipelago, which features as the setting for many of Priest's short stories, collected as *The Dream Archipelago* (1999), and two novels: *The Affirmation* (1981), a metafictional account of a writer's imagination, and *The Islanders* (2011), which takes the form of a gazetteer.

Priest's ninth novel *The Prestige* (1995), winner of both the James Tait Black Memorial Prize and the World Fantasy Award, features the scientist and electrical pioneer Nicola Tesla as a supporting character to its complex story of feuding stage magicians in the closing years of the Victorian period. In 2006, Christopher Nolan directed the film adaptation of the novel; a commercial and critical success. *The Separation* (2002), narrates the divergence of twin brothers Joe and J. L. Sawyer on to alternate historical tracks during the Second World War, and went on to win both the BSFA and the Arthur C. Clarke awards.

Critical work on Priest includes Andrew M. Butler's edited collection, *Christopher Priest: The Interaction* (2005), Ruddick's *Christopher Priest* (1989), and a number of essays in Paul Kincaid's *What It Is We Do When We Read Science Fiction* (2008). In a rare moment of mainstream visibility, Priest was selected, alongside Martin Amis, Pat Barker, Ian McEwan and Salman Rushdie, as one of 20 writers to be featured as 'The Best of Young British Novelists 1983', in the first instance of an exercise that has since been repeated by the magazine *Granta* at ten-year intervals. Priest's characteristically acerbic memoir of the photo-shoot and launch party, 'Where Am I Now?' (2008), mercilessly condemns the whole process as a charade. A decade after a badly-researched article for *The Observer* asked 'Whatever Happened to Christopher Priest?' he remains a thorn in the side of both the literary and SF establishments.

Works Cited

Butler, Andrew M. (2005). *Christopher Priest: The Interaction*. London: Science Fiction Foundation.

Kincaid, Paul (2008). *What It Is We Do When We Read Science Fiction*. Harold Wood: Beccon Publications.

Nolan, Christopher (dir.) (2006). *The Prestige*.

Priest, Christopher (1968). 'The Tankless Task of Thinking'. *Vector* 50. 10–14.

—(1974). *Inverted World*. London: Faber and Faber.

—(1977). *A Dream of Wessex*. London: Faber and Faber.

—(1981). *The Affirmation*. London: Faber and Faber.

—(1995). *The Prestige*. London: Touchstone.

—(1999). *The Dream Archipelago*. London: Earthlight.

—(2002). *The Separation*. London: Scribner.

—(2008). 'Where Am I Now?'. *"It" Came from Outer Space*. Hastings: Grim Grin Studio. 223–36.

—(2011). *The Islanders*. London: Gollancz.

Ruddick, Nicholas (1986). 'Priest's Abandonment of Science Fiction'. *Modern Fiction Studies*. 32. 1 (Spring). 43–52.

—(1989). *Christopher Priest*. Mercer Island, WA: Starmont.

Suvin, Darko (1979). *Metamorphoses of Science Fiction*. New Haven, NJ: Yale University Press.

Kim Stanley Robinson (1952–) grew up in Southern California and subsequently gained his BA and PhD in English Literature at the University of California, San Diego (completing an MA at Boston University in between the two). His PhD thesis was supervised by Fredric Jameson and published as *The Novels of Philip K. Dick* (1984). Robinson began publishing short stories in 1976 and some of the component parts of *Icehenge* (1984) were workshopped with Ursula Le Guin in 1977 but his first published novel was *The Wild Shore* (1984). This became part of a linked sequence, together with *The Gold Coast* (1988) and *Pacific Edge* (1990), variously referred to as the *Three Californias* or *Orange County Trilogy*. The books represent three different, but also internally linked, possible future scenarios for California respectively (and broadly speaking), post-nuclear war, dystopia and Utopia. The combined effect is one of a 'messy' heterogeneity, reminiscent of earlier novels like Dick's *Dr*

Bloodmoney (1965) and Le Guin's *The Lathe of Heaven* (1971) but with more up-to-date environmental concerns.

Robinson's next major work was the *Mars Trilogy*, consisting of *Red Mars* (1993), *Green Mars* (1994) and *Blue Mars* (1996), which has already gained the status of a classic within the SF genre; the first volume winning a Nebula and the second and third winning Hugo Awards. *Red Mars* begins with the colonization of the planet in the 2020s by the First Hundred and follows the progress of the settlement, and the shifting personal and political alliances within it, as it grows and further settlers arrive. Over the course of the trilogy, Mars is terraformed to become fit for habitation, but while a wealth of attendant biological and scientific detail enriches Robinson's narrative, his focus always remains squarely on the human consequences of building a new society. The short stories comprising *The Martians* (1999) share the same setting.

The Years of Rice and Salt (2002) is, in effect, a collection of very long linked stories spanning an alternate history in which the population of Europe is wiped out by the Black Death and the rise of the West never happens. Instead, by the equivalent of our twentieth century, geographical Europe has become part of a wider Muslim modernity, in which Robinson has a group of students discuss whether if the plague had never happened the 'Franks' (i.e. the Europeans) could have become a global power. This, in turn, leads to a discussion of the value of counterfactual history in general and so makes explicit the novel's interrogation both of our understanding of history in general and of the assumptions of Western historiography in particular. Robinson followed this with the three novels, *Forty Signs of Rain* (2004), *Fifty Degrees Below* (2005) and *Sixty Days and Counting* (2007), collectively known as the *Science in the Capital* series, which depict the consequences of escalating environmental disaster on the American political and scientific establishment in the capital city, Washington D.C. The books combine scientific extrapolation with a cynical, satirical attitude to the mechanisms of government and elections. However, as always with Robinson, the human element of the story remains paramount; especially in the middle volume, which finds protagonist Frank Vanderwal living in a tree in the capital's Rock Creek Park.

Galileo's Dream (2009), which recounts a fictionalized life of Galileo complete with Stapledonian interaction with future humans, is Robinson's most ambitious work to that point. It is a huge complex novel which recapitulates all of the concerns from across his previous work by dealing with the inter-relationship between history, science, patriarchy and the function of writing within the physical universe, while simultaneously self-consciously exploring the possibilities of SF as a genre. 2009 also saw the publication of a collection of essays on Robinson's work, *Kim Stanley Robinson Maps the Unimaginable: Critical Essays* edited by William J. Burling. Robinson's most recent novel,

2312 (2012) may be even more significant than its predecessor. Set, as the title indicates, 300 years in the future, it employs stylistic and formal innovation to present its space-dwelling bisexually-gendered protagonists as living not only free of the Earth, but also of its inherently hierarchical and politically repressive values. As the twenty-first century progresses into deepening economic and environmental crisis, Robinson increasingly stands out as a writer still capable of allowing us to believe in a future through the strength and breadth of his vision.

Works Cited

Burling, William J. (ed.) (2009). *Kim Stanley Robinson Maps the Unimaginable: Critical Essays*. Jefferson, NC: McFarland.
Dick, Philip K. (1965). *Dr Bloodmoney*. New York: Ace Books.
Le Guin, Ursula (1971). *The Lathe of Heaven*. New York: Charles Scribner's Sons.
Robinson, Kim Stanley (1984). *Icehenge*. New York: Ace Books.
—(1984). *The Novels of Philip K. Dick*. Ann Arbor, MI: UMI Research Press.
—(1984). *The Wild Shore*. New York: Ace Books.
—(1988). *The Gold Coast*. New York: Tor Books.
—(1990). *Pacific Edge*. London: Unwin Hyman.
—(1993). *Red Mars*. London: Harper Collins.
—(1994). *Green Mars*. London: Harper Collins.
—(1996). *Blue Mars*. London: Harper Collins.
—(1999). *The Martians*. London: Harper Collins.
—(2002). *The Years of Rice and Salt*. London: Harper Collins.
—(2004). *Forty Signs of Rain*. London: Harper Collins.
—(2005). *Fifty Degrees Below*. London: Harper Collins.
—(2007). *Sixty Days and Counting*. New York: Bantam Books.
—(2009). *Galileo's Dream*. London: Harper Voyager.
—(2012). *2312*. New York: Orbit.

Joanna Russ (1937–2011) was born in the Bronx, New York, to teacher parents. She gained her BA in English from Cornell University in 1957, where she studied under Vladimir Nabokov, and then received a Master of Fine Arts in Drama from Yale in 1960. She went on to work as an academic, lecturing at various US universities before taking up a post at the University of Washington, Seattle, in the 1970s, where she rose to full Professor of English; eventually retiring in 1994. She came out publicly as a lesbian in the 1970s. Most of her fiction was written in the 1960s, 1970s and 1980s, as her later life was dominated by Chronic Fatigue Syndrome and back pain.

Russ published her first SF story, 'Nor Custom Stale', in 1959. Her first novel, *Picnic on Paradise* (1968), was a vehicle for her time-travelling mercenary protagonist, Alyx; it was later collected with other Alyx stories as *The Adventures of Alyx* (1976). The entry for Russ in the second edition of *The Encyclopaedia of Science Fiction* notes the impact that the character had simply through being a female autonomous agent: 'The liberating effects of the Alyx tales has been pervasive, and the ease with which later writers now use active female protagonists in adventure roles, without having to argue the case, owes much to this example' (Clute and Nicholls, 1035). Her second novel, *And Chaos Died* (1970), features a male protagonist and contrasts conditions of a future, dystopian and overcrowded Earth with a different, more egalitarian and spiritually-inclined planet.

Her third and best-known novel, *The Female Man* (1975) is a landmark text in the genre and was written some years before publication; her Nebula-Award winning short story, 'When It Changed' (1972), appeared first. This story (discussed in Chapter 4) is set on the planet Whileaway, where a plague killed all the men centuries before creating a women only society. Both Whileaway and the protagonist of 'When It Changed', Janet Evason, reappear in *The Female Man* as one of four interlinked scenarios featuring genetically identical women in very different social contexts. As well as Janet, we also encounter Jeannine in a bankrupt US where the Second World War never happened, Joanna in a recognizable 1970s America and Jael in a world where women are involved in a violent war against men. One possibility suggested towards the end of the novel is that Janet's world was not the consequence of a plague but is in fact the future of Jael's world and the product of victory over the men: 'the Whileawayan flowers nourish themselves on the bones of the men we have slain' (Russ, 1985: 211). However, bare summary does no justice to the wit of Russ's writing which is darkly humorous and eventually transcends the anger, which also animates the novel, in the optimistic ending that envisages a time when gender suppression is a thing of the past.

Russ's other novels include *We Who Are About To* (1977), in which the female protagonist rejects the survivalist demands of the group she is stranded with on a deserted planet, *The Two of Them* (1978), in which a woman on earth dreams about a young woman growing up on another planet, and the children's book *Kittatinny: A Tale of Magic* (1978). She wrote numerous critical articles, essays and reviews; many of which are collected in books such as *How to Suppress Women's Writing* (1983), *To Write Like a Woman* (1995) and *The Country You Have Never Seen: Essays and Reviews* (2007). Critical studies of Russ or featuring extensive discussions of her work include Sarah Lefanu's *In the Chinks of the World Machine: Feminism and Science Fiction* (1988), Jeanne Cortiel's *Demand My Writing: Joanna Russ/ Feminism/ Science Fiction* (1999) and Farah Mendlesohn's edited collection, *On Joanna Russ* (2009).

Works Cited

Clute, John and Peter Nicholls (eds) (1993). *The Encyclopaedia of Science Fiction*. London: Orbit.

Cortiel, Jeanne (1999). *Demand My Writing: Joanna Russ/ Feminism/ Science Fiction*. Liverpool: Liverpool University Press.

Lefanu, Sarah (1988). *In the Chinks of the World Machine: Feminism and Science Fiction*. London: The Women's Press.

Mendlesohn, Farah (ed.) (2009). *On Joanna Russ*. Middletown, CT: Wesleyan University Press.

Russ, Joanna (1959) 'Nor Custom Stale'. *The Magazine of Fantasy and Science Fiction* 17 (3) (September). 75–85.

—(1968). *Picnic on Paradise*. New York: Ace Books.

—(1970). *And Chaos Died*. New York: Ace Books.

—(1972). 'When It Changed'. *Again Dangerous Visions*. Harlan Ellison (ed.). New York: Doubleday. 229–241.

—(1975). *The Female Man*. New York: Bantam Books.

—(1976). *The Adventures of Alyx*. Boston: Gregg Press.

—(1977). *We Who Are About To*. New York: Dell Books.

—(1978). *The Two of Them*. New York: Berkley Books.

—(1983). *How to Suppress Women's Writing*. Austin: University of Texas Press.

—(1985). *The Female Man*. London: The Women's Press.

—(1995). *To Write Like a Woman*. Bloomington: Indiana University Press.

—(2007). *The Country You Have Never Seen: Essays and Reviews*. Liverpool: Liverpool University Press.

Geoff Ryman (1951–) was born in Canada but moved to the US at the age of 11, going on to gain degrees in History and English at the University of California, Los Angeles, before moving to Britain in 1973. He is a prominent gay writer who has won numerous awards for his short stories, novellas and novels, including the Arthur C. Clarke, Philip K. Dick, and James Tiptree, Jr awards. Outside his writing career, Ryman led the web design team at the Central Office of Information in 1994, which helped the UK government establish their website. He also led the design teams responsible for the first official British Monarchy and 10 Downing Street websites, and worked on the UK Government's DirectGov website. He currently lectures in Creative Writing at the University of Manchester.

Ryman's first published SF story, 'The Diary of a Translator', appeared in *New Worlds* in 1976, but his career only really took off from the mid-1980s, with 'The Unconquered Country' (1984), a story about a young woman in Southeast Asia who is forced to rent out her womb to grow machinery in. This long story was revised as a novella in 1986 and subsequently collected in *Unconquered Countries: Four Novellas* (1994). Ryman has travelled in Asia, which also forms the setting (or the basis for fictionalized settings) of some of his works: *Air* (2004) is set in the imaginary country of Karzistan and *The King's Last Song* (2006) is set in Cambodia across several timespans including the present, the twelfth century and the Pol Pot era.

His first novel, *The Warrior Who Carried Life* (1985), is a fantasy quest adventure and Ryman is better known for the two that followed it, *The Child Garden* (1989) and *Was* (1992). The former is set in a transfigured future England and 'complexly massages an array of themes – drugs, dystopia, ecology, feminism, hive-minds, homosexuality, medicine and music – into a long rich novel about identity and the making of great art' (Clute and Nicholls, 1041). *Was* portrays three characters linked by their relationship with L. Frank Baum's 1900 novel *The Wizard of Oz* and its famous cinematic adaptation in 1939. It deals with themes surrounding the loss of innocence in the harsh world of the American frontier, as well as the powerful, long-lasting resonance of effective art and, for its portrayal of a gay male actor who has AIDS, has been heralded by Robert Drake as part of the 'Gay Canon' (1998: 456). In contrast, the gay protagonist of Ryman's later comic novel, *Lust* (2001), is a laboratory-based research scientist who suddenly develops the ability to conjure willing sexual partners out of thin air, including variously Johnny Weissmüller (as Tarzan), Pablo Picasso, a road protestor called Stumpy and the cartoon wife of a cartoon duck. The result is an invigorating mixture of broad farce and serious interrogation of the nature of desire.

Ryman's expertise in web and software design often informs his fiction, such as 'Fan' (1994), a novella about a lonely single mother who becomes obsessed with a virtual incarnation of her favourite pop music star, and *Air*, which tells of how the immanence of a kind of universal wireless neural interfacing changes the last village in the world to go online. This techno-logical expertise has also influenced the format he has chosen for publishing his work in the case of *253, or Tube Theatre*, which first appeared (and is still available) as a website (http://www.ryman-novel.com/) in 1996 and only appeared in book form two years later. Readers were able to use hypertext links to explore the relationships between the 252 passengers (and driver) travelling in the seven carriages of a London Underground train on the Bakerloo Line running between Embankment and Elephant & Castle on 11 January 1995. The paperback edition is necessarily more restricted in its options but does contain footnotes, an index, diagrams and maps; not to mention such playful additions as a reader satisfaction survey ('What are your views of the author?') and activity pages ('Take the pain out of serious fiction').

Ryman is a co-founder of the 'Mundane' movement, which originated at the 2002 Clarion Writers' Workshop. Mundane SF is not only SF that sticks to plausible scientific extrapolation, hence no interstellar travel, but also SF that takes a more holistic approach to change so that any technological shift depicted is accompanied by linked changes to the wider culture and society around it. Interest in the movement has grown steadily and Ryman was one of the guest fiction editors of the June 2008 special 'Mundane-SF' issue of *Interzone*, to which he also contributed the story 'Talk is Cheap'. He subsequently edited *When It Changed: Science into Fiction* (2009), an anthology collecting original SF stories by authors including Paul Cornell, Gwyneth Jones, Ken MacLeod, Justina Robson, Adam Roberts and Ryman himself, which are based on real science and paired with a short commentary from a scientist in the relevant field. A critical text, which addresses and draws links between Ryman's interests in Mundane SF and questions of sexuality and identity, is the summer 2008 special Ryman issue of *Extrapolation*, edited by Susan Knabe and Wendy Gay Pearson.

Works Cited

Clute, John and Peter Nicholls (eds) (1993). *The Encyclopaedia of Science Fiction*. London: Orbit.

Drake, Robert (1998). *The Gay Canon*. New York: Anchor.

Knabe, Susan and Wendy Gay Pearson (eds) (2008). *Extrapolation*. 39. 2 (Summer).

Ryman, Geoff (1976). 'The Diary of a Translator'. *New Worlds Ten*. Hilary Bailey (ed.). London: Corgi. 149–64.

—(1985). *The Warrior Who Carried Life*. London: Allen & Unwin.

—(1989). *The Child Garden*. London: Unwin Hyman.

—(1992). *Was*. London: Harper Collins.

—(1994). 'Fan'. *Interzone* 81 (March). 6–24.

—(1994). *Unconquered Countries: Four Novellas*. New York: St. Martin's Press.

—(1998). *253*. London: Flamingo.

—(2001). *Lust*. London: Flamingo.

—(2004). *Air*. New York: St. Martin's Griffin.

—(2006). *The King's Last Song*. London: Harper Collins.

—(ed.) (2008). 'Mundane-SF Special'. *Interzone* 216 (June).

—(ed.) (2009). *When It Changed: Science into Fiction*. Manchester: Comma Press.

Olaf Stapledon (1886–1950) was born into a wealthy shipping family living near Liverpool on the Wirral peninsula, where he spent much of his life and which is the narrator's starting location for experiencing the cosmos in his 1937 novel *Star Maker*. He was educated at a progressive public school, Abbotsholme, and subsequently went to Balliol College, Oxford. A pacifist, Stapledon worked in an Ambulance Unit during the First World War, before going on to lecture for the Workers' Educational Association and extramurally for the University of Liverpool, also gaining a doctorate in philosophy from the latter in 1925. The ethical idea of the necessary goodness and, therefore, imperative of individual fulfilment within collective and universal frameworks, which he developed in this period, went on to underpin the speculative fiction he wrote throughout his career beginning with his first novel, *Last and First Men* (1930).

The influence of Wells on Stapledon is readily apparent in *Last and First Men*, particularly in the sequences describing a future Martian invasion. The novel charts the evolution of the human race through the rise and fall of successive distinct species until the advent of the eighteenth and 'Last Men' of the title, now living on Neptune rather than the Earth. The vast cosmic perspective of this history narrated from 2,000,000,000 years in the future, necessarily decentres recognizable contemporary human experience and turns the book into an unsettling and estranging experience for the reader. However, 75 years after its first publication, the novel continues to offer relevant insight into the politics, culture and society of the world around us. For example, Stapledon's imaginative projection of future history predicts the emergence of the US and China as the dominant, and sometimes warring, superpowers of the third millennium, and posits the eventual development of a composite cultural consensus between the two, blending science with religion and Puritanism with sexual license, which initiates what he describes as an Americanized World State. Stapledon describes a resultant universal lifestyle, in which everyone is a healthy, independent individual, working short hours, taking long holidays and retiring at 80 with the expectation of another century of active life ahead of them. Yet by concluding, that for all this material prosperity, the citizens of this World state are 'slaves' prevented 'from living a fully human life' (1972: 85), Stapledon offers a powerful critique of the neoliberal values now dominant in the Anglophone World of the twenty-first century, whose roots he clearly discerned in the 1930s. In a foreshadowing of Cormac McCarthy's *The Road* (2006), he goes on to portray this Americanized World collapsing (albeit after persisting for two millennia) into 'an orgy of cannibalism' (1972: 96).

Of Stapledon's later novels, *Odd John* (1935) investigates the possibilities of human development through the character of a mutant 'supernormal' man, and *Star Maker* is another epic account of the breadth of a cosmic perspective, but *Sirius* (1944), about a dog with enhanced intelligence and consciousness, is, somewhat ironically, more recognizably human in its scope. *Last Men in London* (1932), the sequel to *Last and First Men*, is often considered to be less significant than the works listed above, but such an attitude neglects the importance of socialism to Stapledon. In particular, the novel's uneasy blend of its future-narrator's cosmic consciousness with the restrictive opportunities its contemporary protagonist experiences in growing up and living in London, functions as an imaginative and enabling critique of the repressive social and sexual values of the time. Therefore, the novel not only further demonstrates Stapledon's continuation and development of Wells's novel-istic practice but also demonstrates how both Wells and Stapledon were part of a socialist tradition of writing that produced works such as Lionel Britton's *Hunger and Love* (1931) and Lewis Grassic Gibbon's *A Scots Quair* (1946; originally published as separate volumes 1932–4), as well as being representatives of a British tradition of Scientific Romance. Stapledon needs to be acknowledged as a full participant in the unique and distinctive literary culture of 1930s Britain: he was a friend of Naomi Mitchison, published in the Searchlight Books series that was co-organized by George Orwell, and exchanged letters with Virginia Woolf about *Star Maker*, which she read. As Kim Stanley Robinson has argued, Woolf's last novel, *Between the Acts* (1941), may be read as framed by a Stapledonian cosmic consciousness. His influence and significance, therefore, is not just restricted to SF narratives of vast dehumanizing scope, such as Arthur C. Clarke's *Childhood's End* (1953), but can also be seen in those works that forcibly harness this scope to human ends for the purpose of political critique, such as Doris Lessing's *Shikasta* (1979) and Robinson's *Galileo's Dream* (2009).

Works Cited

Britton, Lionel (1931). *Hunger and Love*. London and New York: Putnam.
Clarke, Arthur C. (1953). *Childhood's End*. New York: Ballantine.
Gibbon, Lewis Grassic (1946). *A Scots Quair*. London: Jarrolds.
Lessing, Doris (1979). *Shikasta*. London: Jonathan Cape.
McCarthy, Cormac (2006). *The Road*. New York: Knopf.
Robinson, Kim Stanley (2009). *Galileo's Dream*. London: Harper Voyager.
Stapledon, Olaf (1930). *Last and First Men*. London: Methuen.
—(1932). *Last Men in London*. London: Methuen.
—(1935). *Odd John*. London: Methuen.
—(1937). *Star Maker*. London: Methuen.
—(1944). *Sirius*. London: Secker & Warburg.
—(1972). *Last and First Men and Last Men in London*. Harmondsworth: Penguin.
Woolf, Virginia (1941). *Between the Acts*. London: The Hogarth Press.

Neal Stephenson (1959–) was born in Fort Meade, Maryland, into a family which featured engineers and scientists for more than one generation on both sides. They soon moved to the university town of Champaign-Urbana, Illinois, which Stephenson has described as an an archetypal 'Midwestern American College Town', or 'MACT', with a characteristic egalitarian, educated, science-friendly culture that valued intelligence, practical inquiry and experimentation. In 1966, the family moved to Ames, Iowa, another MACT, where Stephenson would stay until graduating from the high school there and going on to study at Boston University. Famously, he initially specialized in Physics but eventually graduated in Geography, because that subject allowed him to spend more time using computers at the University.

Stephenson's first novel was *The Big U* (1984) but he really came to prominence in the SF world (and beyond) with *Snow Crash* (1992), a post-cyberpunk romp through a Balkanized America and the Metaverse, a virtual-reality domain, with a main character helpfully identified to readers as Hiro Protagonist. The plot and characters are lively and engaging, but it is the continual focus on language across contexts as varied as ancient Sumerian culture and computer programming that both forces its readership to question their basic assumptions about communication, and presages the concern of Stephenson's key later works with the need for information to be free. *The Diamond Age* (1995), set in a neo-Victorian future, has a similar didactic element in that its story of a book that teaches young women to think for themselves is, itself, a demand to its readership to think for themselves.

Stephenson's most important works are *Cryptonomicon* (1999), acclaimed by Gary K. Wolfe as 'very possibly the most important non-science fiction SF novel in decades' (214), and *The Baroque Cycle* (2003–4) which followed it. None of these are easily summarized due to length and complexity; nor, as the Wolfe quote above suggests, are they conventional works of SF. Instead, they are all historical novels written in the style of SF, which is to say that the elements highlighted are the evolution of ideas, rational thought and conceptual breakthroughs, rather than cultural continuity and character development. For example, *Cryptonomicon* features the Second World War codebreaking team at Bletchley Park that played a key role in the Allies' eventual defeat of Nazi Germany; not to try and anchor the plot in verisimilitude, but to imply that the important history underlying the survival of democracy in the second half of the twentieth century is actually that of systems and patterns of information. In short, Stephenson's aim is to change the way we understand the world around us.

The ancestors of some of main characters from *Cryptonomicon* appear in the three volumes of *The Baroque Cycle*; *Quicksilver* (2003), *The Confusion* (2004) and *The System of the World* (2004). The overall story arc concerns the feud between Isaac Newton and Gottfried Leibniz as to who was the originator of the calculus, but further encompasses the birth of the global finance system and the collapse of the *ancien regime* of Europe. The effect once more is to challenge conventional notions of history as driven by dynastic power or material wealth, and place the emphasis on ideas and information. In distinction to this epic global history, Stephenson's most recent novels have assumed more familiar generic forms. *Anathem* (2008) eventually reveals itself to be an old-fashioned space opera, although its plot could be read as manifesting a characteristic authorial didactic intent with, in this case, Stapledonian overtones; namely, that the point of centuries of cloistered learning should be to get out into the world and beyond in order to change not just things but the human species itself for the better. *Reamde* (2011) is a near-future thriller, dealing amongst other topics with the threat of an international terrorist attack on the American homeland.

Despite some critical work on themes raised by Stephenson, there is no sustained critical engagement with his body of work as a whole; the most useful resource being perhaps his own collected non-fiction, *Some Remarks* (2012). This includes two interviews, a lengthy account of the history of underwater cable laying and a transcript of a 2008 lecture he gave at Gresham College (one of the locations featured in *The Baroque Cycle*), in which he reflects on SF as a genre. Two of the most recent essays, 'Locked In' (2011) and 'Innovation Starvation' (2011), discuss the causes and consequences of the decline of the US space program and other big science projects. If innovation is impossible, he suggests that Westernised society is faced with collapse and disappearance from history in the manner of the Ottoman Empire. Confronted with this serious context, a key task of the SF writer is to disseminate intelligence and grand visions; a process which clearly animates Stephenson's oeuvre.

Works Cited

Stephenson, Neal (1984). *The Big U*. New York: Vintage Books.
—(1992). *Snow Crash*. New York: Bantam Spectra.
—(1995). *The Diamond Age*. New York: Bantam Spectra.
—(1999). *Cryptonomicon*. New York: Avon Books.
—(2003). *Quicksilver*. New York: William Morrow.
—(2004). *The Confusion*. New York: William Morrow.
—(2004). *The System of the World*. New York: William Morrow.
—(2008). *Anathem*. New York: William Morrow.
—(2011). *Reamde*. New York: William Morrow.
—(2012). *Some Remarks*. New York: William Morrow.
Wolfe, Gary K. (2010). *Bearings: Reviews 1997–2001*. Harold Wood: Beccon Publications.

James Tiptree, Jr (Alice Sheldon) (1915–87) emerged on to the science fiction scene in the late 1960s and had an immediate impact with a succession of challenging and disturbing stories; going on to win Hugo and Nebula awards. However, although he made many friends by correspondence, nobody ever met him. It was not until 1977, following the death of Tiptree's mother late the previous year and the obituaries' mention of an only daughter, that it finally became known that Tiptree was really a woman. Alice Sheldon was born in Chicago to a wealthy family. Her father was a lawyer who led three expeditions to unmapped Central Africa, and her mother was a successful author and travel writer. Before becoming Tiptree, Sheldon had previously worked as a painter, an art critic, an intelligence analyst with the army during the War and later with the CIA and, finally, a research psychologist while studying for a PhD in experimental psychology at George Washington University in the 1960s. She also occasionally wrote SF under the pseudonym Raccoona Sheldon. In 1987, aged 71, Sheldon first took the life of her husband, and then her own.

The first Tiptree short story published was 'Birth of a Salesman' (1968) but the first to gain real attention was 'The Last Flight of Dr Ain' (1969), in which the eponymous doctor travels round the globe spreading a virus in order to kill the human race and save the Earth, who he personifies as a woman. This was followed in the next few years by stories such as 'And I Awoke and Found Me Here on the Cold Hill's Side' (1972), concerning the unrequited sexual desire of humans for aliens, the Hugo-winning 'The Girl Who Was Plugged In' (1973), a satire on consumerism and corporate control which anticipates the emergence of cyberpunk a decade later, and 'A Momentary Taste of Being' (1975), in which the human race discovers its purpose in the scheme of the universe is to 'act as a gamete in a cosmic coupling' (Clute and Nicholls, 1231); the Encyclopaedia of Science Fiction goes on to conclude that it is 'one of the darkest genre-SF stories ever printed' (ibid).

Arguably, Tiptree's two most important stories are 'The Women Men Don't See' (1973) and 'Houston, Houston, Do You Read?' (1976), which won both the Hugo and the Nebula for Best Novella. In the former, a plane crash throws the male protagonist, Don, together with a mother and daughter couple, Ruth and Althea, who he has previously registered as no more than a 'double female blur' and forces him to try and make sense of them. However, every motive he ascribes to them, from bourgeois morality to women's liberation, proves to be spectacularly wide of the mark as it transpires – in a beautifully-realized twist – that actually they are waiting for aliens to take them off the planet; preferring to live in outer space with occasional returns for breeding purposes rather than participate in the patriarchal order. At the story's end, a bemused Don swills margaritas pondering Ruth's claim that despite equal rights legislation, women only survive 'by ones and twos in the chinks of your world-machine' but, nonetheless, failing to understand how a woman could 'choose to live among unknown monsters, to say goodbye to her home, her world' (2004: 142–3). 'Houston, Houston' is about the slow realization of three astronauts returning from space that somehow they have been thrown forward into the future and that the Earth has now become an all-female planet. They react in different ways, variously trying to take command or asserting an aggressive sexuality, but it eventually becomes clear that the women are in control and have no intention of letting the men back on to Earth. The punch line is that they do not consider themselves to have created a Women's World or Amazon society, but simply see themselves as humanity; a humanity to which men could no longer meaningfully contribute.

There are also two Tiptree novels: *Up the Walls of the World* (1978) is a complex space opera, and *Brightness Falls from the Air* (1985) concerns interaction between species on a distant planet. However, it is her stories that ensure her place in the SF canon. Critical and biographical works on the author include Mark Siegel's *James Tiptree, Jr* (1986), Julie Phillips's *James Tiptree, Jr: The Double Life of Alice B. Sheldon* (2006), and the extensive discussion in Sarah Lefanu's *In the Chinks of the World Machine: Feminism and Science Fiction* (1988), which takes its title from the line in 'The Women Men Don't See' discussed above. In 1991, the James Tiptree, Jr Award was established in Sheldon's honour for works of SF and fantasy that expand notions of gender and sexuality.

Works Cited

Clute, John and Peter Nicholls (eds) (1993). *The Encyclopaedia of Science Fiction.* London: Orbit.

Lefanu, Sarah (1988). *In the Chinks of the World Machine: Feminism and Science Fiction.* London: The Women's Press.

Phillips, Julie (2006). *James Tiptree, Jr: The Double Life of Alice B. Sheldon.* New York: St. Martin's Press.

Siegel, Mark (1986). *James Tiptree, Jr.* Mercer Island, WA: Starmont House.

Tiptree, Jr, James (1968). 'Birth of a Salesman'. *Analog Science Fiction.* LXXXI. 1 (March). 73–84.

—(1969). 'The Last Flight of Dr Ain'. *Galaxy Magazine.* (March). 121–7.

—(1972). 'And I Awoke and Found Me here on the Cold Hill's Side'. *The Magazine of Fantasy and Science Fiction.* 42. 3 (March). 68–76.

—(1973). 'The Girl Who Was Plugged In'. *New Dimensions 3.* Robert Silverberg (ed.). New York: Nelson Doubleday. 60–97.

—(1973). 'The Women Men Don't See'. *The Magazine of Fantasy and Science Fiction.* 45. 6 (December). 4–19.

—(1975). 'A Momentary Taste of Being'. *The New Atlantis and Other Novellas of Science Fiction.* Robert Silverberg (ed.). New York: Hawthorn. 87–180.

—(1976). 'Houston, Houston, Do You Read?' *Aurora: Beyond Equality* Susan Janice Anderson and Vonda N. McIntyre (eds). New York: Fawcett Gold Medal. 36–98.

—(1978). *Up the Walls of the World.* New York: Berkley.

—(1985). *Brightness Falls from the Air.* New York: Tor.

—(2004). *Her Smoke Rose Up Forever.* San Francisco: Tachyon Publications.

H. G. Wells (1866–1946) was born in Bromley, where his parents, former domestic servants, were running a shop. His education was varied, depending on his parents' financial situation, and interspersed with periods as an apprentice: briefly with a chemist and for three unhappy years as a draper.

In 1884, he won a scholarship to the Normal School of Science in London, where he studied biology under T. H. Huxley. Although he did not manage to complete his degree at this time (later gaining a BSc in Zoology in 1890), he managed to earn a living via teaching work and became interested in social reform through the Fabian Society. Although he started writing in the 1880s, it was only after ill health forced him to retire from teaching in the early 1890s that he began publishing the stories, and subsequently novels, which would bring him to world fame and earn him a fortune.

Wells's' first major scientific romance, *The Time Machine* (see discussion in Chapter 4), was published in 1895 but originated in a short story, 'The Chronic Argonauts', written some years earlier. *The Island of Dr Moreau* (1896) and *The Invisible Man* (1897) quickly followed, but his most significant SF novel is probably *The War of the Worlds* (1898). This was a powerful and popular (it initially ran as a serial in the mass-market *Pearson's Magazine*) tale of a Martian invasion of southern England, which included the unforgettable imagery of giant tripods wading up the Thames and laying waste to the south-western suburbs of London with their 'Heat-Ray'. The inversion of British colonial history, by which the most powerful country on the planet is reduced to seeming helplessness as its people are exterminated like vermin, acts as a powerful social critique that is not simply directed at imperialism *per se* but also at the complacency of late Victorian Britain. The novel implicitly calls for a modern, scientific approach to society and government. In subsequent years, with the exception of the comedy of *The First Men in the Moon* (1901), much of Wells's' output was overtly concerned with social reorganisation: such as *A Modern Utopia* (1905) and *In the Days of the Comet* (1906).

Therefore, it can be seen that most of the SF that Wells is famous for was written in the first ten years of his career; indeed, arguably, his best works in the genre were all published before 1900. However, a case can be made that an attitude similar to that displayed in his SF animates the major modern novels he went on to write. For example, the desire of the 'New Woman' heroine of *Ann Veronica* (1909) to study biology is intrinsically linked to the novel's message of free love and sexual liberation. *Tono-Bungay* (1909) not only includes a sub plot concerning radioactive material, but also more importantly charts the emergence of modernity within an England formerly dominated by the great country houses, while closing with its first-person narrator protagonist, George Ponderevo, escaping from a decaying society as he sails down the Thames in a destroyer he has designed himself. Some of Wells's' later books, written after the First World War, can more conventionally be labelled as SF. *The Dream* (1924) details how a scientist from 2,000 years in the future finds himself inhabiting the life of Henry Mortimer Smith in the early decades of the twentieth century and *The Shape of Things to Come* (1933) outlines future history. In this period between the wars, Wells was also brought to the attention of an American popular audience by the regular reprinting of his stories in Hugo Gernsback's *Amazing Stories* and other magazines from 1926 onwards.

Above all else, however, Wells's perennial attraction remains that of the visionary outsider who can see through the pomp and bombast of a society to the rot and emptiness below and offer the promise of an alternate future. The romantic appeal of this position was summarized by his 1904 short story, 'The Country of the Blind' (1904), in which the sighted hero, far from becoming King as the famous proverb suggests, ends up dying an outcast rather than submit to having his eyes surgically removed. The story allegorizes the inhospitality of late Victorian and Edwardian England to new ways of seeing. Wells's enduring legacy is the development of the 'scientific romance' as a device for contesting the stasis and reaction of any social order; the 'science' guarantees the progressiveness of the social and cultural themes, while the 'romance' provides the point of identification for the readers and the fictional space in which to stage opposition to the restrictive cultural and social norms of the day.

Works Cited

Wells, H. G. (1895). *The Time Machine*. London: Heinemann.
—(1896). *The Island of Dr Moreau*. London: Heinemann.
—(1897). *The Invisible Man*. London: Pearson.
—(1898). *The War of the Worlds*. London: Heinemann.
—(1901). *The First Men in the Moon*. London: Newnes.
—(1904). 'The Country of the Blind'. *The Strand Magazine* (April).
—(1905). *A Modern Utopia*. London: McLean.
—(1906). *In the Days of the Comet*. London: Century.
—(1909). *Ann Veronica*. London: Fisher Unwin.
—(1909). *Tono-Bungay*. London: Macmillan.
—(1924). *The Dream*. London: Cape.
—(1933). *The Shape of Things to Come*. London: Hutchinson.

John Wyndham (1903–69), the son of a barrister, was born John Wyndham Parkes Lucas Beynon Harris in Warwickshire but spent most of his childhood in a succession of preparatory and boarding schools, ending up at the relatively liberal Bedales School in Hampshire. While Wyndham only came to fame after the publication of *The Day of the Triffids* in 1951, his first published SF story had actually appeared in 1931, under the name John Beynon Harris, and inaugurated a steady career writing for both UK and US magazines, under various permutations of his given names. As John Beynon, he published two early novels, *The Secret People* (1935) and *Planet Plane* (1936). This latter appeared in several different formats in the 1930s and, following the success of *The Day of the Triffids*, was republished as *Stowaway to Mars* by John Wyndham. During the Second World War, he worked for the Ministry of Information before serving in the army with the Royal Corps of Signals.

His wartime experience clearly affected Wyndham because his fiction changed from space opera to work that was predominantly concerned with the needs of people to respond to some form of extreme disaster and deal with the trauma that arose from it. In *The Day of the Triffids*, the hero, Bill Masen, is recovering in hospital from the sting of a triffid, giant walking plants that are cultivated for their productive oils. When he wakes to silence on a weekday morning, he realizes something is wrong, and takes off his bandages to find that seemingly everyone else in the world has been blinded by what they thought was a meteor shower but was in fact a malfunctioning satellite weapon. The opening chapters of the novel, in which Masen avoids the chaos and falls in with another sighted person, Josella Playton, socialite and author of *Sex is My Adventure*, appears to be the archetypal form of what Brian Aldiss later dubbed the 'cosy catastrophe', in which 'the hero should have a pretty good time (a girl, free suites at the Savoy, automobiles for the taking) while everyone else is dying off' (280). However, the novel proceeds to become a much darker tale as various competing social groups take the steps they consider necessary for the survival of the fittest. Rather than for the reasons Aldiss implies, therefore, the pleasure of the novel, and the reason it was so attractive to a middle-class readership in particular, stems from the fact that the order being overthrown by Wyndham's triffids was the collectivized social democracy of the Welfare State as established by the 1945 Labour Government.

Wyndham's style of disaster fiction, which can also be found in the novels of John Christopher and early works by writers such as J. G. Ballard, Christopher Priest and Keith Roberts, created a space that allowed readers to envision a new dynamic social order in place of the complacent and hidebound post-war British society that existed around them. Therefore, Wyndhamesque fiction can be seen as a direct continuation of the social critique of Wells and Stapledon, with the vital difference that the post-war establishment that it opposed did not have the same historical weight behind it as the Victorian and Edwardian hierarchy of values that Wells challenged. That Wyndham was aware of this relationship to Wells is made clear in the scene in *The Day of the Triffids* in which Bill and Josella discuss 'The Country of the Blind'. Bill is able to reassure Josella that they can escape the mess post-war society has become because: 'there's no organized patria, no State, here – only chaos. Wells imagined a people who had adapted themselves to blindness. I don't think that's going to happen here ...' (2000: 66). And it didn't, of course, because Britain was subsequently transformed by the social and cultural revolutions of the 1960s; an upheaval that *The Day of the Triffids* anticipates.

However, Wyndham, himself, remained ambivalent about such wide-reaching social change. *The Chrysalids* (1955) is a post-nuclear war story of the threat of mutation to the human race and while the readers' sympathies lay with the mutants, the ending is uneasy. Wyndham's next novel, *The Midwich Cuckoos* (1957), was even bleaker in its depiction of a societal and generational divide. The English village of Midwich is subject to an alien visitation, which leaves all women of childbearing age simultaneously pregnant. As it becomes clear that the resulting children have psychic powers and will eventually exert complete control over those around them, an increasingly troubled debate as to what should be done takes on ever more social Darwinist terms before the chilling denouement.

During the 1960s and after, Wyndham's critical reputation, if not his popularity, waned as he came to be seen as no more than a purveyor of cosy catastrophes. However, over recent years this decline has been reversed and the archiving of his papers at the University of Liverpool has led to a renewed interest and even the publication of an hitherto unknown novel, *Plan for Chaos* (2009). As the certainties of the late twentieth century continue to erode, and Britain is faced by the possibility of constitutional break-up, the bleak world of social struggle depicted in his best novels seems once again to be relevant and timely.

Works Cited

Aldiss, Brian and David Wingrove (2001). *Trillion Year Spree*. London: House of Stratus.

Beynon, John (1935). *The Secret People*. London: Newnes.

—(1936). *Planet Plane*. London: Newnes.

Wyndham, John (1951). *The Day of the Triffids*. London: Michael Joseph.

—(1955). *The Chrysalids*. London: Michael Joseph.

—(1957). *The Midwich Cuckoos*. London: Michael Joseph.

—(2000). *The Day of the Triffids*. Harmondsworth: Penguin Classics.

—(2009). *Plan for Chaos*. Liverpool: Liverpool University Press.

Case Studies in Reading 1: Key Primary Literary Texts

Christopher Daley

Chapter Overview

This chapter aims to provide a comprehensive introduction to five literary texts that have played significant roles in the ongoing evolution of Science Fiction or SF. Each text will be analysed in terms of its social and literary context, while close readings will draw out a collection of pertinent themes in each work. Additionally, emphasis will be placed upon the ways in which the five works interact, drawing out a series of convergences and divergences that provide further insights into the constantly changing terrain of SF.

H. G. Wells, *The Time Machine* (1895)

H. G. Wells is regularly cited as the godfather of modern Science Fiction and his influence on the genre is abundant. Nonetheless, his early writings are also particularly important in the history of a distinctly British form of SF writing. David Dalgleish has stated that Wells is accordingly 'central to the British SF tradition' (330) while Brian Stableford has argued that he was 'perhaps the most important thread which bound British scientific romances together' (4). Wells's brand of SF was therefore tied to the initially Victorian genre known as 'scientific romance', which pre-dated the coining of the term 'Science Fiction' by Hugo Gernsback in the 1920s and emerged from speculative non-fiction of the period that littered scientific journals and magazines. Stableford goes on to provide a succinct definition of this fictional offshoot and its relationship with the scientific language of the late nineteenth century:

> A scientific romance is a story which is built around something glimpsed through a window of possibility from which scientific discovery has drawn back the curtain [...] The distinguishing characteristic is not that scientific romances *are* scientific, but that they pretend to be, and they pretend to be in order to serve some rhetorical purpose. (8)

The Time Machine, the first of many scientific romances by Wells during the early stages of his career, succeeds through its harmonious combination of the fantastic (time travel and evolved visions of mankind in the far future) with seemingly rational, scientific discourses represented through the detailed discussions between men of science either side of the Time Traveller's tale and the speculative application of scientific theory within his subsequent adventure.

The structure of *The Time Machine* expertly navigates this revelatory mix of science and the fantastic, beginning with a discussion between the Time Traveller and his dinner guests who consist of, amongst others, a Psychologist and a Medical Man. Within the 'luxurious after-dinner atmosphere' (3) of Victorian suburbia the men discuss time and space, each eagerly displaying their scientific and mathematical acumen. Narration is then handed to the Time Traveller following his declaration concerning the possibility of time travel and his demonstration of a miniature model of his machine. His adventure into the future world of 802,701 occupies the majority of the novel, before his return to Richmond in the final stages of the text unnerves the certainty and security of the Victorian gentlemen in attendance. The descriptions of the Eloi and Morlocks followed by the dying earth 30 million years into the future utilizes nineteenth-century science to speculate on its potential outcomes, consequently offering an unsettling reflective vision to a nineteenth-century audience.

There was good reason for Wells to draw upon contemporaneous science, as the late nineteenth century had ushered in a variety of scientific discoveries and inventions. As Marina Warner explains:

> The last decade of Queen Victoria's reign, when Wells was making up his pioneering scientific romances, was an era of unsurpassed

scientific discovery, and many Victorian scientists were developing the technologies that would create the modern world. Electromagnetism, radio waves, X-rays, new gases (neon, argon, crypton, xenon) brought modernity into being (submarine cables were connecting the world, cities were illuminated, moving pictures started, followed by the telephone and, later, by television). (xx)

Additionally, Wells had studied biology under one of Darwin's key allies, Thomas Henry Huxley, and the influence of evolutionary theory upon *The Time Machine* is clearly marked. Yet despite these scientific successes, their revelatory nature provoked deep unease in Victorian society, with evolutionary theory raising particular questions about the natural desires and motivations of humankind and the potential for degeneration. Also, as is imagined in *The Time Machine*, Darwin's discoveries forced a reappraisal of humanity's relationship with time, and it is through the Time Traveller's journey that Wells is able to articulate the slowness of biological and geological transformations over vast periods of deep time.

Social anxieties around evolutionary theory are therefore scrutinized in the future world that the Time Traveller encounters. The Eloi – who are seemingly descendants of the Victorian upper classes – inhabit grand, but crumbling palaces surrounded by overgrown gardens containing deteriorating statues. The Time Traveller notes the 'ruinous splendour' (29) of the landscape and comments on the lack of other animals whom he assumes have 'followed the Icthyosaurus into extinction' (29). When greeted by the Eloi he notices that they resemble children in both appearance and mannerism, observing that 'they would come to me with eager astonishment, like children, but like children they would soon stop examining me and wander away after some other toy' (28). The representation of the Eloi as effete beings living unthinking and unproductive lives within the ruins of a former Utopia demonstrates the prospect of degeneration once a species reaches its productive peak. Indeed, Peter Firchow explains that Wells was 'the first writer of Utopian fiction to argue that the achievement of Utopia will inevitably lead to stagnation and degeneration' (131). The Time Traveller expresses this in the text, detailing how civilization had eventually broken free from the rigours of nature, but by investing 'energy in security' had ultimately succumbed to 'languor and decay' (33). The degenerative condition of the Eloi acts as a cautionary statement on Victorian optimism, with Wells warning that change and adaption may be biologically inevitable as conditions alter, yet change does not always result in improvement and can just as likely facilitate decline and extinction.

The Eloi's decline therefore makes them prey for the shadowy figures of the Morlocks who have successfully adapted to their enforced position underground and reversed the social and biological subjugation they previously encountered. Indeed, the Morlocks are outlined through a series of visceral descriptions, at one point being likened to a 'human spider' (46). Unlike the Eloi, whose energy has dwindled following their defeat of nature, the Morlocks have maintained a connection to the natural world, struggling within their muddy, dark subterranean world and waiting for their chance to exploit the inefficiency of their Eloi neighbours. While these two sub-species of humanity further illustrate how the eradication of external evolutionary struggle leads to the remaining strands of humanity degenerating into, as Firchow states, 'ever more hopeless states of unfitness' (131), the division between the two also reflects the consequences of persistent class division and social Darwinism. The Eloi's Utopia was brought about through centuries of oppression and Wells grimly imagines the ultimate folly of such a process as the Morlocks overpower their old foe: 'Ages ago, thousands of generations ago, man had thrust his brother man out of the ease and the sunshine. And now that brother was coming back – changed! Already the Eloi had begun to learn one old lesson anew' (58).

Robert Crossley explains how this tussle between the Eloi and Morlocks is accordingly a reflection on the dangers of contemporaneous class segregation: 'The rich who once (metaphorically) devoured the poor become in future time (literally) the food of their former victims. The anonymous inventor who travels through time undergoes something he had not anticipated: the political and moral education of his imagination' (355). Crossley concludes that *The Time Machine* ultimately entices a 'reflection on self, society and the universe' (355) as it is within this future world that the policies of the late nineteenth century have achieved their logical end. Furthermore, the Time Traveller himself realizes that the roots of the Morlocks' struggle reside in his own time, explaining that the conditions he finds had proceeded 'the problems of our own age' (48) and asks his audience whether 'even now, does not an East-end worker live in such artificial conditions as practically to be cut off from the natural surface of the earth?' (48). Wells, here, uses the future setting to describe a social injustice ingrained within his own time and by speculating on the bleakness of its eventual conclusion aims to engender a reaction against such societal mismanagement.

While *The Time Machine* offers a solemn political message through the battle between Eloi and Morlocks, its most startling and disquieting reflection on the nineteenth century is found in the Palace of Green Porcelain that the Time Traveller discovers amongst 'the ruins of some latter-day South Kensington!' (65). The location, content and description of the palace is analogous to the South Kensington museums that are still present today and would have been prominent features of nineteenth-century London. Indeed, the Time Traveller soon uncovers more familiarities in the palace, including recognizable paraphernalia: 'Going towards the side I found what appeared to be sloping shelves, and, clearing away the thick dust, I found the old familiar glass cases of our own time' (65). The fragments of the previous civilization illustrates, as Crossley notes, 'the fragility of culture' (355), but they also demonstrate the vastness of geological time as the specimens uncovered in the nineteenth century have, in 802,701, become redundant artefacts from a long forgotten stage in man's evolution. Correspondingly, Frank McConnell has noted that a major effect of evolutionary theory was 'not simply the idea of man's heritage from lower animals, but rather the disorientating discovery of the immense vistas of time upon which any definition of "man" – or of man's success – has to be imagined' (80). The journeys of the Time Traveller do not confirm the greatness of his age, but expose its smallness within the giant span of human-kind's gradual rise and eventual fall.

The unsettling revelations within the Palace of Green Porcelain are then expanded in the final moments of the Time Traveller's journey where he glimpses an even more distant future as the earth is reaching its final moments. This closing vision, of 30 million years into the future, again points to degeneration and near extinction as he sees only a 'black object flopping about' (84) as the earth cools to uninhabitable temperatures. The Time Traveller's final description reveals the bareness of the dying earth: 'Silent? It would be hard to convey the stillness of it. All the sounds of man, the bleating of sheep, the cries of birds, the hum of insects, the stir that makes the background of our lives – all that was over' (85). Wells once more applies nineteenth-century science, this time the principles of entropy – which states the inevitability of energy loss from a system over time – to elucidate the terminal route for humanity as the world slows to a natural equilibrium. As mentioned previously, it is through this combination of probable science and fantastical imaginings that *The Time Machine* creates an unsettling style where encounters with giant crabs, sickly Eloi and grotesque Morlocks overlap with the discourse of evolution, class politics and the second law of thermodynamics.

While largely pessimistic in tone, the novel's epilogue provides a final message of hope as the unnamed narrator contemplates the Time Traveller's findings, reasoning that fatalism must not dominate humanity's relationship with futurity:

> If that is so, it remains for us to live as though it were not so. But to me the future is still black and blank – is a vast ignorance, lit at a few casual places by the memory of his story. And I have by me, for my comfort, two strange white flowers – shrivelled now, and brown and flat and brittle – to witness that even when mind and strength had gone, gratitude and mutual tenderness still lived on in the heart of man. (91)

The flowers are, of course, samples that the Time Traveller has acquired from the garden of the Eloi estate and it is in the timidity and kindness of the Eloi that the narrator imagines the final remnants of modern man to lie. The epilogue, which also wonders if the once more disappeared Time Traveller may be 'beside the lonely saline lakes of the Triassic Age' (91), again points to the immensity of geological time, but unlike the Time Traveller's description of far future demise, the narrator takes comfort in the prolonged nature of evolutionary transformation and the near endless expanses of deep time, declaring himself to live for the otherwise uncharted 'black and blank' (91) spaces of the future.

Works Cited

Crossley, Robert (2005). 'The Grandeur of H. G. Wells'. *A Companion to Science Fiction*. David Seed (ed.). Malden, MA and Oxford: Blackwell. 353–63.

Dalgleish, David (1997). 'The Ambivalent Paradise: Or, Nature and the Transcendent in British SF'. *Extrapolation*. 38. 4. 327–42.

Firchow, Peter (2004). 'H. G. Wells's Time Machine: In Search of Time Future – and Time Past'. *The Midwest Quarterly*. 45. 2. 123–36.

McConnell, Frank (1981). *The Science Fiction of H .G. Wells*. Oxford and New York: Oxford University Press.

Stableford, Brian (1985). *Scientific Romance in Britain: 1890–1950*. New York: St. Martin's Press.

Warner, Marina (2005). 'Introduction'. In H. G. Wells, *The Time Machine*. London and New York: Penguin. xii–xxviii.

Wells, H. G. (2005). *The Time Machine*. London and New York: Penguin.

Westfahl, Gary (2012).'Hugo Gernsback'. *The Encyclopaedia of Science Fiction* (3rd edn). Available online: http://www.sf-encyclopedia.com/entry/gernsback_hugo [accessed 01 October 2012].

J. G. Ballard, *The Drowned World* (1962)

On the surface, J. G. Ballard's post-apocalyptic novel is far removed from the methodical outline of geological time in Wells's earlier scientific romance. Indeed, Ballard's novel – set in a lagoon above a flooded London following a catastrophic solar event that has melted the polar ice caps and submerged much of the earth – focuses on the surrealist visualizations brought about by disaster along with the psychological trauma experienced by the protagonist of the text, Robert Kerans. Yet, in many ways, Ballard's novel is both indebted to the Wellsian tradition of scientific romance and represents a natural progression from it, with Kerans's descent into 'ancient organic memory' (74) signalling a hallucinogenic re-engagement with the immense vistas of geological and evolutionary time that had fascinated Wells's Time Traveller

nearly 70 years earlier. In addition, Ballard's quartet of ecological apoca-
lypses during the 1960s – *The Winds from Nowhere* (1962), *The Drowned World*
(1962), *The Drought* (1965) and *The Crystal World* (1966) – are all reactions to
a particular tradition of British disaster fiction which can be traced back to
texts such as *The War of the Worlds* (1898) and subsequently continued as
a distinctive sub-genre up to the writings of John Wyndham in the 1950s.
These apocalyptic thrillers invariably seized upon contemporaneous anxieties
and often charted the plight of a protagonist seeking to rebuild a rapidly
crumbling society. Brian Aldiss, in his work *Trillion Year Spree*, famously
dismissed Wyndham for being 'the master of the cosy catastrophe' (315) due
to his reluctance to engage with the terror of social collapse, instead clinging
to the remnants of middle-class culture as the apocalypse unfolds outside.
The Drowned World is, in part, a rebuttal of this style as Kerans exhibits
no desire to save himself but instead succumbs to the mysterious forces
of the transformed landscape. Nonetheless, viewed contextually Ballard's
novel resembles more of a natural adaption of the British disaster genre,
re-imagining the formula to fit his experimentation into what he called 'inner
space', which will be discussed shortly, while also providing a more troubling
response to the prospect of societal collapse during the increasingly 'hot'
moments of the Cold War.

Ballard, alongside Michael Moorcock, was a major force in the British New
Wave in science fiction. Centred by Moorcock's editorship of *New Worlds*
magazine in the 1960s, the movement sought to overturn what it saw as
outmoded SF conventions while also producing a new aesthetic that incorporated avant-garde art and literature. In 1962, Ballard wrote an editorial piece
for *New Worlds* entitled 'Which Way to Inner Space?', which summarized
the style pioneered in his disaster novel of the same year and in many of his
subsequent narratives of the period:

> ... I'd like to see s-f becoming abstract and 'cool', inventing fresh
> situations and contexts that illustrate its theme obliquely. For example,
> instead of treating time like a sort of glorified scenic railway, I'd like
> to see it used for what it is, one of the perspectives of the personality,
> and the elaboration of concepts such as the time zone, deep time and
> archaeopsychic time. (198)

Ballard's 'inner space' writing, and *The Drowned World* in particular, therefore
aim to enact this aesthetic vision as the novel turns away from linear descriptions of attempts to rebuild civilization after catastrophe, and instead turns
towards introspection and internalized time systems as a way of unpicking
the latent content of psychological evolution once the restraints of civilization
have been removed.

This desire to explore 'inner space' is accomplished in *The Drowned World* through the actions of Kerans – a scientist assigned to a testing station which surveys the post-apocalyptic world in the hope of re-establishing some form of societal structure. Kerans quickly becomes disillusioned with his work on the station, declaring that 'the biological mapping had become a pointless game, [...] and he was sure that no one at Camp Byrd in North Greenland bothered to file his reports, let alone read them' (8–9). The testing station therefore becomes a hopeless symbol of the old world and Kerans soon abandons his research and heads south into the increasingly intolerable heat. Unlike comparable disaster texts such as John Wyndham's *The Day of the Triffids* (1951) or John Christopher's *The Death of Grass* (1956), where a group of survivors look to salvage as much of the pre-apocalyptic world as possible, *The Drowned World* sees Kerans move away from the other survivors and into the catastrophe itself. The aim here is to turn the British disaster tradition on its head, overturning the expected actions of the central protagonist. But there is also a wider aesthetic and philosophical drive behind Kerans's journey south, which corresponds with Ballard's 'inner space' style. As Kerans continues his voyage he is accompanied by vivid dreams and visions that appear to resonate from the transformed landscape around him: 'The light drummed against his brain, bathing the submerged levels below his consciousness, carrying him downwards into warm pellucid depths where the nominal realities of time and space ceased to exist' (83). As he immerses himself further, Kerans is offered revelatory glimpses of ancient memories and traumas otherwise suppressed by the mask of civility, with the transformed Triassic-like topography feeding the residual traces of evolutionary memory. As the perceptive Dr Bodkin explains to Kerans: 'we really *remember* these swamps and lagoons' (74).

Yet despite this dual impulse to both overthrow the expectations of the British disaster genre and imagine a more radical relationship with time and space in a post-catastrophe landscape, *The Drowned World* nonetheless tussles with a collection of comparable themes to those articulated in *The Time Machine*. As with Wells, whose Time Traveller revels in exploring the great vistas of deep time, Ballard's landscape, which offers glimpses of huge alligators and a 'sail-backed lizard with a gigantic dorsal fin' (9), has also undergone its own journey into a different temporality. What differs is that Wells's Time Traveller aims to record his findings and report back to his eminent dinner guests, while the Ballardian traveller abandons scientific process and submits to the new environment and its abundance of psychological revelations. Similarly, the redundancy of the testing station and the usurping of humanity by natural forces both correspond with the evolutionary anxieties in Wells's earlier work, but whereas Wells imagined a dying earth, Ballard's drowned landscape is flourishing after humankind's expulsion as giant plants emerge from the decaying remains of modern buildings. This vision highlights a recurring motif in Ballard's disaster fiction of discordant juxtaposition where ecology catastrophe paves the way for the emergence of a surrealist landscape characterized by natural phenomena erupting from the remnants of high modernity.

Indeed, the influence of surrealism on Ballard's career has been boldly stated by literary scholars and the author himself. In another of his non-fiction pieces for *New Worlds* entitled 'The Coming of the Unconscious', Ballard proclaimed that 'the images of surrealism are the iconography of inner space' (84), while Jeannette Baxter has argued that Ballard's oeuvre represents 'a radical Surrealist experiment in the writing of post-war history and culture' (2). The landscape of *The Drowned World* is vividly described as London adopts an appearance more akin to the dreamscapes of Salvador Dali, Paul Delvaux or Max Ernst than that of a sprawling modern city. This is particularly noticeable in the opening passages of the text where the rapidity of the topographical revolution is marked out:

> In the early morning light a strange mournful beauty hung over the lagoon; the sombre green-black fronds of the gymnosperms, intruders from the Triassic past, and the half-submerged white-faced buildings of the 20th century still reflected together in the dark mirror of the water, the two interlocking worlds apparently suspended at some junction in time, the illusion momentarily broken when a giant water-spider cleft the oily surface a hundred yards away. (10–11)

Such intense descriptions allow Ballard to accomplish a distinct painterly quality to his fictional worlds, but there is also a broader contextual purpose to these fantastical landscapes. Many contemporaneous disaster works centred around a collection of Cold War anxieties about nuclear war, the increasingly authoritarian nature of national governments or the consequences of unchecked scientific experimentation – anxieties that these works invariably exploited and at times sought to ameliorate. In Ballard's lagoon world these concerns have been obliterated and simultaneously, as Simon Sellars notes, the 'deadening aids of civilized society' (233) have been pushed aside. As a result, Ballard's over-determined setting, filled with ghostly apparitions of human biological ancestry, welcomes a psychoanalytic exploration of the otherwise dormant drives underpinning human endeavour.

By the novel's conclusion Kerans has committed entirely to his journey south into the heat and near-certain death. Fuelled by his belief that he is embarking on a 'neuronic odyssey' (174) he ploughs on in search of further glimpses of ancient memories and psychic states. Again, a parallel can be drawn with Wells's Time Traveller who disappears once more at the novel's close, this time vanishing for three years. Kerans, conducting his own internalized time travel into the unconscious, is on the brink of disappearance at the end of *The Drowned World*, removing himself from the fragments of the surpassed social order of the twentieth century and becoming a mythical 'second Adam searching for the forgotten paradises of the reborn sun' (175). Whereas Wells offers a glimmer of hope through the narrator's stoical determination to carry on regardless of the Time Traveller's entropic experience, Ballard's conclusion seems less hopeful as Kerans submits to the apocalypse. H. Bruce Franklin has resultantly criticized Ballard for providing a pessimistic view of unconscious energies and failing to dig deeper in search of more hopeful conclusions:

> My criticism is that Ballard does not generally go down far enough below the unconscious to the sources of the alienation, self-destruction, and mass slaughter of our age. He therefore remains incapable of understanding the alternative to these death forces, the global movement toward human liberation which constitutes the main distinguishing characteristic of our epoch. (93)

However, *The Drowned World* intentionally shies away from an encounter with any 'global movement toward human liberation' and instead aims to explore the consequence of freeing an individual from both the shackles of Cold War nervousness and an affectless consumer culture that was emerging in the early 1960s. The result is not mere fatalism in the face of a destroyed civilization but a temporary glimpse at unconscious dreamscapes and repressed psychologies that are otherwise denied.

John Gray partly aligns himself with Franklin's view, explaining that Ballard's fiction 'takes a certain nihilism as given. Ballard regards with suspicion all schemes – liberal, environmentalist – that aim to make the world over. Such schemes repose a faith in human society that Ballard plainly lacks'. However, Gray then concludes that the purpose of this entrenched scepticism is to expose 'what individual fulfilment might mean in a time of nihilism'. *The Drowned World* therefore enacts a purposeful realignment of the British catastrophe tradition by revealing the inherent hopelessness in doggedly rebuilding civilization after disaster and instead reaches the unsettling conclusion that apocalypse may answer powerful death drives lingering beneath the surface of co-operative, functional society. Coupled with this, Ballard's drowned landscape along with the proceeding visions of dried-out rivers in *The Drought* and crystallized forests in *The Crystal World*, establishes fertile locales for Ballard to enforce his surreal visualization of the mid-century world, with the wreckage of modernity co-existing alongside the natural beneficiaries of ecological transformation.

Works Cited

Aldiss, Brian and David Wingrove (1988). *Trillion Year Spree: The History of Science Fiction*. London: Paladin.

Ballard, J. G. (2008). *The Drowned World*. London: Harper Perennial.

—(1997) 'Which Way to Inner Space?' *A User's Guide to the Millennium: Essays and Reviews*. London: Flamingo. 195–8.

—(1997). 'The Coming of the Unconscious'. *A User's Guide to the Millennium: Essays and Reviews*. London: Flamingo. 84–8.

Baxter, Jeannette (2009). *J. G. Ballard's Surrealist Imagination: Spectacular Authorship*. Surrey and Burlington, VT: Ashgate.

Franklin, H. Bruce (1979). 'What Are We To Make Of J. G. Ballard's Apocalypse?'. *Voices for the Future: Essays on Major Science Fiction Writers*. Thomas Clareson (ed.). Ohio: Bowling Green Popular Press. 82–105.

Gray, John (1999). 'Modernity and its Discontents'. *New Statesman*. (10 May). Available online: http://www.newstatesman.com/199905100041. [accessed 22 September 2012].

Sellars, Simon (2012). '"Zones of Transition": Micronationalism in the Work of J. G. Ballard'. *J. G. Ballard: Visions and Revisions*. J. Baxter and R. Wymer (eds). New York and Basingstoke: Palgrave Macmillan. 230–48

Joanna Russ, 'When it Changed' (1972)

Winner of the Nebula Award for best short story in 1972, 'When it Changed' is a defining piece of feminist SF from the period alongside Russ's slightly later novel *The Female Man* (1975). The story follows the narrator, Janet, who lives on a human colony named Whileaway that exists some distance from Earth. The colony is inhabited only by women following a plague that wiped out the male population 'thirty generations ago' (274). Reproduction is carried out through a form of parthenogenesis whereby the colonists enact foetus development through the 'merging of ova' (275). The major event of the story consists of a group of male astronauts from earth landing on the colony and questioning the female inhabitants about their way of life, insisting that they would be happier if men returned to the planet. The narrative concludes with Janet melancholically pondering the imminent return of men and the potential subjugation for the female inhabitants that might ensue. Subtle in style, but containing a series of crucial political messages, 'When it Changed' expertly interrogates the conventions of SF writing and its inherent gender assumptions while also making broader comments – similarly to Ballard and other New Wave writers – about the visions of modernity that dominate SF discourse, with the story looking to investigate the legitimacy of certain forms of hero-worshipping SF.

Accordingly, the opening passages of 'When it Changed' articulate Russ's aim to challenge assumptions about gender roles. At first we are not informed of the narrator's sex as she describes the behaviour of her wife, Katy. We are told that Katy 'drives like a maniac' (271) and that she maintains an intricate knowledge of mechanics, to the extent that 'I've seen her take the whole car apart and put it together again in a day' (271). This is followed by an account of the dreams of the couple's daughter, Yuriko, who we are told imagines 'love and war' (272) and 'hunting in the North' (272). It is not until a few paragraphs later, when Yuriko discovers the astronauts, that it becomes apparent that Whileaway is an all-female society. The purpose of these opening passages is twofold, with Russ primarily confronting the way in which gender roles are rigidly ascribed by portraying Katy and Yuriko as in possession of a number of supposedly 'masculine' interests and attitudes. These opening descriptions expose the constructed nature of gender roles and force the reader to speculate as to the societal changes that may have facilitated such a transformation. But accompanying this, Russ is also making a comment on the expectations of genre. By not revealing the sex of the narrator in the initial passages, Russ plays with readerly assumptions about the narrative voice within SF texts. By explaining Katy's proficient skills as a mechanic and her occasional desire to go 'hiking in the forests above the 48th parallel without firearms' (272), the conventionally masculine traits of the SF hero are projected on to the wifely figure, therefore distorting gendered expectations housed within certain forms of SF writing.

Continuing from this, Russ's questioning of generic assumptions aligns with certain political and aesthetic aims articulated by New Wave SF in the 1960s and 1970s. Russ's story – regardless of being set on a far-future planet – moves away from the anticipated tropes of 'space operas', turning instead to introspection and general suspicion at the forces governing advanced, technological societies. Indeed, Janet outlines the nature of Whileaway's society, making constant pleas to be able to expand at their own pace rather than through hurried industrialization:

> I told him the district caucuses handled problems too big for the
> individual towns. And that population control was not a political issue,
> not yet, though give us time and it would be. This was a delicate point in
> our history; give us time. There was no need to sacrifice the quality of life
> for an insane rush into industrialization. Let us go our own pace. Give us
> time. (274)

While we do not necessarily believe Whileaway to be entirely Utopian – Janet mentions that there are 'so few, so very few who can be free' (274) in the agricultural community – it is nonetheless imagined as resistant to certain processes that have produced mixed effects on Earth and resulted in the desperate visit from astronauts. By imagining a scenario where the follies of previous generations are dismissed in favour of slow, reasoned progress, Russ's story aims to challenge the cyclical histories of certain post-apocalyptic narratives – notably Walter M. Miller's *A Canticle for Leibowitz* (1959) – which imagine an endless repetition of historical paradigms followed by increasingly destructive conflicts.

Indeed, the astronauts who arrive on Whileaway mention that those on earth have suffered 'too much genetic damage in the last few centuries. 'Radiation. Drugs' (276). They therefore seek to colonize Whileaway in order to acquire redemption by overthrowing the female community and, as Janet explains, 'produce a carbon copy of their mistakes!' (278). While the broader aim of this is to challenge the assumptions of patriarchy (which will be discussed below in greater detail), the attempted planting of earthly attitudes on Whileaway further challenges certain SF conventions. As Russ notes in her 1970 essay 'The Image of Women in Science Fiction', many far future SF works imagine societies that are socially analogous to contemporaneous civilization. Russ argues that despite being set *'very* far in the future' (206) even the most intelligent fictional texts at times carry 'today's values and standards into its future Galactic Empires' (206). Whileaway depicts a future female colony that has adjusted to its new environment through a mixture of cultural redefinition and biological adaption. Consequently, Whileaway has resisted a replication of the follies associated with humanity's earthly history and instead speculates on the potential for future transformation and reinvention.

In addition, the sexual politics of 'When it Changed' provide a sustained challenge to certain assumptions about gender in preceding SF writings, especially the masculine attitudes inherent in many 'Golden Age' works. As pointed out by Adam Roberts in *The History of Science Fiction*, 'Golden Age' SF 'valorises a particular sort of writing: "Hard SF", linear narratives, heroes solving problems or countering threats in a space-opera or a technological-adventure idiom' (195). Confronting this formula in 'The Image of Women in Science Fiction', Russ wonders why SF is happy to imagine the likelihood of technological change, but invariably imposes an 'intergalactic suburbia' (206) upon its characters, with her criticism also extending to more literary SF writers:

> In general, the authors who write reasonably sophisticated and literate science fiction (Clarke, Asimov, for choice) see the relations between the sexes as those of present-day, white, middle-class suburbia. Mummy and Daddy may live inside a huge amoeba and Daddy's job may be to test psychedelic drugs or cultivate yeast-vats, but the world inside their heads is the world of Westport and Rahway *and that world is never questioned.* [...] In short, the American middle class with a little window dressing. (206–7)

In calling for a reconsideration of relationships between the sexes in future worlds, Russ goes on to identify the problem of simply replacing a patriarchal suburbia with an antithetical form of matriarchy. Russ argues that many attempts at imagining a female only society represent the community as static or reliant on biological determinism to anticipate the actions of women (see Russ, 2007: 212–13). Therefore, 'When it Changed' aims to dismantle these tendencies towards both comparably orthodox sexual relationships and unconvincing representations of stagnant matriarchy. Whileaway is not a rigid society, but is instead governed by a sense that social roles and responsibilities can be fluidly negotiated amongst the female inhabitants, while both biologically and socially, community members have developed beyond the determining features of mixed-sex relationships and established new forms of sociobiological cohesion.

'When it Changed' therefore interrogates the presumed naturalness of heterosexual relationships and their assumed social functions. The astronauts condescendingly question the functionality of the Whileaway community, mocking their choice of clothing and explaining that 'where I come from, the women don't dress so plainly' (275), before later stating that the female society 'is unnatural' (276). This final comment provokes one of the residents, Katy, to declare that 'humanity is unnatural' (276) to which the astronaut responds with partial agreement followed, ultimately, by continued refusal of the legitimacy of Whileaway:

> 'Humanity is unnatural. I should know. I have metal in my teeth and metal pins here.' He touched his shoulder. 'Seals are harem animals,' he added, 'and so are men; apes are promiscuous and so are men; doves are monogamous and so are men; there are celibate men and homosexual men. […] But Whileaway is still missing something.' (276)

Regardless of the astronaut's momentary recognition of diversity in sexual orientation, he soon reasserts that he believes 'in instinct' (277) and deterministically reasons that impulse will see women long for the return of men. Here, Russ not only satirizes the suggestion that sexuality can be crudely determined by seemingly innate biology, but also subverts certain stereotypes in SF. The astronaut is not a liberating figure, boldly discovering a semi-rural world and offering technological salvation, but rather he is a traveller from a dying earth aiming to colonize a largely harmonious community and reinstate the social failings of his race.

Yet, the stubborn resistance of the Whileaway inhabitants is counteracted in the final passages of the story as Janet downheartedly anticipates the likely aggressive overthrow by the astronauts. Janet concedes that technologically the astronauts are likely to succeed in imposing the return of men, explaining that 'when one culture has the big guns and the other has none, there is a certain predictability about the outcome' (277). This matches with her earlier description of the physical size of the men who appear on the planet, noting how they 'are bigger than we are. They are bigger and broader. They were taller than me, and I am extremely tall, 1m, 80cm in my bare feet' (273). The story's renegotiation of gender roles in an all-woman community is therefore offset by the realization that some biological features, notably male physical strength, are harder to repel. Russ makes specific mention of this in the afterword to the story, expressing that 'human beings are born with instincts (though fuzzy ones) and that being physically weaker than men and having babies makes a difference' (280). As Eileen Donaldson points out, the archetypal hero in SF exhibits 'aggression and ferocity' (156) which 'have gendered the hero masculine' (156). Donaldson continues by emphasizing that 'it is now perfectly acceptable to have a woman warrior hero' (156) despite the broader question as to whether such a character 'furthers the feminist cause or undermines it' (156). Russ's narrative questions the extent to which the female hero can out-manoeuvre biological constraints. Indeed, Janet is described as having scars from a series of duels and has, to an extent, adopted conventionally masculine traits, but accepts that in confronting the bludgeoning force of the astronauts she faces 'a duel so big that I don't think I have the guts for it' (278). 'When it Changed' is on the one hand a text determined to override assumptions about the rigidity of gender roles, particularly when explored through the lens of far future SF, but on the other hand equally enters a dialogue about the reasons for such assumptions, weighing up the amount to which characterizations are governed by patriarchal definitions of female instinct or by natural inequalities in the physical composition of men and women.

The success of 'When it Changed' lies in its meticulous combination of sharp political comment with a broader philosophical sensibility. Douglas Barbour expands this sentiment by describing it as a regular feature of Russ's fiction more generally: 'A savage intelligence and a subtle understanding of the smallest nuances of mood and emotion make for narratives of innuendo, implication, and often jarring lacunae; yet these narratives also argue the most pertinent politics of the personal within carefully constructed sf possibilities' (191). Regardless of its short story form, 'When it Changed' contains a wide collection of themes and issues that are expertly overlapped. Its introspective examination of an otherworldly colony reassesses the style of 'space opera', whilst the Whileaway community simultaneously examines the possible sociological formations of a matriarchal society. Add to this the narrative's complex exploration of biological instinct, and its status as a key work in feminist SF becomes eminently clear. But, more widely than this, Russ's precise combination of competing themes into a lucid social commentary makes 'When it Changed' a crucial text in revealing the possibilities of the SF short story.

Works Cited

Barbour, Douglas (2010). 'Joanna Russ'. *Fifty Key Figures in Science Fiction*. In Mark Bould et al. (eds). London and New York: Routledge. 190–5.

Donaldson, Eileen (2010). 'Hail the Conquering Campbellian S/Hero: Joanna Russ's Alyx'. *Practicing Science Fiction: Critical Essays on Writing, Reading and Teaching the Genre*. K. Helleksen et al. (eds). Jefferson, NC: MacFarland. 154–67.

Roberts, Adam (2005). *The History of Science Fiction*. New York and Basingstoke: Palgrave Macmillan.

Russ, Joanna (1977). 'When it Changed'. *Again, Dangerous Visions*. Harlan Ellison (ed.). London: Pan Books. 271–9.

—(1977) 'Afterword'. *Again, Dangerous Visions*. Harlan Ellison (ed.). London: Pan Books. 279–81.

—(2007). 'The Image of Women in Science Fiction'. *The Country You Have Never Seen: Essays and Reviews*. Liverpool: Liverpool University Press. 205–18.

Octavia Butler, *Kindred* (1979)

Kindred is Octavia Butler's most famous work and, as Michael Levy explains, 'is primarily responsible for the respect Butler achieved outside of sf as an explicitly African-American writer' (43). The novel is narrated in the first person by Dana, a black woman living with her white husband, Kevin, in 1976 California. Unexpectedly, she is pulled back in time to the early nineteenth-century South where she repeatedly saves the life of her distant white ancestor, Rufus. Despite the brutal treatment she receives from both Rufus and numerous white characters, Dana continually returns to rescue Rufus as she learns that he has fathered children with her black ancestor, Alice. The text is in part SF, using time travel to articulate the horrors of slavery and its historical legacies within twentieth-century America. Yet, its firsthand retelling also offers a postcolonial reinterpretation of the slave narrative and it is this renegotiation of genre boundaries that has led to the novel remaining an important text both inside and outside SF.

While ostensibly a time travel narrative, *Kindred* subverts the popular expectations of the SF sub-genre. Unlike the Wellsian time travelling tale, which relies on meticulous pseudo-scientific descriptions of both the concept of time travel and its theoretical potential, Butler's novel intentionally ignores any attempts at explaining the precise reason for Dana's transportation to the antebellum South, with the event remaining a mysterious occurrence:

> I raised my head and discovered that I could not focus on him.
> 'Something is wrong with me,' I gasped.

> I heard him move toward me, saw a blur of gray pants and blue shirt.
> Then, just before he would have touched me, he vanished.
> The house, the books, everything vanished. Suddenly, I was outdoors
> kneeling on the ground beneath trees. (13)

The scientific or technological potentials of time travel are not important points for discussion within *Kindred*, but rather it is the literary and political possibilities of temporal disruption that assists the narrative's vivid exposition of slavery and its historical resonances. Furthermore, Dana's transportation back in time also allows for the application of another literary genre, the slave narrative, on top of the SF time traveller story to create a text that supplies new social terrain for both styles, while equally unsettlingly their generic functions. Nadine Flagel provides an accurate description of the application of this in the text, pointing out that 'while generic conventions in *Kindred* sometimes overlap, more often it is precisely the terms of one genre that allow Butler to interrupt and interrogate the assumptions and expectations held by the other' (217). With this in mind, Dana's journey from the late twentieth century to the early nineteenth facilitates an examination of the slave narrative tradition, while the interweaving of the slave narrative into a time travel adventure redefines the political scope of such a traditional SF style.

Indeed, by rewriting the slave narrative through use of the speculative imagination Butler seeks to reconnect modern black culture with an ancestry dominated by oppression. Dana's transportation back in time does not therefore see her merely observe the sufferings of her ancestors, but she too endures the physical and emotional torment. This is highlighted by the conditions necessitating her time travel as she only travels back when Rufus is in mortal danger and only returns to 1976 when she is close to death herself. Consequently, throughout the text she is beaten, whipped and eventually loses an arm in her final confrontation with Rufus at the narrative's climax. As Sherryl Vint explains, while Dana's embodied experience brings her great physical damage, it also allows her to fully appreciate, understand and engage with the past:

> To project one's current consciousness back in time is not sufficient to recreate the experience of slavery. As long as Dana envisions herself as a disembodied subject, she deludes herself that the experience of slavery is safely contained in the past. Over the course of the novel, she begins to recognize that her subjectivity is not something that she can separate from bodily experience – it cannot remain hermetically sealed and unchanged by the enslavement and suffering she undergoes – and that mind and body are both parts of her self. A past that can affect her body affects this self. Once she realizes this, she is able to take action about the past instead of passively waiting for it to capture her. (249)

Furthermore, it becomes impossible, from the outset, for Dana to distantly observe the events she witnesses. Unlike Wells's white Victorian time traveller who is relatively unrestrained in his exploration of the future world, Dana is immediately interpellated by her black skin, being unavoidably immersed within the all-pervasive system of racism and slavery in early nineteenth-century America. As soon as she steps into this past amongst plantation owners and slaves her black skin dictates that she will have no choice but to experience the full ferocity of the dehumanizing system.

This is contrasted with the experiences of Kevin, who is at one point flung back into the past alongside Dana. As a white man Kevin is relatively secure in the antebellum world. Indeed, he comments that 'this could be a great time to live in' (97) explaining the potential to 'go West and watch the building of the country, see how much of the Old West mythology is true' (97). For Kevin, time travel allows for a revelatory exploration of official national history, of the grand moments and achievements that dominate patriotic narratives. In contrast, Dana experiences the intimate suffering of slaves. Reacting to Kevin's desire to remain curious observers, Dana declares that 'you might be able to go through this whole experience as an observer' (101) but, despite her own efforts to do likewise and have 'nineteen seventy-six shielding and cushioning eighteen nineteen for me' (101), finds that she 'can't maintain the distance. I'm drawn all the way into eighteen nineteen, and I don't know what to do' (101). Surrounded by her ancestors and witnessing their daily struggle, Dana is unable to keep history at a distance but feels compelled to bring it fully to life by immersing herself within their world, carrying the physical and emotional scars that subsequently arrive. Returning to 1976, Dana still maintains the cuts, bruises and lacerations of a slave. She cannot merely compartmentalize the historical moment she briefly experienced, instead the marks of slavery remain permanently upon her body as reminders of its enduring and unsettling legacy within American history.

Both Dana's visceral experiences and the fantastical concept of time travel are also combined to entice a broader reflection on contemporary culture and its connectivity with a past otherwise forgotten. While reminiscing about their engagement, Kevin recalls his sister's unexpected disapproval of his intention to marry Dana, while Dana also recounts the views of her aunt on the prospect of mixed-race children: 'I think my aunt accepts the idea of my marrying you because any children we have will be light. Lighter than I am, anyway. She always said I was a little too "highly visible"' (111). Despite the black civil rights movement of the 1950s and 1960s proving ultimately successful in removing certain forms of overt racism, *Kindred* uses time travel to emphasize the way in which the politics of race are bound up not just in the broad histories of the nation, but that their legacies filter into everyday interaction. As Vint once more explains:

Kindred's present-day setting can be understood as being in the future imagined by nineteenth-century slave narratives, a future in which slavery has ended. This future is not the utopian one sf might rig through time travel, nor the dystopian one sf might use time travel to warn us about. Instead, *Kindred* focuses our attention on the fact that the future is not sufficiently different from the past; that, despite the Emancipation Proclamation, systemic racism persists in ways akin to the continuation of slavery. (243)

Expanding from this, contemporaneous mid-1970s America is – despite the obvious abolition of slavery – represented as being a nation still likely to produce exploitation. Kevin and Dana meet whilst working in menial jobs, with Dana 'working out of a casual labor agency' (52) and Kevin being a 'bottom-of-the-ladder type' (53). Indeed, Dana at one point refers to agency work as a 'slave market' (52), but soon readjusts her assessment and characterizes it as 'just the opposite of slavery. The people who ran it couldn't have cared less whether or not you showed up to do the work they offered. They always had more job hunters than jobs anyway' (52). Mid-1970s life is therefore not a Utopia for Dana, even though it is here that she escapes the brutality of slavery. Instead, by representing 1976 as a place of listlessness, boredom and unstable employment, Butler is able to demonstrate that, regardless of social and political emancipation, the twentieth century still fails sufficiently to overcome the forces of inequality, poverty and cultural dissatisfaction.

Just as Russ's story intentionally complicates and disrupts the expectations of specific strands of SF writing, Butler's novel also succeeds in reinterpreting the political potency of the time travel narrative. Using the fantastical invention of temporal transportation as merely a necessary tool rather than as a key scientific focus, Butler is able to expose, in graphic detail, the lived experience of slavery while simultaneously jumping into the future in order to contemplate the historical legacies of such a brutal history. By fusing realism with time travel, Butler is also able to reignite representations of slavery, with Levy pointing out that 'Butler's novel strips away the veneer of romanticism that imbues such popular books about the old South as *Gone with the Wind* (1936), portraying plantation life as brutal and ugly' (43). This generic fusion ultimately creates a novel that both redefines the social and political boundaries of time travelling SF, while also reviving the slave narrative and exploring its relevancy to twentieth-century culture.

Works Cited

Butler, Octavia E. (1988). *Kindred*. London: The Women's Press.
Flagel, Nadine (2012). '"It's Almost Like Being There": Speculative Fiction,

Slave Narrative, and the Crisis of Representation in Octavia Butler's *Kindred.'* *Canadian Review of American Studies*. 42. 2. 216–45.

Levy, Michael (2010). 'Octavia E. Butler'. *Fifty Key Figures in Science Fiction*. Mark Bould et al. (eds). London and New York: Routledge. 42–7.

Vint, Sherryl (2007). '"Only by Experience": Embodiment and the Limitations of Realism in Neo-Slave Narratives'. *Science Fiction Studies*. 34. 2. 241–61.

William Gibson, *Neuromancer* (1984)

William Gibson is arguably the most prominent and recognizable writer of cyberpunk fiction and his novel *Neuromancer* is rightly labelled as a defining literary text of the genre. The first in a trilogy of works (*Count Zero* and *Mona Lisa Overdrive* would follow in 1986 and 1988 respectively), *Neuromancer* depicts a near-future cityscape consisting of both a chaotic and messy urban sprawl and a competing virtual landscape known as cyberspace. The term cyberspace would become widespread in the 1990s with the growth of the World Wide Web but its popularization is also partly indebted to Gibson's novel, which describes it accordingly:

> Cyberspace. A consensual hallucination experienced daily by billions of legitimate operators, in every nation, by children being taught mathematical concepts … A graphic representation of data abstracted from the banks of every computer in the human system. Unthinkable complexity. Lines of light ranged in the nonspace of the mind, clusters and constellations of data. Like city lights, receding … (67)

The novel's protagonist, Case, has fed off this alternate, virtual city, operating as a hacker. At the novel's opening Case is expelled from cyberspace after stealing from an employer who has subsequently denied him access to the matrix by damaging his nervous system with a 'Russian mycotoxin' (12). Case is resultantly trapped within 'the prison of his own flesh' (12). Seemingly rescued by a shady new employer, Armitage, Case soon discovers that Armitage has not removed the toxins but rather positioned them as slowly dissolving 'toxin sacs' (60) near vital organs to ensure that he follows commands. As the novel progresses Case realizes that Armitage is working for a powerful Artificial Intelligence (AI) named Wintermute that seeks to be connected with its sibling AI, Neuromancer. *Neuromancer*'s depiction of a hypermodern city operating in both physical and virtual terms is a startling vision of the transforming topographies of urban environments in the late twentieth and early twenty-first century, while the intimate relationship between individuals and hi-tech machinery provides a unique view of biological and technological hybridity.

The memorable opening sentence of *Neuromancer* outlines this hyperreal environment: 'The sky above the port was the color of television, tuned to a dead channel' (9). Looked at alongside the descriptions of cyberspace and nanotechnology that follow, it is immediately clear that the novel's locale is awash with advanced technology. However, the cityscape is also defined by its sprawl, existing over vast distances and containing a series of near-slum districts full of detritus and shadowy transactions. Similarly to the overlapping of genres seen in *Kindred*, the representation of squalid, sordid streets in *Neuromancer* is reminiscent of the rugged descriptions of city life in the 'hard-boiled' detective novels of writers such as Raymond Chandler and Dashiell Hammett, and is characteristic of cyberpunk's continual combination of futuristic modernity with its grimy underbelly. Just a few paragraphs after the digital vision in the opening sentence, we are introduced to the scenery of Ratz's bar, which neatly demonstrates this fusion:

> Ratz was tending bar, his prosthetic arm jerking monotonously as he filled a tray of glasses with draft Kirin. He saw Case and smiled, his teeth a webwork of East European steel and brown decay. Case found a place at the bar, between the unlikely tan on one of Lonny Zone's whores and the crisp naval uniform of a tall African whose cheekbones were ridged with precise rows of tribal scars. (9)

Case, a drug addict as well as a hacker, lingers within these seedy territories, unable to access the transcendent realm of cyberspace. Indeed, the apparent lawlessness of the urban sprawl co-exists with the infinite play of the matrix where inhabitants of the city are able to plug in to an alternate reality and conjure a parallel virtual city.

As a consequence of this ludic, provisional quality, *Neuromancer*, and cyberpunk more generally, has often been associated with theories of postmodernity. The inevitability of the relationship can be partly read through converging visualizations of the Western city, with both expressing it as a decentred site mixing overlapping cultural and political forms. The heterogeneous cities of *Neuromancer* are, in Dani Cavallaro's terms, 'hard to *measure*' (152), being a fluctuating, ever changing mass, and operating on 'diverse temporal planes' (Cavallaro, 151). Case perpetually struggles to map his surroundings, instead having to use drugs and alcohol to acquire any perception of the indeterminate technological and cultural mesh surrounding him:

> Get just wasted enough, find yourself in some desperate but strangely arbitrary kind of trouble, and it was possible to see Ninsei as a field of data, [...] Then you could throw yourself into a highspeed drift and skid,

totally engaged but set apart from it all, and all around you the dance of the biz, information interacting, data made flesh in the mazes of the black market ... (26).

Gibson's megalopolises are densely layered, making them difficult to chart and rationalize. On the one hand we are presented with the seemingly logical systems of advanced technology, offering a clean digital landscape existing as part of an infinite matrix, whilst at the same time this technology is seen to intersect with the material city, present within crowded, corrupt and dilapidated locales, making the cities of *Neuromancer* both hi-tech, digitalized corporate arenas and treacherous urban sprawls.

Despite the seeming chaos of *Neuromancer's* cities, they are also monitored and surveyed by omnipotent, but often undetectable, corporations. Again, there is a convergence with postmodern definitions of global capitalism, notably Fredric Jameson's characterization of the 'global multinational and decentred communication network in which we find ourselves caught as individual subjects' (1992: 176). Case constantly seeks autonomy, trying to find spaces outside of the view of the plutocratic Tessier-Ashpool family and the drones that circle overhead as part of 'the spindle's security system' (180). While state control has seemingly evaporated in *Neuromancer* what emerges in its place is a totalizing network of multinational organizations whose control is displayed through either the 'towering hologram logo of the Fuji Electric Company' (13) or the subtle surveillance systems that police both the material world and cyberspace. Gibson's vision of a near-future dystopia is therefore very different to the one famously imagined by George Orwell in *Nineteen Eighty-Four* (1949) as it does not fear the rise of totalitarianism, but rather the redundancy of nation-states when faced with increasingly powerful corporate bodies and multinational systems of economic control.

For Case his role as a hacker within cyberspace frees him from the tyranny of this lingering surveillance culture. However, Armitage, who is discovered to be a former military officer, soon explains to Case how his seemingly counter-cultural role has its roots in military operations:

You're a console cowboy. The prototypes of the programs you use to crack industrial banks were developed for Screaming Fist. For the assault on the Kirensk computer nexus. Basic module was a Night-wing microlight, a pilot, a matrix deck, a jockey. We were running a virus called Mole. The Mole series was the first generation of real intrusion programs. (39)

Armitage continues by announcing to Case that he was 'there when they invented your kind' (39). Armitage therefore exposes the role of state and corporate bodies in the development of hacker culture, with Lisa Yaszek consequently stating in her book *The Self Wired* that

> if hacking originally was created as a corporate weapon and if hackers themselves originally were objects of corporate experimentation, then Case's own sense of autonomy, his sense of opposition to the corporate system, no longer makes sense. (105)

Case has to concede that regardless of his radical desires, his trade as a cyberspace cowboy has its antecedence in the totalizing systems he seeks to subvert.

Thus, to use Yaszek's terms, 'the tendrils of corporate power' (104) invade every part of *Neuromancer's* cityscapes. While the 'consensual hallucination' (67) of cyberspace ostensibly offers the hope of transcendence beyond the corporate surveillance of the city, it soon emerges as another route for coercion. The 'unthinkable complexity' (67) of cyberspace accordingly mimics the chaotic space of the material city along with its corruption and manipulation, as Cavallaro explains:

> Gibson radically questions the association of cyberspace with a clean and rationalized geography. In stating that the computer matrix resembles an image of Los Angeles captured from 5,000 feet up in the air, he actually equates it to an urbanscape of bodily and cultural corruption. (144)

The advanced technology in *Neuromancer* therefore does not liberate, but is instead as prone to exploitation as the organizing forces of the material world. Indeed, Darko Suvin notes that cyberpunk fiction places technology 'inside, not outside, the personal body and mind itself' (352). In Gibson's novel, technology does not operate separately from Case, instead penetrating his physical body through either the chemicals placed within him by Armitage or the act of plugging in to cyberspace. Rather than aiding escape from the body, technology becomes a source of its invasion.

Whereas Case is often beleaguered by penetrative technologies, one of his fellow characters, Molly Millions, is enhanced through the use of bio-technology. Molly is an assassin sent by Armitage to protect Case and is immediately described as possessing an array of technological augmentations: 'She shook her head. He realized that the glasses were surgically inset, sealing the sockets. [...] The fingers curled around the fletcher were slender, white, tipped with polished burgundy. The nails looked artificial' (36–7). Coupled with this, Molly maintains an aggressive attitude, reluctantly putting her gun away upon meeting Case and warning him that if he attempts to 'fuck around with me, you'll be taking one of the stupidest chances of your whole life' (37). Similarly to Russ's representation of female characters readily adopting typically 'masculine' roles, Molly can be seen as overthrowing conventional models of femininity by co-opting supposedly macho technology and occupying the role of a bodyguard . However, as Stacy Gillis explains in her article 'The (Post)Feminist Politics of Cyberpunk', cyberpunk's re-invention of female roles also presents problems:

> These women are positioned as very much at home in the traditionally masculine domains of both technology and physicality [...]. Yet this articulation of female agency is mediated by the ways in which the bodies of these cyborgic women are reduced to either a sexualised or monstrous femininity. (9–10)

Despite being a dominant figure who challenges patriarchal authority, Molly is also to be feared as she readily exhibits the 'ten double-edged, four-centimetre scalpel blades' (37) that appear from underneath her nails. Molly is therefore a human-machine hybrid who cuts across traditional forms of gender classification, which accordingly makes her as much the source of terror as she is a new visualization of femininity. Additionally, Molly labels herself a 'working girl' (41) implying that she has previously been involved in prostitution, which Gillis notes as a significant problem as despite her challenge to 'the tropes of traditional femininity through her physical presence'(12), ultimately her opposition is in some ways 'contained by the language of sexuality' (12).

Neuromancer's vision of cities and their inhabitants transformed by unfettered urbanization, technological innovation and the creeping presence of corporate surveillance marks it as an important text in articulating a literary response to the cultural transformations of the late twentieth century. Jameson, in his influential theoretical work *Postmodernism, or, the Cultural Logic of Late Capitalism* (1991) praises Gibson and cyberpunk fiction for creating a 'new type of science fiction' (38) that 'is fully as much an expression of transnational corporate realities as it is of global paranoia itself' (38). Unlike certain 'Golden Age' SF works, which exhibited extreme confidence in both technology and the hero of the story, Gibson's novel sees technology as a corporate instrument as much as a saviour, whilst the hard-boiled, punk aesthetic aids the creation of a drug-using, morally ambivalent antihero in Case and a ferocious, technologically enhanced female lead in Molly. Additionally, by imagining the erosion of conventional structures of the nation-state in the face of late capitalism's extensive social, economic and technological proliferation, *Neuromancer* has become a landmark novel in anticipating the emergence of contemporary trends in political economy, computing and architecture.

Yet, Neil Easterbrook explains that *Neuromancer's* political sentiment has not been without resistance:

Proponents praised the dark new vision of human life under global capitalism and the energetic vigor it injected into what they perceived as a moribund genre. Detractors disparaged its cynicism, nihilism, diffidence, overwrought style, and romanticization of addiction, criminality, and depravity. (87)

Gibson's work has persistently expressed ambivalence and suspicion towards contemporary urban existence, drawing attention to the affectless nature of cultures dominated by hi-tech consumerism and depicting forms of resistance within transient subcultures that skirt the fringes of legality. The importance of *Neuromancer* is twofold: on the one hand it paved the way for a transformation in SF style by creating a genre that intertwined contemporaneous movements in popular culture (punk and cybernetics particularly) and wove them into a literary framework that borrowed from 'hard-boiled' detective fiction, New Wave Science Fiction and noir thrillers. On the other hand, it has emerged as a prescient companion to exploring contemporary phenomena, successfully outlining the precarity of existence in societies experiencing the traumas of late capitalism and mapping humanity's increasingly addictive relationship with hi-tech consumables.

Works Cited

Cavallaro, Dan (2000). *Cyberpunk and Cyberculture: Science Fiction and the Work of William Gibson*. New Brunswick, NJ: The Athlone Press.

Easterbrook, Neil (2010). 'William Gibson'. *Fifty Key Figures in Science Fiction*. Mark Bould et al. (eds). London and New York: Routledge. 86–91.

Gillis, Stacy (2007). 'The (Post) Feminist Politics of Cyberpunk'. *Gothic Studies*. 9. 2. 7–19.

Gibson, William (1993). *Neuromancer*. London: Harper Collins.

Jameson, Fredric (1991). *Postmodernism, or, the Cultural Logic of Late Capitalism*. London: Verso.

—(1992). 'Postmodernism and Consumer Society'. *Modernism/Postmodernism*. Peter Brooker (ed.). London and New York: Longman. 163–79.

Suvin, Darko (1991). 'On Gibson and Cyberpunk SF'. *Storming the Reality Studio: A Casebook of Cyberpunk and Postmodern Fiction*. Larry McCaffery (ed.). Durham: Duke University Press. 349–65.

Yaszek, Lisa (2002). *The Self Wired: Technology and Subjectivity in Contemporary Narrative*. New York and London: Routledge.

Case Studies in Reading 2: Key Theoretical and Critical Texts in Science Fiction Studies

Jessica Langer

Introduction

The works discussed in this chapter have been chosen because of their influence in science fiction studies – they have been cited so much that each has become a foundational text of the critical field. Hence, by providing an overview of such critically persuasive texts this chapter serves as a starting point for the reader aiming to understand the key debates that animate much of the discussions in science fiction studies, from the late 1970s to today. For each section, I have provided a list of further texts that the reader may find interesting. These will help guide them if they choose to do further research into this academic field.

I have elected to focus on texts by four very different critics, Darko Suvin, Ursula K. Le Guin, Donna Haraway and Fredric Jameson, who offer a diversity of approaches, backgrounds, perspectives and conclusions. Readers may well find themselves agreeing and disagreeing with each in turn. Science fiction studies is a robust, diverse and ever-changing field, and since its critics draw upon a hetergenous range of theoretical backgrounds, it has been important to include a multiplicity of such perspectives in this study.

SF is full of inherent contradictions, being about humans and not about them, radically different from and incredibly pertinent to our own experiences, about which it can be most enlightening. Pulling away from ordinary existence allows a better view of our lives, even estrangement offers a closer understanding, and imagining Utopias allows us to look critically at our own flawed world. One might even call science fiction itself a 'cyborg genre', after Haraway's exploration of the cyborg as political myth (which I discuss in the section dedicated to her work in this chapter): it works well to describe the inherent liminality of the genre. It pushes at the edges to better illuminate the centre – and the critics discussed in this chapter are doing their part to expand that horizon.

It is important, when studying science fiction, to remember that SF texts are not 'only' science fiction, but are almost always multiple in terms of their genre. The critic Carl Freedman provides a definition that echoes the current thinking of most genre theorists:

> It is possible to conceptualise genre in a radically different and thoroughly dialectical way. In this understanding, a genre is not a classification but an element or, better still, a *tendency* that, in combination with other relatively autonomous generic elements or tendencies, is active to a greater or lesser degree within a literary text that is itself understood as a complexly structured totality. In other words: a text is not filed under a generic category; instead, a generic tendency is something that happens within a text. (20)

Helpfully and suggestively such a definition allows for more than one 'generic tendency' in a work, and in doing so the concept of genre functions more broadly and diversely than it appears to do when used on bookstore shelves. That is, this definition lends itself, and therefore the genres of science fiction and others that might coexist within science fiction texts, to a broader and richer range of possibilities than it would have if cultural producers felt the need to only work with the set boundaries of a well-defined SF field.

Works Cited

Freedman, Carl (2000). *Critical Theory and Science Fiction.* Hanover: Wesleyan University Press.

Darko Suvin, *Metamorphoses of Science Fiction* (1979)

Darko Suvin, born in the former Yugoslavia and later a professor at McGill University in Montreal, Canada, was one of the first academic scholars of science fiction. His first book of science fiction criticism was published in Croatian in 1965, and much of that material was translated into English and revised for his 1979 book *Metamorphoses of Science Fiction* (hereafter *Metamorphoses*). This section focuses primarily on this study, which was one of the first, and remains one of the most influential, academic texts on science fiction studies to date. Suvin has written prolifically on many different aspects of SF, including socialist/communist and Victorian SF, and has always been very interested in the role of politics in the genre. Like Fredric Jameson, who we will come to later in this chapter, he has written at some length on the concept of Utopia. Primarily, though, Suvin is a science fiction *theorist*. His main focus has generally been the study of science fiction itself: what is and is not SF, what its important features are, what distinguishes it from other genres, and how it works. This section of the chapter will provide insight into Suvin's key arguments about SF. These are some of the earliest and most foundational elements of science fiction studies, and almost all later criticism takes them into account, whether it is to build on them or disagree with them. Although Suvin is primarily a literary critic, most of his ideas can be applied successfully to science fiction in other media – film, art, television, video games and so forth.

Why Science Fiction is Important

From the very beginning of his career as a critic, Suvin put forward a passionate defence of the study of science fiction, in part because it was – and remains – so popular and well-read among the general populace. He begins *Metamorphoses* by writing that 'a justification for paying serious attention to science fiction may by now be necessary only for other literary critics and scholars' (vii). This is important because he is acknowledging both the popularity of science fiction and the viewpoint, common at the time among critics, that science fiction is *too* popular and is therefore 'paraliterature', or literature that is removed from the true form of the art – in other words, junk. Suvin writes that 'a discipline which refuses to take into account 90 per cent or more of what constitutes its domain seems to me not only to have large zones of blindness but also to run serious risks of distorted vision in the small zone it focuses on' (vii): that is to say, a serious study of science fiction is important not only to understand science fiction itself, but also to understand literature – and film studies, and later new media and video games – as a whole.

Suvin suggests that disdain of science fiction is nothing new, that it has *always* been 'a suppressed and neglected, often materially and most always ideologically persecuted tradition' (87). It has always been important, though, for the very reason that it is so often oppressed: it 'comes always from the yearnings of a repressed social group and testifies to radically other possibilities of life' (89). Science fiction is, he argues, in part the wishful thinking of those who are marginalized in some way by their society, and who are exploring a world in which they are no longer repressed.

Defining Science Fiction

Suvin also spends the first few chapters of *Metamorphoses* discussing the *definition* of science fiction: what exactly one means by the term, when speaking about it. For Suvin, it is very important to define the genre: to

understand science fiction, we need to understand its parameters and limitations, what it is and what it is not.

Ultimately, Suvin settles on a general definition of science fiction as the
'literature of cognitive estrangement' (4). By defining it this way, he assigns a
definitional characteristic to the genre while at the same time distinguishing
it from other kinds of literature that do not do this, particularly other
non-naturalist literature – such as folk tales and fantasy literature – that
include other kinds of estrangement and that are often lumped in or confused
with science fiction. Although Suvin acknowledges that these genres are
related to science fiction, particularly the Utopian 'pastoral' (9), he draws a
clear line of delineation between them and SF. In an earlier essay, 'Radical
Rhapsody and Romantic Recoil in the Age of Anticipation', Suvin defines
the difference in this way: 'Myth asks ahistorically about The Man and The
World. SF asks, What kind of man?, In what kind of world?, and Why such
a man (or indeed non-man) in such a world?' (255). It is not the fact that the
science fictional world is different from our world that matters, according to
Suvin. It is not even, primarily, the effects of the difference, although this is
closer to the crux of things. Rather, the starting point of science fiction is *why
and how* there is a difference

Cognitive Estrangement

What, then, *is* cognitive estrangement? Suvin defines it as a 'creative approach
tending toward a dynamic transformation rather than toward a standard
mirroring of the author's environment', one that is 'not only reflecting *of* but
reflecting *on* reality'. (10) The theorist Carl Freedman, in his discussion of
Suvin's idea of cognitive estrangement, suggests that the world of a science
fiction book or film exists in a 'cognitive continuum with the actual' (xvi). The
two worlds, the diegetic world – i.e. the fictional world in which the events
of the story occur – of the text, and the real world in which we live, are both
similar and different: perhaps the text is set on our earth but a few hundred
years in the future, or features beings who are sentient like humans but are
not human.

There is a tension here. On the one hand, science fiction requires cognitive
estrangement: it is distinguished by something that is fundamentally different
from our 'zero world' – the term Suvin uses to describe the world of the
implied reader (that is, the world of the non-diegetic person who is reading
the text, as opposed to the diegetic world within the text). On the other hand,
it also requires a cognitive *link* with our world: there need to be some similarities between the diegetic world and the reality in which we spend most of
our time and whose physical laws we experience on a daily basis. Therefore,
science fiction needs to be *both* similar to *and* different from our world, in

some measure, in order to be successful. We need a familiar context in which we can appreciate the weirdness and sense of wonder that results from the shrewd inclusion of a 'novum' – plural: 'nova' – a term which Suvin borrows from the Marxist philosopher Ernst Bloch, and which he defines as a 'novelty [or] innovation validated by cognitive logic' (63) – a logical outgrowth of our current scientific understanding, like a flying car, a robot or a generation spaceship.

The Novum

Suvin argues that estrangement is actualized through the novum, which implies a 'relationship deviating from the author's and implied reader's norm of reality' (64). The 'narrative dominance or hegemony' of the novum is therefore one – in fact, possibly the most – important distinctive feature of the science fiction genre which distinguishes it from other genres. In other words, science fiction is unique in that it not only includes, but emphasizes, something that is completely and fundamentally different from the reality in which we live, our 'zero world'. The novum is the vehicle of cognitive estrangement. It is the way in which a science fiction story establishes itself as not just fictionally but functionally separate from the world in which we live. As Freedman has written about the novum: 'The science fictional world is not only one different in time or place from our own, but one whose chief interest is precisely the difference that such difference makes' (xvi–xvii). This is to say that SF depends on the *effect* of its inherent disjunction between story and reality.

It might be objected that the fairy princess of the fantasy genre or the vampire of the Gothic genre also produce fundamental differences between the story and reality. However, Suvin argues that the science fictional *novum* is unique in that it includes the 'presence of scientific cognition' (65). From his perspective, in order to be science fiction, a story needs to be based on the rational principle of scientific thinking (see also the discussion in Chapter 8 of this book). This does not mean that the actual science in science fiction needs to be possible according to our current understanding of science. For instance, as far as we know, faster-than-light travel is not possible according to the laws of our universe, but it occurs throughout science fiction. However, many SF stories typically include a diegetic world in which scientists, rather than wizards or ghosts, have somehow found a way around the conventional laws of physics, whether it is *Star Trek*'s fictional dilithium crystals or the rudimentary wormholes of Joe Haldeman's classic *The Forever War* (1975). Even if it is not scientifically plausible for us, it needs to be scientifically plausible, rather than supernatural, in the world of the story.

The Historical Development of Science Fiction

Suvin discusses the evolution of science fiction from 'a prescientific or proto-scientific approach of debunking satire' – for example, More's *Utopia* (1516) or Swift's *Gulliver's Travels* (1726) – to 'a diagnosis, a warning, a call to understanding and action, and – most important – a mapping of possible alternatives' (12). In fact, Suvin sees modern science fiction as the latest iteration of a literary strand that extends back to the first folk tales. Although modern science fiction is defined by its use of *cognitive* estrangement, it is based in and descended from literature that uses other kinds of estrangement for similar purposes.

In terms of time period, Suvin divides the history of science fiction into six 'clusters' (87):

1 Hellenic (ancient Greek legends and folktales, repurposed in philosophy and drama)
2 Hellenistic-cum-Roman ('Virgil to Diogenes and Lucian')
3 Renaissance-Baroque, or Columbus-to-Louis XIV (c. 1500–1660)
4 The democratic revolution (c. 1770–1820)
5 The 'fin-de-siècle cluster' (c. 1870–1910)
6 Modern science fiction (c. 1920 onwards)

These groupings are important, Suvin tells us, because they represent moments in which science fiction – which, as I discuss above, Suvin sees as a historically marginalized genre – pushed its way into 'officially accepted, normative, or "high" Literature and Culture' (88). This happened only at points in time in which the historical and social conditions supported it: for instance, times of great social or technological change. Let us focus, as an example, on one of these moments of change: what Suvin calls the 'shift to anticipation' (115). This is, according to Suvin, the point in science fiction's history in which its focus shifted from *space* to *time*. This moment is located in Suvin's fourth cluster, the 'democratic revolution', which incorporates the Industrial Revolution and the accompanying origins of democracy. This unprecedented social and technological upheaval led to widespread anxiety. These changes were unique, Suvin argues, in that they represented a wholesale shift in how power worked in society. Before, social and economic power rested in the land where most people lived and worked and, therefore, the novum of previous science fiction was often the fictional land presented in terms of 'radical otherness and/or debunking parody' (116). (Think again of the fictional island in More's *Utopia*, or of the lands of Lilliput and Brobdingnag in *Gulliver's Travels*.) Now, however, power became located in 'the quantification of everyday, economically based practice' with 'money as the universal yardstick for life's values' (116). That is to say that society became capitalist.

The result of these social shifts was a tradition of science fiction that also changed. Whereas previously, most science fiction had been focused on new fictional *places* and how they differed from the reader's own home, authors were beginning to focus on other *times*. Specifically, many authors began to look to the future, to explore what might happen if a particular social rule (say, sexual repression, in Charles Fourier's *Theory of the Four Movements* [1808]) or a particular technological roadblock (for instance, our inability to create a living being out of spare parts, in Mary Shelley's *Frankenstein* [1818]) were to be changed or removed. Instead of exploring other worlds, this kind of science fiction anticipates future times.

Works Cited

Fourier, Charles (1996) [1808]. *Theory of the Four Movements.* Gareth Stedman Jones and Ian Patterson (eds). Cambridge: Cambridge University Press.

Freedman, Carl (2000). *Critical Theory and Science Fiction.* Hanover: Wesleyan University Press.

Haldeman, Joe (1975). *The Forever War.* New York: St. Martin's Press.

More, Thomas (1965) [1516]. *Utopia.* Trans. Paul Turner. Harmondsworth: Penguin.

Shelley, Mary (2003) [1818]. *Frankenstein.* Harmondsworth: Penguin Classics.

Suvin, Darko (1974). 'Radical Rhapsody and Romantic Recoil in the Age of Anticipation: A Chapter in the History of SF.' *Science Fiction Studies* 1. 4 (Fall). 255–69.

—(1979) *Metamorphoses of Science Fiction.* New Haven, NJ: Yale University Press.

Swift, Jonathan (2003) [1726]. *Gulliver's Travels.* Harmondsworth: Penguin Classics.

Further Reading

Critical Works:

Clute, John and Nicholls, Peter (eds) (1993). *The Encyclopedia of Science Fiction* (2nd edn) London: Orbit.

Heinlein, Robert A. (1959). *The Science Fiction Novel.* Basil Davenport (ed.). Chicago: Advent.

Huntington, John (1982). *The Logic of Fantasy: H.G. Wells and Science Fiction.* New York: Columbia University Press.

Moylan, Tom (2000). *Scraps of the Untainted Sky.* Boulder, CO: Westview.

Parrinder, Patrick (ed.) (2001). *Learning from Other Worlds: Estrangement, Cognition, and the Politics of Science Fiction and Utopia.* Liverpool: Liverpool University Press.

Parrinder, Patrick (ed.) (1979). *Science Fiction: A Critical Guide.* London: Longman.

Roberts, Adam (2006). *The History of Science Fiction.* London: Palgrave Macmillan.

Slusser, George E., et al. (eds) (1980). *Bridges to Science Fiction.* Carbondale: Southern Illinois University Press.

Novels and stories:
Lem, Stanislaw (1970) [1961]. *Solaris*. Trans. J. Kilmartin. New York: S. Cox.
Miller Jr, Walter (1960). *A Canticle for Liebowitz*. Philadelphia: J. B. Lippincot.
Zelazny, Roger (1967). *Lord of Light*. New York: Doubleday.

Ursula K. Le Guin, *The Language of the Night: Essays on Science Fiction and Fantasy* (1979)

Ursula K. Le Guin provides a sharp contrast to Darko Suvin. While Suvin is an academic critic whose work is based heavily in philosophy and political theory, Le Guin is primarily a writer of science fiction and fantasy whose criticism takes the form of beautiful and incisive essays. While he advocates a relatively strict definition and limitation of SF, her conception of the genre is much more fluid and inclusive.

This fluidity is evident in Le Guin's fiction as well. Her famous SF novels *The Left Hand of Darkness* (1969) and *The Dispossessed* (1974), both feature a technical device, called the 'ansible', which allows instantaneous communication between two points in space – a concept and name that is used as well in a number of subsequent SF works such as Orson Scott Card's *Ender's Game* (1985). However, this novum shares the stage with meditations on anthropology, sociology and psychology; considerations typically associated with what is sometimes called 'social' or 'soft' SF. Nor does she limit herself to SF: her *Earthsea* series (1969–72) is classical magic-based fantasy, and some of her other works, such as the devastating short story 'The Ones Who Walk Away from Omelas' (1973) or the far-future pastoral book-and-music-CD *Always Coming Home* (1985), resist easy classification.

Le Guin's and Suvin's conceptions of science fiction do, however, have one crucial thing in common. Where Suvin puts forth cognitive estrangement as the central conceit of science fiction, Le Guin writes of 'distancing, the pulling back from "reality" in order to see it better' as 'perhaps the essential gesture of SF' (19). Both recognize the critical difference and the essential similarity between our world and the world of the SF text. An understanding of this central contradiction, which creates much of the tension we see in science fiction, is shared by almost all critics of SF.

It is important to remember, too, that Le Guin's criticism of science fiction specifically, and her social critique more generally, is carried out through her fiction as well as through her essays and other criticism. In this way, she is unique among the four critics covered in this chapter, although not unique among science fiction writers: there is a distinguished tradition of writer-critics in SF, such as Damon Knight, Robert A. Heinlein, Joanna Russ, Samuel Delany and Gwyneth Jones to name some of the more prominent.

Defining Science Fiction – or Not

Unlike Suvin and many other SF critics such as Freedman and Heinlein, Le Guin does not exclude fantasy from the genre of science fiction. In fact, she claims, 'the two overlap so closely as to render any effort at exclusive definition useless' (21). In all of her criticism and in most of her creative work, in fact, she is preoccupied with this slippage between the two categories, which are both different from each other and connected to each other. In her introduction to her early novel *Rocannon's World* (1974), which is science fictional and yet also outside of what Suvin would name as the generic boundaries of SF she writes:

> When asked to 'define the difference between fantasy and science fiction',
> I mouth and mumble and always end up talking about the spectrum,
> that very useful spectrum, along which one thing shades into another.
> Definitions are for grammar, not literature, I say, and boxes are for bones.
> But of course fantasy and science fiction *are* different, just as red and blue
> are different; they have different frequencies; if you mix them (on paper –
> I work on paper) you get purple, something else again. *Rocannon's World*
> is definitely purple. (133)

It may be wise to note that this viewpoint is becoming more common in contemporary science fiction criticism; in the past 20 years or so, science fiction literature and other media have themselves become less rigid in defining themselves: a good example of this is China Miéville's literary works, for which he prefers the catch-all term 'weird fiction', which 'blurs the boundaries between science fiction, fantasy and horror' (Bradford para. 12). While the critic Eric S. Rabkin does distinguish between science fiction and what he calls 'fairy tales', he rejects the idea that the estrangement of science fiction is purely cognitive, arguing that it can be spiritual as well: 'miracles are just as easily accepted in science fiction as they are in fairy tales' (79). And as SF has been used increasingly by writers in various cultures, some of whose scientific world views – or 'indigenous scientific literacies', as the critic Grace L. Dillon calls them (23) – differ from the scientific givens with which many people in Western countries might be familiar, elements of SF have been combined with fabulism, folktale, myth, *orature* and other kinds of native or indigenous non-realist stories. Some examples of this blending can also be seen in the works of Nalo Hopkinson, Larissa Lai, Minister Faust, N. K. Jemisin, Nnedi Okorafor, Ben Okri, Hiromi Goto, Eden Robinson and many others. We can see, then, that Le Guin has plenty of company in her resistance to a rigid definition of science fiction: there is, as she says, plenty of 'purple'.

Science Fiction, Mythology and Psychoanalysis

Le Guin's essay 'Myth and Archetype in Science Fiction' in *The Language of the Night* is one of the first, and one of the most elegant, to engage in a deep exploration of the importance of foundational myths in SF. She begins by stating that 'science fiction is the mythology of the modern world' (73). This appears an effective definition which seems at first glance to make perfect sense. Immediately, though, she complicates the question by calling it a 'half-truth' that, 'when used carelessly, as a whole truth, can cause all kinds of confusion' (73). Le Guin is fond of this strategy in all of her criticism, questioning the ideas and ideals, the past assertions and assumptions, which seem to constitute the understood truths of SF. Throughout the essay, Le Guin critiques what she calls the 'reductionist' view of 'scientism', which sees scientific development as a 'progressive draining dry of the content of mythology' (74). She notes as well that this is a hallmark of Freudian psychoanalysis (81), which sees mythology as a hallmark of the unconscious, and sees psychoanalysis as a method by which the unconscious is drained (and the patient is therefore cured of his or her anxiety). Instead, in this essay as in others, Le Guin follows the Jungian concept of a 'mutually creative relationship' between conscious and unconscious (81).

This idea of a mutually creative, mutually beneficial relationship between conscious and unconscious is writ large in Le Guin's understanding of the productive relationship between SF and mythology, and between rationality and desire. For Le Guin, there is no conflict between SF and mythology: it is not a zero-sum game, with one replacing the other. Rather, she sees them as overlapping or, more acurately, as speaking to a different part of the self. Human beings are rational creatures, she writes, but we are also 'sensual, emotional, appetitive, ethical beings, driven by needs and reaching out for satisfactions which the intellect alone cannot provide' (74). Although both science and mythology are frameworks of understanding the world, they are not – in fact, Le Guin believes, they *cannot* – be mutually exclusive. Instead, they speak to different parts of ourselves: science to our rational sides (or at least the part of us that craves rationality), and mythology to our irrational sides. Because we are both rational *and* irrational beings, we need both kinds of literature, and because these needs coexist within us, they can also coexist within a work of literature (or other form of cultural production). One of the best-known examples of this coexistence is Le Guin's own *The Word for World is Forest* (1972), which includes both science fiction and mythological elements. Another, more recent example is Nalo Hopkinson's *Brown Girl in the Ring* (1998), which blends dystopian science fiction with Caribbean mythology.

'Is Gender Necessary?': Le Guin, Gender Identity and Feminism

One of Le Guin's most famous novels is *The Left Hand of Darkness*, set on a world called Gethen where the indigenous humanoid inhabitants are of a sex that is neither male nor female (although they all use the male pronoun 'he'). Instead, they are androgynous most of the time; every month or so, they go into a phase of sexual and reproductive readiness called 'kemmer' and develop temporary male or female genitalia. Each person goes through both male and female kemmer states in his life, and has no control over which he will be in each kemmer. And following on from this, each person may be both a mother and a father at different times.

One thing accomplished by this odd arrangement is the separation of *sex* and *gender* – a separation that is accepted by most gender theorists in contemporary criticism. The term 'sex' normally refers to one's physical state: whether one has male or female genitalia, or in rare cases, both or neither. Gender, on the other hand, is *socially* determined, and may or may not match up with one's body. Those who identify as transsexual and have not had surgery, for instance, may identify as female in sex but male in gender, or vice versa, or even somewhere in between; the sexologist Arthur Kinsey believed that gender was a spectrum, not an either-or. Some societies recognize gender identities outside of male or female, like the *hijra* in India.

Le Guin's own viewpoint on the gender identity of the Gethenians is interestingly changeable: in her initial introduction to *The Left Hand of Darkness*, which is also collected in *The Language of the Night*, she focuses not on gender but on the theme of the SF writer as seer or prophet. In fact, she mentions the sex/gender construct of the Gethenians only in passing, and only in relation to this theme: 'Yes, indeed the people in [the book] are androgynous, but that doesn't mean that I'm predicting that in a millennium or so we will all be androgynous ...' (158). Her use of the word 'androgynous' here is also significant. The fact is, the Gethenians are not androgynous in the human sense: they are something *different*, entirely different. They represent, in terms of sex and gender, a novum, and *The Left Hand of Darkness* is therefore, in the words of Freedman as discussed above, in large part about the difference that such difference makes. It is not about an androgynous society. It is, rather, about a society in which sex and gender function in the specific way that Le Guin has imagined, a way that is impossible in our own reality, and the story that follows from this functioning has at its centre that difference.

In her essay 'Is Gender Necessary?' (1976), one of the earliest and most important essays on gender in science fiction, Le Guin revisits the question of androgyny in *The Left Hand of Darkness*. She acknowledges that her invention of the Gethenians, who are sexually inert and entirely without either sex or gender (as we understand them in zero-world) most of the time, was a 'heuristic device, a thought-experiment', as science fiction often is (1979: 163). She describes the subject of the experiment in the following terms:

> Because of our lifelong social conditioning, it is hard for us to see clearly what, besides purely physiological form and function, truly differentiates men and women. Are there real differences in temperament, capacity, talent, psychic processes, etc? If so, what are they? (1979: 163)

There are many ways of answering these questions: scientists might conduct controlled studies of gender differences, journalists might interview people of all different gender identities. An SF writer like Le Guin, on the other hand, uses the tools of SF – the *novum*, the pulling back to see more clearly, the simultaneous cognitive estrangement and emotional immediacy – to ask the same questions, and to come to interesting answers.

Le Guin's own answer points to three differences between Gethen and our world, which she posits as being due to the difference in sex and gender between the two contexts. First, on Gethen there is no war; there are plenty of quarrels between people, and the people themselves are no more moral than we are here on Earth, but these quarrels are on a small scale – murders, assassinations, fights and the like – rather than massively organized violence. Second, they do not exploit their planet – or rather, as Le Guin significantly puts it, 'rape their world' – and they do not have what Le Guin considers to be a particularly male drive for 'Progress', the 'pushing forward to the limit, the logicality that admits no boundary' (165). Third, because of the Gethenians' discontinuous sexuality, it is not a factor in their daily lives. This is not to say that their sexuality is somehow easy, or even lesser; Le Guin allows that the 'extreme, explosive, imperative quality' of kemmer causes problems that we, as more or less continuously sexual beings, do not have (167). However, the *distinction between men and women* is not a social factor on Gethen, because there is no such thing as men or women; everyone is both, and neither, in a way that is estranged from our reality. We pull back to Gethen, to a world with no men or women and therefore no difference between them, to look more clearly at our own world in which being a man or a woman often matters a great deal, in some very specific ways. Le Guin's thought experiment has reached a conclusion: these aforementioned three factors are the difference that such difference makes.

The 'Other' in Science Fiction

Le Guin is one of the first theorists to make the connection between the science-fictional Other – alien or otherwise – and the social, political, cultural and other kinds of Others that we encounter in, and often exclude from, our own systems of knowledge. I discuss this at length in my own book, *Postcolonialism and Science Fiction* (2012):

> The figure of the alien – extraterrestrial, technological, human-hybrid or otherwise – and the figure of the far-away planet ripe for the taking are deep and abiding twin signifiers in science fiction, are perhaps even the central myths of the genre. They are, to riff on the most famous work of Robert A. Heinlein, one of science fiction's most famous writers, the Stranger in a Strange Land [...]. These two signifiers are, in fact, the very same twin myths of colonialism. (3)

These are themes that run through all of Le Guin's work, both critical and artistic. The Other she is talking about is, quite simply, one who is different from oneself in some quantifiable or socially significant way: 'There is the sexual Alien, and the social Alien, and the cultural Alien, and finally the racial Alien' (Le Guin, 1979: 97).

Le Guin makes the argument that much of SF fails to accurately or sufficiently represent these kinds of otherness, and that most SF has been 'regressive and unimaginative. All those Galactic Empires, taken straight from the British Empire of 1880 [for instance]' (98). She points to the classic dichotomy of the science fictional alien, which echoes the old Orientalist construction of otherness: either 'the only good alien is a dead alien' (98) or 'we get all these wise and kindly beings who deign to rescue Earth from her sins and perils' (98–9). What's missing, Le Guin argues, is a represen-tation of alienness – which, of course, closely represents sexual and social and cultural and racial otherness in our own zero-world – that does not fall back on archetype. And, of course, this is a dilemma that is not limited to science fiction: depictions and representations of otherness have long wanted for nuance and realism. Science fiction, Le Guin suggests, has the power to change this; it is specifically situated to challenge these things. And it ought to.

Works Cited

Bradford, Kimberley (2002). 'China Miéville – City Animal'. *The Fortean Bureau* 5 (December). Available oneline: http://www.forteanbureau.com/dec2002 interview.html. [accessed 3 May 2008].

Card, Orson Scott (1985). *Ender's Game*. New York: Tor Books.

Dillon, Grace L. (2007). 'Indigenous Scientific Literacies in Nalo Hopkinson's Ceremonial Worlds'. *Journal of the Fantastic in the Arts*. 18. 1. 23–41.

Hopkinson, Nalo (1998). *Brown Girl in the Ring*. New York: Warner Aspect.

Langer, Jessica (2012). *Postcolonialism and Science Fiction*. Basingstoke and New York: Palgrave Macmillan.

Le Guin, Ursula K. (1966). *Rocannon's World*. New York: Ace Books.

—(1968). *A Wizard of Earthsea*. Berkeley, CA: Parnassus Press.

—(1969). *The Left Hand of Darkness*. New York: Ace Books.

—(1971). *The Tombs of Atuan*. New York: Atheneum.

—(1972). *The Farthest Shore*. New York: Atheneum.

—(1972). 'The Word for World is Forest'. *Again Dangerous Visions*. Harlan Ellison (ed.). New York: Doubleday. 26–108.

—(1973). 'The Ones Who Walk Away from Omelas'. *New Directions 3*. Robert Silverberg (ed.). New York: Doubleday. 1–8.

—(1974). *The Dispossessed*. New York: Harper & Row.

—(1985). *Always Coming Home*. New York: Harper & Row.

—(1976). 'Is Gender Necessary?'. *Aurora: Beyond Equality*. Susan Janice Anderson and Vonda N. McIntyre (eds). New York: Fawcett Gold Medal. 130–9.

—(1979). *The Language of the Night: Essays on Fantasy and Science Fiction*. New York: Putnam.

Rabkin, Eric S. (1980). 'Fairy Tales and Science Fiction'. *Bridges to Science Fiction*. George E. Slusser, George R. Guffey and Mark Rose (eds). Carbondale: Southern Illinois University Press. 78–90.

Further Reading

Critical texts:

Malmgren, Carl D. (1993). 'Self and Other in SF: Alien Encounters'. *Science-Fiction Studies*. 20. 1 (March). 15–33.

Marez, Curtis (2004). 'Aliens and Indians: Science Fiction, Prophetic Photography and Near-Future Visions'. *Journal of Visual Culture*. 3. 3 (December). 336–52.

Rieder, John (2008). *Colonialism and the Emergence of Science Fiction*. Middletown, CT: Wesleyan University Press.

Rose, Mark (1981). *Alien Encounters: Anatomy of Science Fiction*. Cambridge, MA: Harvard University Press.

Novels and stories:

Hopkinson, Nalo and Uppinder Mehan (eds) (2004). *So Long Been Dreaming: Postcolonial Science Fiction and Fantasy*. Vancouver: Arsenal Pulp Press.

Donna Haraway, 'A Cyborg Manifesto' (1985)

Donna Haraway, like Le Guin, is very interested in gender and how it functions in SF. Haraway holds a PhD in biology and has a dual degree in zoology and philosophy; her work is at the crossroads of science and philosophy, a position that scholars often call 'intersectional' or 'interdisciplinary'. Much of her work has to do with *metaphor*: how we associate certain things with others, how phenomena become linked in our consciousness, and how the terms we use to describe things can have an enormous impact on the way we look at, live in and engage with the world. Haraway's 1991 collections of essays, *Simians, Cyborgs and Women: The Reinvention of Nature*, looks from many different perspectives at the way we think about and the terms we use to describe the body – in particular, the female body – in our capitalist, postmodern, scientifically advanced, putatively but not entirely egalitarian society. Of these essays, 'A Cyborg Manifesto', first published in 1985, is the most famous and most-cited. Although not a work of SF criticism as such, it refers to a number of SF writers and works (as discussed below). However, its true significance to the field lies in the tremendous influence that its ideas have had for fiction and, especially, criticism (see the further discussions in Chapters 8 and 11 of this book). One way to approach this essay is to regard it as a work of non-fictional SF in its own right.

An 'Ironic Political Myth'

Haraway opens the essay by describing it as 'an effort to build an ironic political myth faithful to feminism, socialism and materialism' (149). Here, Haraway makes it easy for us by laying out her framework quite clearly (and certainly many more critics could usefully adopt such a strategy!). So why is this myth 'ironic'? Irony is, Haraway argues, about 'contradictions that do not resolve into larger wholes, even dialectically, about the tension of holding incompatible things together because both or all are necessary or true' (149). Haraway is setting us up to look at what she sees as a set of deep conflicts, and at the *same time* deep truths: much of criticism, science fiction and otherwise, is learning to look at and live with the fact that most debates shake out in shades of grey – or purple – rather than one simple answer. Irony, the use of the cyborg metaphor, is Haraway's method of dealing with the deep contradictions she sees in the way that femininity, and humanity more generally, is conceptualized in her society.

The Cyborg and Hybridity

The first contradictory metaphor Haraway sets up is between fiction and reality: 'A cyborg is a cybernetic organism, a hybrid of machine and organism, a creature of social reality as well as a creature of fiction' (149). This simultaneous distinction and link between fiction and social reality, what is sometimes called the 'materialist/discursive divide' (para. 10), poses the same questions as any art or cultural production that comments upon the world in which we live – that is, all art and all cultural production. Is a cyborg a person or a robot? Is it real or fictional? Does it represent science fiction, or does it represent science fact? In all cases, Haraway would argue, it is both. A cyborg is a *hybrid* thing: it is two things at once, and as such, it includes both fictional and real representations. This hybridity, this both-ness, this ability to be more than one thing at the same time – even if those two things sometimes seem to conflict – is at the centre of Haraway's theory. Not only does the cyborg represent more than one different thing at the same time, Haraway argues, but its hybridity also functions as a metaphor for society more generally. The cyborg is a 'fiction mapping our social and bodily reality' (150), which expresses both the contradictions and the possibilities of living in the modern world:

> Contemporary science fiction is full of cyborgs – creatures simultaneously animal and machine, who populate worlds ambiguously natural and crafted. Modern medicine is also full of cyborgs, of couplings between organism and machine, each conceived as coded devices, in an intimacy and with a power that was not generated in the history of sexuality. Cyborg 'sex' restores some of the lovely replicative baroque of ferns and invertebrates (such nice organic prophylactics against heterosexism). Cyborg replication is uncoupled from organic reproduction. Modern production seems like a dream of cyborg colonization work, a dream that makes the nightmare of Taylorism seem idyllic. And modern war is a cyborg orgy [....]
> By the late twentieth century [...] we are all chimeras, theorized and fabricated hybrids of machine and organism; in short, we are cyborgs. (149–50)

Haraway's analysis is deep and layered. She codes a cyborg as both mechanically sexless and inherently sexual, both emotionless and emotional, both organic and inorganic. And, crucially, the cyborg represents both freedom and oppression, both powerful to create change and powerless to keep from being co-opted as what Haraway sees as agents of destruction. The most productive way to utilize the cyborg metaphor for the purposes of political anti-oppression work, Haraway suggests, is to attach it to the notion of what she calls the 'fractured identit[y]' of modern feminism. 'Identities seem contradictory, partial and strategic', she writes, and suggests that the solution is similarly partial and conglomerated: 'affinity, not identity' (155). It may be useful here to think back to the definition of genre at the beginning of this chapter: how genre is often seen in academic study as a *tendency* rather than a category, which opens up the possibility of being more than one thing at the same time. Haraway is doing the same thing here with feminism, using the cyborg metaphor. Just as a cyborg embodies more than one kind of thing, so can a woman embody more than one kind of thing. Haraway uses the theorist Chela Sandoval's example of the Black or Chicana American woman, who has often been silenced as such, and the construction of the category 'woman of colour' to create *both* an alliance between women of various identities *and* a differentiation between this category and the simple 'non-innocent' category of 'woman' (157). Thus, one use of cyborg theory is to conceptualize this kind of identity that is both fractured and whole.

Technology, Capitalism and Cyborg Identity

Haraway sees our contemporary world as one in the midst of a fundamental shift from one way of thinking and being to another, a shift as wholesale and essential as that of the Industrial Revolution, which led to the inception of large-scale capitalism (of which Haraway is very critical):

> I argue for politics rooted in fundamental changes in the nature of class, race and gender in an emerging system of world order analogous in its novelty and scope to that created by industrial capitalism; we are living through a movement from an organic, industrial society to a polymorphous, information system ... (161)

From here, she sets up a list of 'transitions from the comfortable old hierarchical dominations to the scary new networks [that she has] called the informatics of domination' (161). The transitions most germane to a discussion of science fiction are 'Representation/Simulation', 'Bourgeois novel, realism/Science fiction, postmodernism' and 'Second World War/Star Wars' (161–2), each of which replaces a theoretical or cultural construct with one that, to echo Le Guin and Suvin, 'pulls back from reality' and creates cognitive estrangement in the way that SF does. Rather than pulling back in order to see or understand reality better, however – and rather than being straightforward transitions from 'natural' to 'artificial', which they may seem to be but are not – Haraway argues that these transitions are incomplete and complex 'cyborg semiologies' (163) which both reinscribe and continue the domination of our bodies by capitalist forces and hold the ability to critique those same forces. Most of all, they are both descriptors of reality, and myths and metaphors by which we try to understand our reality: 'The boundary is permeable between tool and myth, instrument and concept, historical systems of social relations and historical anatomies of possible bodies, including objects of knowledge. Indeed, *myth and tool mutually constitute each other* (164, emphasis added). This comes back to Haraway's original 'ironic political myth' of the cyborg, which is also a mimetic description: the way we understand things and those things themselves are always linked and are always at the same time disjointed. Haraway resolves this contradiction into a boundary that exists and yet is always crossed, that is inherently hybrid.

That is not to say that these 'cyborg semiologies' are somehow neutral. Haraway's 'informatics of domination' does, after all, represent a new kind of domination of humanity under late capitalism in general and of women more specifically. In particular, Haraway challenges the popular conception that the advent of technology has freed women from household labour and enabled them to join the public sphere. Rather, she argues, 'the extreme mobility of capital and the emerging international definition of labour are intertwined with the emergence of new collectivities, and the weakening of familiar groupings' (166). It is not just the technological structure of global society that is changing, but our social structure is changing as a result, with effects as world-altering as anything in SF.

Haraway and Science Fiction

In this changing world dominated by the flow of information, Haraway identifies writing – one of the earliest fusions of human and machine (formerly the pen or pencil; now the laptop, tablet or smart phone) – as the key technology for cyborgs. As we know from the work of Suvin and Le Guin, the main characteristic of SF texts is that they express a contradictory mix of difference and similarity between their world and ours. For this reason, Haraway sees the practice of SF as crucial to cyborg existence, providing an understanding of not only the world's present but also its potential futures; SF writers 'are our story-tellers exploring what it means to be embodied in high-tech worlds. They are theorists for cyborgs' (173).

Haraway looks to feminist science fiction both for inspiration and for further metaphors by which we can come to understand both the current situation of femaleness and femininity and the future promise of 'a monstrous world without gender' (181) – thus making her argument directly relevant to male readers as well – in the midst of all of this shifting, changing and breaking down of boundaries: 'The cyborgs populating feminist science fiction make very problematic the statuses of man or woman, human artefact, member of a race, individual entity, or body' (178). Remember that all of these things are categories that Haraway aims to problematize, that the notion of the category itself is problematic and that Haraway's theory depends on hybridization and boundary-crossing. She discusses authors such as Joanna Russ, Samuel R. Delany, James Tiptree Jr and Octavia Butler amongst others. Their science fiction, Haraway argues, explores the various ways in which the categories that seem to bind us, and the boundaries that seem to limit us, can be broken down. If we are all cyborgs, then SF, more than any other art form, can help us to understand who and what we are.

Works Cited

Haraway, Donna (1991). 'A Cyborg Manifesto'. *Simians, Cyborgs and Women: The Reinvention of Nature.* London: Free Association Books.

Further Reading

Critical texts:

Ahmed, Sara (2000). *Strange Encounters: Embodied Others in Post-coloniality.* London: Routledge.

Carr, Brian (1998). 'At the Thresholds of the "Human": Race, Psychoanalysis, and the Replication of Imperial Memory'. *Cultural Critique.* 39. (Spring). 119–50.

Chaney, Michael A. (2003). 'Slave Cyborgs and the Black Infovirus: Ishmael Reed's Cybernetic Aesthetics'. *Modern Fiction Studies.* 49. 2 (Summer). 261–83.

Haraway, Donna (1997). *Modest_Witness@Second_Millennium.FemaleMan© Meets_ OncoMouse™: Feminism and Technoscience.* New York: Routledge.

Hoagland, Ericka and Reema Sarwal (eds) (2010). *Science Fiction, Imperialism and the Third World.* Jefferson, NC: McFarland.

Jeffress, David, Julie McGonegal and Sabine Milz (2006). 'Introduction: The Politics of Postcoloniality'. *Postcolonial Text.* 2. 1 (2006). Available online: http://postcolonial.org/index.php/pct/article/view/448/162 [accessed 26 July 2013].

Melzer, Patricia (2006). *Alien Constructions: Science Fiction and Feminist Thought.* Austin: University of Texas Press.

Ryan, Marie-Laure (ed.) (1998). *Cyberspace Textuality: Computer Technology and Literary Theory.* Bloomington: Indiana University Press. 137–63.

Novels and stories:

Butler, Octavia E. (2000). *Lilith's Brood.* New York: Grand Central.

Effinger, George Alec (1987). *When Gravity Fails.* New York: Orb.

McDonald, Ian (2005). *River of Gods.* London: Pocket Books.

Piercy, Marge (1992). *Body of Glass.* London: Michael Joseph.

Shiva, Vandana (2008). *Distances.* Seattle: Aqueduct Press.

Fredric Jameson, *Archaeologies of the Future: The Desire Called Utopia and Other Science Fictions* (2005)

Fredric Jameson, like Donna Haraway, is not primarily known as a science fiction theorist; however, like Haraway, he sees science fiction as a useful and sometimes essential way to understand the world in which we live. Jameson is one of the world's leading literary critics, and works in the Western Marxist tradition. He has published extensively on structuralism, formalism, narrative, modernism and postmodernism. His well-known work on the latter subject, *Postmodernism or, The Cultural Logic of Late Capitalism* (1991), includes significant analysis of Philip K. Dick and is generally relevant to SF (see the discussion in Chapter 8). Since the early 1970s, Jameson has written a number of essays on SF for the journal *Science Fiction Studies* and in various collections, many of which are collected in the second half of *Archaeologies of the Future*. These essays chiefly analyze the work of various authors – such as Dick, Le Guin and A. E. Van Vogt – and specific novels – such as Brian Aldiss's

Starship (1958; better known by its UK title *Non-Stop*), Vonda McIntyre's *The Exile Waiting* (1975) and Kim Stanley Robinson's *Mars* trilogy (1993–6) – as Utopian discourses. The first 233 pages of the book, consisting of new material, present a dense theoretical argument on the nature of Utopia and the problems of writing it as SF. Here, I am focusing primarily on this first part, but, as with the other critical texts discussed in this chapter, this section should be read as an introduction to some of the key themes raised in the work, rather than a summary or full accounting; interested readers should seek out the full text of the book to learn more.

Science Fiction, Categorization and Liminality

In his discussion in *Archaeologies of the Future* of the generic difference between fantasy and science fiction, Fredric Jameson comes at this same problem from a slightly different angle to Suvin, suggesting that 'generic undecidability', the corollary to generic distinction, is a key concept in understanding the SF genre (68). Jameson also refers to the 'spaces between fantasy and SF' (68), placing the work of Gene Wolfe and the early SF novels of Ursula K. Le Guin within those spaces; though he does not mention Le Guin's novels by name here, I would suggest that *Rocannon's World* (1966), *Planet of Exile (1966)* and *City of Illusions* (1967) are meant. This provision of liminal space can be seen as an acknowledgement of the possibility of multiply-located generic tendencies. Perhaps, being in the 'spaces between', they are rather *within* both spaces at the same time—or even in many spaces at once, hybrid and multiple rather than marooned between. These intersections provide the opportunity not only to examine the characteristics of such a meeting-space, but also to follow each intersecting thread outward, multiplying and layering the significance of each text.

At the same time as Jameson allows for liminality, however, he – like Suvin does – tends towards categorization in his discussions of the development of science fiction in general and Utopia in particular. In his comprehensive discussion of *Archaeologies of the Future*, the science fiction writer and theorist Adam Roberts (see Chapter 9 of this book), sets these categories out clearly:

> *four* levels of Utopian allegory (anagogic, moral, allegorical and textual, p.9), *four* 'dimensions or cardinal points' of More's *Utopia* (Greece, medieval Europe, the Incas, Protestantism) […] here are *six* historical stages of SF (adventure, science, sociology, subjectivity, aesthetics and cyberpunk) with an implied *seventh* stage, feminism, running concurrently with the last two, and *four* historical stages in the representation of alien-ness in SF: first the Golden Age 'account of

bodily and social dispositions' of the 1950s and 1960s, which is to say the 'classic exotic alien'; second the 'Other as the Same' of *Blade Runner* and the 1980s; thirdly the 1990s in which the alien represents 'everything non-normative and perverse', and nowadays, when apparently the alien has 'reverted to magic and dragons'. (140–1)

This is a relatively intricate base upon which to balance one's understanding of SF, and is perhaps more rigid than is necessary since there are so many works that *are* liminal and that *do not* fit so easily into categories. However, this categorization can also be helpful in teasing out differences and, particularly, shifts in focus or theme between temporal or other modes of SF production. As an example, at the very beginning of the book, Jameson distinguishes between the 'Utopian form' or the 'written text or genre' of Utopian writing or other cultural production, *and* the 'Utopian wish' or the 'Utopian impulse in daily life', the ways in which we structure our lives according to our striving for what we see as a better or more perfect way to live (1). Following this, he suggests a third category, 'Utopian vision', to describe the political practice of attempting to create a Utopian society, before going on to comment on the 'futility' of definition, and the fact that attempting to define terms will – much like attempting to define Utopia itself – inevitably leave out something interesting. This see-sawing between rigorous definition and the drawbacks of that very practice is something of a theme in *Archaeologies of the Future*.

Why Utopia?

A hallmark of science fiction since its inception has been the concept of *Utopia*: simply put, the idea or desire for a system – political, cultural, economic, social, etc. – that is in some way free of the associated problems inherent in whatever the current system is. In fact, Utopian writing represents a significant portion of science fiction production up to the 1960s, at which point authors such as Le Guin, Delany and others began to publish work that challenged the Utopian ideal in various ways.

Like Suvin, Jameson takes inspiration from the Utopian philosophy of Ernst Bloch, the same thinker from whom Suvin borrowed the term and concept of the *novum*. He suggests that 'to see traces of the Utopian impulse everywhere, as Bloch did, is to naturalize it and to imply that it is somehow rooted in human nature' (10). Although Jameson follows this observation with the qualification that those who have made actual 'attempts to realize Utopia'— that is, literary and/or political projects—'have always been maniacs and oddballs' (10). Herein one encounters one of the fundamental contradictions of Utopia. It is certainly nearly, if not entirely, universal amongst humans to wish and dream for something better. And, historically, humans have always imagined a better or more perfect place, from Plato's theory of Forms to More's *Utopia* (1515), the Ur-text of the Utopian genre. However, the actual *realization* of Utopia has always been fairly impossible. I refer again to Roberts' excellent discussion to explain Jameson's ultimate take on the purpose of Utopia, which is

> *not* a coherent vision of radical otherness; and neither is it a straightforward blueprint for a 'better world' which could be magically transferred into this world in which we actually live. Rather it is *always the historically and culturally specific response to particular social dilemmas.* (para. 9, emphasis in Roberts)

In Jameson's own words:

> I believe that we can begin from the proposition that Utopian space is an imaginary enclave within real social space, in other words, that the very possibility of Utopian space is itself a result of spatial and social differentiation. But it is an aberrant by-product, and its possibility is dependent on the momentary formation of a kind of eddy or self-contained backwater within the general differentiation process and its seemingly irreversible forward momentum […].
>   [O]n the one hand, its very existence or emergence certainly registers the agitation of the various 'transitional periods' within which most Utopias were composed (the term 'transitional' itself conveying this sense of momentum); while, on the other, it suggests the distance of the Utopias from practical politics. (15)

Therefore, the discussions throughout *Archaeologies of the Future* of various Utopias in various specific texts ought to be read not as pragmatic blueprints, but as political aspirations or imagined possibilities. Jameson argues that the Utopian space is quite distinct from 'zero world' space. The function of Utopia is, to echo Le Guin again, to 'pull back from reality' in order to critique or explore it, not to attempt to create our own Utopia.

A Few Problems with Utopia

As critics such as Jameson and Joan Gordon suggest, the Utopian impulse, so integral to the heritage of science fiction, is inherently one which invites a prejudiced world view – in its perfection, it is inherently *exclusionary* of whatever is deemed imperfect according to the rules and desires of whatever Utopia in particular is at issue. As Jameson writes in the introduction to *Archaeologies of the Future*,

> The fundamental dynamic of any Utopian politics (or of any political Utopianism) will therefore always lie in the dialectic of Identity and Difference, to the degree to which such a politics aims at imagining, and sometimes even at realizing, a system radically different from this one. (xvii)

It is not just *political* or *systemic* difference, however, that Utopianism imagines: it is also individual difference. Gordon writes that there is a 'sensitive dependency among Utopia, genocide and the alien Other' and that 'genocide is a utopian project' (205). Perfection requires the absence of the imperfect, or rather, the different: those who bear what Gordon calls 'the contamination of difference', therefore, are either excluded or eradicated.

Although he is strangely silent on the implications to Utopia's structure of the alien body, Jameson believes that the institution of Utopia itself is implicated in a discussion of colonialism, which Le Guin also mentions in her discussion of otherness in science fiction (as I discuss above). His strongest critique is that Utopia is

> very much the prototype of the settler colony […] my own feeling is that the colonial violence thus inherent in the very form or genre itself is a more serious reproach than anything having to do with the authoritarian discipline and conformity that may hold for the society within Utopia's borders. (205)

Interestingly, Jameson identifies one group that he sees as somehow immune from the exclusionary force of Utopia: that of the *family*, 'persist[ing] like a foreign body within the new society', 'secured no doubt by biology, threaten[ing] the geometrical Utopian diamond with a flaw that cannot be theorized or fantasized away' (207). This is not to say that the concept of the family is in any way standardized, or even similar, across Utopian cultural production. Rather, in every Utopia there is *some* kind of family, whether it is idealized or problematized, anxiety-producing or comforting, along the lines of the 'bourgeois' nuclear family that dominates capitalist societies (208) or any number of alternative family arrangements, biological or chosen. Even in negation, there is an echo of the family – just as even in negation of difference, even in its absence, there is an echo of difference. The suggestion here is that the family, like difference itself, is an inherent feature of the human condition; Utopia can include or exclude it, but cannot ignore it.

Works Cited

Aldiss, Brian (1958). *Starship*. New York: Criterion Books.
Gordon, Joan (2002). 'Utopia, Genocide and the Other'. *Edging Into the Future: Science Fiction and Contemporary Cultural Transformation*. Veronica Hollinger

and Joan Gordon (eds). Philadelphia: University of Pennsylvania Press. pp. 204–16.

Jameson, Fredric (1991). *Postmodernism, or, the Cultural Logic of Late Capitalism*. London: Verso.

—(2005). *Archaeologies of the Future: The Desire Called Utopia and Other Science Fictions*. London: Verso.

Le Guin, Ursula K. (1966). *Rocannon's World*. New York: Ace Books.

—(1966). *Planet of Exile*. New York: Ace Books.

—(1967). *City of Illusions*. New York: Ace Books.

McIntyre, Vonda N. (1975). *The Exile Waiting*. New York: Nelson.

More, Thomas (1965) [1516]. *Utopia*. Trans. Paul Turner. Harmondsworth: Penguin.

Roberts, Adam (2005). Review of *Archaeologies of the Future*. *The Valve*. Available online: http://www.thevalve.org/go/valve/article/jamesons_archaeologies_of_the_future/ [accessed 26 July 2013].

Robinson, Kim Stanley (1993). *Red Mars*. London: Harper Collins.

—(1994). *Green Mars*. London: Harper Collins.

—(1996). *Blue Mars*. London: Harper Collins.

Further Reading

Critical texts:

Booker, M. Keith (1994). *The Dystopian Impulse in Modern Literature: Fiction as Social Criticism*. Westport, CT: Greenwood.

Gordon, Joan (2003). 'Hybridity, Heterotopia, and Mateship in China Miéville's *Perdido Street Station*'. *Science Fiction Studies*. 91 (November). 456–77.

Gordon, Joan and Veronica Hollinger (eds) (2002). *Edging Into the Future: Science Fiction and Contemporary Cultural Transformation*. Philadelphia: University of Pennsylvania Press. 204–16.

Kristeva, Julia (1982). *Powers of Horror: An Essay on Abjection*. Trans. Leon S. Roudiez. New York: Columbia University Press,

Wolfe, Gary K. (1979). *The Known and the Unknown: The Iconography of Science Fiction*. Kent, OH: Kent State University Press.

Novels and stories:

Christopher, John (1964). *The World in Winter*. London: Penguin.

Dick, Philip K. (1974). *Flow My Tears, The Policeman Said*. New York: Doubleday.

Huxley, Aldous (1932). *Brave New World*. London: Chatto and Windus.

Le Guin, Ursula K. (1971). *The Lathe of Heaven*. New York: Avon.

Miéville, China (2000). *Perdido Street Station*. London: Macmillan.

Stapledon, Olaf (1930). *Last and First Men*. London: Methuen.

Strugatsky, Arkady and Boris (1978). *Roadside Picnic*. Trans. Antonina W. Bouis. London: Gollancz.

6 Key Critical Concepts, Topics and Critics

David M. Higgins and Roby Duncan

Part One: Concepts and Topics

Alien: A strange or foreign being. In SF, 'alien' often refers to a creature from another world. Although the term was deployed to describe extraterrestrial visitors as early as 1820 by Thomas Carlyle, this definition of the alien as an extraterrestrial was not more generally established until the early twentieth century. One of the earliest uses of the word in SF occurs in Edgar Rice Burroughs' *A Princess of Mars* (1912; originally published as 'Under the Moons of Mars' by Norman Bean). While aliens can sometimes serve as mindless antagonists in SF stories, David Seed suggests that SF often uses the alien to interrogate questions of identity and difference: aliens can encourage readers 'to re-examine their self-conceptions as a result of their confrontation with the Other, with beings whose culture is rarely explored in its own right, but rather to highlight the markers of difference' (27).

Cognitive Estrangement: A term developed by Darko Suvin to describe the experience of encountering unusual elements in SF that are significantly different from the reader's reality, particularly when the unusual elements are based on scientific or technological extrapolations rather than elements of fantasy. Suvin argues that the defamiliarization of taken-for-granted reality that occurs when a reader encounters such unusual elements causes the reader to imagine the world from a different perspective, and this allows familiar settings and experiences to be seen from an outside critical position. The term cognitive estrangement was adapted into English from the German *Verfremdungseffekt*, or 'alienation effect', a term coined by twentieth-century German playwright Bertolt Brecht, who used it to describe the distancing effect produced in an audience when the action taking place on stage is strange enough to prevent passive emotional identification with the characters.

Cyberpunk: A term created by Bruce Bethke for the title of his short story 'Cyberpunk' (1983) and later used to describe a subgenre of SF which came to prominence in the 1980s and 1990s in the work of William Gibson, Pat Cadigan, Bruce Sterling, Rudy Rucker, John Shirley and many others. Cyberpunk fictions are often characterized by near-future urban environments, harsh socio-economic circumstances and morally ambiguous characters. The term entered popular usage following the release of William Gibson's *Neuromancer* (1984), a work which defined the genre for many readers. A portmanteau combining cybernetics and punk, the genre came to be identifiable by the combination of these elements, and cyberpunk stories often centre around fiercely individualistic characters (often criminals) embroiled in conflict with authoritarian trans- or post-national corporate syndicates. Such narratives are often set against a dystopian background in which class warfare and environmental collapse occur within a context defined by global information exchanges and advanced technology. Cyberpunk fictions often include representations of transglobal cultures, massive interlinked data networks, virtual realities and marginal characters who exist on the outskirts of established society and culture. Flows of information hold a privileged position in the genre, and they often occur simultaneously as environments (in the case of virtual cyberspaces into which a user can project her disembodied consciousness) and as characters (in the form of artificial intelligences).

Cyborg: A contraction of the term 'cybernetic organism', this term refers to a creature whose body has been artificially modified to adapt or extend its normal abilities. The term was developed by two NASA scientists, Manfred E. Clynes and Nathan S. Kline, in their 1960 paper 'Cyborgs and Space', which explored the idea of altering an astronaut's body to adapt to harsh conditions rather than creating an artificial environment to sustain the astronaut. The term was later popularized by David Rorvik in his 1971 book *As Man Becomes Machine: The Evolution of the Cyborg*. The definition of the term has since been expanded from a machine-man hybrid to include the notion of a human-technology interface that adapts immaterial/digital cybernetic information technologies into human communication and cognition. Further extrapolations, by authors such as Donna Haraway in her 1991 essay 'A Cyborg Manifesto', see the boundary-dissolving hybridity of the cyborg as a conceptual means for marginalized and economically disenfranchised subjects to 'contest for meanings, as well as for forms of power and pleasure in technologically mediated societies' (154).

Empire: A superior political, economic and/or cultural dominion that exerts its influence over subordinate states or colonies. An empire that rules over colonies directly can be referred to as a *formal empire*; the indirect influence wielded over foreign states by a superpower is often referred to as *informal empire*. SF narratives often portray the colonization of other worlds by explorers from Earth (or the colonization of Earth by invaders from other worlds), and questions concerning the morality of imperialism are often central to SF extrapolations. John Rieder's book *Colonialism and the Emergence of Science Fiction* (2008) argues that the early SF genre emerges from (and is conceptually shaped by) the most aggressive historical phase of Western formal imperial expansion in the late nineteenth and early twentieth centuries. Early pulp SF was often influenced by the generic conventions of the American Western genre, and Richard Slotkin's *Gunfighter Nation: The Myth of the Frontier in Twentieth-Century America* (1992) also suggests that early SF is influenced by the imperial imaginaries associated with the conquest of the American West. New Wave SF authors in the 1960s often reacted against what they experienced as an imperial emphasis in 'outer space' SF, and they instead attempted to subvert the imperial fantasy tradition in SF by turning their attention to 'inner space' explorations (see for example Thomas Disch's 1968 novel *Camp Concentration*). Some of these authors, such as Ursula K. Le Guin and Samuel Delany, use SF to critique the emergence of an informal American empire in the post-war period and beyond. Early twenty-first century SFs, such as the television show *Battlestar Galactica* (2004–2009), use SF extrapolations in order to challenge and defamiliarize American imperial discourses in the post-9/11 era.

Extrapolation: In mathematics, extrapolation is the process of constructing new data points by estimating the value of variables outside a known range by assuming that the projected values will follow logically from known ones. Extrapolation can similarly refer to the projection of human experience into an unknown future: a driver, for example, might extrapolate road conditions beyond his or her current line of sight based on available information. In 1947, Robert Heinlein suggested that extrapolation was central to SF imaginings: in a successful SF story, 'science and established facts are extrapolated to produce a new situation, a new framework for human action' (17). The term has subsequently become a frequent way to refer to science fictional imaginings that begin from established facts in order to predict alternative plausible circumstances.

Golden Age: A term used to refer to the period from 1937 (when John W. Campbell took over as editor of *Amazing Stories*) through the late 1950s in US SF publishing. The Golden Age followed the pulp era of the 1920s and 30s, and Campbell used his editorial influence to cultivate a greater sense of realism and psychological depth in SF than had been generally present in the preceding years. Many recognizable SF tropes were established during the Golden Age, and stories during this time began to return to metaphysical themes that earlier pulp SF had disavowed. According to M. Keith Booker and Anne-Marie Thomas, 'Golden Age sf was characterised by a faith in the inevitability of dramatic scientific and technological progress, often accompanied by an optimistic belief that this progress would lead to social, political, and economic progress as well' (326). Popular Golden Age writers included Isaac Asimov, Arthur C. Clarke, Robert A. Heinlein, Frederik Pohl, A. E. Van Vogt, Theodore Sturgeon, Lester Del Rey, Leigh Brackett and C. L. Moore.

Hard SF: A term used to denote fiction that focuses on established scientific knowledge and principles or carefully considered extrapolation from said knowledge and principles. The distinction between 'Hard' and 'Soft' SF often runs parallel with the same distinction in the sciences: most Hard SF is identifiable by its emphasis on physics, astronomy, chemistry, engineering and biology. The work most often cited as a representative example of Hard SF is Tom Godwin's 'The Cold Equations' (1954), in which a young girl stows away on a space ship not knowing that the success of the ship's voyage depends on an exact calculation of the weight of its cargo. This type of fiction is often characterized by a respect for established scientific knowledge and principles and an aversion to supernatural or transcendental phenomena. Some fans and scholars criticise Hard SF for what they perceive as its shallow character development, frequent sexism and an oversimplified moral narration. Hard SF is also noteworthy for the rigor with which its fan base analyzes, criticizes and explores the 'realism' of the fantastic elements included in the stories.

Megatext: A term used to describe the interlinked body of tropes, conventions, texts and archetypes that are shared by SF and Fantasy narratives. In *Reading By Starlight: Postmodern Science Fiction* (1995), Damien Broderick describes the megatext as:

> [a] vast intertextual 'hyper-text': part encyclopaedia of knowledge drawn from current scientific data and theories, part iconography established

in previous sf, part generic repertoire of standard narrative moves, their probability-weighted variants, and their procedures for generating new moves. (68)

According to Charles Segal, the classicist who pioneered the concept in reference to the interconnectedness of mythological narrative frameworks, megatexts can be regarded as inclusive of not only previously created themes and stories, but also the 'subconscious patterns or "deep structures" … which tales of a given type share with one another' (176). While SF as a whole may be considered a megatext, and the various subgenres of SF (Cyberpunk, Hard SF, etc.) also considered megatexts, individual cross-textual settings may also be considered as more specific megatexts (e.g. Michael Moorcock's Multiverse, The Star Trek Universe, etc.) The consistencies and inconsistencies that exist among texts produced within a single megatextual framework can provide a reference set allowing for a deeper understanding of the individual works composing the megatext.

New Wave SF: A transatlantic avant-garde SF movement that occurred during the 1960s and 1970s. New Wave writers sought to combine SF's extrapolative power with avant-garde literary experimentation and an emphasis on 'soft' sciences (such as psychology and sociology) rather than the 'hard' physical sciences (physics, biology, mathematics) championed by traditional SF. New Wave writers were critical of technological progress, suspicious of nation-alism and imperialism and devoted to a celebration of cultural revolution; some romanticized the dystopian decay of Western culture in order to critique the social and political conditions of their time. The New Wave emerged from four major publication sites: the British SF magazine *New Worlds* under the editorship of Michael Moorcock beginning in 1964, Harlan Ellison's *Dangerous Visions* anthologies in 1967 and 1972, Damon Knight's *Orbit* anthol-ogies beginning in 1966, and Judith Merril's *England Swings SF* (1968) and her *Annual of the Year's Best Science Fiction* anthologies. Some may add Robert Silverberg's *New Dimensions* anthologies beginning in 1971 as a fifth New Wave publication node; by this time the impact of the New Wave had become widespread in the SF world. A wide variety of authors were part of the New Wave movement. Some of them, such as J. G. Ballard, Samuel R. Delany, Ursula K. LeGuin, Joanna Russ and Philip K. Dick have achieved critical attention in the literary mainstream. Many others are known primarily as SF writers, and a short list of these includes Brian Aldiss, Barrington J. Bayley, John Brunner, Thomas M. Disch, Harlan Ellison, Philip Jose Farmer, M. John Harrison, Langdon Jones, Damon Knight, Michael Moorcock, Charles Platt, James Sallis, Robert Silverberg, John T. Sladek, Norman Spinrad, Roger Zelazny and Pamela Zoline. Colin Greenland's *The Entropy Exhibition* (1983), the first and most notable book-length study of the New Wave, analyzes the theme of entropy in the fiction of Aldiss, Ballard and Moorcock.

Novum: A term used to identify the primary feature of a work of SF which differentiates the setting from the reader's own world and generates an experience of cognitive estrangement. The unusual element might be a new technology, the discovery of life on other worlds or the identification of a new scientific law. A novum can be described as the set of material innovations and modifications in the history of the setting from which the reader can recognize the possibility that the future can be different from the present, and that the present could also have been different given plausible changes in historical circumstance. Darko Suvin, the critic to establish the term in SF criticism, argues in *Metamorphoses of Science Fiction* (1979) that the novum of an SF story must be validated by cognitive logic, and he therefore contrasts it to the magical elements one might find in fantasy fiction.

Parabola: A term originally used by Brian Attebery to describe the shape of a general SF archetype as it appears repeatedly in different specific stories. The idea that a SF narrative can proceed like an open-ended parabola contrasts it to the closed nature of a generic formula story. In 'SF, Parables, and Parabolas' (2005), Attebery argues that narrative parabolas are 'unlike formulas' because they 'do not dictate either a story's ending or the writer's ends. Stories that utilize such scenarios may start in the same place, but then they go wherever their thematic concerns may lead. If a formula is a closed circle, the sf scenario is an open curve, a swing toward the unknown: a parabola' (14). He further suggests that the parabola also functions as a parable: it is 'both an open ended curve and a vehicle for significance' (14). This notion of the parabola as an 'open curve' and as a 'vehicle for significance' attempts to trace the transformation of an SF narrative as it is reiterated in new contexts; different authors reshape a parabola's recognizable pattern in different ways with different endings and alternative thematic concerns as they revisit a given story in new and subsequent narrative repetitions.

Posthumanism/Transhumanism: A pairing of terms used to denote the transformation of humans into modified, possibly superior beings often characterized by a transcendence of human physical frailty and a ceasing of the aging process. People who have not yet completed this transformation, but who have either begun the process or have embraced a posthumanist philosophy, are often identified as 'transhuman'. Transhumanist fiction is often identified by the presence of technologically-advanced utopian settings, transformative self-modification, and by a recognition of the constructedness of contemporary cultural, gender and class norms. Transhumanism is not just a genre or element within SF; it is also an SF-inspired philosophy and cultural movement which often focuses on technological self-modification, life extension and control over the direction of evolution.

Postmodernism: A term used to describe both a constellation of late twentieth- and early twenty-first-century aesthetic productions and a paradigm that occurs in such productions (and throughout culture at large). Postmodernism is often considered to be an aesthetic style that succeeds, while continuing aspects of, early twentieth-century modernism. Postmodern art is generally characterized by a mixing of styles and genres and a tendency to draw upon a wide range of sources from both high culture and popular culture. M. Keith Booker and Anne-Marie Thomas suggest that 'postmodernist art tends to be complex and experimental in the mode of modernist art, but more playful, irreverent, and ultimately sceptical of the power of art to change society' (329). In *Postmodernist Fiction* (1987), Brian McHale argues that SF is the quintessential postmodern genre because it focuses on questions of ontology (or being) rather than questions of epistemology (or knowing). In his view, the modern detective novel focuses on how to correctly or incorrectly know the world (correct knowledge of the world enables the detective to solve the crime in question). SF, in contrast, offers a plurality of possible worlds to know, and McHale suggests that this ontological multiplicity is a bedrock of postmodern aesthetics. In *Postmodernism* (1991), Frederic Jameson suggests that the postmodern emphasis on playful shallow surfaces indicates a deeper cultural resistance to the process of mapping the social, political and economic complexity of late capitalism; he therefore suggests that postmodernism is complicit in the underlying logic of contemporary capitalist hegemony. A variety of literary postmodern authors use SF tropes and conventions: John Barth, Jorge Luis Borges, Christine Brook-Rose, Italo Calvino, Angela Carter, Don Delillo, Umberto Eco and Thomas Pynchon all foreground science-fictional elements in their postmodern works. Some SF authors whose works have been characterized as postmodern include Philip K. Dick, J. G. Ballard, Samuel R. Delany, William Gibson, Michael Moorcock, Rudy Rucker, Kurt Vonnegut Jr and Joanna Russ.

Sense of Wonder: A term first used by H. P. Lovecraft in 1935 to characterize a feeling of awakening or awe triggered by an expansion of one's awareness or by a confrontation with the vastness of space and time. The phrase came into popular usage in SF in the 1960s, and it is often considered to be a cliché term; sometimes it is derided in SF fandom for its overuse in pulp SF and for the variety of 'cheap tricks' that can be used (such as gratuitous depiction of differences in scale) to provoke a sublime emotional response in a reader.

Singularity: A term coined by author Vernor Vinge in 1983 to refer to a theoretical future moment when a level of technological advancement will be achieved such that no predictions of what might follow can be accurately made. The concept of singularity has its roots in Moore's law, which predicts that the processing power of computers will grow more or less exponentially every two years. The idea of technological singularity references the cosmological singularities located at the centre of black holes; the gravity of these objects is so intense that light cannot escape, and consequently we can have no direct knowledge of them. Singularity stories, such as Charles Stross's *Accelerando* (2005), often emphasize the emergence of artificial intelligences which progressively improve themselves to the point where their functions are no longer comprehensible to human beings. These stories often also involve the uploading, or digital encoding, of human minds into technological devices and the development of nanotechnological devices allowing for posthuman development.

Slipstream: A contested term often used to refer to a type of fiction which straddles or transgresses the usual boundaries between SF, fantasy and literary fiction. The term was first used by Bruce Sterling in an article published in *SF Eye* #5 (July 1989) where he wrote that slipstream is 'a kind of writing which simply makes you feel very strange; the way that living in the twentieth century makes you feel, if you are a person of a certain sensibility' (78). Some describe slipstream as a genre opposed to mainstream literature, but others, such as James Patrick Kelly and John Kessel, claim that slipstream is less a genre and more an effect of cognitive dissonance that certain fictions have upon readers. Still others claim that slipstream is a term that lumps together metafiction, magical realism, surrealism, experimental fiction and counter-realism; it is sometimes applied to stories simply because they display postmodern sensibilities in their rejection of mimetic reality.

Subjunctivity: A term coined by Samuel Delany in his essay 'About Five Thousand One Hundred and Seventy Five Words' (1969; reprinted in *The Jewel-Hinged Jaw* in 1977) to describe the nature of language in SF narratives. In grammatical usage, the subjunctive mood (unlike the indicative or imperative moods) designates states of possibility that have not occurred. Delany draws upon this basis to distinguish between different degrees of subjunctivity that occur in different types of writing: naturalistic fiction deals with events that 'could have happened', fantasy addresses things that 'could not have happened' and SF focuses on things that 'have not happened' (1977: 31–2). Delany further notes that SF narratives can be divided into four major subcategories: things that might happen (predictive futures), things that will not happen (science-fantasy stories), things that have not happened yet (cautionary dystopias) and things that have not happened in the past (alternate histories). Delany suggests that SF's subjunctive nature offers it a richer and more diverse field of possibilities than can typically be found in the pages of literary realism. In her essay 'Speculations: The Subjunctivity of Science Fiction' (1973), Joanna Russ expands on Delany's thoughts and argues that SF occupies a position suspended precisely between fantasy's events that could not happen and the events that could happen in realistic fiction.

Sublime: A term used to identify an overpowering or overwhelming feeling, usually created by perceiving something that is vast, obscure or of tremendous scale; the sublime object often induces a feeling akin to terror. Examples of sublime experiences include encounters with mountain ranges, oceans, new planets and other similarly epic vistas. The concept of the sublime dates back to the Greek rhetorician Longinus, who described it as the quality in certain works of art that allowed audiences to experience *elestasis*, or a sense of being transported. The concept was further refined by Edmund Burke in the eighteenth century, when he described the Sublime as the opposite of Beauty, and claimed that the former overwhelms, awes and ravishes the viewer, while the latter can be appreciated in a more calm, serene manner. Burke also insisted that both art and nature can create experiences of sublimity. Due to Burke's influence, the sublime was referenced in Immanuel Kant's *A Critique of Judgment*, where Kant associates the sublime with the concept of the infinite. The experience of the sublime in SF is often associated with generating the genre's 'sense of wonder', and in *The Seven Beauties of Science Fiction* (2008), Istvan Csicsery-Ronay Jr examines the importance of the sublime in Mary Shelley's Frankenstein (1818), Stanley Kubrick's *2001: A Space Odyssey* (1968), the Wachowski siblings' *The Matrix* (1999) and James Tiptree Jr's *Up the Walls of the World* (1978).

Works Cited

Attebery, Brian (2005). 'Science Fiction, Parables, and Parabolas'. *Foundation* 34. 95 (Autumn). 7–22.

Bethke, Bruce (1983). 'Cyberpunk'. *Amazing Science Fiction*. (November) 1983. 94–105.

Booker, M. Keith and Anne-Marie Thomas (2009). *The Science Fiction Handbook*. Chichester: Wiley-Blackwell.

Broderick, Damien (1995). *Reading by Starlight: Postmodern Science Fiction*. London: Routledge.

Burroughs, Edgar Rice (1917) [1912]. *A Princess of Mars*. Chicago: A. C. McClurg & Co.

Clynes, Manfred E. and Nathan S. Kline (1960). 'Cyborgs and Space'. *Astronautics*. (September). 26–7, 74–6.

Csicsery-Ronay Jr, Istvan. (2008). *The Seven Beauties of Science Fiction*. Middletown, CT: Wesleyan University Press.

Delany, Samuel R. (1969). 'About 5,175 Words'. *Extrapolation*. 10. 2 (May). 52–66.

—(1977). *The Jewel-Hinged Jaw: Essays on Science Fiction*. Elizabethtown, NY: Dragon Press.

Disch, Thomas (1968). *Camp Concentration*. London: Hart-Davies.

Ellison, Harlan (ed.) (1967). *Dangerous Visions*. New York: Doubleday.

—(ed.) (1972). *Again Dangerous Visions*. New York: Doubleday.

Gibson, William (1984). *Neuromancer*. New York: Ace Books

Godwin, Tom (1954). 'The Cold Equations'. *Astounding Science Fiction*. 53. 6 (August). 62–84.

Greenland, Colin (1983). *The Entropy Exhibition*. London: Routledge.

Haraway, Donna (1991). 'A Cyborg Manifesto: Science, Technology, and Socialist-Feminism in the Late Twentieth Century'. *Simians, Cyborgs and Women: The Reinvention of Nature*. New York: Routledge. 149–81.

—(1991). *Simians, Cyborgs, and Women: The Reinvention of Nature*. New York: Routledge.

Heinlein, Robert (1965). 'On the Writing of Speculative Fiction'. *Of Worlds Beyond*. Lloyd Arthur Eshback (ed.). London: Dobson.

Jameson, Fredric (1991). *Postmodernism, or, the Cultural Logic of Late Capitalism*. London: Verso.

Kubrick, Stanley (1968). *2001: A Space Odyssey*. USA: MGM.

Lovecraft, H. P. (1995). 'Some Notes on Interplanetary Fiction'. *Miscellaneous Writing*. Sauk City: Arkham House Publishers. 119.

McHale, Brian (1987). *Postmodernist Fiction*. New York: Routledge.

Merril, Judith (ed.) (1968). *England Swings SF*. New York: Doubleday.

Rieder, John (2008). *Colonialism and the Emergence of Science Fiction*. Middletown, CT: Wesleyan University Press.

Rorvik, David (1971). *As Man Becomes Machine: The Evolution of the Cyborg*. New York: Doubleday.

Russ, Joanna (1973). 'Speculations: The Subjunctivity of Science Fiction'. *Extrapolation*. 15. 1 (December). 51–9.

Seed, David (2011). *Science Fiction: A Very Short Introduction*. New York: Oxford University Press.

Segal, Charles (1983). 'Greek Myth as a Semiotic and Structural System and the Problem of Tragedy'. *Aresthusa*. 16.

Slotkin, Richard (1992). *Gunfighter Nation: The Myth of the Frontier in Twentieth-Century America*. New York: Atheneum.

Sterling, Bruce (1989). 'Slipstream'. *Science Fiction Eye*. 5. 1 (July). 77–80.

Stross, Charles (2005). *Accelerando*. New York: Ace Books.

Suvin, Darko (1979). *Metamorphoses of Science Fiction: On the Poetics and History of a Literary Genre*. New Haven, CT: Yale University Press.

Tiptree, Jr, James (1978). *Up the Walls of the World*. New York: Berkley.

Wachowski, Larry and Andy (dir.) (1999). *The Matrix*.

Part Two: Critics

Aldiss, Brian: A UK writer, anthologist and critic. Aldiss was a prolific SF writer in the 1950s, and during the 1960s he became one of the central figures in the British New Wave movement (along with Michael Moorcock and J. G. Ballard). In the mid-1960s, Aldiss and Harry Harrison started the first short-lived journal of SF criticism, *Science Fiction Horizons*, which published two issues and featured articles by James Blish, Kingsley Amis and William S. Burroughs. Aldiss is best known in SF criticism for his literary history *Billion Year Spree* (1973), which was revised and expanded, with David Wingrove, as *Trillion Year Spree* in 1986. *Billion Year Spree* was one of the most influential early works that helped establish SF as a legitimate academic object of study. In it, Aldiss emphasises SF's historical origins and development; he argues that SF emerges from the gothic romance as it examines the impact of the industrial revolution on the human condition. According to Aldiss, Mary Shelley can be identified as one of the first SF writers, because *Frankenstein* (1818) relies on science rather than magic as its central fantastic element.

Amis, Kingsley: A UK writer, poet, critic, knight and father of UK writer Martin Amis. Amis was a well-known writer of social comedies in the 1950s and early 1960s; often regarded as one of the 'Angry Young Men', he was also a popular poet. In addition, he was the co-editor of a number of influential SF anthologies in the 1960s (such as *Spectrum* volumes I–V), and he was the sole editor of *The Golden Age of Science Fiction* anthology in 1981. In 1959 Amis delivered a series of lectures on SF at Princeton University in which he portrayed SF as a literature of satire and sociological exploration rather than as one focused on technology and juvenile adventure. These lectures were revised and published as *New Maps of Hell* (1960), one of the first critical volumes that established SF as an object for serious academic consideration. Amis was responsible for a number of SF and SF-influenced novels such as *The Anti-Death League* (1966), *The Green Man* (1969), *The Alteration* (1976) and *Russian Hide-and-Seek* (1980).

Delany, Samuel: A US novelist and critic who teaches creative writing at Temple University. Delany has written over 40 fiction and non-fiction books, and is recognized as a major contributor to SF literature and criticism. He has won four Nebula Awards, two Hugo Awards and the Pilgrim Award for lifetime achievement in SF criticism and scholarship. Carl Freedman notes that 'with the lone exception of Darko Suvin, no other critic has done as much as Delany to professionalise the study of sf, to make it as intellectually rigorous and as theoretically deft and resourceful as any other area of literary criticism' (65). Delany deploys the image of light diffracting through a gem or jewel as a metaphor for critical reading: just as white light is broken up into a spectrum of colours as it passes through a jewel, the illusion of singular meaning within a text is divided into a plural range of interpretive possibilities when a narrative is subjected to deconstructive close reading. Delany's foundational critical essays on SF are collected in *The Jewel-Hinged Jaw: Notes on the Language of Science Fiction* (1977), *The American Shore: Meditations on a Tale of Science Fiction by Thomas M. Disch – Angouleme* (1979) and *Starboard Wine: More Notes on the Language of Science Fiction* (1984). In these volumes, he advances SF criticism by avoiding straightforward thematic readings and the literary defences of SF that characterized much preceding work in the field; instead, Delany focuses on the structural elements of SF as a linguistic practice. Delany coined the term 'subjunctivity' to describe SF's structural differences from mimetic fiction, and the deconstructive close reading approach he models in *The American Shore* closely resembles Roland Barthes's' critical methodology in *S/Z* (1970). In his criticism, Delany is also notable for his rejection of traditional literary canonization and for his attention to the importance of subjectivity and difference; in this regard, his memoir of his own experience of coming of age as an openly gay dyslexic African American SF writer is chronicled in his autobiographical book *The Motion of Light in Water* (1988).

Freedman, Carl: A Professor of English at Louisiana State University. Freedman won the 1999 SF Research Association Pioneer Award for his essay 'Kubrick's *2001* and the Possibility of a Science-Fiction Cinema', and he has written critical scholarship on Samuel Delany, Ursula K. Le Guin, Isaac Asimov and many other SF authors. He is best known for his book *Critical Theory and Science Fiction* (2000), which expands on ideas he originally developed in an essay he wrote for *Science Fiction Studies* in 1987. In this book, Freedman offers critical readings of Stanislaw Lem's *Solaris* (1961), Ursula K. LeGuin's *The Dispossessed* (1974), Joanna Russ's *The Two of Them* (1978), Samuel Delany's *Stars in My Pocket Like Grains of Sand* (1984) and Philip K. Dick's *The Man in the High Castle* (1962). Freedman privileges the writings of 1960s and 1970s New Wave authors as examples of the best critical possibilities offered in SF, and he contrasts these against the mundane creative possibilities offered by mainstream popular SF writers and the pulp SF tradition. Drawing upon Darko Suvin's definition of SF as a literature of 'cognitive estrangement', he argues that SF and critical theory are united in their mutual aspiration to defamiliarize taken-for-granted cultural norms and to offer realistic alternative utopian counter-possibilities. For this reason, he suggests that Marxists and other cultural theorists should pay particular attention to the best works of SF rather than dismissing them as inconsequential popular fantasies.

Haraway, Donna: A US science and technology scholar who teaches in the History of Consciousness department at the University of California, Santa Cruz. Haraway studied zoology and philosophy at Colorado College before completing her PhD in Biology at Yale in 1972. She is the author of several books, including *Primate Visions* (1989), *Simians, Cyborgs, and Women* (1991), *Modest_Witness@Second_Millennium. FemaleMan(C)Meets_OncoMouse*™ (1997), *The Companion Species Manifesto* (2003) and *When Species Meet* (2008). Her work has won the Gustavus Myers Human Rights Award (1990), the Ludwick Fleck Prize (1992), the Robert K. Merton Award (1992), the American Book Award (1992) and the J. D. Bernal Prize (2000) for lifetime achievement in social study of the sciences. In SF scholarship, Haraway pioneered critical approaches to cybernetics and to human/animal relations. Her influential 'Cyborg Manifesto' (originally published in 1985, then later revised and expanded in *Simians, Cyborgs, and Women*) argues that the cyborg offers a metaphor for hybrid subjectivity that challenges Western conceptual binaries (such as the imaginative binary that defines 'humans' and 'machines' as separate epistemological categories). Haraway often asserts common ground between her work and the concerns of feminist SF writers; both challenge the essentialization of gender, sexuality, and reproduction, and both strive to discover and/or create new ways of thinking about identity and difference. Haraway's cyborg scholarship and her ground-breaking work in animal studies eschews a social and political praxis founded upon the presumed sameness of shared essential identities in favour of a postmodern politics of shifting tactical affinities; her work demonstrates that epistemologies of identity facilitate destructive conceptual limitations, while epistemologies of affinity enable expansive creative collaborations. Her work, similarly to the writing of the SF authors she frequently cites (such as Joanna Russ), attempts to deconstruct myths of wholeness and to explore alternative intersections of science, technology and social narrative.

Jameson, Fredric: A Marxist political theorist and literary critic who holds the William A. Lane Professorship in The Program in Literary and Romance Studies at Duke University; Jameson is the author of over 20 books of literary and cultural criticism, many of which examine SF in order to make claims about the relationships between postmodernity and capitalism. One of Jameson's notable early works was *The Political Unconscious: Narrative as a Socially Symbolic Act* (1981), in which he offered a Marxist analysis of the interpretive frameworks by which literary texts are constructed. His major breakthrough, however, was his article 'Postmodernism, or, the Cultural Logic of Late Capitalism' (originally published in *New Left Review* in 1984) where he argued that postmodern aesthetics represent a celebration of the failure to understand the complexity of global economic, social and political connectivity within the advanced stages of capitalist hegemony. Jameson was an active early contributor to the journal *Science Fiction Studies* starting in 1973, and when he later revised his 'Postmodernism' essay into his longer book *Postmodernism, or, the Cultural Logic of Late Capitalism* (1991), his analyses of the relationships between aesthetic forms and economic structures examined the works of Margaret Atwood, J. G. Ballard, Samuel Delany, Philip K. Dick, William Gibson, Ursula K. Le Guin and many other SF figures. In *Postmodernism*, Jameson famously argued that cyberpunk SF was a quintessential expression of postmodern values and ideas. Jameson continues to write about SF, and his recent book *Archaeologies of the Future: The Desire Called Utopia and Other Science Fictions* (2005) investigates the origins of the utopian narrative form and interrogates a variety of SF novels in order to question the value of utopian imaginings in the contemporary world.

Lefanu, Sarah: A Royal Literary Fund Fellow at the University of Exeter who enjoys a broad background as a scholar, editor and broadcaster, she is also a previous Artistic Director for the Bath Literature Festival (2003–9). Lefanu is best known in SF studies for her book *In the Chinks of the World Machine: Feminism and Science Fiction* (1988), which won the MLA Emily Toth Award in 1990. In this book, Lefanu argues that science fiction offers women a greater range of freedoms than mainstream literature because it affords authors the ability to extrapolate beyond the patriarchal norms of the existing social realities reproduced in mimetic fictions. The book begins with a series of essays examining a variety of topics, such as early female SF writers, female characters in SF and feminist utopias and dystopias. It concludes with an examination of approaches to gender essentialism in the work of James Tiptree, Jr, Ursula Le Guin, Suzy McKee Charnas and Joanna Russ. Lefanu has edited several fiction anthologies, including *Dispatches from the Frontiers of the Female Mind* (1985), a collection of SF stories by female authors that she co-edited with Jen Green. She has also written introductions or forewords to several of Joanna Russ's works.

Le Guin, Ursula Kroeber: A US writer, essayist and critic who has written over 20 novels in addition to her short fiction, poetry, children's books and critical essays. Her work regularly addresses critical topics such as feminism, gender, sexuality, imperialism and cultural relativism. Much of her fiction can be read as critical theory; her early Hainish novels interrogate the emergence of imperial globalization in the aftermath of Western European decolonization, and *The Left Hand of Darkness* (1969) extrapolates alternative ways of imagining gender and sexuality while at the same time innovating cosmopolitan alternatives to imperial political and economic relations. Her award-winning novel *The Dispossessed* (1974) explores how language shapes thinking and culture, and it offers a Cold War-era critique of capitalism and utopian socialism. In addition to the extrapolative work accomplished by her fiction, Le Guin has also written a variety of non-fiction essays that offer critical contributions to SF studies. In her essay 'Is Gender Necessary' (1976) she responds to prevalent criticisms of *The Left Hand of Darkness* by noting that she might have taken a more radical approach to her portrayals of gender and sexuality in the novel, and she later revises her view in 'Is Gender Necessary? Redux' (1987) by taking an even stronger position distancing herself from her earlier and more incomplete critical stance; in this regard, it is often appropriate to read Le Guin's fiction and non-fiction as part of an ongoing critical conversation. Le Guin's most notable non-fiction essays on SF, fantasy and gender are collected together in *The Language of the Night: Essays on Fantasy and Science Fiction* (1979).

Rieder, John: A Professor of English at University of Hawaii at Manoa. Rieder earned his PhD from Yale in 1980; his early work focused on English Romanticism (particularly Wordsworth and Percy Shelley). He is known in SF scholarship for his ground-breaking research on early SF and colonialism; his book *Colonialism and the Emergence of Science Fiction* (2008) argues that 'SF addresses itself to the ideological basis of colonial practice itself, by engaging various aspects of the ideology of progress' (30). Along with Gwyneth Jones, Istvan Csicery-Ronay and Patricia Kerslake, Rieder is one of the first scholars to focus attention on the role of imperial fantasy in SF; *CESF* is widely regarded as the first substantial study on SF and colonialism. Rieder argues that SF emerges in the late nineteenth century during the most aggressive phase of Western imperial expansion; SF first becomes visible in imperialist countries (primarily France and England), and then it quickly gains popularity in other nations pursuing imperial projects (including the United States, Germany and Russia). His work asserts that 'allusions to colonial history and situations are ubiquitous features of early SF motifs and plots. It is not a matter of asking whether but of determining precisely how and to what extent the stories engage colonialism' (3). Rieder is also notable for his approach to genre in SF scholarship; he was the winner of the 2011 SFRA Pioneer Award for his essay 'On Defining SF, or Not' (2010) which argues that SF 'has no essence, no single unifying characteristic, and no point of origin' (193), and that a more realistic approach to SF would more properly regard it as an historically constituted mode of categorization deployed by specific 'communities of practice' (206).

Russ, Joanna: A feminist SF writer and academic who taught English at the University of Washington until 2011. Russ is the author of eight novels, two short story collections and five volumes of critical essays; her non-fiction writing has won the Florence Howe Criticism Award and Science Fiction

Research Association Pilgrim Award. Her most famous fictional work is *The Female Man* (1975), an avant-garde postmodern feminist novel which deconstructs gender, sexual identity and the sexism of SF narrative conventions and reader expectations. Her critical essay collections *To Write Like a Woman: Essays in Feminism and Science Fiction* (1995) and *The Country You Have Never Seen* (2007) interrogate the ways in which SF writers and critics approach gender in stereotypical ways. Her non-SF novel *On Strike Against God* (1980) challenges the sexism often present in SF fan and academic communities, and her non-fiction collections *How to Suppress Women's Writing* (1983) and *Magic Mommas, Trembling Sister, Puritans and Perverts* (1985) investigate the treatment of women in the pages of SF. Russ also offers an analysis of the radical feminisms of the 1960s and 1970s (with bold statements concerning the possible futures of such feminisms) in *What Are We Fighting For? Sex, Race, Class, and the Future of Feminism* (1998).

Suvin, Darko: A SF theorist, editor and poet who earned his PhD from Zagreb University in the former Yugoslavia and later emigrated to North America, where he taught English and Comparative Literature at McGill University in Montreal from 1968 until 1999. Along with R. D. Mullen, Suvin was a co-founder in 1973 of *Science Fiction Studies*, the top-ranking peer-reviewed journal of SF scholarship. Suvin's work on SF has been collected in *Metamorphoses of Science Fiction* (1979), *Victorian Science Fiction in the UK* (1983), *Positions and Presuppositions in Science Fiction* (1988) and *Defined by Hollow* (2010). In 1979, he was the winner of the Science Fiction Research Association Pilgrim Award for his lifetime contributions to SF criticism and theory. Suvin was one of the most influential scholars in establishing the legitimacy of SF as an object of serious academic study in the 1970s. His early work refutes the marginalization of SF as 'paraliterary' art and instead locates the genre in a long tradition of Utopian literary imaginings that reaches back to Lucian of Samosata, Thomas More and Francois Rabelais. Suvin argues that literary SF performs some of the most critical and transformative work in contemporary literature. Starting with his essay 'On the Poetics of the Science Fiction Genre', collected in *Metamorphoses of Science Fiction*, Suvin theorises SF as a literature of 'cognitive estrangement', and he defines SF as 'a literary genre whose necessary and sufficient conditions are the presence and interaction of estrangement and cognition, and whose main formal device is an imaginative framework alternative to the author's empirical environment' (7–8, emphasis removed). In addition to his extensive writing on Bertolt Brecht, Suvin's own SF scholarship focuses on the Utopian imaginings of modernist SF authors such as Yevgeny Zamyatin, Karek Capek and Olaf Stapledon, and New Wave SF authors like Ursula K. Le Guin, Philip K. Dick and Joanna Russ.

Works Cited

Aldiss, Brian (1973). *Billion Year Spree*. London: Weidenfeld and Nicolson.

Aldiss, Brian and David Wingrove (1986). *Trillion Year Spree*. London: Gollancz.

Amis, Kingsley (1960). *New Maps of Hell*. New York: Harcourt, Brace.

—(1966). *The Anti-Death League*. London: Gollancz.

—(1969). *The Green Man*. London: Jonathan Cape.

—(1976). *The Alteration*. London: Jonathan Cape.

—(1980). *Russian Hide-and-Seek*. London: Hutchinson.

Barthes, Roland (1974) [1970]. *S/Z*. Trans. Richard Miller. New York: Hill and Wang.

Delany, Sanuel (1977). *The Jewel-Hinged Jaw: Notes on the Language of Science Fiction*. Elizabethtown, NY: Dragon Press.

—(1979). *The American Shore: Meditations on a Tale of Science Fiction by Thomas M. Disch – Angouleme*. Elizabethtown, NY: Dragon Press.

—(1979). *Heavenly Breakfast*. New York: Bantam Books.

—(1984). *Starboard Wine: More Notes on the Language of Science Fiction*. Elizabethtown, NY: Dragon Press.

—(1984). *Stars in My Pocket Like Grains of Sand*. New York: Bantam Books.

Dick, Philip K. (1962). *The Man in the High Castle*. New York: Putnam.

Freedman, Carl (1998). 'Kubrick's *2001* and the Possibility of a Science-Fiction Cinema'. *Science Fiction Studies*. 25. 300–18.

—(2000). *Critical Theory and Science Fiction*. Middletown, CT: Wesleyan University Press.

—(2010). 'Samuel R[ay] Delany (1942–)'. *Fifty Key Figures in Science Fiction*. Mark Bould et al. (eds). London: Routledge. 61–5.

Haraway, Donna (1985). 'A Cyborg Manifesto: Science, Technology, and Socialist-Feminism in the Late Twentieth Century'. *Socialist Review*. 15. 2.

—(1989). *Primate Visions*. New York: Routledge.

—(1991). *Simians, Cyborgs, and Women: The Reinvention of Nature*. New York: Routledge.

—(1997). *Modest_Witness@Second_Millennium.FemaleMan©Meets_OncoMouse™: Feminism and Technoscience*. New York: Routledge.

—(2003). *The Companion Species Manifesto*. Chicago: Prickly Paradigm Press.

—(2008). *When Species Meet*. Minneapolis: University of Minnesota Press.

Jameson, Fredric. (1981). *The Political Unconscious: Narrative as a Socially Symbolic Act*. Ithaca, NY: Cornell University Press.

—(1984). 'Postmodernism, or, the Cultural Logic of Late Capitalism'. *New Left Review*.

—(1991). *Postmodernism, or, the Cultural Logic of Late Capitalism*. London: Verso.

—(2005). *Archaeologies of the Future: The Desire Called Utopia and Other Science Fictions*. London: Verso.

Lefanu, Sarah and Jen Green (eds) (1985). *Dispatches from the Frontiers of the Female Mind*. London: The Women's Press.

—(1988). *In the Chinks of the World Machine: Feminism and Science Fiction*. London: The Women's Press.

Le Guin, Ursula (1969). *The Left Hand of Darkness*. New York: Ace Books.

—(1974). *The Dispossessed*. New York: Harper & Row.

—(1976). 'Is Gender Necessary?'. *Aurora: Beyond Equality*. Susan Janice Anderson and Vonda N. McIntyre (eds). New York: Fawcett Gold Medal. 130–9.

—(1979). *The Language of the Night: Essays on Fantasy and Science Fiction*. New York: Putnam.

—(1987). 'Is Gender Necessary? Redux'. *Dancing at the Edge of the World*. New York: Grove Press. 7–16.

Lem, Stanislaw (1970) [1961]. *Solaris*. New York: Walker & Co.

Rieder, John (2008). *Colonialism and the Emergence of Science Fiction*. Middletown, CT: Wesleyan University Press.

—(2010). 'On Defining SF, or Not: Genre Theory, SF, and History'. *Science Fiction Studies* 37.2. 191–209.

Russ, Joanna. (1975). *The Female Man*. New York: Bantam Books.

—(1978). *The Two of Them*. New York: Berkley Books.

—(1980). *On Strike Against God*. New York: Out & Out Books.

—(1983). *How to Suppress Women's Writing*. Austin: University of Texas Press.

—(1985). *Magic Mommas, Trembling Sister, Puritans and Perverts*. Trumansburg, NY: Crossing Press.

—(1995). *To Write Like a Woman*. Bloomington: Indiana University Press.

—(1998). *What Are We Fighting For? Sex, Race, Class, and the Future of Feminism*. New York: St. Martin's Press.

—(2007). *The Country You Have Never Seen: Essays and Reviews*. Liverpool: Liverpool University Press.

Shelley, Mary (2003) [1818]. *Frankenstein*. Harmondsworth: Penguin Classics.

Suvin, Darko (1979). *Metamorphoses of Science Fiction: On the Poetics and History of a Literary Genre*. New Haven, CT: Yale University Press.

—(1983). *Victorian Science Fiction in the UK*. Boston: G. K. Hall.

—(1988). *Positions and Presuppositions in Science Fiction*. London: Macmillan.

—(2010). *Defined by a Hollow: Essays on Utopia, Science Fiction and Political Epistemology*. Bern: Peter Lang.

The Science Fiction Film

7

Aris Mousoutzanis

Science Fiction, Film and the Science Fiction Film: Origins and Early Stages

The increasing popularity of science fiction throughout the twentieth century is indebted to a large extent to cinema, even if some critics would consider the medium to be also responsible for the reputation of SF as a commercial genre with low cultural value. Even today, many people's familiarity with SF derives largely from Hollywood blockbusters and film still remains a major vehicle for the dissemination of the genre. However, SF has become indispensable to Hollywood as well, since it is one of the genres to produce the most profitable blockbuster movies – the 'blockbuster' itself, as a type of cinema, was established through SF, after the release of George Lucas's *Star Wars* and Steven Spielberg's *Close Encounters of the Third Kind* in 1977. There is, in other words, a mutual dependence, even a reciprocal influence, between SF and the cinema: on the one hand, the need for alien landscapes, alternate realities and alien creatures has encouraged technical innovation in cinema, as in the case of computer-generated imagery (CGI) technology. On the other, the film industry has familiarized wider audiences with the generic conventions of SF, indeed even before the late 1970s, during the so-called 'Classic Era' of the SF film of the 1950s. In theoretical terms, the relationship between SF and cinema may be described as a *dialectic* relationship, one in which two distinct concepts, entities or states of affairs interact and influence each other.

The 'history of SF cinema', J. P. Telotte has also pointed out, 'practically coincides with that of the cinema itself' (42). The two of them have been bound up with each other since their very beginnings, which may be traced not just in the same historical period but even in the same year. Many historians consider 1895 to be the year of the birth of cinema, when the Lumière brothers demonstrated to an audience at the Grand Café in Paris their short film, *The Arrival of a Train*. This is the same year of publication of H. G. Wells's *The Time Machine*, an event that may be seen as marking the official beginning of modern SF. When an inventor named Robert Paul read *The Time Machine*, he contacted Wells to discuss a patent for some sort of projection device that would simulate an imaginary journey through time similar to the one described in Wells's text. Even if the patent was not approved, the incident is indicative of the cinematic qualities of Wells's fictional device of time travel. 'Like the cinema spectator', Jonathan Bignell writes, 'the Time Traveller sits on a red plush seat and watches a marvellous spectacle, and the journey into the future depends on a machine, a techno-logical apparatus rather than magic or dream' (88). Wells's Time Machine was essentially a cinematic device: the experience of travelling to the future is described by the Time Traveller as one where he can see his housemaid Mrs Watchett first entering the room 'like a rocket' in fast-forward motion, and later, on his way back to the present, as if she moves in reverse motion: 'The door at the lower end opened, and she glided quietly up the laboratory, back foremost, and disappeared behind the door by which she had previ-ously entered' (66). Around the same period, techniques of fast-forward and reverse-motion were used in early film 'shorts' that are now considered the earliest predecessors of the SF film. The Lumière brothers' *Mechanical Butcher* (1895) from the same year was a one-minute film that was showing a pig being fed into a machine that would make various cuts of pork out of the pig's meat. Audiences could watch the film in reverse motion, a technique parodied by Edwin Porter in his 1904 film, *Dog Factory*, a film showing a machine remaking strings of sausages back into whatever breed of dog the customer wanted. This experimentation with cinematic technique and special effects renders these shorts as the earliest predecessors of SF cinema. Their focus on spectacle and 'trickery' rather than on plot and characteri-zation has led Tom Gunning to refer to this group of films as 'the cinema of attractions' committed to present a 'series of views to audiences' that are 'fascinating because of their illusory power' (57). A well-known example from the period, George Méliès's *Trip to the Moon* (1902) is often discussed in historical accounts of the medium for its pioneering development of costuming and special effects. The film, Mark Bould has argued, is 'primarily a compendium of special effects whose story merely frames a display of cinema's magical possibilities' (80).

The use of state-of-the-art special effects is still one of the most recognizable features of an SF film, something noted by film critics and reviewers, often in a disparaging tone – the underlying assumption being that the genre's heavy reliance on 'eyeball kicks' is often at the expense of plot, theme or characterization. This approach, however, Adam Roberts argues, 'is missing the point. The special effects in any given SF film … *are* the point', they are 'characters in a very real sense' (152–3). According to this approach, the importance of special effects is not just a formal feature of SF but a characteristic tightly connected to its major concerns. '*Spectacle* and *speculation*', for Geoff King and Tanya Krzywinska, 'sum up two key dimensions of the genre' (7), in an argument that suggests that the speculative nature of SF is bound up with its efforts at providing a spectacular cinematic experience. It is due to the major importance of vision and visualization that the SF film is often seen as one of the most self-conscious types of cinema, a visual experience that is about seeing, watching and observing, a cinema that is about cinema itself. In this sense the SF film is one of the most *self-reflexive, meta-textual* or *meta-cinematic* genres. An SF film is more likely than many other types of movies to involve scenes with other visual media in their setting: monitors, telescopes, microscopes, hologram tubes, view-screens, scanning devices and X-ray visions. Often the camera may assume a first-person perspective either in scenes that involve exploring alien or unknown environments or in films that present the action from the perspective of the video-vision of cyborgs like Robocop or the Terminator. 'Cinematic movement becomes an essential mode of comprehension' in a genre whose most significant meanings are often found 'in their visual organisation and their emphasis on perception' (Bukatman, *Blade Runner*, 9). The discussion of major films and stages in the history of SF below will be referring to the self-reflexive nature of SF cinema as a common denominator around which to introduce a number of major themes and concerns of the genre and the way in which it has interacted with literary SF.

The early Science Fiction Film: *Metropolis* (1927)

The first full-length SF films were produced during a period ranging roughly between the mid-1920s and the mid-1930s in Russia (*Aelita*, Protozanov, 1924), Germany (*Metropolis*, Lang, 1927), the USA (*The Mysterious Island*, Hubbard, 1929), France (*The End of the World*, Gance, 1931) and the UK (*Things to Come*,

Menzies, 1926). *Metropolis* is the film with the most long-lasting influence on the genre and it is generally considered to be the first official SF feature film. References to Lang's film abound in later classic SF films, such as *Star Wars* (Lucas, 1977) or *Blade Runner* (Scott, 1982); Superman's city was named after the film by the superhero's creators Jerry Siegel and Joe Shuster. References to the film may be also found in the music videos for 'Radio Ga Ga' by The Queen and Madonna's 'Express Yourself', and more recently the videos and performances of pop stars like Kylie Minogue, Beyoncé and Lady Gaga. These are only a few of the influences of Lang's seminal work that still resonates in popular culture even almost one century later.

Metropolis started a trend that would be reproduced in later classic SF films discussed below, it received mixed responses by critics and audiences alike that concentrated on two apparently contradictory aspects of the film: its plot seemed quite simplistic, derivative and predictable whereas its visual aesthetic looked very original, futurist and impressive. The film follows Freder, the son of the master of Metropolis Joh Fredersen, who follows Maria, a leading figure among the working classes that delivers sermons about the advent of a 'mediator' that will negotiate better working conditions with the city rulers. Freder chooses to rebel against his father who collaborates with the scientist Rotwang to create a robot identical to Maria in order to infiltrate the workers and discredit her cause. The real Maria is kidnapped and her double unleashes chaos in the city as she convinces the workers to destroy the machines and let the city vaults flood. Eventually the workers are persuaded to end their rebellion by their manager Grot and they turn their fury against the robot Maria who is burnt on a stake while the real Maria is rescued from Rotwang by Freder, who brings about a reconciliation between the workers and his father. The film ends with a title card of its central message: 'the mediator between the head and the hands must be the heart'. The story seems as naïve and predictable today as it was seen to be when the film was first released but it is indicative of the strong *intertextual* nature of the SF film. The plot of *Metropolis* is woven through a tissue of quotations from previous texts – Mary Shelley's *Frankenstein* (1818), E. T. A. Hoffmann's *The Sandman* (1826), Villiers de l'Isle Adam's *Future Eve* (1886) and H. G. Wells's *When the Sleeper Wakes* (1910) are just a few. This has become a standard feature of SF films that often acknowledge their indebtedness to previous novels or films.

Reviews of the film's plot also concentrated on its political messages and in this way also represent another feature of the SF film, its engagement with contemporary politics. The critical perceptions of the film's politics have been divided between those who see *Metropolis* as a prototypical Marxist film and those who believe that Lang's work reproduces a fascist aesthetic. On the one hand, the film may be seen as reflecting Karl Marx's theory of history as a *dialectic* conflict between the working classes (in Marx's terms, the *proletariat*) and the middle classes (the *bourgeoisie*). The film's opening scenes first introduce the audience to the 'Eternal Gardens' and the 'Clubs of the Sons' that include theatres, libraries and stadiums – the sphere of culture and ideas that Marx termed the ideological *superstructure* of society, dominated by the bourgeoisie. We then see the underground machine rooms operated by the workers, what Marx termed the material *base* of society associated with the proletariat. It is therefore quite easy to find in *Metropolis* a representation of Marxist theory as its plot stages the clash and reconciliation between the lower and upper classes. However, other critics suggested that underneath the film's all-too-obvious Marxist concerns there lurked an underlying fascist orientation. The most well-known critique was the one launched by Siegfried Kracauer, who saw *Metropolis* as a right-wing Utopia not only in its emphasis on images of violence and destruction, but also in its representation of crowds in symmetrical geometrical forms that anticipated the Nazi aesthetic of the 'mass ornament', the crowd arranged in a tightly ordered and perfectly symmetrical shape. The term that Kracauer used to refer to this stylistic effect of the film is 'excessive ornamentation', a technique employed even in scenes that represents moments of rest that prepare for revolution, such as the one where the workers listen to Maria delivering her sermon. The film's closure, for Kracauer, suggests 'that the industrialist acknowledges the heart for the purpose of manipulating it; that he does not give up his power, but will expand it over a realm not yet annexed – the realm of the collective soul' (164). This approach to the film gained even further currency after the Second World War, when the crowd imagery in the underground scenes became eerily reminiscent of Nazi concentration camps.

In his own response to these accusations, Lang admitted a degree of naivety even as he defended his work by suggesting that this was not his main concern: 'One cannot make a politically conscious film by claiming that the heart mediates between the hand and the brain – that's a fairy tale, really. I was more interested in machines' (cited in Boglanovich, 124). In this respect the film is also prototypical of the SF film's recurring concern with technological development and industrialization. In its creation of the robot Maria, *Metropolis* prepared the ground for the robots, androids and cyborgs that have become stock characters in the genre, even as its preoccupation with the relationship between the human and the technological would become one of its major concerns. The film's robot is only the most obvious embodiment of this concern: Rotwang has also already become a 'Machine Man' as he has an artificial hand after having lost his own hand during his work on the robot. The workers, on the other hand, have been turned into machines by Fredersen, even as machines are represented as living creatures that consume the workers. This overt technophobia in the film's plot, however, contrasts with the aestheticization of technology in the film's directing, which includes scenes and images that still look visually impressive. The very first SF film is emblematic of the genre's meta-cinematic status also because many of its scenes involve watching and observing. One of these scenes in the film also introduces another major concern of criticism on the SF film, its gender politics: Fredersen and Rotwang send the robot Maria to perform a strip show in a nightclub in order to test how convincing she is as a 'real woman' in a sequence that juxtaposes shots of Maria performing her dance and images of a surrealist collage of the eyes of the male spectators observing her during her show. The female body, in this scene, is a 'projection' of the male gaze. The camera assumes the perspective of the male spectator and places the audience in a position occupied by the men of the film. The scene is a perfect illustration of the theory of the 'male gaze' by Laura Mulvey, who has demonstrated the ways in which the female body is objectified in classic Hollywood cinema, where women are portrayed erotic objects either for the characters in the film or for the spectators in the auditorium: 'A woman performs within the narrative: the gaze of the spectator and that of the male characters in the film are neatly combined without breaking narrative verisimilitude' (27). The objectification of the female body in the film's directing also corresponds to the objectification of Maria in the plot, who is literally turned into an object, a robot to obey Fredersen and Rotwang. Furthermore, the 'doubling' of Maria reproduces the two dominant ways in which women have been represented in patriarchal narratives: as either virgins or whores. The film's narrative resolution privileges the former over the latter even as it attests to its misogyny, another feature of the SF film that would not be challenged before the 1970s with the advent of the Second Wave of feminism.

The Classic Era: *The Day the Earth Stood Still* (1951)

The classic era of the American SF film is less indebted to those early films mentioned above and more in line with an American tradition of serialized narrative both from fiction, the pulp magazines of the 1920s and the 1930s, and from film, the 'movie serials' that emerged in the 1910s and became increasingly popular during the 1930s until they gradually declined in popularity by the mid-1950s. These were short films shown in cinemas in weekly episodes that ran in 12 or 15 instalments. Their plot was formulaic, characterization was stereotypical and special effects were limited, but they were driven by a fast pace, packed with action and established some classic characters of the genre like Flash Gordon or Buck Rogers. The serials also familiarized a wider audience with a stock of SF conventions and in this way prepared the ground for the classic era of the 1950s, that includes a number of SF classics produced by small companies specializing in low-budget B-movies aimed at a predominantly teenage audience.

The boom in the genre was inaugurated by the critical and commercial success of two films in 1950, Irving Pichel's *Destination Moon* and Kurt Neumann's *Rocketship X-M*, two films that were seminal to the revival of the genre in their own distinct way. *Destination Moon* was produced by George Pal, who would become a key figure of the classic era as the producer of several SF movies at the time, and the film is now remembered for its Oscar-winning special effects and discussed as 'a colourful special effects extravaganza' (Jancovich and Johnston, 72). Its visual aesthetic is indicative of a common major feature of the numerous films that were produced during the decade, 'that they deploy the special effects of their day to create a sense of unfamiliarity and spectacle' (King and Krzywinska, 6). The influence of *Rocketship X-M*, on the other hand, lay less in its form and more in its plot; the discovery on Mars of the radioactive ruins of an extinct civilization at the aftermath of a nuclear conflagration betrayed a more overt preoccupation with issues pertinent to the Cold War era that would become typical of the American SF film of the 1950s.

The most recurring theme of the era was that of alien invasion, which received a renewed popularity at the prospect of a nuclear conflict with the Soviet Union in films such as of *War of the Worlds* (Haskin, 1953), *Invaders from Mars* (Menzies, 1953) or *Earth vs. the Flying Saucers* (Sears, 1956). It has been quite common to see the alien in these films as the Soviet Other, although more recent approaches has demonstrated the ways in these films articulate anxieties endemic to American society. The case of Siegel's *Invasion of the Body Snatchers* (1956) is probably the most representative, whose alien 'pod people' that replace human citizens with emotionless clones have been typically seen as a metaphor for Communist infiltration. The film, however, according to Bould, 'offers little to support such a reading':

> the movie's imagery of contagion and dehumanisation, often associated
> with communism, was also central to contemporary discourses about
> everything from mass culture, marijuana, motherhood and McCarthyism
> to homosexuality, civil rights, juvenile delinquency and rock'n'roll. (86)

Regardless of their symbolism, aliens were evil and threatening in the majority of these films. A notable exception is one of the most 'respectable' and influential movies from the period, Robert Wise's *The Day the Earth Stood Still*. Based on Harry Bates's short story 'Farewell to the Master' originally published in the pulp SF magazine *Astounding Science Fiction* in 1940, *The Day the Earth Stood Still* was the first film produced in A-format by Hollywood and aimed at an adult audience. The benevolent alien Klaatu who arrives on Earth to warn humanity against their use of nuclear weapons introduced the type of the 'alien envoy' that would figure again in later films such as *Close*

Encounters of the Third Kind or *E. T. The Extra-Terrestrial* (Spielberg, 1982). His ten-foot-tall robot Gort with its cyclops' eye found later incarnations in other robots and cyborgs whose flashing eye, often staring directly at the camera, is a defining feature of their figure, such as the Terminator, the Borg of *Star Trek* or the Centurion Cylons from *Battlestar Galactica* – in this way participating in the recurrent imagery of eyes that attests to the self-reflexive nature of the genre.

In its use of a story involving the arrival of an alien on Earth in order to articulate Cold War fears and anxieties, *The Day the Earth Stood Still* is typical of its time. The way in which it engages with these fears, however, is quite distinct. The film does not evoke any sense of threat or hysteria through its alien character but through the responses of official institutions to his arrival. The sense of paranoia is introduced in the film's opening sequence that juxtaposes shots from newspaper headlines interspersed with broadcasts by radio and television stations on the arrival of a flying saucer. The film targets the media more than any other institution as the major source of fear and hysteria throughout its entire course: the media circulate rumours that Klaatu may be a Russian spy, they trigger 'menace from another world' hysteria when Klaatu escapes from the hospital where he has been kept after being accidentally shot by a nervous soldier, and they produce 'Monster from Mars' headlines after Klaatu brings about a power cut around the world in demonstration of his power. In a similar vein, government and military representatives are persistently portrayed as impulsive and prone to violence and in several action sequences they threaten and shoot out of fear and without cause. Unlike the average SF movie of the time, *The Day the Earth Stood Still* is not militarist or reactionary but pacifist and liberal. Klaatu's plea for an end to war is matched by his respect for human life, as the power cut he causes around the world does not affect hospitals or flying airplanes, while even his robot Gort does not kill people but disintegrates weapons. The film's pace is also much more restrained than other movies of the time and it is more of a low-key, minimalist drama with focus on characterization and a matter-of-fact directing the gives the film a realist style. After his escape from the hospital, Klaatu decides to mingle with ordinary people and settles down in a boarding house under the name Mr Carpenter, where he befriends young widow Helen Benson and her son Bobby. There is a sequence where Klaatu and Bobby visit the Arlington National Cemetery and the Lincoln memorial that has an elegiac, even mournful tone about it, as the film finds hope for humankind in the words of the Gettysburg Address inscribed on the memorial or the scientific humanism of Professor Barnhardt, an Einstein-like character that Klaatu contacts in order to arrange a meeting with the world's leading scientists. The film's gender politics were also slightly better than those of the average SF film at the time. Even if Helen is a secondary character that ends up screaming as Gort approaches her in a later scene, she is still no scantily-clad damsel-in-distress that has her clothes ripped but a working mother raising an intelligent child and a woman ready to stand up to difficult situations and help the film's protagonist.

The Christian symbolism introduced in the film was intended to be part of its pacifist message. Klaatu is a messianic Christ-like figure that descends from the sky with a message of salvation for humanity, lives among everyday people as a 'Carpenter' until he is betrayed by an acquaintance (Helen's boyfriend who reports him to the authorities), killed by the authorities and resurrected by Gort in order to deliver his message to a crowd: if humanity pursues its present course, it will be obliterated. They must disarm or their planet will be eliminated. Then he ascends to the sky, leaving those behind him to either accept or reject his guidance. These references were first intro-duced by scriptwriter Edmund North without Wise's knowledge and they were meant to be only subliminal, and Klaatu's resurrection was made to be temporary only at the request of the Motion Picture Associations of America, after which a line was added to the dialogue where Klaatu says that the power over life and death is 'reserved to the Almighty Spirit'.

There is, however, a certain irony in Klaatu's ultimatum, whose pacifist message is delivered with an aggression that is at odds with the film's liberal pretensions and suggests a form of benevolent dictatorship. Jancovich and Johnston consider *The Day the Earth Stood Still* to be 'a highly authoritarian film, in which Klaatu's warning is also a threat: humanity is too irrespon-sible to handle nuclear power, and must surrender itself to a robot police force which will punish aggression with global extinction' (74). Released in the midst of the Korean War, the film's approach of 'stop fighting or we will destroy you' resonates with the containment policy of President Harry S. Truman during that war.

Art Science Fiction: *2001: A Space Odyssey* (1968)

For most of the 1960s, the American film industry produced only isolated instances of considerable or profitable SF. It is only towards the end of the decade that the genre witnesses a revival, with films such as *The Planet of the Apes* (Schaffner, 1968), the first major SF 'film series' with extensive cross-marketing that is often read as an allegory of contemporary racial conflicts during the Civil Rights movement. One of the most important films of this period is Stanley Kubrick's *2001: A Space Odyssey*, a film whose significance lies in its combination of different strains of SF produced at the time. Even if it may be seen as yet another space travel film in response to J. F. Kennedy's space race, *2001* was also co-written by Arthur C. Clarke whose work is often associated with the 'hard SF' of the Golden Age of SF, and yet it was executed with a New Wave aesthetic and betrayed similarities with a series of films influenced by European art cinema, such as *Alphaville* (Godard, 1965), *La Jetée* (Marker, 1965) or *Solaris* (Tarkovsky, 1972) – the latter often considered to be the Soviet 'answer' to *2001*.

The film consists of four different parts. The first part, 'The Dawn of Man', shows two tribes of hominids in prehistoric Africa fighting for access to a water hole when a black monolith mysteriously appears out of nowhere. A member of one tribe touches the monolith, which leads him to use a bone as a tool, a weapon that helps his tribe reclaim the water hole. In one of the film's most famous sequences, the leader of the tribe throws the bone triumphantly into the air as the camera jump-cuts from the falling bone to an orbital satellite millions of years in the future, the starting point of the second part of the film, 'TMA-1'. The plot now focuses on Dr Heywood R. Floyd who travels to a US outpost on the Moon to investigate a reported incident at a moon base. Floyd discusses with Russian scientists the rumours of a mysterious epidemic at the base that are revealed to be a cover story to hide the discovery of a monolith identical to the one of the first part of the film. When Floyd joins a team that visits the monolith, they pose for a photograph in front of it when it starts emitting a high-pitched radio signal, and the film moves to the third and longest part of the film, 'Jupiter Mission'. The story takes place 18 months later aboard a spaceship on a classified mission to Jupiter whose operations are controlled by a sentient computer named HAL while most of the crew is in suspended animation. The two humans on duty, Dr David Bowman and Dr Frank Poole are getting suspicious of HAL's performance when he reports non-existent technical malfunctions and they consider deactivating it. The computer has been overhearing their conversation and when the two of them exit the spaceship to fix the reported faults, HAL severs Poole's oxygen hose and prevents Bowman from entering back into the ship, while it turns off the life support functions of the rest of the crew. Bowman manages to enter the ship and eventually deactivate HAL and then watches a pre-recorded video message from Dr Floyd, who reveals that the ship's mission is to trace the radio signal emitted by the monolith of the previous part that seems to originate from Jupiter. The last part of the film, 'Jupiter and Beyond the Infinite', presents Bowman's trip to Jupiter inside a pod in a psychedelic sequence that follows a tunnel of colour light as his pod races at great speed across vast distances of space. He finally finds himself middle-aged in a bedroom where he sees progressively older versions of himself until he becomes an elderly man lying in bed. Another black monolith appears next to the bed and when Bowman reaches for it he turns into a foetus-like creature that floats in space and ends up gazing at the Earth.

This is only a basic summary of a lengthy film whose merit lies less in its slow-paced plot and more in its look that still looks impressive and technically immaculate. Many of the film's shots look like still photographs. In its aspirations towards a 'non-verbal, universal experience', the film 'embodies the dream of absolute cinema' (Chion, 2001: v), a contemporary trend, mostly among European directors, towards a cinema relieved of the constraints of language and narrative. *2001* was intended to be a non-verbal experience that had to be seen rather than narrated, and seeing is very important in the plot itself whose character exchanges are often mediated through screens: we see Floyd speaking to his daughter through a monitor before he is scanned and questioned by another screen that lets him aboard the ship, whereas Poole and Bowman talk to their families through other screens and watch themselves on the news. The most representative scene in this respect would be the one in which HAL can understand Poole and Bowman's conversation about him while they've hidden in a pod to prevent it from overhearing them, only by monitoring them, by reading their lips. The self-reflexive nature of this film also lies in the recurrent imagery of eyes: we see a shot of a tiger's eye in the first part, HAL's eye observing the ship in the third, and several shots of Bowman's eye during the film's psychedelic sequence. *2001*, for Kubrick, was 'a visual experience, one that bypasses verbalised pigeonholing and directly penetrates the subconscious with an emotional and philosophical content' (cited in Kagan, 145).

Kubrick's references to inner levels of consciousness and to the emotional rather than the intellectual impact of the film betray its similarities with the New Wave of SF, which is perhaps one reason why established SF novelists reacted with hostility to the film. Lester del Rey, for instance, thought that this was not a 'normal science-fiction movie at all' but 'the first of the New Wave-Thing movies, with the usual empty symbolism' (38). Other writers chose to support Clarke's writing over Kubrick's cinema. Ray Bradbury, on the other hand, found the dialogue 'banal beyond extinction', and thought Kubrick was 'a very bad writer who got in the way of Arthur C. Clarke, who is a wonderful writer' (cited in Agel, 299). Responses like these make sense when looking at the differences between Kubrick's and Clarke's visions of this work. Clarke's novelization of the film describes an outward, expansionist Odyssey of an ingenious humanity that explores the universe with the help of their technology. Kubrick's film is closer to the spirit of the original Odyssey, it is a journey backwards, back to the origins of humanity, a return back to childhood. Unlike Clarke's novel, it is a film whose fascination with technical perfection and technological progress is in contrast to its cold and distant portrayal of human characters.

2001 is about evolution, both in a Darwinian sense and in a more spiritual sense of transcendence and rebirth. The first part of the film may be seen as a post-Darwinian Eden whose Tree of Knowledge is a monolith that helps the ape-men to stand on their feet for their first time. Later scenes or images of the film reproduce events of previous parts according to a cyclical narrative that leads to the final image of a newborn baby, a symbol of both a new beginning and of everyone's past. Michel Chion's suggestion that the 'impossibility of escaping from the cradle' is 'at the heart of Kubrick's work' (2) certainly applies to *2001*. However, this portrayal of humanity as a species in need of nurturing by a superior alien intelligence has been one of the most questionable aspects of the film. Norman Kagan has suggested that the film provides a very authoritarian story that 'preaches submission': 'All human accomplishments are implied to be automatic responses to the monolith's inspiration: "Make tools!" ... the only real superiority of the monolith is overwhelming power to manipulate and control. The monolith knows best, man is nothing. (161–2). Such a reading is certainly encouraged by the film's cold and alienating portrayal of humanity. The society of 'TMA-1' is devoid of feelings and emotions, the stewardesses serving technologically processed food on board of the spaceship are passionless and machine-like, a portrayal hardly flattering from a feminist perspective. This was one of the film's aspects criticized by Bradbury: 'what you're missing is humanity. There are no sympathetic characters' (cited in McAleer, 203). This is in stark contrast to the meticulously stylized sequences of spaceships that betray an almost fetishistic fascination with technical innovation in a film that portrays technology as becoming increasingly more powerful than the humans. One of the most succinct critiques of this aspect of the film was launched by Pauline Kael, who admired the beauty and elegance of Kubrick's film but objected to its passionless, almost inhuman characters: 'Kubrick's message is that people are disgusting but things are lovely' (68).

The Science Fiction Blockbuster: *Star Wars* (1977)

Whereas the period between the late 1950s and the late 1970s witnessed the release of a few noteworthy and commercially successful SF films, the genre's general popularity had declined considerably until the release of Spielberg's *Close Encounters* and Lucas's *Star Wars* in 1977, two films that marked what Vivien Sobchack describes as 'a sudden and radical shift in generic attitude and a popular renaissance of the SF film' (226). These two films signalled the rise of the SF film among the dominant genres to generate blockbuster movies. Spielberg's *Jaws* (1975) was the film that triggered the trend towards producing high-cost, high-tech, high-speed thrillers stylized with cutting-edge special effects and promoted with extensive cross-marketing. Films like *Jaws* and *Star Wars* epitomize the new tendency towards 'increasingly plot-driven' films that were 'increasingly visceral, kinetic and fast-paced, increasingly reliant on special effects, increasingly "fantastic" (and thus apolitical) and increasingly targeted at younger audiences' (Schatz, 30).

A second major feature of the generic shift identified by Sobchack lay in the genre's combination of a futuristic outlook – through the films' SF storylines and their recourse to state-of-the-art special effects – with a prevailing mood of nostalgia. The tremendous popularity of the movies by Spielberg and Lucas led to immediate attempts to replicate their success with other films such as *Superman* (Donner, 1978) or *Star Trek: The Motion Picture* (Wise, 1979). These, however, were not new stories but adaptations for the big screen of classic SF texts from comic books and television. Furthermore, part of the revival of the genre consisted in a series of remakes of classic films of the 1950s, such as *Invasion of the Body Snatchers* (Kauffman, 1978), *The Thing* (Carpenter, 1982) or *The Fly* (Cronenberg, 1986). This combination of futurism and nostalgia was, for Sobchack, 'clearly evidenced by *Star Wars*'s shiny evocation of the future as "Long, long ago ...", by *Close Encounters*' yearning for childhood rather than for its end and by the blatant pronouncement of the very title of *Back to the Future*' (229). The nostalgic mood of *Star Wars* did not lay just in its setting but also in its rich intertextual references to literally every previous stage in the history of SF.

An examination of the intertextual relations of *Star Wars* to the SF tradition helps understand the film's success as well as the reasons for which the SF film emerged as the dominant genre to generate blockbuster movies. The film's aim to provide a spectacular cinematic experience is reminiscent of the early cinematographers' attempts to experiment with the new medium of cinema during the period of short 'trickery films'. Its emphasis on plot over character is indebted to the work of pulp SF writers like Edgar Rice Burroughs and Edward E. Smith. *Star Wars* follows the tradition of the writings of Burroughs, as its plot is more action-driven than character-based and establishes clear-cut distinctions between heroes and villains, Good and Evil, Self and Other. Perhaps a stronger influence would be the writings of E. E. Smith, whose distinctive features include an effort at creating a sublime 'sense of wonder' through the evocation of tremendous power, size and scale in their plots where everything is magnified to vast proportions: stories about scientists with superior intelligence travelling in massive spaceships over millions of light years to destroy powerful enemies with super-powerful force-beams. This influence is evident in the very first shots of *Star Wars*, right after the opening text, where we see an enormous spaceship slowly entering the screen, and the Death Star – the artificial planet intent on destroying other planets – is a reference to one of Smith's Lensman stories featuring an entire planet aimed and fired at Earth at faster-than-light speeds.

The film's narrative pace, on the other hand, was indebted to movie serials of the 1930s such as *Flash Gordon*. The opening credits of *Star Wars* are a clear reference to the visual style of this series, whereas Darth Vader has been compared to Gordon's arch-enemy, Ming the Merciless. The influence of the serials, however, lies more in the way in which the plot reaches a climax every 15 minutes or so. The fact that the film was released as 'Episode 4' gives the sense that it starts *in medias res*, as if the audience is watching the fourth episode of a series. However, its clean-cut, well-spoken white heroes seemed as if they arrived from an idealized version of the 1950s, and the clear-cut division between Good and Evil may be seen as a metaphor for the polarities of the Cold War. In this sense, *Star Wars* was referencing classic works of the Golden Age of SF; its plot revolving around a decadent Empire reminiscent of texts such as Isaac Asimov's *Foundation* series, whereas its robots C3P0 and R2D2 seemed an allusion to Robbie the Robot from *Forbidden Planet* (Wilcox, 1956).

This combined attention to the new and the old attracted both dedicated SF fans that could recognize these references and other viewers who enjoyed the film as a new type of cinema. Its presentation of an old-fashioned romantic story with the aid of computer-driven camera effects attracted both male and female, older and younger audiences. The film's nostalgia, however, was also matched by its conservative cultural politics. Whereas *Star Wars* may seem like a radical film in its staging of a rebellion against an oppressive empire, this rebellion does not seem to challenge the gender stereotypes or race relations of its universe. Instead, the clear-cut distinctions between heroes and villains, Self and Other, seems to apply to its representations of women and members of different 'races'. The active heroes of the film are always men, whereas Princess Leia mainly serves the traditional stereotype of the damsel in distress. *Star Wars* is a male initiation narrative that stages Luke Skywalker's coming-of-age through his Oedipal conflict with Darth Vader, who is revealed in the sequel *The Empire Strikes Back* (Kershner, 1980) to be his biological father. Furthermore, the heroes and those who are in positions of authority are always white in the film. The rebels are clean-cut, white Americans who are friends with life-like machines, whereas the Empire's militarists are machine-like men and the villain of the story, Darth Vader, is presented as black. The aliens, on the other hand, who are supposed to stand in for ethnic variation are either represented as dangerous, as in the 'freak show' at the bar scene, or as sidekicks, as in the case of Chewbacca, the only alien among the small group of heroes. In *Star Wars*, Peter Lev has argued, 'man is the measure of all things' (34).

The film's conservatism was part of Lucas's wish to distance his work from the more experimental films of the 1960s like *2001* or the social critiques of the bleak dystopias of the 1970s, like *Soylent Green* (Fleischer, 1973) or *Logan's Run* (Anderson, 1976). *Star Wars* represents a conscious effort to return to traditional morality and family entertainment. According to Dale Pollock,

> Lucas wanted to present positive values to the audience. In the 1970s
> traditional religion was out of fashion and the family structure was

disintegrating. There was no moral anchor. Lucas remembered how protected he had felt growing up in the cocoonlike culture of the 1950s, a feeling he wanted to communicate in *Star Wars*. (143)

However, 'positive values' that serve to reinforce dominant social institutions like the nuclear family often disregard the interests of minority groups of gender, sexuality or race. Family values are often invoked in political campaigns of American conservative parties and the regressive, conservative politics of *Star Wars* has led critics to suggest that the film anticipated the rise and popularity of the neoconservative politics of Ronald Reagan during the 1980s. In fact, 'Star Wars' was the name chosen by Reagan for his Strategic Defence Initiative against the 'Evil Empire' of the Soviet Union during the 1980s. According to Michael Rogin, the film encapsulates a new 'alliance' between Hollywood and Washington that would be formed during the 1980s, whose president was a 'former actor who capitalised on his confusion of film with the world outside it' (28). This is not to suggest that Lucas is either responsible for or predicted the use that politicians would make of his film, but the fact that his ideas were put into these specific political and military ends is indicative of the underlying politics of the film itself.

Horror Science Fiction: *Alien* (1979)

Ridley Scott's *Alien* triggered a second major development of the SF film in the late 1970s. Its release at the same year with John Carpenter's *Halloween* brought about both a rebirth of the horror movie and its cross-fertilization with SF. Horror and SF – or, in the case of fiction, the Gothic – had always been in a constant dialogue with each other throughout their history. Classic Gothic novels such as Shelley's *Frankenstein* are now considered to be also seminal SF texts. Late Victorian fictions that have been foundational to the future development of SF demonstrate elements of body horror that are a direct influence of the Gothic tradition – Wells's Morlocks in *The Time Machine*, the animal hybrids of *The Island of Doctor Moreau* or the vampiric Martians of *War of the Worlds* would be some of the most representative examples. Classic Era films like *Invasion of the Body Snatchers*, *The Thing* or *The Fly* are also categorized as horror movies. But despite these connections, the futurist societies of SF films tended to be very clean, sterilized and antiseptic – *2001* has been seen as parodying the banal futures portrayed in the average SF film. *Alien*, by contrast, had a gritty realism in its portrayal of the spaceship *Nostromo*, whose dark and dirty interiors are more reminiscent of a submarine than a spaceship. Furthermore, any monstrous transformations or bodily amputations in earlier films were only hinted at or occurring off screen; *Alien* was the film to start a tendency to visualize these transformations onscreen

157

that would become a distinctive feature of both the 'new horror' and the 'horror SF' genre. This subgenre was distinguished by 'a further hyperbole of the body – a meticulous lingering upon the destruction or transformation of the human body' (Bukatman, *Terminal Identity*, 265). The most widely known example of this new tendency would be the work of David Cronenberg that includes films such as *Scanners* (1981), *Videodrome* (1983), *Dead Ringers* (1988) and *Crash* (1996). One of the most famous scenes of *Alien* is indicative of this new trend: after receiving an unknown transmission, the ship diverges from its return trip to Earth and members of the crew are sent to explore a derelict alien spaceship that is the source of the transmission. One of the crewmembers, Kane, discovers a chamber with alien eggs, one of which releases a creature that attaches to his face. Kane is brought back to the ship and the creature eventually falls dead, but soon afterwards, a new alien creature is 'born' by bursting out of Kane's chest. This scene had made people vomit in the first screenings of the film and is exemplary of the genre's focus on arousing horror through bodily penetration, mutilation and transformation. For Scott Bukatman, *Alien* signalled 'the return of the repressed – the body – to the *space* of the science fiction film' (*Terminal Identity*, 262). As he elaborates,

> The organic, almost intestinal, spaces of both the alien craft and the
> corridors of the Nostromo are invaded by a silicon-based life form
> that blends easily with the pipes and protrusions of human machinery
> … *Alien* is the film in which the *body* invades the pristine and sexless
> rational spaces of the science fiction films. The genre hasn't been the same
> since. (266–7)

Bukatman's discussion suggests that horror and monstrosity in the film emerges at the encounter between biology and technology; the alien's ability to blend with the machinery of *Nostromo* was 'doubled' by the crewmember Ash's ability to blend with the rest of the crew without them realizing that he is an android secretly assigned to the mission by the Corporation. In this respect, *Alien* prefigured the persistent concern with the interface between the human and the technological in cyberpunk novels and films of the next two decades, represented by the recurring imagery of cyborgs in films such as *The Terminator* (Cameron, 1984) and *Robocop* (Verhoeven, 1987). The film, however, also anticipated cyberpunk in its underlying critique of corporate capital; *Nostromo* is not a spaceship on a scientific mission, it is a commercial towing vehicle that, it is revealed towards the end, has been sent by the generically titled 'Company' to return the alien to Earth for the purpose of studying it even at the cost of the crew's lives. In this sense, the film presented 'a future in which the individual struggles to escape from the tyranny of the multinational' (James, 193).

The film's indebtedness to the horror tradition has invited interpretations from a psychoanalytic perspective. The 'alien birth' scene has been seen by Barbara Creed as a re-enactment of what Freud termed 'the primal scene', the childhood fantasy of witnessing parental intercourse for the sake of under-standing the 'mystery' of one's existence. For Creed, this was an identifying feature of the subgenre: 'One of the major concerns of the science fiction horror film (*Alien, The Thing, Invasion of the Body Snatchers, Altered States*) is the reworking of the primal scene in relation to the representation of other forms of copulation and procreation' (129). In fact, this theme seemed to be a recurring convention of the SF film: 'when smaller craft or bodies are ejected from the mother-ship into outer space; although sometimes the ejected body remains attached to the mother-ship by a long lifeline or umbilical cord' (130). A first interpretation of this concern might relate it to the genre's ontological concerns and its existential interrogations of human nature. For Creed, however, this was more consistent with the genre's gender politics. *Alien* was praised for its strong female leading character Ripley that would become one of the most classic SF heroines. The influence of the second wave of feminism of the 1970s was obvious in the screenplay that was written so that each character could be played by either a male or female actor. A closer examination, however, reveals the film's underlying gender politics to be less innocent. According to Creed, the persistent restaging of the primal scene in the film was part of its recurring scenes of monstrous or 'un-natural' reproduction and motherhood – the film's opening scene is a typical instance where the ship's computer, named 'Mother', awakens the crewmembers from suspended animation after receiving the mysterious signal, a 're-birthing scene which is marked by a fresh, antiseptic atmosphere' (129). The most obvious example, however, was the alien itself, which was read by Creed as a representation of 'the monstrous feminine', pre-Oedipal archetypes of motherhood dedicated exclusively to reproduction with no concern for the patriarchal Law which, however, are portrayed as monstrous in patriarchal genres such as the SF film. In Creed's own words, the 'archaic mother', whose defining characteristic is 'her total dedication to the generative, procreative principle' (135) is 'reconstructed and represented as a *negative* figure' in 'patri-archal signifying practices, particularly the horror film' (135). By contrast, 'there is an attempt in *Alien* to appropriate the procreative function of the mother, to represent a man giving birth, to deny the mother as signifier of sexual difference – but here birth can exist only as the other face of death' (136). Mary Anne Doane has discussed this mode of representation of the maternal in films like *Alien* with specific reference to 'the revolution in the development of technologies of reproduction (birth control, artificial insemination, *in vitro* fertilisation, surrogate motherhood, etc.)' that has brought about 'a contem-porary crisis in the realm of reproduction' and 'an overwhelming extension of the category of the maternal, now reaching monstrous proportions' (169). The 'horror' of these films lies in 'the traumatic impact of these technologies – their potential to disrupt given symbolic systems that construct the maternal and the paternal as stable positions. It is a trauma around which these films obsessively circulate and which they simultaneously disavow. (175)

Postmodern Science Fiction (I): *Blade Runner* (1982)

Ridley Scott's *Blade Runner* was hardly a commercial success at its first release and received very mixed responses by critics and audiences. Most of the negative reviews concentrated on the film's plot that was seen as too slow, predictable and clichéd. The voiceover of the main character Rick Deckard, added to the first 'cut' of the film after negative responses during preview screenings, did not help either – rumour has it that Harrison Ford intentionally delivered his lines as badly as he could in the hope that the voiceover would not be included in the film. Over the years, however, *Blade Runner* eventually earned a cult following, especially after the release of a 'director's cut' in 1992 without the voiceover and with a different ending, among other changes. By now it is considered a classic film and one of the most representative films of 1980s SF cinema.

A common praise, even during the film's first release, was, as with most of the above films, its visual aesthetic. In fact, *Blade Runner* is perhaps the most representative example of the self-reflexive nature of the SF film, as it abounds in images of viewscreens, photographs and eyes. One of the film's very first shots is the image of a disembodied eye staring at the cityscape of Los Angeles, followed by a sequence where Leon, one of the films androids – called 'replicants' – is subjected to the so-called 'Voigt-Kompff test', an 'empathy test' that determines whether the subject is a human or a replicant by concentrating on the subject's eye contractions during a series of emotionally provocative questions. One of the film's most well-known scene, it has been seen by Bukatman as a 'reflection on the status of the cinematic image' (*Blade Runner*, 46): during his mission to hunt down a group of renegade replicants that have returned to Earth illegally, Deckard is analyzing a photograph owned by Leon with a computer that zooms at different details of the photograph in search of evidence. The scene may be seen as symbolic of the act of film-making itself as Deckard sounds like a film director while giving instructions to the computer ('Track right … now pull back, pan left'). These are only a few instances of the recurring imagery of eyes, screens and photographs that have led Bukatman to describe the film as 'a drama about vision' (10).

Positive reviews of the film's visual style, however, concentrated specifically on its vision of a dark futurist Los Angeles, whose overcrowded areas were juxtaposed with abandoned neighbourhoods and derelict buildings and whose various different structures were demonstrating styles from diverse periods and places – Egyptian pyramids, Roman columns, Chinese dragons placed next to futuristic high-rise buildings and flying spaceships. This technique of juxtaposing the old and the new was called by designer Syd Mead as 'retrofitting': 'upgrading old machinery or structures by slapping new add-ons to them' (cited in Sammon, 79). A similar argument may be made for the film's generic identity. A loose adaptation of Philip K. Dick's novel *Do Androids Dream of Electric Sheep?*, with a title borrowed form a novel by William Burroughs, the film's visuals reminded of Lang's *Metropolis* or Batman's Gotham City – the latter originally considered to be the film's title by Scott – whereas its SF themes were combined with elements from film noir, the hardboiled detective novel or the Western. In this sense, the film may be seen as reproducing the combination of futurism and nostalgia established by *Star Wars*, but the way in which *Blade Runner* engaged with 'retro-futurism' was markedly different from Lucas's film. The juxtaposition of diverse styles from different periods and cultures is less indicative of a neoconservative nostalgia and more iconic of a defining feature of postmodern culture, what the neo-Marxist critic Fredric Jameson discussed as *pastiche*, an 'aesthetic of quotation' that 'incorporates dead styles' and 'attempts a recollection of the past, of memory, and of history' (Bruno, 67). Furthermore, its littered post-industrial cityscape was embodying the 'inverted millenarianism' of the postmodern in which, for Jameson, 'premonitions of the future, catastrophic or redemptive, have been replaced by the senses of the end of this or that' (1). Its juxtaposition of different cultures with advertising billboards and commercials embodies Jameson's central argument that the postmodern was marked by the increasing convergence of the cultural and the economic, of the Marxist base and superstructure, in a combined process of the commercialization of culture and the 'culturalization' of the economy – a process registered in works such as Andy Warhol's billboards of Campbell's soup cans or Coca Cola bottles. Postmodernism, for Jameson, represented the 'cultural logic of late capitalism', and *Blade Runner* was symptomatic of this logic even beyond its visual style, in its thematic preoccupation with themes such as the power of multinational corporations, represented in the film by the Tyrell Corporation, who were producing replicants. It is for this reason that the film is also often considered to be an example of cyberpunk cinema, a series of films released during the 1980s and 1990s such as *Robocop*, *Total Recall* (Verhoeven, 1990), *Johnny Mnemonic* (Longo, 1995), and *Strange Days* (Bigelow, 1995) amongst others.

On the other hand, the replicants have been read against the theory of another major philosopher of the postmodern, Jean Baudrillard's theory of simulation and hyperreality. For Baudrillard, the proliferation of media technologies in every aspect of advanced capitalist societies in the West had led to a general perception and experience of the mediated image as more 'real' than the real itself, as 'hyperreal'. Humanity had immersed itself in a universe of simulation – 'the generation by models of a real without origin or reality' (*Simulacra*, 1). Mediated images are no longer copies but simulacra – copies of other copies with no originals. In a classic article on *Blade Runner*, Giuliana Bruno has suggested that the film's replicants provide 'almost a literalisation of Baudrillard's theory of postmodernism as the age of simulacra and simulation' (67). *Blade Runner* blurs the distinctions between humans and replicants more than Dick's original novel and encourages the audience to sympathize with their replicants. The main theme of Dick's novel was Deckard's gradual dehumanization during his hunt for androids that were cruel, cold and heartless. Scott's replicants, on the other hand, have the ability to develop emotions and empathy when their mental circuits reach a certain level of complexity, which is why a self-destruct mechanism incorporated in their design is activated after a four-year cycle. The replicants are near the end of their lifespan and therefore emotionally developed – for instance, their leader Roy Batty is reluctant to reveal to Pris the deaths of Leon and Zhora and he cries when Pris dies as well. However, from the opening Voigt-Kompff test scene the film establishes empathy as one of the defining features of the human, and in this respect this difference between novel and film is one of the main ways in which *Blade Runner* blurs the boundaries between the human and the replicant. A second way is its engagement with the intertwined themes of memory and history, represented by the photographs that the replicants cling to in order to affirm a sense of a past, a history and an identity. When Rachael, first introduced in the film as Tyrell's assistant, is revealed to be a replicant despite her knowledge, she visits Deckard to show him a photograph of herself with her mother when she was a child, but Deckard reveals to her that her memories belong to Tyrell's niece. Even if this may suggest, at a first level, that this is indicative of the pervasiveness of commodification under late capitalism, which reaches areas as personal as memory and identity, it is more the case that even human memory has been theorized as malleable and subject to revision. In fact, it is through the film's engagement with the theme of memory that the film, particularly the director's cut, suggests that Deckard himself may be a replicant, through the addition of a sequence where Deckard dreams of a unicorn. In that version's final scene, Deckard is just about to run away with Rachael when he stumbles upon a parting gift from officer Gaff, a small tin-foil unicorn that suggests that he could access Deckard's implanted dreams.

For all its exemplary representations of postmodern culture, the film has received critiques for its identity politics, and specifically its representations of gender. As in the film that it quotes, *Metropolis*, the portrayal of women in *Blade Runner* falls within the virgin/whore dichotomy in which female characters are either innocent and docile, like Rachael, or promiscuous and aggressive, like Iris and Zhora. The scene where Deckard is almost forcing Rachael to have sex with him and admit that she loves him in particular makes for uncomfortable viewing. The film is essentially a male narrative: whereas the plot begins by concentrating on the quest of the replicants to find their creator Tyrell and request to extend their lifespan, by the end of the film this quest has been converted to an Oedipal confrontation between their leader Roy and his 'father'. *Blade Runner* certainly invites such an interpretation as Roy kills Tyrell when he finds out that an extension of their life cycle is not possible by crushing his skull and poking his thumbs through Tyrrell's eyes in one more detail that focuses on eyes that reproduces 'the Oedipal topos of blindness recurs, reversed' (Bruno, 1987: 71). 'In the scene in which Roy kills Tyrell', Bruno suggests, he '*simulates* the Oedipus complex' (172)

Postmodern Science Fiction (II): *The Matrix* (1999)

Unlike *Blade Runner, The Matrix* was a film that was hailed as a classic SF film fairly soon after its release. The wide perception of the film as a new type of SF cinema only affirmed its status of a postmodern text whose claim to 'newness' lay in its heavy use of a pastiche of themes, motifs and imagery from previous SF texts. Its hackers, underground clubs, cybernetic implants, mirror shades and its central concept of the Matrix seemed to disprove Bruce Sterling's announcement that '[c]yberpunk is not there anymore'. Its major premise that everyday 'reality' is not real was a recurring theme of the work of Philip K. Dick, whose work received increasing attention by Hollywood from the release of *Blade Runner* onwards, in film adaptations of his works such as *Total Recall* (1990), *Screamers* (Duguay, 1995), *Minority Report* (Spielberg, 2002) and *A Scanner Darkly* (Linklater, 2006). At the same time, the film's visual style and action scenes recalled Japanese anime, manga and King Fu movies, combined with elements from the American super hero movie, the romance and the Western. Its AIs appeared to be out of *Men in Black* (Sonnenfeld, 1997), whereas the messianic role of Neo recalled Luke Skywalker in *Star Wars*. The film's Christian symbolism was also reminiscent of *The Day the Earth Stood Still*: Neo is the 'One' who becomes a Christ-like figure that dies and is reborn to redeem mankind with the help of a character named Trinity, whereas Cipher may be seen as enacting the part of Judas. The Christian references were combined with allusions to other religions, philosophies, mythologies and fairy tales – Buddhist ideas of reality, ancient Greek mythological figures like Morpheus, references to Socrates's 'Know Thyself', the White Rabbit of *Alice in Wonderland*, amongst others.

The central conceit of the film was self-consciously relying on Baudrillard's philosophy; the phrase 'the desert of the real' is a direct quotation from

Simulations and Simulacra, a copy of which is shown in an early scene of the film. An earlier draft of the film's script from 1996 in fact has Morpheus directly referring to the work of Baudrillard, and the Wachowskis approached the philosopher to request that he collaborated for the two sequels. His decline of the offer is understandable both for the way in which his theory was incorporated in the plot and for the type of cinema that *The Matrix* represents. Baudrillard used to be much less critical of the medium of cinema; unlike television, that was always described as a cold, indifferent and banal medium, cinema was discussed by Baudrillard as a 'special ceremonial' (*Symbolic,* 31), a modern ritualistic experience whereby a group of people gather in a dark space to share a common experience. This was the case, however, for the traditional filmmaking of classical Hollywood, unlike the CGI-driven blockbuster cinema whose development marked a 'trajectory from the more fantastic and the mythical to the realistic and the hyperrealistic' (*Simulacra,* 46). One is left to wonder, then, to what extent a film that is exemplary of this type of cinema is capable of articulating a critique of the hyperreal universe of which it is a part. If there was anything distinctively new about *The Matrix,* it was not its plot but its innovative use of special effect technology and it was often discussed mainly for its use of the technique of 'bullet-time', a shot sequence where the frame appears to freeze in time, and the camera angle turns around 180 degrees or more around static actors – a technique often parodied in films such as *Scary Movie* (Wayans, 2001) or *Shrek* (Adamson and Jenson, 2001). According to William Merrin, it is 'the technical capacities of the medium' that are 'the point and the advertised star of the film'; what attracted audiences was precisely the *look* of the film, its 'cybernoir tones, shades, and metals of the fashion and technology on display'. For Merrin, this is *'film itself* as a techno-chic object of consumption; as style, statement, and pure sign-object'. And whereas this argument reaffirms the self-reflexive quality of SF cinema, it problematizes the film's engagement with its subject matter. If the plot of *The Matrix* stages a rebellion against the universe of simulation, its very form and style embraces the film's object of critique.

The problems with the film's application of Baudrillard's philosophy are even more obvious in the way in which his theory of hyperreality has been incorporated in the plot. If the everyday life of 1999 is revealed to be an intricate virtual reality in which humanity lives with no memory of its enslavement by evil Artificial Intelligences in the future, underneath this simulation exists the real post-apocalyptic world of 2199 where humans are grown in pods that drain their 'bioelectric energy' for the maintenance of the Matrix. In this sense the film reproduces the distinction between 'appearance' and 'reality' that has been the topic of philosophical speculation since the days of ancient Greece, a distinction that Baudrillard's postmodern philosophy sought to challenge. The main point about his theory of hyperreality is that this distinction does not exist anymore: simulation is not opposed to reality, it *is* reality. As Merrin points out, the only scene from *The Matrix* that comes closer to conveying this aspect of Baudrillard's philosophy is the one in which Neo watches everyday life from inside his car with a confused look as he is struggling to reconcile with the fact that this is an electronic illusion: 'We do not have to look to the year 2199 for this: the virtualisation of everyday life is already well underway'. Baudrillard himself underlined this misinterpretation of his work in the film where 'the new problem posed by simulation' was 'confused with its classical, Platonic treatment' (2004). Indeed, the film's portrayal of simulation seems less indebted to Baudrillard's theory and more to Plato's 'theory of forms', according to which abstract forms and ideas are more real and easy to understand than material objects.

The film's engagement with this specific topic was only the culmination of a trend of 'virtual reality' films in SF cinema during the decade that saw the explosion of the Internet: whereas the trend started with *Tron* (Lisberger, 1982), it gained pace with films such as *The Lawnmower Man* (Leonard, 1992), *The Thirteenth Floor* (Rusnak, 1999) and *eXistenZ* (Cronenberg,1999), among others, demonstrating 'a depthless sense of space and of infinite spatial relationships' and 'an aesthetic of the limitless and the borderless, of groundless life' (Redmond, 138). Films like these were made alongside the formations of the first online communities and discussions on 'cybercultures' in academic discussions, accompanied by a recurring argument on the extent to which reality itself had already become 'science-fictionali,ed' after the advent of space travel, satellite networks, information technology and mobile communications. Donna Haraway had suggested in her 'Cyborg Manifesto' that 'the boundary between science fiction and social reality has become an optical illusion' whereas for Istvan Csicsery-Ronay Jr, science fiction had 'ceased to be a genre *per se*, becoming instead a mode of awareness about the world.' (308). Indeed, *The Matrix* was shortly caught up in a curious, uncanny relationship with 'reality': two years after the release of the film, Slavoj Žižek was comparing the terrorist attacks of 9/11 to the scene in the film where Morpheus awakens Neo to 'the desert of the Real': 'Was it not something of a similar order that took place in New York on September 11? Its citizens were introduced to the "desert of the real" – for us, corrupted by Hollywood, the landscape and the shots of the collapsing towers could not but be reminiscent of the most breathtaking scenes in big catastrophe productions' (15). Not unexpectedly, imagery of 9/11 would proliferate in SF films produced after the attacks, such as *Ever Since the World Ended* (Grant and Little, 2001), *28 Days Later* (Boyle, 2002), *War of the Worlds* (Spielberg, 2005) or *Children of Men* (Cuarón, 2006), but the fact the event itself was briefly mistaken for a disaster movie by many people switching on their TV set that morning was only proof of the primacy of simulation over reality registered in *The Matrix*.

The film's engagement with terrorism enhanced these associations even further. *The Matrix* is a 'home-based terrorist allegory' (Redmond, 138) where Neo leads the terrorist project organized by Morpheus that has been described by Merrin as 'a hyper-paranoid, anarcho-libertarianism, combining Old Testament fundamentalism, new-age mysticism, *X-Files* hyper-conspiracy, backwoods militia, Japanese doomsday cult, and a proto-Fascistic aestheticisation of violence, fashion, and military hardware'. From this perspective, it makes less sense to see the film as 'anticipating' 9/11 and more as symptomatic of the climate generated by events such as the Oklahoma City Bombing, the Heaven's Gate suicide cult or the first terrorist attempt at the World Trade Center. The climate of terrorism is a major reason for the re-emergence of the invasion narrative during the decade. According to Sean Redmond, films such as *Species* (Donaldson, 1995), *Independence Day* (Emmerich, 1996), *Mars Attacks!* (Burton, 1996) or *Starship Troopers* (Verhoeven, 1997) 'speak to the fear of terrorism and to "wish for" terrorist acts' (137–8), even as they were 'wholly in keeping with *fin-de-siècle* fantasy' (Keane, 75) generated by the advent of the millennium.

Finally, a plot detail of *The Matrix* that perhaps has not been given enough critical attention renders the film representative of another trend in contemporary SF cinema: the Matrix is sustained by the 'bioelectric energy' of the humans of 2199, who are grown in vast fields and kept alive in pods, plugged into a massive energy-generating tower. The imagery in these short scenes is reminiscent of the Oscar-winning work of Swiss artist H. R. Giger for *Alien* and that part of the story is representative of a different orientation in the genre towards the limits and the economy of the body in the days of the Human Genome Project, biological warfare and global epidemics – films figuring viruses and epidemics such as *12 Monkeys* (Gilliam, 1995), or *28 Days Later,* or cloning and genetic engineering such as *Gattaca* (Niccol, 1997) and *The Island* (Bay, 2005). The film, in this respect, is representative of an emerging dialectic in SF cinema between movies that register the immersion of the human subject in virtual environments and those that concentrate more directly to the corporeal nature of human subjectivity.

Works Cited

Adamson, Andrew and Vicky Jenson (dirs) (2001). *Shrek.*
Agel, Jerôme (1970). *The Making of Kubrick's 2001.* New York: Signet.
Aldiss, Brian and Wingrove, David (1986). *Trillion Year Spree: The History of Science Fiction.* London: Gollancz.
Anderson, Michael (dir.) (1976). *Logan's Run.*
Baudrillard, Jean (1993 [1973]). *Symbolic Exchange and Death.* London: Sage.

—(1994). *Simulacra and Simulation*. Trans. S. F. Glaser. Ann Arbor: University of Michigan Press.

—(2004). '*The Matrix* Decoded: *Le Nouvel Observateur* Interview with Jean Baudrillard'. Trans. G. Genosko. *International Journal of Baudrillard Studies*. 1.2. Available online: http://www.ubishops.ca/baudrillardstudies/vol1_2/ genosko.htm. [accessed 3 March 2013].

Bay, Michael (dir.) (2005). *The Island*.

Bigelow, Kathryn (dir.) (1995). *Strange Days*.

Bignell, Jonathan (1999). 'Another Time, Another Space: Modernity, Subjectivity, and *The Time Machine*'. *Alien Identities: Exploring Difference in Film and Fiction*. Deborah Cartmell, I.Q. Hunter, Heidi Kaye and Imelda Whelehan (eds). London: Pluto Press. 87–103

Boglanovich, Peter (1967). *Fritz Lang in America*. London: Studio Vista.

Bould, Mark (2003). 'Film and Television'. *The Cambridge Companion to Science Fiction*. Edward James and Farah Mendlesohn (eds). Cambridge: Cambridge University Press. 79–95.

Boyle, Danny (dir.) (2002). *28 Days Later*.

Bukatman, Scott (1993). *Terminal Identity: The Virtual Subject in Postmodern Science Fiction*. Durham and London: Duke University Press.

—(1997). *Blade Runner*. London: British Film Institute.

Bruno, Giuliana. (1987). 'Postmodernism and *Blade Runner*'. *October* 41. 61–74.

Burton, Tim (dir.) (1996). *Mars Attacks!*

Cameron, James (dir.) (1984). *The Terminator*.

Carpenter, John (dir.) (1982). *The Thing*.

Chion, Michel (2001). *Kubrick's Cinema Odyssey*. Trans. C. Gorbman. London: British Film Institute.

Creed, Barbara (1990). '*Alien* and the Monstrous-Feminine'. *Alien Zone: Cultural Theory and Contemporary Science Fiction Cinema*. Annette Kuhn (ed.). London: Verso. 128–41.

Cronenberg, David (dir.) (1981). *Scanners*.

—(1983). *Videodrome*.

—(1986). *The Fly*.

—(1988). *Dead Ringers*.

—(1996). *Crash*.

—(1999). *eXistenZ*.

Csicsery-Ronay Jr, Istvan (1991). 'Science Fiction and Postmodernism'. *Science Fiction Studies* 18:3, 305–8.

Cuarón, Alfonso (dir.) (2006). *Children of Men*.

Doane, Mary Anne. (1990). 'Technophilia: Technology, Representation, and the Feminine'. *Body/Politics: Women and the Discourses of Science*. Mary Jacobus, Evelyn Fox Keller, and Sally Shuttleworth (eds). London: Routledge, 163–76.

Donaldson, Roger (dir.) (1995). *Species*.

Donner, Richard (dir.) (1978). *Superman*.

Duguay, Christian (dir.) (1995). *Screamers*.

Emmerich, Ronald (dir.) (1996). *Independence Day*.

Fleischer, Richard (dir.) (1973). *Soylent Green*.

Gance, Abel (dir.) (1931). *The End of the World*.

Gillam, Terry (dir.) (1995). *12 Monkeys*.

Godard, Jean-Luc (dir.) (1965). *Alphaville*.

Grant, Callum and Little, Joshua Atesh (dirs) (2001). *Ever Since the World Ended*.

Gunning, Tom (1990). 'The Cinema of Attractions: Early Film, Its Spectator and the Avant-Garde'. *Early Film: Space, Frame, Narrative*. Thomas Elsaesser (ed.). London: British Film Institute. 56–62.

Haskin, Byron (dir.) (1953). *War of the Worlds*.

Hubbard, Lucien (dir.) (1929). *The Mysterious Island*.

Huyssen, Andreas (2000). 'The Vamp and the Machine: Fritz Lang's *Metropolis*'. *Fritz Lang's Metropolis: Cinematic Visions of Technology and Fear*. Michael Minden and Holger Bachmann (eds). Rochester, NY: Camden House. 198–217.

James, Edward (1994). *Science Fiction in the 20th Century*. Oxford: Oxford University Press.

Jameson, Fredric (1991). *Postmodernism or, the Cultural Logic of Late Capitalism*. London: Verso.

Jancovich, Mark and Johnston, Derek (2009). 'Film and Television, the 1950s'. *The Routledge Companion to Science Fiction*. Mark Bould, Andrew M. Butler, Adam C. Roberts and Sherryl Vint (eds). London: Routledge. 71–80

Kael, Pauline (1975). 'Kubrick's Golden Age'. *New Yorker*. (27 Dec). 68.

Kagan, Norman (1972). *The Cinema of Stanley Kubrick*. New York: Continuum.

Kaufmann, Philip (dir.) (1978). *Invasion of the Body Snatchers*.

Keane, Stephen (2001). *Disaster Movies: The Cinema of Catastrophe*. London: Wallflower.

Kershner, Irvin (dir.) (1980). *The Empire Strikes Back*.

King, Geoff and Krzywinska, Tanya (2000). *Science Fiction Cinema: From Outerspace to Cyberspace*. London: Wallflower.

Kracauer, Siegfried (1947). *From Caligari to Hitler: A Psychological History of the German Film*. New York: Princeton University Press.

Kubrick, Stanley (dir.) (1968). *2001: A Space Odyssey*.

Lang, Fritz (dir.) (1927). *Metropolis*.

Leonard, Brett (dir.) (1992). *The Lawnmower Man*.

Lev, Peter (1998). 'Whose Future? *Star Wars*, *Alien* and *Blade Runner*'. *Literature/Film Quarterly*. 26. 1.30–7.

Linklater, Richard (dir.) (2006). *A Scanner Darkly*.

Lisberger, Steven (dir.) (1982). *Tron*.

Longo, Robert (dir.) (1995). *Johnny Mnemonic*.

Lucas, George (dir.) (1977). *Star Wars*.

Lumière, Auguste and Louis (dirs) (1895). *Arrival of a Train*
—(1895). *Mechanical Butcher*.

Marker, Chris (dir.) (1965). *La Jetée*.

McAleer, Neil (1992). *Arthur C. Clarke: The Authorised Biography*. Chicago: Contemporary Books.

Méliès, Georges (dir.) (1902). *A Trip to the Moon*.

Menzies, William Cameron (dir.) (1926). *Things to Come.*
—(1953). *Invaders from Mars.*
Merrin, William (2003). '"Did You Ever Eat Tasty Wheat?": Baudrillard and *The Matrix'. Scope: An Online Journal of Film Studies.* Available online: http://www. scope.nottingham.ac.uk/article.php?issue=may2003&id=257&section=article [accessed 3 March 2013].
Mulvey, Laura ([1975] 1992). 'Visual Pleasure and Narrative Cinema'. *The Sexual Subject: A Screen Reader in Sexuality.* Mandy Merck (ed.). London: Routledge, 22–34
Neumann, Kurt (dir.) (1950). *Rocketship X-M.*
Niccol, Andrew (dir.) (1997). *Gattaca.*
Pichel, Irving (dir.) (1950). *Destination Moon.*
Pollack, Dale (1990). *Skywalking: The Life and Films of George Lucas.* Hollywood: Samuel French.
Porter, Edwin (dir.) (1904). *Dog Factory.*
Protozanov, Yakov (dir.) (1924). *Aelita.*
Redmond, Sean (2009). 'Film Since 1980'. *The Routledge Companion to Science Fiction.* Mark Bould et al. (eds). London: Routledge. 134–43.
del Rey, Lester (1969). 'Review of *2001: A Space Odyssey'. Best SF: 1968.* Brian W. Aldiss and Harry Harrison (eds). New York: Putnam, 38.
Roberts, Adam (2000). *Science Fiction.* London: Routledge.
Rogin, Michael (1998). *Independence Day, or How I Learned to Stop Worrying and Love the Enola Gay.* London: British Film Institute.
Rusnak, Josef (dir.) (1999). *The Thirteenth Floor.*
Sammon, Paul (1996). *Future Noir: The Making of Blade Runner.* New York: HarperCollins.
Scanlon, Paul (1977). 'The Force Behind George Lucas: Interview with George Lucas by Paul Scanlon'. *Rolling Stone.* (25 Aug), *43.*
Schaffner, Franklin J. (dir.) (1968). *The Planet of the Apes.*
Schatz, Thomas (2003). 'The New Hollywood'. *Movie Blockbusters.* Julian Stringer (ed.). London: Routledge. 15–44.
Scott, Ridley (dir.) (1979). *Alien.*
—(1982). *Blade Runner.*
Sears, Fred F. (dir.) (1956). *Earth vs. the Flying Saucers.*
Siegel, Don (dir.) (1956). *Invasion of the Body Snatchers.*
Sobchack, Vivien (1993). *Screening Space: The American Science Fiction Film.* New York: Ungar.
Sonnenfeld, Barry (dir.) (1997). *Men in Black.*
Spielberg, Steven (dir.) (1975). *Jaws*
—(1977). *Close Encounters of the Third Kind.*
—(1982). *E. T.: The Extra-Terrestrial.*
—(2002). *Minority Report.*
—(2005). *War of the Worlds.*
Sterling, Bruce (1998). 'Cyberpunk in the Nineties'. *Interzone.* 23 May. Available at: http://lib.ru/STERLINGB/interzone.txt. [accessed 3 March 2013].

Tarkovsky, Andrei (dir.) (1972). *Solaris.*

Telotte, J. P. (2009). 'Film, 1895-1950.' *The Routledge Companion to Science Fiction.* Mark Bould et al. (eds). London: Routledge. 42–51

Verhoeven, Paul (dir.) (1987). *Robocop.*

—(1990). *Total Recall.*

—(1997). *Starship Troopers.*

Wachowskis (dirs.) (1999). *The Matrix.*

Wayans, Keenan (dir.) (2001). *Scary Movie.*

Wells, H. G. (1895). *The Time Machine.* London: Heinemann.

Wilcox, Fred (dir.) (1956). *Forbidden Planet.*

Wise, Robert (dir.) (1951). *The Day the Earth Stood Still.*

—(1979). *Star Trek: The Motion Picture.*

Zemeckis, Robert (dir.) (1982). *Back to the Future.*

Žižek, Slavoj (2002). *Welcome to the Desert of the Real.* London: Verso.

Science Fiction Criticism

Andrew M. Butler

Chapter Overview

Introduction

There is a moment in the first issue of *Amazing Stories* when Hugo Gernsback describes the magazine as specializing in a kind of 'a charming romance intermingled with scientific fact and prophetic vision [...]. Not only do these amazing tales make tremendously interesting reading [...] [t]hey supply knowledge [...] in a very palatable form' (3). He dubbed it 'scientifiction', although readers relabelled it 'science fiction' and abbreviated it to 'stf' or 'sf'. While there had been earlier SF – Gernsback lists Edmund Bellamy, Jules Verne, Edgar Allan Poe and H. G. Wells, and the mode might be traced back to Mary Shelley or Lucian of Samosata – this editorial coalesced SF as a genre. While, like most genres, it is impossible to define, the field is shaped by the statements and criticisms of its authors, editors and readers in the discourse about the form. Damon Knight (1956) argued that science fiction was what people pointed at when they said 'science fiction'; the writings on SF of critics, reviewers and academics form a corpus outlining where an interpretive community is pointing. This chapter will give an overview of the history of SF criticism, emphasizing the post-1968 era when academic study blossomed in the wake of student protests on campuses across the world. I discuss eight loose groupings, by necessity omitting some key names because their work cannot be reduced so easily to a category – M. Elizabeth Ginway, Roz Kaveney, Rob Latham, Roger Luckhurst, Kathleen L. Spencer, Patricia Warrick and Gary Westfahl all spring to mind as unique and varied voices from whom I have learned much. The chapter is also inclined towards the Anglophone critics and to analysts of prose fiction.

The First Science Fiction Critics

Early SF magazines began the practice of printing readers' letters commenting on stories, and some of these readers, who began to identify themselves as fans, also wrote to each other. They started publishing their own amateur or fan magazine (fanzines), the first of these probably being *The Comet* in 1930. Not all of them actually discuss SF – some fanzines are a semi-public autobiography of or platform for the individual fan, often confessional, but usually leavened with humour. At the other extreme, some fans have produced a significant body of critical work – K. V. Bailey, John Foyster, Bruce Gillespie, Jeanne Gomoll, Paul Kincaid, David Langford, Cheryl Morgan, Jeffery Smith, Maureen Kincaid Speller and Susan Wood, to pick ten names at random – that on occasions has appeared in professional or academic venues, although criticism is no less important for being non-professional. Fans have worked to catalogue the genre, to create archives or, in the case of the Hugo Awards, to recognize achievements in the field by writers, artists, editors and fans. In Australia, Bruce Gillespie edited the fanzine *SF Commentary* from 1968, publishing among other things significant criticism by and on Stanisław Lem, Philip K. Dick and Christopher Priest. *Foundation*, a British academic journal, is published by the Science Fiction Foundation, which was largely formed by fans. Fans have also had significant input into the Science Fiction Research Association. The interaction between fans and academics has been fruitful, although occasionally hostile. The fan Dena Brown wrote 'Let's take science fiction out of the classroom and put it back in the gutter where it belongs' on a blackboard at the Science Fiction Research Association meeting in 1971. When James Kneale and myself were trying to set up a network of people interested in the fantastic in the early 1990s, one professor warned us that we would be 'deluged' by amateur enthusiasts.

Author Critics

Authors have also reviewed other authors, Lem and Priest have both been mentioned, as has Knight – who became notorious for 'Cosmic Jerrybuilder:

A. E. van Vogt', and whose early criticism was collected in *In Search of Wonder* (1956). Novelist James Blish wrote criticism under the pseudonym William Atheling Jr – collected in *The Issue at Hand* (1964) and *More Issues at Hand* (1970) – and writers such as Damian Broderick, Avram Davidson, Thomas Disch, M. John Harrison, Colin Greenland, Gwyneth Jones, Ursula Le Guin, Joanna Russ and many more have reviewed SF for magazines, or written autobiographical reflections on their own fiction. One early book-length work on SF – actually a collection of lectures – was *New Maps of Hell* (1960), by British novelist Kingsley Amis. The British SF writer Brian Aldiss wrote a literary history of the genre, *Billion Year Spree* (1973), which situated Mary Shelley's *Frankenstein* (1818) as the first true work of SF and argued that the form focused on 'the search for a definition of man and his status in the universe which will stand in our advanced but confused state of knowledge (science) and is characteristically cast in the Gothic or post-Gothic mould' (8). John Clute is one example of someone who has moved in the other direction from critic to novelist. Since the 1960s he has been one of the most challenging and honest of the genre's analysts, although arguably his work has suffered from a piecemeal approach that has precluded the emergence of a unified agenda. His third edition of the *Encyclopedia of Science Fiction* looks set to be a gold standard for reference works in the field.

Perhaps the most sophisticated analysis of SF by a professional fiction author is to be found in the work of Samuel R. Delany, who in 'About Five Thousand One Hundred and Seventy Five Words' (1969) defined SF as a reading protocol, in which readers interpreted the individual words of SF sentences in terms of a science-fictional world. In a realist novel, 'Her world exploded' would be a metaphor for someone having a bad day; in SF it would be a literal description of an apocalypse. Delany describes how each new word modifies meaning in the science-fictional sentence 'The red sun was high, the blue low', describing an imaginary world. Alongside collections, beginning with *The Jewel-Hinged Jaw* (1977), Delany also wrote a book-length semiotic study of Thomas M. Disch's 'Angouleme' (1971), *The American Shore* (1978), splitting the story down into tiny analyzable fragments or lexemes. Delany's interest in semiotics, Roland Barthes, Jacques Derrida and Michel Foucault, was to feed into his own fiction, especially the *Return to Nevèrÿon* sequence (1979–87).

Marxist Criticism

Karl Marx and Frederick Engels's engagement with the work of Robert Owen, Charles Fourier and other Utopian socialists in *The Communist Manifesto* (1848) offers the first Marxist analysis of SF, criticizing the various possible futures envisaged because they were not sufficiently radical or communist. Raymond

Williams published a short piece in a 1956 edition of *The Highway*, a Workers' Education Association journal, recommending three types of SF as being worth serious attention: putropia (Utopian fiction for a populist audience), doomsday (various apocalyptic scenarios) and space anthropology (imaginative traveller's tales). In response to the SF trope of a division between a rational few and the masses, Williams worries that 'to think, feel, or even speak of people in terms of "masses" is to make the burning of the books and the destroying of the cities just that much more possible' (1988: 358), noting the alienation which individuals feel as part of being faced with the mass market. Williams's piece was largely forgotten, although he taught Patrick Parrinder, an H. G. Wells expert, and suggested to him the idea for the edited collection *Science Fiction: A Critical Guide* (1979). Parrinder's monograph *Science Fiction: Its Criticism and Teaching* (1980) still deserves attention for its resistance to a totalizing model of SF as unified in favour of concentrating on its relations to the romance, the fable and the epic.

The first major theorization of SF occurred within a Marxist paradigm, in the work of Darko Suvin. Suvin took the ideas underlying the theatrical practice of *Verfremdungseffekt* – estrangement or alienation – from the German playwright Bertolt Brecht. Brecht wanted his audiences to think through the ideas of his plays, rather than simply empathize with his characters, and used a number of techniques to wake them up in their viewing. When reading a work of SF, the reader becomes conscious that they are observing a different world from their own which is unfamiliar to them; when they are then faced with the real world, they may see it in a new way. But the reader does not come to the fictional world entirely as a blank tablet to be impressed upon – the reader has a sense of the structures and interrelationships within the world they are familiar with, and comes to the fiction with the same sense of expectations. This process is known as cognition, and is associated with knowledge, especially scientific, logical knowledge. Brecht connects cognition to Galileo's ability to deduce the path of a pendulum from observation of its swing. Having seen a chandelier move, Galileo could predict the motion of a clock pendulum. By analogy, the reader of SF takes their expectations of how the world works – especially in the realm of scientific knowledge – and uses them to build up a series of assumptions about the fictional world being described by the SF writer. Suvin thus defines SF as a 'literary genre whose necessary and sufficient conditions are the presence and interaction of estrangement and cognition, and whose main formal device is an imaginative frame-work alternative to the author's empirical environment' (1979: 9) – to some extent the notion of 'cognition' maps on to science, the 'estrangement' on to fiction, although the two impulses are connected in a sort of dialectical relationship, in the oscillation between the familiar being unrecognizable and recognizing the unfamiliar, the fictional science and scientific-flavoured fiction.

Suvin borrowed the term 'novum' from the Marxist Ernst Bloch to describe the textual unit of novelty, such as 'spaceship', 'ray gun', 'Martian', which would be part of the estrangement of the reader and which would be in need of a cognitive reading to explain. Nova include invented vocabulary and terminology, which need to be decoded from context rather than through an authorial explanation. While the concept of the novum has remained a mainstay of SF criticism, it was this that Delany objected to and countered with his earlier described sense of SF as a reading protocol (1969), arguing that there could be a work of SF that described unfamiliar experiences without resorting to neologisms.

Suvin's coinage of 'cognitive estrangement' as definitional of SF has become part of the critical orthodoxy of SF, although it often excludes a large amount of the genre. Suvin's book-length accounts of SF – such as *Metamorphoses of Science Fiction* (1979), *Victorian Science Fiction in the UK* (1983) and *Positions and Presuppositions in SF* (1988) – have focused more on nineteenth-century works than pulp SF, and exclude many works, such as Robert Louis Stevenson's *Strange Case of Dr Jekyll and Mr Hyde* (1886), from the genre's canon. For many years he dismissed fantasy from consideration, a position criticized by China Miéville in 'Cognition as Ideology: A Dialectic of SF theory' (2009), but he has written about it in 'Considering the Sense of "Fantasy" or "Fantasy Fiction": An Effusion' (2000). As an early editor of *Science Fiction Studies* he helped edit special issues on Dick and Le Guin, part of the process of canonizing those authors, and has since written on Soviet SF, William Gibson and cyberpunk, as well as returning to Dick and Le Guin.

Along with Suvin, early issues of *Science Fiction Studies* featured essays by Peter Fitting and Fredric Jameson, which gained the journal a reputation for being Marxist – indeed Dick allegedly wrote to the FBI about his fears of a visit by Fitting and Jameson to discuss his work. The journal subsequently widened its scope, and was to include much work on postmodernism, and it remains the most theoretically inflected of the major SF academic journals. Fitting contributed an essay on Dick to the 1975 special issue, '*Ubik*: The Deconstruction of Bourgeois SF', which in part claimed Dick for Marxism, and subsequently did much work in Utopian studies, as well as showing an interest in feminist SF. Jameson also worked on Dick in 'After Armageddon: Character Systems in *Dr Bloodmoney*' (1975), which applied A. J. Greimas's semiotic squares of paired binary oppositions to the organization of Dick's characters. Jameson was to return to discuss Dick in relation to postmodernism, as will be discussed below. Jameson's work on Utopia has also been influential – in particular 'Progress Versus Utopia; or, Can We Imagine the Future' (1982) with its contention that SF is engaged with the past rather than the future – and *Archaeologies of the Future* (2005) collects most of his significant work in the field. His ideas have been engaged with from a range of theoretical perspectives in part because of his attempt to synthesize a plurality of models – Marxist, structuralist, Lacanian and so on. While Jameson's arguments make convincing cases for the significance of SF to the contemporary world, his discussions of the details of specific texts are not always as accurate as might be desirable.

A focus on Utopia – the 'respectable' side of SF – also features in the work of Tom Moylan, whose *Demand the Impossible* (1986) describes the 'critical utopia', a depiction of an imagined world which comes out of a revolution from an oppressive old society, with a particular reflection upon class, social, sexual or ecological relations and power structures. Moylan's volume focused on Le Guin's *The Dispossessed* (1974), Russ's *The Female Man* (1975), Marge Piercy's *Woman on the Edge of Time* (1976) and Delany's *Triton* (1976), significant not so much for their blueprints for a better society – although some of their authors would aspire to practice what their novels preach – but rather for the critique they make of the context in which they were written. Moylan has continued to work on Utopian, as well as dystopian, fiction, most notably in his collection *Scraps of the Untainted Sky* (2000).

Back in the 1920s, a group of German-based Marxist critics, the Frankfurt School, had begun to engage with various forms of popular and mass culture, in particular seeing how such outputs would perpetuate and support the dominant power structures in society and how the mass market standardized and simplified aesthetic outputs as a repetitive product to be consumed. Some of them also took on board the ideas of Sigmund Freud and (later) Jacques Lacan in their analysis of mass culture. The American academic Carl Freedman sees himself as continuing their work. His reading of SF is an explicitly political one, which is aware of the place of SF within the mass market place. *Critical Theory and Science Fiction* (2000), a book that intends to do for science fiction what Georg [György] Lukács did for historical fiction with *The Historical Novel* (1937), treads a familiar path through the works of Delany, Dick, Le Guin and Lem, rather than the more populist end of the genre. More recently, Freedman used SF in his *The Incomplete Projects* (2002), with chapters on Stanley Kubrick's *2001: A Space Odyssey* (1968), George Orwell's *Nineteen Eighty-Four* (1949) and Dick, and has demonstrated a sustained interest in the works of Miéville.

If anything, the collapse of the Berlin Wall and the end of the Cold War has led to a greater interest in Marxist thinking in SF circles, rather than less. William J. Burling edited a collection of essays on Marxist SF writer Kim Stanley Robinson, *Kim Stanley Robinson Maps the Unimaginable* (2009), and left-leaning SF writers such as Ken MacLeod, Iain M. Banks and China Miéville have all had collections, special issues or conferences devoted to their work. Miéville, wearing multiple hats of author, academic and political campaigner has been particularly visible, co-editing with Mark Bould both a special issue of *Historical Materialism*, reclaiming fantasy for Marxist attention, and *Red Planets* (2009), a collection of essays on SF and Marxism. He attended and responded to a conference devoted to his oeuvre in London in 2012. Jameson and Suvin continue to be influential points of reference, even as later generations argue with their ideas. Istvan Csiscery-Ronay, for example, has developed Freedman's definition of the 'cognition effect', which has softened the aspect of science operating in mass market fiction in favour of a more generalized sense of the scientific, and downplayed the importance of a single novum in works of SF.

Postmodernism

Postmodernism was a controversial aesthetic mode, too loose and plural-istic to be called a movement, which had its origins in post-war architecture and boomed in the 1980s and 1990s in literature, art, film, television and theatre. Postmodern texts are often playful in nature; they variously quote and allude to other objects, resist hierarchies of high and low art, show an awareness of their status as created objects – for example, novels in which their authors appear, such as Kurt Vonnegut's *Breakfast of Champions* (1973) or, arguably, Russ's *The Female Man* – and are steeped in irony or camp. The theoretical, philosophical and political underpinnings of the mode were in part derived from thinkers associated with Marxism – most notably Jameson – but, equally, its main critics were also Marxist, such as the Frankfurt School sociologist and philosopher Jürgen Habermas and Trotskyist political theorist Alex Callinicos, who see it as neoconservative. Irrespective of the politics of postmodernism – and its sense of irony does not help to resolve the question – its adherents made ample use of science fiction in its attempt to describe the world in the days of the home computer and video revolution and the emergence of the internet. Dick Hebdige notes that the French postmodernist Jean Baudrillard 'has introduced Philip K. Dick into the body of "serious" social and critical theory rather like a mad or malevolent scientist might assist the *Invasion of the Body Snatchers* by introducing a pod from outer space into a small, quiet mid-western town' (1986/7: 9). Baudrillard's examination of how economic systems of exchange are being undermined by the creation of simulacra, copies with no original, owes much to Dick's usage of robotic animals, android doubles, talking taxi cabs and fake fakes.

Baudrillard's attack on '*the evil genius of advertising*' (2001: 134) as something which undermines the Western metaphysical division between truth and falsehood suggests that he rejects Marxism because it does not go far enough – capitalism privileges economic value over utility, whereas communism and socialism want to return to the primacy of needs being met, whereas Baudrillard wants somehow to break out of the whole model of exchange of one item for another. While he discusses the works of Dick and J. G. Ballard in his essays, even SF is not enough to describe the contemporary world: 'the "good old" SF imagination is dead, and [...] something else is beginning to emerge (and not only in fiction, but also in theory). Both traditional SF and theory are destined to the same fate: flux and imprecision are putting an end to them as specific genres' (1991: 309). As the postmodern lens began to use the object of study – SF – as a subject position in its own right, so SF became a means of analyzing the real world. Baudrillard's ideas were picked up by Scott Bukatman, especially in his analysis of postmodern SF cinema *Terminal Identity* (1993), and were directly referenced in the Wachowskis' *The Matrix* (1999). When two articles by Baudrillard were published in *Science Fiction Studies* (1991), the reaction was in part hostile; Ballard took the opportunity to dismiss SF academia in general.

Jean-François Lyotard's *The Postmodern Condition* (1979) made less impact on the criticism of SF than Baudrillard. In a nutshell, Lyotard examined the standards of proof for current knowledge, and found that notions of predictability and repeatability were harder to apply than in the days of the experiments of Galileo. Chaos theory, quantum mechanics and other branches of science meant that experiments were difficult to repeat thanks to the size and expense of the necessary equipment, and that there were limits to the extent of knowledge as the act of observing could determine the result. There was a failure of what Lyotard called 'metanarratives', the stories that give legitimacy to our practices, including the notion of modernity as a kind of progress toward Utopia. Rather than such progress, the modern world had produced trench warfare and concentration camps. Lyotard's ideas questioned the certainties of our cognition, and therefore placed limits on our capacity to know the world. While in the monograph he defined postmodernism as 'an incredulity toward metanarratives' (xxiv), which occurs after some kind of epochal rupture in the late 1950s or early 1960s, in an article 'Answering the Question: What is Postmodernism?' (1982), a response to Habermas, he was more interested in the state of aesthetics in the era of the transnational corporation, and the eclecticism of taste that was now open to consumers. This is very much the world that is the backdrop for cyberpunk and postcyberpunk SF, especially the works of Gibson, Bruce Sterling and Neal Stephenson. Lyotard hardly celebrates this, but his attack on any form of totalitarian thought pits him as much against some aspects of Marxism as it does against Nazism, fascism or capitalism.

Jameson wrote the preface to the English language edition of *The Postmodern Condition* and, in *Postmodernism, or the Cultural Logic of Late Capitalism* (1991), examined postmodernism from within a Marxist paradigm. Marx had argued that the economic base or infrastructure of a given society affected its social, political and cultural superstructure, and that, as the base changed, so did the superstructure. The shift from feudalism to capitalism had been as much a cultural change as a social, political and economic one. Further changes following the two World Wars ushered in an era described as 'late capitalism' or 'post-industrial capitalism'. Jameson defined its aesthetic characteristics variously as depthlessness, obsession with surface and fashion, a dramatic focus on the collapse of individual identity (or death of the subject), use of irony and the consequent undermining of authentic emotions, a failure of originality which led to authorial pastiche and intertextuality, and the embrace of nostalgia. It is the last category which points Jameson back to SF and his analysis of the representation of the 1950s as an epoch looked back on with (questionable) nostalgia in relation to David Lynch's *Blue Velvet* (1986), Jonathan Demme's *Something Wild* (1986) and Philip K. Dick's *Time Out of Joint* (1959). While the two films use the notion of the 1950s as a period before it all went wrong, but which contained the seeds of disaster, *Time Out of Joint* was written in the 1950s *and* looks back to that present as an historical period from the point of view of the novel's present in an imagined 1990s. Jameson declares: 'of the great writers of the period, only Dick himself comes to mind as the virtual poet laureate of this material' (280), and indeed there are passing references to Dick throughout Jameson's book. On the other hand, in an endnote, Jameson confesses: 'This is the place to regret the absence from this book of a chapter on cyberpunk, henceforth, for many of us, the supreme *literary* expression if not of postmodernism, then of late capitalism itself' (419). Again, there is a sense that SF becomes central to the way of understanding the world, but Jameson is no unproblematic endorser of the postmodern world, his attempt is to find a cognitive map with which to comprehend it.

The final postmodern strand of SF criticism I wish to discuss comes from the work of Donna Haraway, one of the first to theorize the notion of the posthuman. Commissioned by the *Socialist Review* to identify ways forward for socialist-feminism in the era of Ronald Reagan, Haraway wrote 'Manifesto for Cyborgs: Science, Technology, and Socialist Feminism in the 1980s' (1985). From the mid-1970s, literary criticism had been questioning the essential nature of personal identity and the power hierarchies which society attached to them – male/female, heterosexual/homosexual, white/black and so on – and began to deconstruct the established perception of these categories as fixed, eternal and natural. Madonna and Michael Jackson were very visible examples of hybrid figures who would not fit in the race or gender pigeonholes of a neoconservative patriarchal society. The word 'cyborg' was coined in the 1960s as a hybrid object, part machine (*cyb*ernetic), part animal (*org*anism), and had been most visible in popular culture in the television series *The Six-Million Dollar Man* (1973–8) and *The Bionic Woman* (1976–8), until the advent of 1980s films such as *The Terminator* (1984). Haraway discussed the significance of cyborgs in the writings of Octavia Butler,

Delany, Vonda McIntyre and Russ, among others, then appropriated the term as labelling a new kind of subject position for humans in the contemporary world. Haraway argued that '[t]he cyborg is a creature in a post-gender world; it has no truck with bisexuality, pre-oedipal symbiosis, unalienated labour, or other seductions to organic wholeness through a final appropriation of all the powers of the parts into a higher unity' (1991: 150). If this risked presenting a subject position for women as monstrous, then this was preferable, for Haraway, to the image of women on pedestals, as goddesses. In parallel with this, in studies of horror – including Ridley Scott's film *Alien* (1979), among others – Linda Williams (1983) suggested that female viewers identify with the monster rather than the patriarchal hero and Barbara Creed (1991) offered the figure of the monstrous feminine as an alternative to the innocent, looked-at, victim, Cyborg theory blossomed beyond Haraway, especially through the analysis of Gibson's *Neuromancer* (1984) and related cyberpunk novels, but Haraway's radical edge was often lost. Cyberpunk looked all too much like a boy's club, with white, male hackers in cyberspace and women often represented as dominatrix fantasies. Critics such as Joan Gordon, N. Katherine Hayles, Veronica Hollinger, Gwyneth Jones and Nicola Nixon asked searching questions about the sexual and humanist politics of cyberpunk and postmodernism – Nixon, for example, rejected the model of cyberpunk as radical because of its masculinist power politics: 'The political (or even revolutionary) potential for SF, realized so strongly in '70s feminist SF, is relegated in Gibson's cyberpunk to a form of scary feminized software; his fiction creates an alternative, attractive, but hallucinatory world which allows not only a reassertion of male mastery but a virtual celebration of a kind of primal masculinity' (231).

A number of collections of essays on cyberpunk were published, of which the best are Larry McCaffery's *Storming the Reality Studio* (1991) and George Slusser and Tom Shippey's *Fiction 2000* (1992); an indication of the importance of the former is that Graham J. Murphy and Sherryl Vint's collection, *Beyond Cyberpunk* (2010), was conceived as beginning where that had left off. But while postmodern critics ostensibly set out to destroy the canon and break down boundaries between high and low culture, in practice most of them focused on *Neuromancer* and Scott's *Blade Runner* (1982). If anything the canon shrank. Furthermore, much criticism of cyberpunk and postmodern SF was written by critics with a rather too narrow knowledge of the genre.

Feminist Criticism

Cyberpunk as a subgenre was dominated by male writers, with Pat Cadigan the only woman to be included in the seminal cyberpunk anthology, *Mirrorshades* (1986), edited by Sterling. Indeed, more male writers than female publish genre SF for adults, get included in anthologies and get shortlisted for awards. In autumn 2010, Niall Harrison wrote 'If we ask how many British women are publishing original adult science fiction with a major genre publisher in Britain, the answer is pretty bleak [...] I think the answer may be just one writer, Jaine Fenn'. The definition is narrow – women are publishing with non-genre imprints, in the children and young adult markets and being labelled as fantasy – but it feels like a gender-conservative market. The standard historical narrative of SF notes an influx of women with the popular success of *Star Trek* (1966–9) and the fandom which surrounds it. However, such histories are all written by men, with the exception of Bould and Vint's *Routledge Concise History of Science Fiction* (2011). The patriarchal bias might seem surprising if we follow Aldiss's assertion that *Frankenstein* was the first SF novel, but it was all too easy for female writers after Shelley to become invisible – indeed, her other SF novel *The Last Man* (1826) is rarely discussed. Most accounts of women's SF begin with the feminist critical utopias of the 1970s and move up to the present day, with female pulp writers – often published under sex-neutral names or initials only, such as Leigh Brackett or C. L. Moore – being largely ignored. More recently the historical gaps have been filled in by a number of revisionist accounts. Justine Larbalestier's *The Battle of the Sexes in Science Fiction* (2002) examines the period 1926–73, from the pulps to the emergence of feminist SF, looking at both the fiction of the period and the critical debates in magazines. Lisa Yaszek's *Galactic Suburbia* (2008) recuperates post-war women's SF, which Russ and others had dismissed as insufficiently feminist, by analyzing its representations of changing women's roles from the mid-1940s to the 1970s. Helen Merrick's *The Secret Feminist Cabal* (2009) offers a cultural history of women's SF, examining female editors, writers and fans from the days of the pulps onwards.

In 'What Can a Heroine Do? or Why Women Can't Write' (1971), Russ notes the limited roles which were open to female fictional characters, and how there seemed to be a psychological narrative which meant that stories 'ought' to be about men. She saw potential for new narratives to be created with women at their heart in genre fiction – the supernatural, crime and SF – and for about ten years wrote challenging SF which did just that. Le Guin, who had been publishing SF in the 1960s and with *The Left Hand of Darkness* (1969) had produced a classic which challenged the biological essentialism of gender, became one of the most celebrated writers within the genre, and crossed over to mainstream attention.

Russ, in *How to Suppress Women's Writing* (1983), analyzes the rhetorical ploys which consistently downplayed women's writing – it was not as good as men's, it was not important, it was not appropriate, they had help from fathers, husbands or brothers, it was just a one-off, and so on – each of which was clearly ideological in nature. Her account is part of the wider history of feminism, which can be traced back to the era of Shelley's mother, Mary Wollstonecraft's groundbreaking *A Vindication of the Rights of Women* (1792). Russ, Le Guin and other feminist SF authors and critics wrote in the context of books such as Betty Friedan's *The Feminine Mystique* (1963), Kate Millett's *Sexual Politics* (1970), Germaine Greer's *The Female Eunuch* (1970) and Shulamith Firestone's *The Dialectic of Sex* (1970). The movement's focus was threefold: an analysis of the representation of women by male writers as victims or monsters, the establishment of publishers to bring neglected writers back into print and promote contemporary women's writers and a philosophical investigation – often within the realm of psychoanalysis and French philosophy – into the nature of feminine consciousness, narratives and styles. The emergence of two new academic journals, *Science Fiction Studies* and *Foundation* – alongside the older *Extrapolation* – in the early 1970s offered more space for feminist criticism to be published, and the work of Le Guin and Russ, as well as of Delany, was the centre of much of this. It was not just women who engaged in this work; in *The Feminine Eye* (1982), Tom Staicar collected work by both male and female critics on Brackett, Marion Zimmer Bradley, Suzy McKee Charnas, C. J. Cherryh, Suzette Haden Elgin, Moore, Andre Norton, James Tiptree Jr and Joan Vinge. There has also been the deliberate production of all-female anthologies, such as Pamela Sargent's three collections beginning with *Women of Wonder* (1974), the establishment of specialist presses and imprints, and criticisms of the sex ratio of authors nominated for and winning the major awards.

In 1974, the Canadian *The Witch and the Chameleon*, edited by Amanda Bankier, was the first feminist fanzine, and in 1975 SF fan Jeffrey D. Smith published an issue of *Khatru*, devoted to a discussion of women in SF. He had invited Charnas, Delany, Virginia Kidd, Le Guin, McIntyre, Raylyn Moore, Russ, Tiptree, Luis White, Kate Wilhelm and Chelsea Quinn Yarbro to exchange letters discussing the gender politics of SF and wider society. The two male contributors, Delany and Smith, were clearly well-intentioned in what they wrote, but were criticized by the female participants. Russ warned Smith: 'Every time you open your mouth, your foot goes in deeper. Stop it, man! There is nothing more disgusting than a belligerent/apologetic husband telling all us (women) how he was the one who *made* his marriage egalitarian because of course *she* would never have thought of it on her own' (*Khatru* 57). McIntyre told him 'Both you and Chip [Delany] are doing a standard liberal male guilt trip on the rest of us. You excuse your flaws by admitting guilt and failure. This gives you the chance to reveal how well-meaning you are – doing women's work! – and at the same time get lots of nice positive feedback and sympathy for your martyr number' (*Khatru* 58). At this point, it was not known that Tiptree was a pseudonym for Alice Sheldon so everyone assumed Tiptree was a man when she wrote a contribution rejecting the division between monstrous men and angelic women, in favour of male violence or aggression and female mothering. She was eventually asked to leave the project. As described in Julie Philips's *James Tiptree Jr*, Sheldon was eventually revealed to be a woman masquerading as a man when Smith read an obituary of her mother and recognized enough detail to realize that the daughter mentioned was Tiptree.

Fandom also organizes an annual convention devoted to feminist SF, Wiscon (1976–), and an APA (a sort of shared fanzine for which the same group of people contribute and read materials, distributed by mail) for women, *A Woman's APA*. More recently, in 1991 two writers who had attended Wiscon, Karen Joy Fowler and Pat Murphy, established a series of annual awards, in memory of James Tiptree Jr, recognizing SF which questioned issues surrounding gender, although it need not necessarily be feminist. (There is also a feminist wiki, wiki.feministSF.net/)

A number of significant feminist SF critics have emerged from academia. Marleen S. Barr edited several collections of criticism, beginning with *Future Females* (1981), and has written four books on SF, beginning with *Alien to Femininity* (1987). In her coinage of 'Feminist Fabulation' for a 1992 book of that name – drawing upon Robert Scholes's use of 'fabulation' to describe SF as a kind of literary endeavour – she argues that feminist SF is a significant location for the exploration of postmodern feminist identity, and for the proposal of alternatives to the patriarchal structure of contemporary society. Indeed, she argues that SF and the contemporary world are growing ever closer. She rightly lambasts the suppression of women's writing, attacking one overly masculinist account of postmodernism and SF as 'perpetuat[ing] a story about how the feminist frog remains in the backwaters and drowns in obscurity' (2005: 153). However, her positive association of feminist SF and postmodernism generally ignores criticisms (as discussed above) of postmodernism as neoconservative. An account of postmodernism and feminist SF was also provided by Jenny Wolmark in her *Aliens and Others* (1994), offering cogent discussion of Butler, Cadigan, Charnas, Cherryh, Sally Miller Gearhart, Jones, McIntyre, Piercy, Sargent and others. Sarah Lefanu's *In the Chinks of the World Machine* (1988), which coincided with a period when the Women's Press were publishing feminist SF in Britain as a distinct imprint, offered another account of SF by women from a feminist perspective. Lucie Armitt edited a collection of feminist essays on SF, *Where No Man Has Gone Before* (1991), but subsequently approached the genre from the perspective of fabulation, in books such as *Theorising the Fantastic* (1996) and *Contemporary Women's Fiction and the Fantastic* (2000).

Batya Weinbaum and Robin Anne Reid together founded *Femspec*, a feminist SF journal active from 1999, with particular strengths in analysis of African American, Jewish and pulp SF. The efforts of Gordon, Hollinger,

Carol McGuirk, Farah Mendlesohn, Wendy Gay Pearson, Vint, Yaszek and others as current or previous co-editors of the other academic journals has helped keep feminist SF criticism on the agenda.

Queer Theory

Queer theory grew to prominence in the early 1990s, developing in part out of feminist thinking. Judith Butler's *Gender Trouble* (1989) argued that gender was something which was performed rather than innate. If gender identity was fluid, then sexuality needed to be rethought as something more than just a heterosexual/homosexual binary. 'Queer', both as a word being reappropriated from a term of abuse and as a word which could mean 'to blur', 'to muddy', was the label adopted by theorists such as Eve Kosofsky Sedgwick and Michael Warner. It had also been a label adopted by the overlapping gay, lesbian, transgendered, transsexual and bisexual communities who found common cause in their reaction to HIV and campaigns for equality and rights. Queer readings not only examine the nature and power structures of different sexualities, but also explore the ways in which various sexualities are coded within cultural texts. For example, it had become a common understanding that Alfred Hitchcock's film *Rope* (1948) focused on a murder committed by two gay men, but D. A. Miller (1990) noted that the words 'gay' and 'homosexuality' were not used in the film, nor was there any sex scene or kiss to disclose their sexuality. The common reading of the characters as gay had been a product of assumption and innuendo.

An earlier analysis of SF from the perspective of sexuality had been in Fredric Wertham's *Seduction of the Innocent* (1954), in which he questioned the nature of the relationship between Batman and Robin in the comic books. At a time when homosexuality was illegal, it was feared in the West second only to communism as something which would corrupt individuals and destroy lives. Homosexuality rarely appeared explicitly in SF prior to 1970 – Theodore Sturgeon's 'The World Well Lost' (1953) being a rare exception. The sidelining of female characters, which is part of the genre's avoidance of dealing with sexuality, leaves it open to the suggestion that depictions of homosociality (relationships between those of the same sex, not necessarily but usually men) are actually of homosexuality. Thomas M. Disch, in a lecture which suggests that SF is really a branch of children's literature, notes the homoerotic charge in Robert A. Heinlein's *Starship Troopers* (1959): 'The hero is a homosexual of a very identifiable breed. By his own self-caressing descriptions one recognizes the swaggering leather boy in his most flamboyant form. There is even a skull-and-crossbones earring in his left ear' (1976: 154). The readerly game of spotting the subtext is one that led to a subgenre of often pornographic fan fiction, slash, discussed below in the section on Fan Studies.

Susan Sontag's 'Notes on "Camp"' (1964) was a sort of manifesto describing a post-eighteenth century sensibility of aestheticism, in which the artificial was celebrated and bad taste was raised to high. Sontag's anatomy of camp 'degayed' a branch of taste commonly associated with homosexuals, although while not all camp people are homosexual, it needs to be emphasized that not all homosexuals are camp. But if homosexual taste and camp sensibility are aligned, then Sontag's championing of naïve over deliberate camp is part of the attempt to sideline homosexuality. As well as describing Jayne Mansfield, Jane Russell, Victor Mature, Tiffany lamps, feather boas and *Swan Lake* as camp, she also mentioned Cooper and Schoedsack's *King Kong* (1933) and *Flash Gordon* comics. Camp is thus a way of reading film, especially the films of the so-bad-they're-good variety. Bould has analyzed the camp qualities of Hodge's *Flash Gordon* (1980) and *Blade Runner*, noting how the critical reception of the former was extremely negative, regarding it as tainted by a sense of deliberate camp. It needs to be asserted that distinctions between naiveté and deliberateness fall prey to the intentional fallacy assuming that, say, the makers of *The Giant Claw* (1957) did not know how bad their film looked.

One academic who has done more than most to introduce queer theory into SF criticism is Wendy Gay Pearson, whose outputs include two pieces in the 'Science Fiction and Queer Theory' special section of *Science Fiction Studies* (1999), writing an essay on Geoff Ryman for the Lesbian and Gay themed issue of *Foundation* (2002) and the chapter on queer theory for *The Routledge Companion to Science Fiction* (2009) and co-editing *Queer Universes* (2008). In 'Alien Cryptographies' (1999), she begins by noting the absence of homosexual characters from *Star Trek* in its various televisual and cinematic guises, as well as from most SF, but questions how far the addition of individual characters would challenge the genre's heteronormativity (the standardization of heterosexuality as the default form of sexuality). She notes the power of queer readings to unpack paranoia inherent in classic texts; offering an analysis of John W. Campbell's 'Who Goes There?' (1938) in which the anxieties about a body-snatching alien mimicking the appearance of a friend can be seen as a metaphor for homophobic witch hunts. She concludes the article with an analysis of a Tom Reamy story, 'Under the Hollywood Sign' (1975), which complicates the traditional notions of sex, gender and sexuality and challenges the notion of heteronormativity, but at the same time is a text that is open to multiple readings which 'queer' our understanding of it. For Pearson, queer theory and queer readings not only contest heteronormativity, but also homonormativity, the establishment of a fixed, quasi-official definition of what gay identity should be.

Chris West also challenged questions of normativity and even of 'the queer' itself in his readings of SF, arguing that the genre is full of queers.

Two of his essays focus on Heinlein's *The Puppet Masters* (1951), a narrative about an invasion of America by parasitic slugs who control human bodies. The Cold War parallels are obvious here; in one scene the characters first consider if the aliens could conquer Russia, then wonder if they already have. Alongside political paranoia are anxieties about homosexuality, with possessed men being mounted by aliens and feminised. SF and horror often displaces anxieties about perceived threatening cultural identities – non-men, non-whites, non-heterosexuals, non-adults, non-capitalists, non-Christians – on to aliens, cyborgs and monsters. Depictions of aliens that look like us but are somehow *different* mark points where sexual, gendered, political and other forms of difference collapse into each other – there is an indiscriminating fear of the Other. In 'Perverting Science Fiction' (2005), West traces the connections between the notion of the other and the 'perverse', preferring the latter term to queer, and arguing that SF 'is, and always has been, deeply troubled, certainly marked by and, we might say, obsessed with the perverse' (115). In 'Yesterday's Myths Today and Tomorrow' (2007), he discussed the difficulties of identifying homosexual characters, focusing on 'The World Well Lost' and two 1970s short stories, and how homosexuality operates at the level of connotation, of myth, rather than denotation. Sexuality cannot be detected by reading signs; if only because those signs point to the fluidity of sexual identity as defined by genitals rather than to homosexuality.

Race

While significant numbers of women were writing SF in the 1970s and subsequent decades, there have been very few African American or African Caribbean writers of Anglophone SF. Delany and Butler have rightly gained much critical attention, but Steven Barnes, Levar Burton, Tananarive Due, Sutton E. Griggs, Nalo Hopkinson, N. K. Jemisin, Peter Kalu, Charles Saunders and George Schuyler have received relatively little, and Walter Mosley is better known for his detective fiction. This is not to say that the rest of SF is white – there is a substantial list of Jewish writers and other countries are producing SF, including Brazil, China, India and Japan – nor that whiteness as an ethnicity does not need critical attention. But it is largely a black heritage – the legacy of British colonialism and the slave trade, the American Civil War and segregation – that forms a thematic backdrop to the analysis of race in Anglophone SF.

The long history of SF would trace the mode from the European encounter with 'otherness' in the early days of the growth of capitalism and exploration – beginning say with Shakespeare's *The Tempest* and Caliban – and be traced through the growth of empire to the scientific romances of the nineteenth century. In *The War of the Worlds* (1898), Wells explicitly makes a parallel between the Martian invasion and the British colonization of Tasmania, but on the negative side were various narratives about conquest by a racial other, such as M. P. Shiel's *The Yellow Danger* (1898), as analyzed by Edward James (1990). John Rieder (2008) has also traced the connections between the emergence of SF and the discourse about the social consequences of colonialism. First contact novels could also be reruns of the American frontier myth and a rewriting of the encounter with First Nation peoples, sometimes as recompense for the genocide, sometimes replicating racist assumptions. Countless planetary romances play out the processes of colonization, and empires and the appropriation of wealth permeate space operas.

If in some early SF there is a fear of faceless, uniform hordes – which survives at least as late as Stephenson's *Snow Crash* (1992) – then the future is often monochrome. Scholes and Eric Rabkin suggest that '[t]he presence of unhuman races, aliens, and robots, certainly makes the differences between human races seem appropriately trivial' (1977: 188), as human identity becomes unified in comparison with an alien species, which itself is often imagined as being monolithic in ethnicity. While this might represent the overcoming of prejudice and advent of racial harmony, it tends to erase the difference which would give humans both individual identity and cultural solidarity. There is a fear that the future has been whitewashed. For all the ethnic mix of the crew of the Starship Enterprise, culturally they all appear American, and the groundbreaking positioning of an African American woman on a major television network (Nichelle Nichols as Uhura) rather obscures the fact that she is little more than a receptionist. Elisabeth Leonard's collection *Into Darkness Peering* (1997) includes some useful analysis of race in white writers, including Dick, Bradbury and the cyberpunk movement.

In science fiction, racial difference gets displaced on to species difference: the encounter with the alien can be a metaphor, parable or allegory of the encounter with a different ethnic group. If this is a knowing representation of racism, then this needs to be undercut or otherwise it could make uncomfortable reading as it risks asserting that non-whites are non-humans. For example, Gardner Dozois's *Strangers* (1978) is an account of a romance between a human and a Cian, articulating hostility towards intermarriage between races. The novel avoids the charge of racism, because the human protagonist turns out to have entirely misunderstood the Cian culture, which is more complex than he had presumed – the novel is a critique of colonial attitudes. The *Planet of the Apes* films (1968–73) are frequently taken to be an account of the civil rights struggles in America. If this is the case and the gorillas are meant to represent African Americans and the orangutans Jews, then the films connote a long history of racist imagery.

Chris Cutler argues that the popular culture of African Americans has offered them 'a unique way to come to terms with the alienation at the heart of the capitalist production and commodity exchange' (1993: 51). Part of this would be the experience of working in the car factories of Detroit – which gave rise to Motown Records – as well as in other working class jobs, and the recording technologies which gave rise to rap and other genres of music. Mark Dery edited a special issue of *South Atlantic Quarterly* (1993) in which he coined the term 'Afrofuturism' to describe: 'Speculative fiction that treats African American themes and addresses African American concerns in the context of twentieth-century technoculture' (1994: 180). Dery suggests that the displacement of the ancestors of African Americans from Africa to the new world positions them within a SF scenario: 'African Americans [...] are the descendents of alien abductees; they inhabit a sci-fi nightmare in which unseen but no less impassable force fields of intolerance frustrate their movements' (1994: 180). Dery seems to be reappropriating the history of white colonialism as one of Black power. The myth of alien abduction underlies the musical cosmologies of Jazz artist Sun Ra, who claimed that he had been teleported to Saturn, and funk band Parliament, who saw music as a means of escape to an earlier, superior, quasi-Egyptian society. Along with such afrofuturist music – to which could be added the work of the hip hop band OutKast – it is also important to consider blaxploitation films, especially *Blackenstein* (Levey 1973), where the black identity of the monster can also be read as an avenger resisting the dominant white order. It has to be admitted that such productions tend to be omitted from many accounts of SF.

Rather than discussing *afro*futurism, De Witt Douglas Kilgore has written about *astro*futurism. Drawing upon the work of Howard P. Segal, he posits 'a type of twentieth-century technological utopianism that takes the human exploration and colonization of space as its goal' (2000: 272). Kilgore notes how on occasions the new start of space travel allows for a reimagining, praising McIntyre for her use of a black, female protagonist in *Starfarer* (1989). Kilgore suggests that the racial power structures of astrofutures could be predicted from the authors' attitudes to the politics of colonialism:

> a writer's political position corresponded to his or her position in relation to the central narrative convention of imperial exploration. For Jerry Pournelle, Larry Niven, and many other space-opera specialists, the militaristic overtones of geographic exploration (past and future) are a necessary component of any future social order we can imagine (2003: 130–1).

Arthur C. Clarke, as a liberal based for much of his life in a former colony, imagines a future in which women and people of colour co-exist with males and whites, but difference has been subsumed under what Kilgore perceives as a process of homogenization, creating 'an ivory-colored humanity' (2003:

147). Despite Kilgore's optimism about Clarke's commitment to pluralism, in several of his novels it seems hardly even skin deep; Clarke imagines futures where people coexist because of sameness, not despite differences.

Fan Studies

Fans are those enthusiasts who are not content to be consumers of the genre, but also produce in relation to SF, whether in print or online – or with groups of other people – publishing fanzines, newsletters, articles, fiction, pamphlets, books, small press books, Tweets, blogs and webpages, organizing clubs, conventions, meetings, Amateur Press Associations (APAs) and fan funds to raise money or documenting the genre in collections, archives, films and so on. Some sociological work has been done on science fiction readers and fans – who are not necessarily the same – of which the most prominent are William Sims Bainbridge's *Dimensions of Science Fiction* (1986) and Brian Stableford's *The Sociology of Science Fiction* (1987). Bainbridge surveyed attendees at the 1978 World SF Convention in Phoenix, Arizona, with a 1979 control group of students from the University of Washington, as well as comparing the results to his survey of Seattle residents on the subject of spaceflight and a 1970 survey of Boston residents by Irene Taviss. He found that SF fans were more likely to be in favour of spaceflight and technology than the general population, and that this was the case whether the reader preferred hard SF, new wave SF or sword and sorcery science fantasy. Scientific rigour was closely associated with notions of new technology, and hard SF writers, perhaps unsurprisingly, were rated as being scientifically rigorous and describing new technology, whereas fantasy was less rigorous and was not perceived as engaging with new technology. More literary writers, such as Ray Bradbury, Lem and Kurt Vonnegut, were associated with new wave writers and connected to social sciences. Stableford's work was based on his 1979 doctoral thesis on the sociology of SF.

Bainbridge and Stableford examined literary SF fans, but subsequent work has mostly focused on film and television fandom, whose conventions have been more commercial. Film and television most likely reaches a wider audience than a book, and perhaps the ongoing form of television is more likely to gain a vocal fandom, demanding new episodes or complaining at failures in the series. Perhaps the most studied fandom is that of *Star Trek*, whose fans orchestrated a letter-writing campaign to bring the series back from cancellation, and showed creator Gene Roddenberry that there was a market for a sequel television series or a cinematic spin off. Some groups have campaigned for gay characters to be introduced into the series, especially *Deep Space Nine* (1993–9), and pressed the producers on the series' heteronormativity. Some fans had been writing slash fiction since 1974 and, between

2000–7, fans produced 50 episodes of their own gay and lesbian themed series, *Star Trek: Hidden Frontier*.

Slash fiction foregrounds the homoerotic subtext within many popular television dramas, imagining a relationship – usually sexual, often porno-graphic – between two male characters. Fans initially imagined a pairing of Kirk and Spock from *Star Trek* – leading the fiction to be labelled Kirk/Spock, K/S or, more commonly, slash fiction – but subsequent fan fictions have used characters from later series of *Star Trek* (1987–2005), *Buffy the Vampire Slayer* (1997–2003), *The X-Files* (1993–2002) and almost all major television series, as well as the Harry Potter books (1997–2007) and films (2001–11) and *The Lord of the Rings* films (2001–3). Initially it was written by women for women, at a point where pornography was being criticized by feminist critics. Some fan writers might have been playing out their sexual fantasies, others were clearly refashioning masculine gender roles into something more complex. This is part of the position that Patricia Frazer Lamb and Diane Veith took in their pioneering 'Romantic Myth, Transcendence and *Star Trek* Zines' (1986), which situated the fiction as romance. Russ came out as a slash fan first in an article 'Another Addict Raves About K/S' (1985) in a fanzine, *Nome*, that she reprinted as 'Pornography By Women for Women with Love' (1985) in a more academic collection, She was interested in the politics of pornography, as well as admitting to writing it herself. She championed the pleasures of slash against the more puritanical aspects of feminism. In *Enterprising Women* (1991) Camille Bacon-Smith records her own discovery of and then initiation into slash culture, in a sort of participant observation. She is open to the charge that she generalizes too much from her own experience, and insists (contrary to Russ) that slash is written by unhappy women to resolve psychological crises in their lives. Constance Penley's study of slash is part of her examination of the ways by which NASA and the *Star Trek* franchise have been mutually dependent in their advocacy of space travel and technology, as well as both being creators of popular legend – in particular she notes how the details surrounding the Challenger disaster have been repressed as part of their narrative.

Slash also raises issues around the legality of representation both in terms of its use of pornographic description and in the use of characters and conventions that are copyrighted by corporate owners. Derivative works are often rigorously policed, whether to protect the reputation of their materials (in the case of fan fiction) and to guard rights which they may wish to exploit themselves (in the case of fan-created reference works). Henry Jenkins has studied the *Star Trek* audiences in terms of what he calls 'textual poaching' – the way in which fans transform copyright or owned materials into what they want them to be for their own purposes. Fandom is a form of 'partici-patory culture', in which the fan is in dialogue with other fans and, to varying degrees, with the producers of that culture. Culture increasingly seems to have meaning in relation to its consumers rather than its producers, although this risks contradicting the arguments of the Frankfurt School about the ways in which dominant culture perpetuates itself. While the audience-as-producers are not passive dupes or dopes, their agency and potential for taking control of the means of production are limited and regulated: a fan is unlikely to make money from fan fiction. An exception might be E. L. James's *Fifty Shades of Grey* (2011), that began as online fan fiction inspired by Stephanie Meyer's *Twilight* saga (2005–8). It was much changed from its source and needed corporate intervention to become a bestseller. Participatory culture is only pseudo-democratic, giving the illusion that the creative power of consumers may have an impact on the overall capitalistic system.

Fan studies continues to focus on media, with research on *Judge Dredd* (1995) and *The Lord of the Rings* by Martin Barker and Kate Brooks (1998), *Alien*, *Blade Runner* and *Star Wars* by Will Brooker (2002), *Doctor Who* by Matt Hills (2002) and so on. The problem for these critics is always how to triangulate from their specific experiences of fandom to fandom as a whole – even if they are 'aca-fans', in Jenkins's terms, their researching hybrid identities raise on the one extreme the problem of 'going native', on the other being incomers or outsiders. Many fans have become suspicious of academic investigation, in some cases fearing that there is an existing theoretical paradigm into which their experiences may be slotted, and doubting the ethics of the researcher's methodology. Fans can fillet a questionnaire for inconsistencies in seconds.

Conclusion

The increasing plurality of critical approaches means that this chapter can only scratch the surface – with art, film, television, radio, music and comics opening up whole new modes of investigation for SF, not to mention the challenges posed by adaptation, advertising, animal studies, architecture, design, economics, future studies, geography, law, philosophy, religion and translation. If SF began as a genre when Gernsback pointed at it in 1926, then today there are thousands of fingers pointing in a bewildering number of directions.

Works Cited

Aldiss, Brian W. (1973). *Billion Year Spree*. London: Weidenfeld and Nicolson.
Amis, Kingsley (1960). *New Maps of Hell*. New York: Harcourt, Brace.
Armitt, Lucie (ed.) (1991). *Where No Man Has Gone Before*. London: Routledge.
—(1996). *Theorising the Fantastic*. London: Arnold.
—(2000). *Contemporary Women's Fiction and the Fantastic*. London: Palgrave Macmillan.

Atheling Jr, William (1964). *The Issue at Hand*. Chicago: Advent.

—(1970). *More Issues at Hand*. Chicago: Advent.

Bacon-Smith, Camille (1991). *Enterprising Women*. Philadelphia: University of Pennsylvania Press.

Bainbridge, William Sims (1986). *Dimensions of Science Fiction*. Cambridge, MA: Harvard University Press.

Ballard, J G. (1991). 'A Response to the Invitation to Respond'. *Science Fiction Studies*. 18.3 (November). 329.

Barker, Martin and Kate Brooks (1998). *Knowing Audiences*. Luton: University of Luton Press.

Barr, Marleen S. (ed.) (1981). *Future Females*. Bowling Green, OH: Bowling Green University Popular Press.

—(1987). *Alien to Femininity*. New York: Greenwood Press.

—(1992). *Feminist Fabulation*. Iowa City: University of Iowa Press.

—(2005). 'Feminist Fabulation'. *A Companion to Science Fiction*. David Seed (ed.). Oxford: Blackwell: 142–55

Baudrillard, Jean (1991). 'Two Essays: "Simulacra and Science Fiction" and "Ballard's *Crash*".' *Science Fiction Studies*. 18. 3 (November). 309–20.

—(2001). 'Barbara Kruger'. *The Uncollected Baudrillard*. Gary Genosko (ed.). London and Thousand Oaks: Sage. 134–7.

Bould, Mark (2002). 'Not in Kansas Any More'. *Foundation*. 86 (Autumn). 40–50.

Bould, Mark and China Miéville (eds) (2002). *Historical Materialism*. 10. 4.

—(eds) (2009). *Red Planets*, London: Pluto.

Brooker, Will (2002). *Using the Force*. New York: Continuum.

Bukatman, Scott (1993). *Terminal Identity*. Durham, NC: Duke University Press.

Burling, William J. (ed.) (2009). *Kim Stanley Robinson Maps the Unimaginable*. Jefferson, NC: McFarland.

Butler, Judith (1989). *Gender Trouble: Feminism and the Subversion of Identity*. New York: Routledge.

Creed, Barbara (1991). *The Monstrous Feminine*. New York: Routledge.

Csiscery-Ronay, Istvan (2008). *The Seven Beauties of Science Fiction*. Middletown, CT: Wesleyan University Press.

Cutler, Chris (1993). *File Under Popular*. New York: Autonomedia.

Delany, Samuel R. (1969). 'About Five Thousand One Hundred and Seventy Five Words'. *Extrapolation* 10. 2 (May). 52–66.

—(1977). *The Jewel-Hinged Jaw*. Elizabethtown, NY: Dragon Press.

—(1978). *The American Shore*. Elizabethtown, NY: Dragon Press.

Dery, Mark (1994). 'Black to the Future'. *Flame Wars*. Mark Dery (ed.). Durham, NC Duke University Press: 179–222.

Disch, Thomas M. (1976). 'The Embarrassments of Science Fiction'. *Science Fiction At Large*. Peter Nicholls (ed.). London: Gollancz: 141–55.

Fitting, Peter (1975). '*Ubik*: The Deconstruction of Bourgeois SF'. *Science Fiction Studies*. 2. 1 (March). 47–54.

Freedman, Carl (2000). *Critical Theory and Science Fiction*. Hanover, NH: Wesleyan University Press.

—(2002). *The Incomplete Projects*. Hanover, NH: Wesleyan University Press.

Gernsback, Hugo (1926). 'A New Sort of Magazine'. *Amazing Stories* 1.1 (April). 3.

Gordon, Joan (1990). 'Yin and Yang Duke It Out'. *Science-Fiction Eye 2* (February). 37–9.

Haraway, Donna J. (1991). *Simians, Cyborgs, and Women*. New York: Routledge.

Harrison, Niall (2010). 'Women and the Clarke'. *Torque Control* (5 October). Available online: http://vectoreditors.wordpress.com/2010/10/05/women-and-the-clarke/

Hayles, N. Katherine (1999). *How We Became Posthuman: Virtual Bodies in Cybernetics, Literature and Informatics*. Chicago and London: University of Chicago Press.

Hebdige, Dick (1986/1987). 'A Report on the Western Front'. *Block.* (Winter). 4–26.

Hills, Matt. (2002). *Fan Cultures*. London: Routledge.

Hollinger, Veronica (1991). 'Cybernetic Deconstructions: Cyberpunk and Postmodernism'. *Storming the Reality Studio: A Casebook of Cyberpunk and Postmodern Science Fiction*. Larry McCaffery (ed.). Durham and London: Duke University Press. 203–18.

James, Edward (1990). 'Yellow, Black, Metal, and Tentacled'. *Science Fiction, Social Conflict and War*. Philip J. Davies (ed.). Manchester: Manchester University Press. 26-49.

Jameson, Fredric (1975). 'After Armageddon'. *Science Fiction Studies* 2.1 (March). 31–42.

—(1982). 'Progress Versus Utopia; or, Can We Imagine the Future'. *Science Fiction Studies*. 9. 2 (July). 147–58.

—(1991). *Postmodernism, or the Cultural Logic of Late Capitalism*. London: Verso.

—(2005). *Archaeologies of the Future: The Desire Called Utopia and Other Science Fictions*. London: Verso.

Jenkins, Henry (1992). *Textual Poachers*. New York: Routledge.

Jones, Gwyneth (1992). 'The Boys Want to be with the Boys'. *New York Review of Science Fiction*. 48 (August). 14–16.

Kilgore, De Witt Douglas (2000). 'Changing Regimes: Vonda N. McIntyre's Parodic Astrofuturism.' *Science Fiction Studies*. 27. 2 (July). 256–77.

—(2003). *Astrofuturism*. Philadelphia: University of Pennsylvania Press.

Knight, Damon (1956). *In Search of Wonder*. Chicago: Advent Publishers.

Lamb, Patricia F. and Diana L. Veith (1986). 'Romantic Myth, Transcendence and *Star Trek* Zines'. *Erotic Universe*. Ed. In Donald Palumbo (ed.). Westport, CT: Greenwood. 235–55.

Larbalestier, Justine (2002). *The Battle of the Sexes in Science Fiction*. Middletown, CT: Wesleyan University Press.

Lefanu, Sarah (1988). *In the Chinks of the World Machine*. London: The Women's Press.

Leonard, Elisabeth (ed.). (1997). *Into Darkness Peering*. Westport, CT: Greenwood Press.

Lyotard, Jean-François (1984). *The Postmodern Condition*. Manchester: Manchester University Press.

McCaffery, Larry (ed.) (1991). *Storming the Reality Studio*. Durham, NC: Duke University Press.

Merrick, Helen (2009). *The Secret Feminist Cabal*. Seattle, WA: Aqueduct Press.

Miéville, China (2009). 'Cognition as Ideology: A Dialectic of SF Theory'. *Red Planets*. Mark Bould and China Miéville (eds). London: Pluto. 231–48.

Miller, D. A. (1990). 'Anal Rope'. *Representations*. 32 (Fall). 114–33

Moylan, Tom (1986). *Demand the Impossible*. London: Methuen.

—(2000). *Scraps of the Untainted Sky*. Boulder. CO: Westview Press.

Murphy Graham J. and Sherryl Vint (eds) (2010). *Beyond Cyberpunk*. New York: Routledge.

Nixon, Nicola (1992). 'Cyberpunk: Preparing the Ground For Revolution Or Keeping the Boys Satisfied'. *Science Fiction Studies*. 19.2 (July). 219–35.

Parrinder, Patrick (ed.) (1979). *Science Fiction: A Critical Guide*. London: Longman.

—(1980). *Science Fiction: Its Criticism and Teaching*. London: Methuen.

Pearson, Wendy Gay (1999). 'Alien Cryptographies'. *Science Fiction Studies*. 26. 1 (March). 1–22.

—(2002). 'Science Fiction as Pharmacy'. *Foundation* 86. (Autumn). 65–75.

—(2009). 'Queer Theory'. *The Routledge Companion to Science Fiction*. Bould, Mark et al. (eds). New York: Routledge. 298–307.

Pearson, Wendy Gay, Veronica Hollinger and Joan Gordon (eds) (2008). *Queer Universes*. Liverpool: Liverpool University Press.

Penley, Constance (1997). *NASA/Trek*. New York: Verso.

Phillips, Julie (2006). *James Tiptree, Jr.*. New York: St Martin's Press.

Rieder, John (2008). *Colonialism and the Emergence of Science Fiction*. Middletown, CT: Wesleyan University Press.

Russ, Joanna (1972). 'What Can a Heroine Do? or Why Women Can't Write?'. *Images of Women in Fiction*. Bowling Green, Ohio: Bowling Green University Popular Press: 2–22

—(1983). *How to Suppress Women's Writing*. London: The Women's Press.

—(1985). 'Pornography By Women for Women with Love'. *Magic Mommas, Trembling Sisters, Puritans and Perverts*. Trumansburg, NY: Crossing Press. 79–99.

Scholes, Robert E. and Eric S. Rabkin (1977). *Science Fiction: History, Science, Vision*. Oxford: Oxford University Press.

Slusser, George and Tom Shippey (eds) (1992). *Fiction 2000*. Athens, GA: University of Georgia Press.

Smith, Jeffrey D. (ed.) (1993). *Khatru*. 3/4. Jeanne Gomoll (ed. additional material). Madison, WI: Corflu.

Sontag, Susan (1966). *Against Interpretation*. New York: Farrar, Straus and Giroux.

Stableford, Brian (1987). *The Sociology of Science Fiction*. San Bernardino, CA: Borgo Press.

Staicar, Tom (ed.) (1982). *The Feminine Eye*. New York: Ungar.

Suvin Darko (1979). *Metamorphoses of Science Fiction*. New Haven, CT: Yale University Press.

—(1983). *Victorian Science Fiction in the UK*. Boston: G.K. Hall.

—(1988). *Positions and Presuppositions in SF*. London: Macmillan.

—(2000). 'Considering the Sense of "Fantasy" or "Fantasy Fiction": An Effusion'. *Extrapolation*. 41. 3 (Fall). 209–47.

Wertham, Fredric (1954). *Seduction of the Innocent*. New York: Reinhart & Company, Inc.

West, Chris (2002). 'Queer Fears and Critical Orthodoxies'. *Foundation*. 86 (Autumn). 17–27.

—(2005). 'Perverting Science Fiction'. *Foundation*. 94 (Autumn). 100–17.

—(2007). 'Yesterday's Myths Today and Tomorrow'. *Extrapolation*. 48. 3 (Winter). 504–19.

Williams, Linda (1983). 'When the Woman Looks'. *Re-Vision*. Mary Anne Doane, Patricia Mellencamp and Linda Williams (eds). Los Angeles: University Publications of America. 83–99.

Williams, Raymond (1988). 'Science Fiction'. *Science Fiction Studies*. 15.3 (November). 356–60.

Wolmark, Jenny (1994). *Aliens and Others*. Brighton: Harvester Wheatsheaf.

Yaszek, Lisa (2008). *Galactic Suburbia*. Columbus: Ohio State University Press.

Changes in the Canon

Adam Roberts

In its most neutral formulation, talk of 'the canon' is only a way of prefacing the query 'what shall I read?' with the qualification *since I cannot read every-thing...*' Now such a question might be asked by different sorts of readers. Some who read very little and wish, as it were, to dip their toe into SF might well want to know where to start; others who read more regularly might want to know how to flesh out their sense of the field; yet others who read a great deal might want to know what they have missed. But no matter how much one reads, one will fall short of total knowledge of all the narratives that constitute SF. Even people who read a very large amount – and I am one such person, as it happens – can devote their entire lives to reading (as I intend to) and make only a small dent on the total body of texts that exist. I am using 'readers' here as shorthand that includes viewers of cinema and TV, attendees at theatres and conventions – the currently fashionable marketing jargon-phrase is 'eyeballs'. Whichever terms are adopted, the case remains unaltered. Human cultural production massively outpaces the capacity of any individual human to take it all in. In such a situation, selection is unavoidable; and it is to be preferred that the processes by which the selection is made are, at least to some extent, visible.

Canon formation is a process of selecting a small group of texts from a large group of texts. That is to say, it is a process of whittling away or discarding. One of the reasons debate can become so heated on this matter is that such discarding manifests a family relationship to the process of censorship, a suppression of a large proportion of texts not by fiat but by neglect, in some ways a more potently dismissive strategy. If an authoritarian regime forbids the reading of a given book, they are tacitly acknowledging that the work is significant, even powerful. But for a book simply to fall into desuetude combines the invisibility of censorship with the taint of mediocrity, or even actual badness.

It is worth rehearsing these points here because changes in any canon, such as the canon of SF, involves (practically speaking) the resuscitation of a number of previously neglected texts. In practice this takes one of two forms: first rescuing texts from unjust suppression, and second re-arguing the case for mediocrity on grounds of aesthetic worth or historical importance. In the former case it is rarely, especially in more recent times, that texts have been actively censored, for instance by a political religious authority. Rather it is more likely to have engaged the action of generalized prejudice, such as widespread default sexism (the belief, actively or tacitly held, that 'women don't produce great art'), racism or homophobia.

Here I will mention one non-SF example to illustrate my point. For many years it was more-or-less axiomatic that 'the novel' was a form invented by men. Across the world, English Literature courses instructed students that Bunyan, Defoe, Fielding, Sterne, Smollett and Richardson constituted the 'canon' of pre-Romantic fiction. The people devising and teaching these courses were in all likelihood no more specifically sexist than the general population (indeed: many of them were women). However, of the many hundreds of novelists working in this period, the chaff had been discarded so as to leave an exclusively male canon. Then in 1986 an American literary critic called Dale Spender published a book called *Mothers of the Novel: 100 Good Women Writers Before Jane Austen*. It caused a kerfuffle in the narrow world of academia; not because it dealt with a large a body of eighteenth-century female writers of fiction, for the existence of these writers was already well known, but because of its insistence that these were *good* writers. If it is tacitly accepted that the canon is a way of separating the good writers from the bad, pointing out not only that a large number of good writers have been excluded nonetheless, but also that these writers are all women, is to raise unavoidable questions about levels of sexism so pervasive as to have become, as background radiation tends to be, invisible.

Since the publication of Spender's book (though not wholly because of it) the situation in the academy has changed in pronounced ways. It is nowadays a rare academic who would feel comfortable teaching a course that excludes female writers; and it is now common for institutions to offer courses designed specifically to address the gender bias of traditional canon formation. Some academics have opposed this change, although the broad consensus amongst university critics and teachers is that it has been a worthwhile one, adding both broadness and richness to our sense of literature. A few years back, faced with a course at my own institution called 'Women, Feminism and Writing', a (male) student objected: 'why are there no courses called *Men, Masculinity and Writing*?' My colleague's reply ('yes, we ran that

The Science Fiction Handbook

course for many years: it was called *English Literature'*) was only slightly flippant. Similar cases can be made for the inclusion of writers of colour, and LGBT writers.

But situations, like the Academy, where a discrete, identifiable group is actively selecting a group of texts with canonical, or pseudo-canonical, status (and who can thus be targeted with arguments to select a more inclusive range of texts) is the exception rather than the rule. I'll mention a couple of parallel examples from the world of science fiction, by way of bringing this essay back to topic. Let us imagine we wish to construct a canon of SF novels published over the last 120 years. This will involve not only selecting a small number of titles from the tens of thousands (and perhaps hundreds of thousands) of possibles; it will mean making those titles available to readers – for although advances in e-book production have made this second portion much easier than it used to be, for much of the period we are talking about it was a capital-intensive proposition. Two possible mechanisms for canon-formation are: publishers' lists, and genre prizes. I'll give a concrete example of the former, because it is one in which I have been, in a small way, involved. Victor Gollancz, a subsidiary of Orion books, publishes a list of 'SF Masterworks'. Although this list makes no claims to being definitive it nevertheless functions as one de facto canon; selecting and making available certain titles to interested readers. Most of the titles on this list are chosen by a small group of editors and critics (I have myself, on occasion, been involved in the process). The selection works with certain constraints, to do with availability and copyright in a large way, and to a lesser extent with commercial potential. My experience of it is that the list has made a conscious effort not to exclude women and writers of colour; yet the resulting 'canon' is overwhelmingly white and male. This has not gone unremarked in the wider world of SF fandom; many blogs and other social media platforms have hosted discussions of gender and race imbalances in the canonical SF with commendable vigour and engagement. One fan, Ian Sales, in neo-Spenderist mode, set up a website called *SF Mistressworks* (sfmistressworks.wordpress.com/), containing reviews of a great many excellent SF novels by women. On the subject of ethnic diversity in the SF canon, both in terms of the representation of race in SF and racial diversity amongst SF writers, the topic is again widely debated; a few years ago this discussion achieved a kind of critical mass, referred to under the stringently polemical moniker 'Racefail'. At its height, 'racefail' involved hundreds of blogs, livejournals and other social media, as well as some print magazines (and of course a great deal of face-to-face discussion, panels at SF conventions and the like) all passionately exercised over the status of people of colour within SF, both as represented within texts and as authors and fans. The place of writers of colour in 'the canon' was part of this larger debate.

198

It is not a mark of complacency to consider this symptomatic of rude health in the community as a whole; although the proof of suchlike puddings, in terms of wider representation of women and a more ethnically diverse SF, is not entirely evident in the eating. Because, to backtrack a little, one objection to arguments of the Dale Spender sort is to challenge the 'good' part of her title – to insist, as it were, that actually white-male-dominated canons are made purely on the basis of the merit of the texts themselves. This assertion can be made in a straightforwardly sexist manner (as it might be: 'women just aren't as good at writing novels as men') but is much more likely to be encountered in the less nakedly offensive but more insidious form: 'I'm not interested in the gender of the author, I am only interested in the quality of the book'.

One way of countering this argument would be to start from the non-sexist and I think inarguable premise that women are, as a whole, no less clever or creative than men, and then reason that: since women constitute approximately half the population, it looks *statistically* unlikely that they would contribute only a tiny fraction of the world's best novels. The difficulty here is that this argument fails to bridge from the general to the particular, which any effective counterargument needs to do since generating a canon is always a process of selecting *specific* texts. The bias can easily become self-reinforcing. In a culture in which female achievement is overlooked, and in which it is harder for any given woman with X amount of ability than it is for any given man with X amount of ability to get published, let alone noticed, the pool from which one selects is already disproportionately male.

Prizes bring this question of specificity to a particular focus. The usual remit of a prize is that it selects one title as 'the year's best'. Now a man winning a prize in any given year has little larger bearing on the question of canon-formation. Even the most committed anti-sexist would have to concede that the year's best could just as well be written by a man as a woman. Diagnosis of incipient sexism needs a larger data pool. For instance, the spread of gender over many decades of the same prize being awarded. This is because (and this is my point) the list of 'winners of the Hugo award for best novel', or 'winners of the Arthur C. Clarke award' constitute a kind of canon, in the same way the list of Booker Prize winners or 'Best Picture' Oscars do. Or it might be closer to the truth to say that such lists represent the kernel of a canon. The idea would be: hopefully you will be aware of *more* than just these titles, but *you should know at least these*. Accordingly it is a limiting fact that – to pick a couple of data from amongst many – no woman won a best-novel Hugo (the prize was established in 1953) until Ursula Le Guin did so in 1970, or that a 1966 poll by leading SF magazine Analog listing 'the All-Time Best SF' did not include any titles written by women. These facts, and others like them, are indicative of a set of quasi-canonical assumptions about genre that have been increasingly challenged. To repeat myself, what is significant about these details is not that women were excluded, but that that exclusion went largely unremarked. However, when Mike Ashley's collection of short fiction, *The Mammoth Book Of Mindblowing SF*, was published in 2009, with none of its 21 stories written by women, it triggered widespread criticism and reaction. While there is not unanimity, there is now widespread consensus amongst SF Fans that any 'canon' ought to include more than just white males.

This brings me to the nub of my argument: canon formation is, actually, an iteration of the wisdom and foolishness of crowds. I can be a little more precise. It is certainly the case that some canons are selected by teachers (choosing to assign certain texts, and not others, as class reading), and it may be the case that publishers or prize-awarding bodies slowly accrete canons over time, by identifying certain texts as noteworthy and not others. But the main thrust of canon-formation works by a process of collective rather than individual selection. 'We' generate canons by bestowing our cumulative favour on certain titles. This is in part an unconscious process, as accretive mass processes often are; but the self-reflexive element of Fandom's habit of critiquing itself builds-in a feedback dynamic. This is what makes the difference: the pressure applied to SF Fandom's collective sense of 'the canon' by SF Fandom itself – that self-reflexive openness to the possibilities of modification manifested by phenomena such as 2009–10's 'racefail' debates, and the ongoing 'SF Mistressworks' discussions. To put it simply: SF fans, by and large, *care* about their genre. Many fans pride themselves on the range and correctness of their knowledge of the genre; and most are politically and ideologically engaged. But underlying all this is a deeper motivation.

Adapting Alain Badiou's definition of philosophy found in *Infinite Thought* (2003) to this discussion, I am going to suggest that the canon is 'prescribed by several conditions that are types of truth procedures or generic procedures' (165). According to Badiou, these types are science, art, politics and love. The last three categories seem to me particularly relevant here. It is certainly the case that there are some SF fans, whose tastes run to what is called 'hard SF' and who might, indeed, self-identify as 'hard-core', for whom 'science' is indeed a key criterion for separating out worthwhile SF from worthless, and thereby constituting a canon. But I want to talk in slightly broader terms, partly because 'SF Fandom' as a whole is a much larger group than 'hard-core fans of hard SF', but mostly because science itself has proven itself historically mutable. Things once considered scientifically plausible, or even scientifically true, are no longer so. It turns out there *are* no oceans upon Venus. Excluding *Frankenstein* (1818), *The Invisible Man* (1897) or *The Left Hand of Darkness* (1969) from 'the SF canon' because these texts get the science 'wrong' to one degree or another would be a patently foolish policy.

The argument I am making, in other words, is that 'art', 'politics' and 'love' all feed very directly and obviously into the business not only of making but of revising and changing canons. The first category speaks to that impulse to say 'such-and-such a novel must be included in the canon *because it is very good*' – it is, in other words, the appeal to aesthetic merit. Political intervention, though dismissed by many under the caricature of 'political correctness', has an equally important if generally remedial role to play. To claim that there are 100 good female novelists working before Jane Austen is to intervene politically as well as aesthetically, since female representation in culture and actual female lives in society are closely linked. Ensuring that a 'canon' of SF texts includes a representative number of texts by women, writers of colour and LGBT writers would only *not* be political in a Utopian world unafflicted by any residuum of sexism, racism and homophobia. We do not live in such a world.

But it's the final term—love—that is, I think, the most interesting. Constructing canons is not a passionless undertaking. SF Fans care about SF because they love it, and another way of describing a canon would be to call it 'a list of SF texts worthy of our love'. There's some point in dwelling on this, because it is often overlooked, especially in discourses of academic enquiry which have, for several reasons, a bias towards 'disinterested objectivity'. But love is behind the process, and one of the attractive things about Badiou's philosophy is the way it insists upon the compossibility of 'love' and 'truth'. To describe the question 'which texts should be included in a SF canon?' as open-ended is not the same thing as pretending it's a wholly subjective, and therefore arbitrary, game. You and I may disagree over particular texts; but there is still some force in considering the truth-functions of canons. This is not just to claim that Shelley's *Frankenstein* is a more influential SF novel than Jane Loudon's *The Mummy* (1827), which is a proposition fairly easily supported evidentially; but also to make the more daring assertion that M. J. Engh's *Arslan* (1976) is a better novel than Michelle Shirey Crean's *Dancer of the Sixth* (1993).

I wonder if one (rather un-Badiouian) way of framing this would be to talk in terms of shame. Since that might look like a non-sequitur, I'll explain what I mean. I'm interested in exploring the utility of this claim: a work of SF can be considered canonical *if you ought to be ashamed not to know it*. This might be anything from mild and readily excused embarrassment that you haven't yet gotten around to reading Lauren Beukes' *Zoo City* (2010); or it might be the more profound shame that you have not read Margaret Atwood's *The Handmaid's Tale* (1985).

This perhaps looks judgmental, but I mean 'shame' in a particular sense, as an affect directly operative of 'love'. The US psychoanalytic theorist Silvan Tomkins has some interesting things to say on this subject. To quote Eve Kososfsky Sedwick and Adam Frank's deft summary, we got our first taste of Silvan Tomkins when we were looking for some usable ideas on the topic of shame. In a sodden landscape of moralistic or maudlin *idées reçues* about what is, to the contrary, the most mercurial of emotions, Tomkins' formulations startle … [he] considers shame, along with interest, surprise, joy, anger, fear, distress [and] disgust to be the basic set of affects. He places shame, in fact, at one end of the affect polarity *shame-interest*, suggesting that the pulsations of cathexis around shame, of all things, are what either enable or disenable so basic a function as the ability to be interested in the world. (Sedgwick and Frank, *Shame and its Sisters*, 4–5)

This is well put I think. For Tomkins 'shame is an innate auxiliary affect and a specific inhibitor of continuing interest and enjoyment'. Talking in terms of personal interaction (although he could as well be talking about other manifestations of social being) he suggests this might be 'because one is suddenly looked at by one who is strange, or because one wishes to look at or commune with another person but suddenly cannot because he is strange, or one expected him to be familiar but he suddenly appears unfamiliar, or one started to smile but found one was smiling at a stranger'. Sedgwick and Frank are surely correct that 'the emphasis in this account on the *strange*, rather than on the prohibited or disapproved' is what is ground-breaking here. In terms of the canon, it is the gap between the strangeness of a text and the wider expectation that it be familiar that generates the affect in question, which in turn will motivate either a withdrawal or else precisely an engagement with (and therefore a reinforcement of) the 'canonical' text. As Tomkins puts it: 'once shame has been activated, the original excitement or joy may be increased again and inhibit the shame or the shame may further inhibit and reduce excitement or joy'. (Sedgwick and Frank, 134–5)

In other words, the salient for SF Fandom, as a canon-forming body, is the community context *in which one can become ashamed* (for instance: of one's ignorance) *precisely as a means* of enabling one's interest in the construction of a non-arbitrary canon of core texts.

Since I am grounding 'the canon' in an aggregation of community decisions, it will be worth saying something, briefly, about that community. SF Fandom represents a fairly small dedicated group of people with similar interests that is part of a much larger generalized group of people with a less focussed interest in, but broadly positive sense of, genre texts. Before the internet core fandom manifested in physical groups, from friends' meetings and small groups in pubs discussing SF to larger-scale get-togethers at conventions. Now with the internet fandom is able to perform 'community' on a global scale, all the year round. This has, perhaps counter-intuitively, not caused physical get-togethers to diminish; on the contrary events like Comicon,

Worldcon and Finncon are now enormous. The relation of this to canon-forming is, I am arguing, the intersection between a Badouian love/art/politics and a Tomkinsian 'shame'.

I'll give an example. Consider the statement: 'I have never seen *Star Wars*'. If I were to say that to a non-SF fan I would not be surprised to hear the reply: 'neither have I; I don't really like sci-fi'. In the context of SF Fandom, however, the reply will more likely consist of a kind of friendly mockery, a chiding, an 'and you call yourself a fan!' The shame entailed is that of a positive affect, in Tomkins's sense, and one that therefore tends towards the establishment of a canon. By this I mean that saying 'I have never seen *Star Wars*' does not entail the sort of shame associated with confessing to a genuinely antisocial act, but neither is it making a merely neutral statement about yourself, along the line of saying (say) 'I have never been fishing' or 'I have never eaten sushi'. To say 'I have never been fishing' is to acknowledge that whilst fishing represents a very popular pastime for many people, that group that happens not to include you. It would not (to labour the point) carry the implication that you feel you *ought* to go fishing. But uttering 'I have never seen *Star Wars*', particularly in the context of Fandom, is much more likely to be delivered with defiance ('so much for your precious genre!') or with a kind of positively-inflected shame, an acknowledgement that it is something you probably should have done. Indeed, there is a long-running UK radio show actually called 'I Have Never Seen *Star Wars*', on which celebrities appear and 'confess' to shameful omissions in their cultural or social practice.

The point of all this for the present essay is that the shame one feels at the admission 'I have never seen *Star Wars*' is an index to the canonicity of that text. It is not that *Star Wars* is a particularly good film; indeed, there are many fans who think it a bad film (artistically and politically, as Badiou might say) but who nevertheless would consider it slightly shaming to admit 'I have never seen *Star Wars*'. Replace the salient in that sentence, and we track the degrees of marginality to the canon: 'I have never seen *Zardoz* (1974)' is much less shaming. 'I have never seen *The Tunnel* (1935)' or 'I have never seen *The Island at the Top of the World* (1974)' is hardly shaming at all, for these are minor films. They are minor – which is to say, non-canonical – because they are artistically weak, because no political point is made in bringing them within the canon, but above all because they are not loved in the way canonical texts are loved.

It perhaps sounds paradoxical to link 'shame' with the positive affect of canon-formation's 'love' (not to mention art and politics) as I do here. But I think it helps explain the success of campaigns to address 'injustices' in canon formation. A book such as Dale Spender's, or academic efforts to rescue texts by writers of colour, gay or trans-sexual writers – or efforts to raise the profile of female SF, or 'Racefail' – apply their leverage not with actual bigots, sexists and racists (who presumably will simply shrug them off), but with that much larger constituency of people who are not themselves knowingly motivated by sexism, racism or prejudice and are moreover aware of the pervasive ubiquity of sexism, racism and prejudice as formative discourses of the society in which we all live. To put it another way, directing our attention to (for instance) '100 good female novelists before Jane Austen' shames us into admitting the extent to which the cultural inertia of ubiquitously sexist attitudes and assumptions had blinded us to female achievement in this area.

According to this reading, it is not coincidental that one key axis of change in the parameters of SF Canonicity has been an articulation of social-political shame, moved in part by a sense that neglecting women, writers of colour and LGBT figures in genre partakes of a broader, shameful societal prejudice against such groups.

In what ways do these questions shape the sense of the SF as a changing or evolving mode? Well, before we can talk about the ways the SF Canon has changed, it is necessary to at least sketch a status quo to which those changes applied. This is harder to do than might be thought, for several reasons. One is that there is little consensus about what SF is in the first place, either in terms of broader definition or in terms of when it begins. Another is that the SF-oriented communities needful for the formation of canons developed, until fairly recently, only patchily, hampered by the difficulties of congregation. But for the sake of argument, I'll propose the second half of the twentieth-century as a place to start. This is not because I think SF only half a century old – in point of fact, I believe it to be a genre of great antiquity, with antecedents amongst the Ancient Greek novel, and established in recognizably modern, pseudo-scientific and culturally Protestant form around 1600 (see my *Palgrave History of Science Fiction*). But for much of its early life SF was a minor component of broader culture. It is not until the twentieth-century that a critical mass of fans emerged, and not until quite late in that century that we find self-reflexive critical discourse (extending beyond book and film reviews into broader analytical appraisals and interrogations, critical historical reviews and theoretical discussions). One of the first book-length works to discuss genre was J. O. Bailey's *Pilgrims Through Space and Time* (1948). Bailey was a professional academic, Professor of Literature at the University of North Carolina at Chapel Hill, and the Science Fiction Research Association honours his memory by calling their prestigious award for excellence in SF scholarship 'the Pilgrim Award'. The genre's major awards were established in subsequent decades – the Hugos in 1953, the Nebulas in 1965 and the Arthur C. Clarke in 1987. By the 1980s there were many works of criticism being published and academic courses taught. Such discursive work was already involved the business of challenging and changing the sense of what was 'canonical' for the genre: Marleen Barr's *Alien to Femininity*

(1987) makes a persuasive case for female writers of SF; Donna Haraway's 'A Cyborg Manifesto' (1985) develops an influential cyborg-feminist thesis, and Ursula Le Guin (herself a very major SF writer) had published *The Language of the Night* in 1979, collected essays that eloquently revised her own attitudes to the place of gender in her writing. This leads us to the striking state of affairs where, rather than there being an established canon that is later challenged, the SF Canon *comes into being* as a contested site of discursive expansion.

It is hard, indeed, to identify a representative 'canon'. We might take the case of Brian Aldiss's influential history of the genre *Billion Year Spree* (1974, republished in expanded form as Aldiss and Wingrove, *Trillion Year Spree*, 1986). Although he discusses earlier works, it is Aldiss's contention that the first science fiction novel is Mary Shelley's *Frankenstein* (1818). From there he traces a lineage of the genre through nineteenth-century Gothic, the commercial successes of Jules Verne and Henry Wells, into a broadening delta of twentieth-century texts, disposed broadly speaking into two sorts: US science fiction of the age of Pulps (1920s–1930s), Golden Age (1940s–1950s) and New Wave (1960s), and UK science fiction, which Aldiss characterizes as more downbeat and smaller-scale (Aldiss coined the phrase 'cosy catastrophe' to describe the work of John Wyndham, John Christopher and others). Many writers are mentioned, but a core of figures gets the greatest attention, including: Poe, Verne, Wells, Hugo Gernsback, Edgar Rice Burroughs, E. E. 'Doc' Smith, Asimov, Arthur C. Clarke, Pohl, Van Vogt, Walter Miller, Robert Heinlein, Frank Herbert, Philip K. Dick and Michael Moorcock. In other words, white men take up the bulk of the book's discussion, even if the larger thesis is that the foundational text of the genre was written by a woman. Many female writers are discussed, although as minor names in a larger narrative. There is a greater emphasis on female contributions to the genre in the 1986 re-issue of the work, itself symptomatic of a shift in critical culture.

Aldiss's is a work of personal history, not an attempt to set-in-stone the canonical limits of the genre. But we can take it as an indicative early 1970s text that says: writers of SF come in many varieties, but the most important, influential and best happen to be white men. To talk, then, of the way this 'canon' has changed in the four subsequent decades is to identify three main areas.

The first is historical, and this is that expansion of the canon with least purchase. I say so with a degree of sorrow, since it is an area that interests me personally. Aldiss argues that SF begins with Frankenstein, in 1818. Other critics have suggested the later nineteenth century as the starting point; or even later still (Hugo Gernsback did not coin the specific term 'science fiction' until 1927). It remains the case today that most critics, as most fans, consider SF to be marked by its modernity, its relationship to recent technological advances and attendant social changes. That said, there have been critics who have attempted to expand the chronological reach of the SF canon back beyond the early nineteenth century, to the Middle Ages and even Antiquity (see Roberts, 2006). The argument can be made on grounds of historical significance, as well as (in some cases) on aesthetic grounds. But the case is not one with wide appeal. The bottom line is that few self-professed SF Fans would be ashamed to admit, even to other SF Fans, that they have never read these texts. We might want to suggest that these texts ought to be included in a separately conceived 'academic study of SF' canon.

A second area – broadly, that of increasing the diversity of the existing modern SF canon in terms of gender, ethnicity and alternate sexualities – has already been discussed. Here there is broader consensus. It would be a brave critic who denied the 'canonical' importance of Andre Norton, C. L. Moore, James Tiptree, Jr, Joanna Russ, Ursula Le Guin, Marge Piercy, Octavia Butler, Nalo Hopkinson, Pat Cadigan and Gwyneth Jones to the genre. Similarly, gay writers such as Samuel Delany and Geoff Ryman merit inclusion in any SF canon. As several critics point out, a genre invested in the representations of aliens is necessarily therefore committed to an engagement with 'alienness' and 'otherness'. It can be uniquely hospitable to the representation of groups 'othered' or alienated from mainstream society. Sarah Lefanu's critical monograph *In the Chinks of the World Machine* (1988) makes this case, taking as its title a line from a story by (female) author James Tiptree, Jr called 'The Women Men Don't See'. Expanding the canon along these lines is, as I have been arguing, an ongoing process. That Nalo Hopkinson and Uppinder Mehan's collection of stories written exclusively by people of colour, *So Long Been Dreaming* (2004) was the first such volume published is in itself, and considering its recent date, shaming. Kenneth M. Roemer's 'Contemporary American Indian Literature' (1994) persuasively makes the case for the importance of anthologies for challenging the canonical status quo.

A third, related area in which the SF canon has been expanded is geographical. The notion that science fiction is a purely 'Western' phenomenon, dominated by US writers, though once common, is no longer tenable. SF has been and continues to be produced all around the world; and it is difficult to see how vigorous SF cultures in India and the Far East, in South America and parts of Africa can be excluded from the canon. The problem here is a lack of consensus as to which Indian, Chinese, Japanese, South American or African writers and works merit selection. Moreover, there may be reasons for a more sanguine view of the matter. Perhaps the SF canon is less amenable to evolution than this essay has been suggesting. Istvan Csicsery-Ronay's article 'Science Fiction and Empire' (2003), argues that the discursive and representational logics of SF are too deeply implicated in myths of technoscientific empire ever to escape the conceptual cosmos of technological development that itself provided the momentum for imperial expansion and control. It may be the case that gender, ethnicity and alternate sexualities will only ever be represented in a tokenistic fashion. Fandom has made fewer inroads here than is the case with gender, race and sexuality. Lavie Tidhar's *World SF Blog* (worldsf.wordpress.com/) works to redress the balance of perspective, but where female writers, writers of colour and gay writers do get nominated for, and sometimes even win, major prizes it is still very much the exception for a non-Anglophone writer to be recognized in this way on the world stage.

Works Cited

Aldiss, Brian (1973). *Billion Year Spree*. London: Weidenfeld and Nicolson.

Aldiss, Brian and David Wingrove (1986). *Trillion Year Spree*. London: Gollancz.

Ashley, Mike (2009). *The Mammoth Book Of Mindblowing SF*. London: Constable and Robinson.

Atwood, Maragaret (1985). *The Handmaid's Tale*. Toronto: McClelland & Stewart.

Badiou, Alain (2003). *Infinite Thought: Truth and the Return of Philosophy*. Translated by Oliver Feltham and Justin Clemens. London: Continuum.

Bailey, J. O. (1947). *Pilgrims Through Space and Time: Trends and Patterns in Scientific and Utopian Fiction*. New York: Argus Books.

Barr, Marleen (1987). *Alien to Femininity*. Westport. CT: Greenwood Press.

Beukes, Lauren (2010). *Zoo City*. Johannesburg: Jacana Publishing.

Boorman, John (dir.) (1974). *Zardoz*.

Crean, Michelle Shirey (1993). *Dancer of the Sixth*. New York: Del Rey.

Csicsery-Ronay, Jr., Istvan (2003). 'Science Fiction and Empire'. *Science Fiction Studies*. 30. 2 (July). 231–45.

Elvey, Maurice (dir.) (1935). *The Tunnel*.

Engh, M. J. (1976). *Arslan*. New York: Warner Books.

Haraway, Donna (1991) [1985]. 'A Cyborg Manifesto: Science, Technology, and Socialist- Feminism in the Late Twentieth Century'. *Simians, Cyborgs and Women: The Reinvention of Nature*. New York: Routledge. 149–81.

Lefanu, Sarah (1988). *In the Chinks of the World Machine: Feminism and Science Fiction*. London: The Women's Press.

Le Guin, Ursula (1969). *The Left Hand of Darkness*. New York: Ace Books.

—(1979). *The Language of the Night: Essays on Science Fiction and Fantasy*. New York: Putnam.

Loudon, Jane (1827). *The Mummy*. London: Henry Colburn.

Lucas, George (dir.) (1977). *Star Wars*.

Roberts, Adam (2006). *The History of Science Fiction*. Basingstoke: Palgrave Macmillan.

Roemer, Kenneth M. (1994). 'Contemporary American Indian Literature: The Centrality of Canons on the Margins'. *American Literary History*. 6. 3. 583–99.

Sales, Ian (2010). *SF Mistressworks*. Available online: sfmistressworks.wordpress.com/

Sedgwick, Eve Kofosky, and Adam Frank (eds) (1995). *Shame and its Sisters: A Silvan Tomkins Reader*. Durham: Duke University Press.

Shelley, Mary (2003) [1818]. *Frankenstein*. Harmondsworth: Penguin Classics.
Spender, Dale (1986). *Mothers of the Novel: 100 Good Women Writers Before Jane Austen*. London and New York: Pandora Press.
Stevenson, Robert (dir.) (1974). *The Island at the Top of the World*.
Tidhar, Lavie (2009). *World SF Blog*. Available online: worldsf.wordpress.com/
Wells, H. G. (1897). *The Invisible Man*. London: Pearson.

10 Issues of Gender, Sexuality and Ethnicity

Pat Wheeler

One of the most conspicuous aspects of science fiction of the late twentieth century and twenty-first centuries is its heterogeneity and its refusal to be contained within a single, paradigmatic framework. Critical theories of sexuality, gender and ethnicity within science fiction writing can forecast potential futures with the absence of socially constructed images and values associated with ideas of femininity and masculinity. What critical theories of race and difference can show is that science fiction can not only forecast futures absent of racism, but also what Kilgore describes as 'futures in which racism persists, taking on new forms around new lines of difference' (16). Science fiction serves to inform through representations of 'other' ways of being, rather than attempting to set standards and norms for women's and men's behaviour. According to Brian Attebery

> In science fiction, androgyny and other sexual alternatives need not be illusions to be dispelled or exceptions to be avoided but can instead represent plausible features of an extrapolated future or an alien world … writers are more than willing to disrupt the binary gender code with such concepts as a literal third sex, a society without sexual division, gender as a matter of individual choice, involuntary metamorphosis from one sex to another, gender as prosthesis, and all manner of unorthodox manifestations of sexual desire. (9)

Science fiction writers provide transgressive reading experiences that disavow the prescriptive nature of representation and offer the space to imagine new cultural assumptions about women and men when the constraints of contemporary society are taken away.

Gendered/Transgendered Futures

The political nature of much of science fiction provides a platform for writers to focus on the hierarchical relations of power, bringing a multiplicity of women's and men's experiences to their texts and challenging dominant gender models by positing other ways of 'being'. The term 'gender' is used to signify a set of cultural assumptions about women and men. Formally the terms 'sex' and 'gender' were virtually synonymous and linked intrinsically to essentialist assumptions about women and men and their role in society. The separation of sex and gender allows critics such as Judith Butler to argue that gender is socially constructed – that it is the product of cultural circumstances and therefore can be changed. Feminist critics argue that women interpret their discrimination through inherited notions of gender identity and through designated roles ascribed to them. They contend that essentialism is a product of patriarchy and privileges men's interests over women's. An essential model of thinking about gender and sexuality is the belief that there are certain ways of thinking and behaving which are 'essentially' manly or 'essentially' womanly. This model deems these characteristics are innate and remain fixed and unchangeable. Although it is acknowledged that notions of gender are historically and socially constructed, it is clear that in science fiction new and resistant identities are formed in reaction to dominant and hegemonic groups. Gender is understood to be instantly recognizable from a series of socially constructed images and values whereby the idea of femininity and masculinity is intrinsically linked to the formation of women's and men's identity. Butler argues that 'when a category is understood as representing a set of values or dispositions, it becomes normative in character and hence, exclusionary in principle'. In other words, when the models of 'woman' and 'man' are unrecognizable to other women and men, they become alienated, or, as Butler (1990: 325) states, they are 'left to conclude they are not ... as they have perhaps previously assumed'. In the culturally determined images with which we are continuously confronted, 'gender anomaly' is invariably missing and in the majority of the signifying images that abound, anyone who stands outside the accepted 'normality' of gender assumptions do not see themselves commonly represented. This absence was taken up by a number of science fiction writers, such as James Tiptree Jr, Jane Palmer, Sally Gearhart, Elisabeth Vonarburg, Josephine Sexton and Jody Scott for example, who both resist and transcend accepted gender definitions in their texts.

Transgender is a term used to signify people who wish to live their lives (or part of their lives) as the opposite gender to their biological sex at birth without necessarily resorting to permanent reassignment. Transgender people and transvestites (crossdressers) frequently have no desire to change their sex (or have not yet decided) and are happy with their bodies including their genitalia. They occupy transgressive subject positions that contradict the binary sex/gender system in that they are not either/or, they are both/ and. In *The Epistemology of the Closet* (1990) Eve Kosofsky Sedgwick argues that we now need to think about a transgender 'continuum' where gender is not fixed, rather it is a continuum, a process, continually renegotiated and never finally realized. Science fiction by its very nature offers a useful site for challenging both the binaries of male/female sex and of the cultural constructions of gender that are attached to those categories. Protagonists can 'perform' gender, they can be male or female, they can be neuters, have no definable sexual category, be intersexed or they can switch between genders. In science fiction the body (whether human or other) is a *tabula rasa*, capable of multiple and contradictory readings.

The transgendered body has been theorized as an 'in-between body' that Halberstam suggests 'retains the marks of its own ambiguity and ambiva-lence' (96). According to Anne Cranny-Francis the familiar polarities of male/ female are destroyed by a 'third term' which is 'both and neither of the polar terms'. She says:

> In the case of transvestites, transsexuals, and bisexuals, those polarities are male/female and heterosexual/homosexual. The importance of the third term is not that it simply breaks down boundaries, however, instead it makes boundaries visible. The third term identifies boundaries that we have been taught (ideologically, culturally) not to see; the homophobia that sustains a heterosexist society, the misogyny endemic to patriarchal attitudes. (148–9)

The notion of a 'third term' was taken up by Ursula Le Guin in *The Left Hand of Darkness* (1969). The novel is set on a planet where the androgynous inhabitants occupy a third space, one where they are sexually inactive and impotent apart from periods of 'kemmer'. When in kemmer, Gethenians secrete hormonal substances until either male or female dominance is established. The individuals have no predisposition to being male or female and as they undergo periods of kemmer throughout their lives they can be male and female, fathers and mothers. The male/female binary is still obvious here, as is the propensity to assign male dominance to the characters in the book, but Le Guin's novel about love and betrayal clearly articulates what has become known as a 'gender continuum'. The novel, ground-breaking and highly praised at the time of publication, has since received a rather more negative criticism in terms of its portrayal of non-gendered races that appear to be mostly endowed with 'masculine' attributes. The novel does, however, maintain its position in the canon of science fiction writing about gender, paving the way for other writers who follow.

Joanna Russ's *The Female Man* (1975) is well known for its queering of the gendered body as is Samuel R. Delany's *Triton* (1976). However, Russ's 'The Mystery of the Young Gentleman' (1982) is more ambiguous, as it is a transgender narrative with a protagonist of unknown gender and race but who 'masquerades' as a man. When confronted she/he/it says, 'a woman pretending to be a man, who pretends he's a woman in order to pretend to be a man? Come, come, it won't work' (88). These and other narratives clearly do work to make the transgendered body a viable and transgressive option. Other fiction that foregrounds transgender protagonists include Octavia Butler's *Dawn* (1987), whose Ooloi occupy transgendered spaces, Maureen McHugh's *Mission Child* (1998), Lois McMaster Bujold's *A Civil Campaign* (1999), Melissa Scott's *Shadow Man* (1995), which has five gender categories: woman, fem, herm, mem or man, and Suzy McKee Charnas's *The Conqueror's Child* (1999), the fourth in the Holdfast series. In the late 1990s Carolyn Ives Gilman's *Halfway Human* (1998), Charnas's *The Conqueror's Child* (1999) and Nancy Farmer's *Sea of Trolls* (2004) reignited the gender debate. See, for example, Brian Attebery, *Decoding Gender in Science Fiction* (2002), Patricia Melzer, *Alien Constructions: Science Fiction and Feminist Thought* (2006) and Wendy Gay Pearson's *Queer Universes: Sexualities in Science Fiction* (2008).

Feminism, Gender and Science Fiction

In 1989 The *Feminist Review* published a special edition, 'The Past Before Us: Twenty Years of Feminism', that reflected upon much of that critical and political thinking by and about women. The preface to the edition proclaimed that what was needed in the latter part of the twentieth century was 'a politics that builds upon the phenomenal advances of women's liberation'. The politics they envisaged took into account 'the limitations of a parochial and ethnocentric feminism' and 'reassessed and changed' the engagement and debate feminism (in particular socialist feminist) has with the 'black and lesbian women's movement, the Left, the peace movement, gay and anti-racist activists'. Such politics, they claim, 'are the most important legacy we inherit from twenty years of feminism' (6). During this period of potentially emancipatory politics many women writers embarked on a challenge to readers' relationships to what Kim Worthington calls, 'the procedural bounds of … inherited literary rules' (30) and to present what in many ways had previously been deemed unrepresentable: women who do not rely on male protagonists to inscribe them with meaning. Women's experimentation with science fiction at this time created what Lorna Sage calls a 'heterocosm', a place where 'atopic texts' that are both plural and placeless work as 'agents of alterneity' for women writers who frequently have 'satiric, didactic specu-lative or combative aims' with their writing (ix–x). The appropriation of and experimentation with male-dominated genres such as science fiction allowed women to address issues of class, gender and sexuality, together with ongoing debates about alienation and economic deprivation.

The major project of feminist science fiction is to call attention to the 'constructedness' of gender and to question those patriarchal ideologies that posit the pervasive belief in 'essential' differences which permanently distinguish men from women and which invariably render women as passive and inferior. Feminist critics argue that women interpret their discrimination through inherited notions of gender identity and through designated roles ascribed to them. They contend that essentialism is a product of patriarchy and privileges men's interests over women's. In a patriarchal system women are frequently negated and demonized and this is internalized in women's self-reflexive precept of femininity. Feminist science fictions written during this period actively engage in the transformation and renegotiation of dominant social orders, and for Maria Lauret these have historically 'come to fulfil an important role … as a site of struggle over cultural meanings' (95). The 20-year period evoked in the review is especially telling in terms of science fiction studies. In her critical appraisal of feminist science fiction, *In the Chinks of the World Machine* (1988), Sarah Lefanu wrote of 'the extraor-dinary relationship between feminism and science fiction that flowered in the 1970s and 1980s' (7). Prior to Lefanu's persuasive examination, feminist critics (most notably Joanna Russ) had argued that men who wrote future worlds tended to place women in the same sort of reductive roles they occupied at the beginning of the twentieth century. Russ, amongst others, argues that much of twentieth-century science fiction 'has in general ignored women's estate and the social problems with which feminism deals' (135). Feminists were tired of the lack of interesting and viable women characters in much of genre writing and so began to appropriate male-dominated genres overtly as part of a strategy for subverting patriarchal discourses. At this time The Women's Press was instrumental in creating the sort of heterocosmic space Sage envisioned when it created its science fiction division in the 1980s. Its aim was to 'publish science fiction by and about women; to present exciting and provocative images of the future that would offer an alternative vision of science and technology, and challenge male domination of the science fiction tradition itself' – these were the aims of the Women's SF Press and this manifesto is printed at the front of all the books in the original series. A number of the 'new' women writers published in the science fiction division were recovered from earlier in the twentieth century but the imprint also brought in women writers who were new to publishing in science fiction. Recovered writers include, for example, Charlotte Perkins Gilman, Naomi Mitchison and Katharine Burdekin; republished established writers such as Joanna Russ, Sally M. Gearhart, Jody Scott and Octavia Butler and new writers such as Jane Palmer, Rhoda Lerman, Josephine Saxton and Sandi Hall were all published by The Women's Press, Science Fiction Division in 1980–90. This notable body of work uses the themes and tropes of the genre in order that women protagonists can break free from the constraints placed on them by reductive or unambiguous representations.

Writing within a specific genre such as science fiction offers a supporting framework on which to construct ideological, politically motivated narratives. Patricia Duncker says in her discussion of genre fiction in *Sisters and Strangers* that 'the writer who chooses a genre that is strongly marked by a traditional array of motifs, characters, plots, locations and emotions' (16) is both supported and confined by those conventions. She believes that the writer of genre fiction is bound by readers' expectations even as they attempt to subvert them from within, but she goes on to say that 'originality will come from clever use of form' rather than abandoning the form itself. Feminist critics such as Anne Cranny-Francis, Lefanu, Russ and Marleen Barr see fictional genres and in particular science fiction as the ideal medium from which women can explore new possibilities and new ways of being. Science Fiction writing with its critical examination of ideology, its temporal and geographical shifts and its conventions of science and technology in pivotal roles is for many women writers the definitive genre from which to explore their disillusionment with socially driven constructions of 'woman'. The genre is interrogative; it asks questions and speculates on possible answers or solutions to those questions and it imagines radically different worlds from those we know. It is, according to LeFanu, a means of 'fusing political concerns with the playful creativity of the imagination' (7). Feminist science fiction draws on an important strand in all science fiction – that of resistance to the dominant ideology.

Charlotte Perkins Gilman's satire *Herland* (1915) is generally accepted as the first SF novel to reflect a preoccupation with gender issues and focus quite specifically on the political character of sex and sexuality; establishing the case for sexual politics as an area of struggle. Subsequent works such as Katharine Burdekin's *Swastika Night* (1937), C. L. Moore's 'No Woman Born' (1944) and Naomi Mitchison's *Memoirs of a Spacewoman* (1962) are also significant in their representation of women in a male-centered genre. However, it was not until the late 1960s and the advent of second-wave feminism that gender itself became recognized as an area for political debate, and writers such as Joanna Russ, James Tiptree Jr and Samuel R. Delany emerged. The resultant feminist science fiction was characterized by narratives of self-discovery that explicitly refused traditional depictions of gendered behaviour. Russ's *Picnic on Paradise* (1968), for example, has one of the first women protagonists, Alyx, who transgresses pernicious gender assumptions. Alyx is a secret agent, a thief and an assassin and although she embodies some of those charac-teristics that have traditionally been associated with masculinity such as rationality, bravery and adventuring on the high seas, she retains a strongly gendered femaleness. She is a wise woman. The 1970s and 1980s proved prolific for such gender-questioning writing: Russ's *The Female Man* (1975), Marge Piercy's *Woman on the Edge of Time* (1976), Suzy McKee Charnas's *Motherlines* (1978), Sally Gearhart's *The Wanderground* (1980) and Elizabeth Vonarburg's *The Silent City* (1988) all debate, among other things, how society might develop if gender constraints were eliminated. Suzette Elgin's *Native Tongue* (1984) and *The Judas Rose* (1987) offer a critique of patriarchy through language. Sandi Hall's *The Godmothers* (1982) examines women's persecution though the past (witch burning), the present (twentieth-century women's liberation) and future (holovids) patriarchal structures. Angela Carter's *The Passion of New Eve* (1977) and Esme Dodderidge's *The New Gulliver* (1988) use reverse gender dialectics in their portrayal of injustices against women. That is, the men are ascribed with gender attributes associated with women and women with those attached to men, a straightforward reversal of their social position and essential natures. In these mainly satirical novels, men, in alter-native and future societies, are forced to take on the sort of subjugated roles that many women occupied in the 1970s and 1980s. This represents a small sample of feminist science fiction writing in the 1970s and 1980s. This sense of history enables us to see both the development of the genre in the early years of second-wave feminism and its expansion from texts that opened up gender debates to ones that focused on radical social change. Feminist science fiction writing at the end of the twentieth century carries within it an ideological relationship with what has gone before. It presents an interaction between the individual and the world, whether it is in the past, present or future.

'Cyberfeminist Simulations'

In *Aliens and Others* (1994) Jenny Wolmark argues that 'cyberpunk has reworked the spatial and temporal dislocation that is the most character- istic feature of science fiction' (109). She believes this to be the 'collapsing of the imaginary distance between the present and the future into a virtual reality' that relocates the ideas of 'spatial/temporal' into 'outside/inside'. The dystopian futures that predominate in twentieth-century science fiction writing are more prophetic or anticipatory than the Utopian ones and come with warnings or forebodings; rather than visions of a better world it presents a grim vision of the future. The strongly inscribed discourses of cyberpunk fictions are overloaded with (supposedly) male preoccupations of cyber technology, matrix hackers, sex, drugs and rock and roll. Wolmark argues that 'cyberpunk has reworked the spatial and temporal dislocation that is the most characteristic feature of science fiction'. She believes this to be the 'collapsing of the imaginary distance between the present and the future into a virtual reality' that relocates the ideas of 'spatial/temporal' into 'outside/inside'. In an often quoted article, 'Some Real Mothers: An Interview with Samuel R. Delany' (1988), Tokayi Tatsumi explores the genesis of new movements in science fiction writing including the move towards dystopian cyberpunk fiction. In the interview, Delany suggests that the most important influence of cyberpunk is 1970s feminist science fiction. The general milieu of cyberpunk is one of environmental degra- dation encountered in post-apocalyptic, post-national enclaves that are the result of man-made catastrophes and the emergence of a new-world order. Cyberspace, the metaphoric space where electronically stored information can be experienced, is, according to Wolmark, 'strongly inscribed with the masculine', where 'jacking in is the new jerking off'. In Wolmark's discussion of cyberspace there is a strong correlation between the genre and feminist science fiction. The machine/human interface and the fear and fascination with new technologies mirror the fear and fascination of women, too often proscribed as the alien other. Cyberspace becomes a place where identity can be transmuted and transformed at will and so necessarily expresses a fundamental ambivalence towards the body which is important to women's writing.

The technical modification of the body and the emergence of the cyborg features significantly in women's dystopian writing of this period. Lise Leroux's strange, evocative book, *One Hand Clapping* (1998) is a series of interlinking stories, set in futuristic urban landscapes. She imagines a possible future where genetic engineering dominates and body parts can be replaced. The grafting of buds on to humans to grow spare body parts provides paid work and clinics advertize on television for clients. The main protagonist,

Marina, moves from one hand implanted, to multiple implants all over her body. In the novel Leroux is concerned with ethical and moral issues surrounding genetic engineering, as well as cybernetics, the 'family' unit and pollution; capitalism with its concomitant qualities of greed and exploitation are shown to be the prime motivations behind medical and genetic experimentation. Donna Haraway's notion of the hybridized body as discussed in 'A Manifesto for Cyborgs: Science, Technology and Socialist Feminism in the 1980s' is a key feature here, where the woman and the implants become a fabricated organism; the body as machine. In the same way Maureen F. McHugh's novel *China Mountain Zhang* (1992) explores diversely imagined future cultures. In the dystopian tradition this is a novel where the hero Zhang cannot change the inequalities of the system. In a future where the People's Republic of China is the dominant world power McHugh draws on a clutch of creative ideas ranging from organic engineering, to architects who 'imagine' biotic, natural houses. She also gives the reader a sexually charged, illicit computer game, capable of giving orgasmic pleasure, and the ability to modify one's looks with human/computer interfaces. In her future there is still racism and sexism, but McHugh synthesizes political and sexual tensions together, and extrapolates both positive and negative elements from the end of the twentieth century.

The spatial and temporal dislocation that is the most characteristic feature of dystopian science fiction is evident in a range of feminist novels published in the 1990s, of which Leroux and McHugh are just an example. Pat Cadigan's *Tea from an Empty Cup* (1998) is set in a future where Japan has been destroyed by an earthquake, lives are lived at the interface of human and machine and net surfers who live in virtual worlds are being murdered online, by displaced persons who are trying to create a virtual New Japan. Cadigan reworks the ideas of 'spatial/temporal' dislocations into the 'outside/inside' of a virtual world. Lieutenant Konstantin must enter the Matrix to hunt down the killers and becomes a hybrid of woman and machine. Cadigan's protagonist, Konstantin is important in that she transgresses forbidden borders and disrupts the rather problematic standards of representation of women in novels such as William Gibson's *Neuromancer* (1984). Sadie Plant calls this 'cyber feminist simulation' and argues that after decades of ambivalence towards technology many feminists are finding a wealth of new opportunities in the virtual worlds created by the technological revolution. In the tradition of hard science fiction, women's dystopias explore the possibilities of intelligent machines, nanotechnology and artificial intelligence in the machine/mind interface of virtual worlds. These worlds open up new spaces for women, spaces where they can deny authority and confuse identity: sexualities and genders within the matrix are ambiguous and unrestrained.

Case Study Gender: Carolyn Ives Gilman, *Halfway Human* (1998, 2010)

> You're not even conscious of [gender], for the most part, but it's always
> there. It's very subtle: levels of formality, types of language, deference,
> rivalry, respect. Even your voices and the way you hold your bodies
> change depending on which sex you're with. I don't know why you
> don't find it oppressive, except that you're so used to it. (Carolyn Ives
> Gilman, 85)

In the late 1960s and 1970s many writers sought to expose ideological
divides and envisioned societies where gender and sexuality were no longer
divisive forces. As noted above, in *The Left Hand of Darkness* (1969), Ursula
Le Guin attempted to define and understand the meaning of sexuality and
gender, both at personal and collective levels of consciousness, stating 'I
eliminated gender to find out what was left. Whatever was left would be,
presumably human. It would define that area that is shared between man
and woman' (177). Le Guin's attempt to eliminate gender constraints left
the supposedly androgynous creatures visibly exhibiting male characteristics. The undertaking to demonstrate that men and women cannot
be cast in any preconceived ideal or assigned to a corresponding role
dependent on expectations of patterns of behaviour in socially constructed
gender roles proved problematic. Le Guin was criticized for *The Left
Hand of Darkness* in that she could not help but inscribe the supposedly
androgynous characters as male. In Carolyn Ives Gilman's *Halfway Human*
(1998, 2010) the author takes Le Guin's attempt a stage further. Whether
she has successfully managed to create a character with no obvious gender
attributes is open to debate. It is a novel that in the tradition of feminist
science fiction interrogates ethical and societal issues and it is no surprise
that Gilman has been called 'the new Le Guin'. Its central protagonist is
Tedla, a bland, who is a neuter from the planet Gammadis. The neuter is
found wandering on Capella Two, a planet colonized by Earth where a
capital market economy rules. The principal export is knowledge; money
and information are the only truly transportable commodities. Tedla is
placed in the care of Valerie Entrada, a xenologist who gradually hears
the story of Tedla's life.

The interaction of the neuter from Gammadis with its protector on Capella
offers a critique of slavery, eugenic experimentation and market forces as well
as an ongoing debate on gender. Tedla was born on a planet where all are
born neuter and where children all live together. In socialization classes they
learn of aliens from other planets who are born with sexual organs and live in
family units; this seem repulsive to the children who apparently do not turn
into male or female until they reach puberty:

The docents (teachers) had always told us that only primitives lived that way, in tribalism and true civil amity was impossible as long as the bonds of biology were allowed to coexist with those of community. We discussed it and I, at least, concluded that the aliens must be more socially primitive than we. (49)

At puberty the children supposedly go through a number of tests that determine what they will be male, female or bland. The blands are seen as less than human, they are reduced to a voiceless, marginalized class who live 'in gray space', literally behind the scenes cooking, cleaning and generally running the everyday lives of the 'humans', leaving them free for more intellectual pursuits. In a strong correlation to how slaves were treated, blands are deemed non-human, slower, more stupid and to have no rights. Gilman draws on the legacy of both the history of slavery and the tradition of speculative writing to foreground Tedla's experiences as a non-human. It is also a story of first contact between the Gammadians and the Capellans and the interaction between the two that leads to rebellion. Tedla escapes from Capella with a member of the first contact team, a xenologist, and is educated on Capella, where it is found after the death of its protector and its own attempted suicide.

Valerie Entrada initially sees Tedla as an opportunity to further her career, the information she learns from Tedla's story is worth a lot of money especially as the big corporate companies that hold the power on Capella seem very interested in it. The reason we learn is that a delegation from Gammadis is expected on Capella and a bland on the loose with an extraordinary tale is going to be a real problem. The corporation for whom Valerie works wants to eradicate Tedla's memories, supposedly to cure its suicidal tendencies, but in effect for political and financial reasons. When we finally hear its story it seems that far from being 'untouchable', the blands' lives are bound to their masters in more ways than imaginable.

What is clear here is that this novel engages in the deconstruction of the textual meaning of gender and power through a variety of narrative techniques. Natalie Rosinsky (107) argues that the challenges to 'hierarchical relationships' that feminist writing offers are important. She believes that women find a 'fundamentally different and dynamic process' in reading and writing science fiction. What is so interesting about reading *Halfway Human* is how the reader imagines the character Tedla, called 'it' throughout the novel. Is it possible to see it as completely without gender attributes? In this extract Valeria tries to get Tedla to put on some clean clothes and goes to her husband's wardrobe:

'nothing too masculine', Tedla said nervously. 'I hate it when people treat me as if I were a man'

> Surprised Val said 'Don't worry, we'll be in the UIC; it's gender neutral'.
>
> 'There's no such thing,' Tedla said. 'You think so but laws can't change people's instincts'.
>
> Val smiled. 'I think you overestimate how steeped in sexuality we are. It doesn't dominate our waking thoughts, you know.'
>
> 'You're not even conscious of it, for the most part, but it's always there. It's very subtle: levels of formality, types of language, deference, rivalry, respect. Even your voices and the way you hold your bodies change depending on which sex you're with. I don't know why you don't find it oppressive, except that you're so used to it'. (85)

This conceptualizing of the body in *Halfway Human* is a 'cultural reconfiguring' of human identity that draws on 'the images and symbols of a culture' to articulate the assumptions predicated on the body. According to Cranny-Francis the 'relationship between our conceptions of ourselves as human beings and the material conditions of our existence' (145) is worked through in the imaginary spaces of fictional texts. In this instance Gilman's use of narrative is one way of 'reinflecting the known – taking a new look at things'. Gilman's two societies work very effectively as extrapolations of the gender assumptions of our own society.

Science Fiction and Sexuality: The 'Queer' Body

Gay and lesbian criticism has over the years sought to reinterpret the heterosexist and homophobic nature of sexuality. Critics and theorists posited that patriarchal cultures, such as Western culture, tended to be focused on what Butler ('Gender Trouble', 336) has termed a 'heterosexual matrix'. However, according to Eve Kosofsky Sedgwick, sexual difference can take many different forms and identities such as 'gay' and 'lesbian' do not allow for more complex sexual border crossings. Her influential text *The Epistemology of the Closet* (1991) sought to question existing tendencies and binary thinking about sexuality. Kosofsky examines the historical legacy of such thinking about heterosexual and homosexual 'norms' and attempts to posit other ways of thinking about sexuality.

Science fiction can concern itself with sexual transformations, debating sexual dissonance through literary representations of difference and otherness that reinscribe sexual identity. It offers an ideal platform from which to debate the denaturalization of heterosexuality. Butler argues the construction of 'coherence' in sex debates conceals 'discontinuities that run rampant within heterosexual, bisexual and gay and lesbian contexts' ('Gender Trouble', 336). To unsettle and defamiliarize heteronormative sexuality as many science fiction writers seek to do is to expose its discontinuities and to provide a reading experience that subverts the unifying affirmation of heterosexuality. Many writers of the genre take the debate quite self-consciously into areas such as transexuality with its inherent renegotiation of sexual reassignment and transvestism with its temporary shifts of gender identity. In order to transform the social relations of 'lived bodies' science fiction writers offer a radical shift in awareness of sexual difference. In 'Gosh Boy George, You Must Be Awfully Secure In Your Masculinity!', Kosofsky Sedgwick argues that male and female sexualities are not on opposite poles but are in different 'perpendicular dimensions' (16). What is interesting is that while Sedgwick happily encompasses other sexualities within this debate, she is not always so clear in her approach to transexuality and transgender. However, in 'Blatantly Bisexual; or, Unthinking Queer Theory', Michael du Plessis draws upon Sedgwick's earlier points and makes a stronger case for the transsexual potential and Sandy Stone's persuasive essay 'The Empire Strikes Back: A Post-Transsexual Manifesto' (294–300) rightly foregrounds the theoretical possibilities of the transsexual body. The transsexual represents the breaking down of boundaries within the corporeal body, not just within the terms of culturally constructed gender. As with transgendered people, transsexuals can be categorized as exhibiting a third gender term. However, critics argue that the transsexual does not simply break down cultural or sexual boundaries; instead they also make those boundaries visible.

The body then is a confining/confined space that can be transcended by transgressive reinscription and science fiction offers an examination of the cultural and ideological positioning of sexuality where identity intersects and undermines any form of substantive representation. It speaks from a place other than the normative and it has the potential to present other transpositions and permutations of sexuality. The transsexual body holds great potential for sexuality debates. Angela Carter's *The Passion of New Eve* (1977) is an early examination of sexual dissonance and recounts the tale of the transsexual Eve, formerly Evelyn, who as a result of his appalling treatment of women as sex objects is captured by radical feminists and forced to undergo surgical reassignment. He is physically a woman but escapes before he/she undergoes the psychological training to 'become' a woman. Carter's savage satire uses transexuality as a metaphor for the unfixed body; Eve is a man inhabiting a body that has been deliberately reassigned in order to invite the male gaze. As a transsexual Eve experiences a specific history of gender and sexuality with its concomitant subjugation and violence.

Carol Emschwiller's *Carmen Dog* (1988) is a satirical and humorous novel that accentuates highly politicized debates on sexuality and gender. Emshwiller leaves the reader in no doubt as to the position of women in her blurring of boundaries between the categories of woman as pet and pet as a colonized feminine object:

> He picked her out, bought her, trained her, and taught her everything she
> knows (or so he thinks, anyway), disciplined her .... Perhaps it could be
> a time of new and strange excesses he never dared to even think about
> let alone perform when he was younger or with his wife (who always
> rather frightened him) after all, Pooch is another kind of creature entirely.
> Courage would hardly be needed with such as her. If, for instance, he
> wanted to tie her, spread-eagled, to the bed, she would not wonder at
> this behaviour (8).

Emshwiller's point that women are 'domesticated' in the same way as animals underpins her writing. While Emshwiller has a point to make about women's state, it is always underpinned by her ironic exegesis on women and their 'domesticated' sexual habits. She of course asks many questions regarding sexuality and is primarily concerned with the dynamics of being female and the destiny of women's biology. These issues are of paramount importance and are rendered highly conspicuous throughout the novel. *Carmen Dog* focuses on the sexualized female body as a commodity and as a site of exchange. The fetishized female body is directly linked to the fabulous feathers and fur the women grow, accentuating women's roles as objects of sexual desire and beauty. The more sexually exotic the creatures are, the more they are 'lionized'. Emshwiller engages specifically with the need for women to negotiate a space for themselves as subjects rather than objects and recognizes that women's sexual needs are heterogeneous. She places women's mutability in the progressive alternation from one condition to another; from woman to animal and animal to woman.

Emshwiller offers a deliberation on women's recognition of themselves as sexual objects in a diverting and surreal way. Women are not a finished product here, they are in a state of metamorphosis. This can be linked in part to the position of women under patriarchy, that is, woman tamed. For as Emshwiller has noted, once women begin to challenge that authority they are no longer needed by a society that is based on the need for women to be subservient:

> Recently several of her rapidly changing friends have had just such a fate
> (whatever it is) having become too hard to handle at home in all sorts of
> ways, for however one may enjoy the possession of an intelligent animal,
> too much intelligence, too many pertinent and impertinent questions,
> and too much independence is always hard to put up with in others, and
> especially so in a creature one keeps partly for the enhancement of one's
> own self-image. (5)

Women, who have been made into domestic 'pets' by their husbands, literally begin to transform into animals and the pets that are obedient and adored begin to turn into fabulous and exotic women. The irony that Emshwiller brings to the representation and thoughts of the female/animals is apparent throughout, although she is clearly not afraid to satirize women:

> 'Anything', she will say to him, 'I'll do absolutely anything: lick your feet, walk one step behind your left heel, just let me stay and serve you …' She hopes that after she says all this and makes the promises he'll see that she is worth keeping (a thought not uncommon to many creatures of her sex). (16)

And in the same way, the women/animals constantly talk about the doctor who has been torturing them. Many of them 'were quite taken with [him] and still are, after all this. They talk about him constantly: how tall! How thin! What secrets do those dark eyes hold?'(34). Again Emshwiller has no problem saying how foolish women are, telling us in an aside that we must remember the doctor is the only male around and that the women find his cruelty attractive and believe that they can change him through their love. There are, she informs us, those 'who nearly swooned with pleasure at the treatment they received … as long as it didn't become *too* painful' (43).

The oppression and training of women is apparent in *Carmen Dog*, but this is of course subverted and undermined by the refusal of some women and animals to be contained. Emshwiller's satire is bitingly surreal, with images of women and pets in a state of change overlapping physically. The women become pack animals, 'brownish creatures heading north […] a huge herd […]. Many have colourful backpacks or colourful, rolled up raincoats slung over their shoulders' (52). The women/animals still wear 'wide-brimmed hats' and 'all have large paper or plastic bags of what is obviously their meals for several days' (52). The humour is very apparent, but it is not always clear whether it is at the expense of women or on behalf of women's perceived gender attributes. It is clear however, that the women and animals recognize the idea of 'difference' in a way that none of the male characters can. Emshwiller uses the woman/animal combination to useful effect in a complex environment that explores the exploitative possibilities of being a woman as well as the potentially liberating ones. In *Carmen Dog*, the bodies *are* the machines, capable of transformation, mediated entirely by the material and physical world that surrounds them. The novel is both an articulation and conceptualization of the category 'woman' and the destabilization of female sexuality.

In science fiction the temporal and geographical dislocations allow the creation of alternate (sexual) worlds, and call existing (sexual) realities into question. In one of the most notable novels of the 1970s, Samuel Delany's *Trouble on Triton* (1976), sexual freedom and sexual diversity are an intrinsic part of the social system on Triton, where there are at least 'forty or fifty different sexes' (99). What Butler calls 'the regulatory fiction of hetero-sexuality' is notably absent and there is a radical disunity of heterosexual coherence and a transfiguration of sexuality. In her discussion of queer theory and science fiction Wendy Pearson argues that queer theory:

> tends to be sceptical about epistemologies which see sexual orientation as a fixed identity so that sf which describes bodies, genders, sexualities as fluid is much more in harmony with approaches that celebrate fluidity, liminality and other radical tactics for deconstructing the rigidity of binary identity categories. ('Queer Theory', 157)

This is most obvious in Delany's novel where he unfixes and transforms essentialist notions of gender, race and sexuality in a world that seemingly has no sexual taboos and where every conceivable desire is catered for. The protagonist Bron starts as a sexist male and changes into a woman. The novel with its complex sexual ambiguities explores the motivations, and, more specifically, the aftermaths of changing sex.

Case Study Queer/Sexuality: Geoff Ryman, *The Child Garden* (1989)

Queer theory and the anti-essentialism that underpins it provide an important platform from which to examine marginality and sexual dissonance. For Sedgwick what makes the 'queerness of a queer reading' ('Paranoid Reading', 2–3) is not necessarily a move towards same-sex, interpersonal eroticism, but that it is rather the texts and readings of them that offer 'a kind of *genius loci* for queer reading' where a 'sense of personal queerness may or may not have resolved into a sexual specificity of proscribed object choice, aim, site or identi-fication'. One such text that lends itself to this reading is Geoff Ryman's *The Child Garden* where scientific and technological innovation has consequential effects on individual sexual experience. Set in a post-revolutionary London, controlled diseases – 'viruses' – are given to all inhabitants. Individual 'Belief' is a disease and because of advances in medicine, acceptable patterns of behaviour can be caught or administered: 'Viruses made people cheerful and helpful and honest. Their manners were impeccable, their conversation well-informed, their work speedy and accurate. They believed the same things' (1). The viruses contain all the knowledge that anyone will ever need including language, knowledge, practical skills and philosophical reasoning. In this world people are considered adult by the time they reach the age of ten when they are 'read' by the Party:

Everyone was Read at ten years old [...]. It was part of their democratic right. Because of advances in medicine, representative democracy had been replaced by something more direct. People were read and models were made of their personalities – these models joined the government, to be consulted. The government was called 'The Consensus'. It was a product of late period socialism. (3)

Milena, the protagonist, has not been 'read' as she was ill with the viruses that were given to her. She is one of the few people not to be part of The Consensus. She is convinced the Party will try to read her and that she will die when they do so. Milena, or rather the person she is will die, because the 'reading' is a form of brainwashing. It works to eradicate any quirks of personality that might destabilize The Consensus. Milena has 'Bad Grammar' in that she likes women and desires them sexually, when everyone else is programmed to be heterosexual: 'There was one virus to which Milena knew she had been immune. There was one thing at least she was sure was part of herself. There was no ignoring the yearning in her heart for love, the love of another woman' (2). In this world, homosexuality is 'a semiological product of late period Capitalism' and has been eradicated (2). Milena suffers from resistance to heteronormativity: 'I need a woman, and there isn't going to be one. They've all been cured' (11). She believes she is the last of her kind in the world.

Ryman presents a world fuelled by performativity, a place where culture replicates itself endlessly, but never gives birth to anything new, and sets this against an inter-species love affair between Milena and Rolfa, a Genetically Engineered polar/human who is designed to survive in sub-zero temperatures of Antarctica. The GEs are not considered human but are an 'intelligent related species'. In Ryman's future world identities and bodies are no longer stable, but are fluid and unfixed with endless possibilities for regeneration and renewal. The body of the bear/woman Rolfa becomes a contested place where sexual identity and queerness are played out. Ryman's exploration of sexuality does not just engage with the homo/heterosexual binary, but through this interspecies relationship he explores the endless possibilities of other sexualities. Rolpha the bear/woman is 'huge and shaggy', covered with fur/hair, has rotten green teeth and she pants like a dog. She possesses 'a long pink tongue hung out of her mouth, curled and quivering to cool (15). She is:

the most fascinating irresolution of opposites. She was huge and coy at the same time [...] she moved with a fearful, tip-toe precision that meant she invariably knocked something over. She was boisterous and coarse and delicate and refined, usually in the same sentence. (37)

Rolpha bestrides the normative/queer continuum like a colossus. Her huge, Rabelaisian figure works to subvert the homo/heterosexual binary. Milena's attraction to the bear/woman's queerness is humorously rendered. She realizes she is sexually attracted to her. She 'lusted after the huge, baggy body. She wanted to do very specific things with it' (30). If the project of queer theory (among other things) is to subject the role of normative sexuality to scrutiny and the project of science fiction is 'cognitive estrangement' then Ryman's futuristic low comedy of manners and sexuality lends itself very specifically to queer readings.

While this reading concentrates on the queering of the body and sexuality, Ryman's novel clearly lends itself to further scrutiny. Indeed Wendy Gay Pearson's reading of the novel in 'Towards a Queer Genealogy of SF' looks at other defining motifs in the novel and is recommended reading. 'Queer', however, remains a contested term with an often discussed inconsistent set of qualifying features. As Pearson astutely points out, '[q]ueer's very slipperiness, however, its tendency towards instability and its pleasure in resisting attempts to make sexuality signify in monolithic ways, are all part of its appeal' ('Alien Cryptographies', 17). In moving away from subject positions that foreground a white, male and heterosexual experience writers such as Ryman open up those contested spaces in discourses about sexuality and the body.

Science Fiction and Ethnicity

'The problem of the twentieth century is the problem of the color-line –
the relation of the darker to the lighter races of men in Asia and Africa, in
America and in the islands of the sea'.
— W. E. B. DuBois *Souls of Black Folk* (1903)

Science fiction, with its ability for reimagining 'strangeness' or 'difference' provides an ideal forum for the examination of race and ethnic identity. However, in historical terms much of science fiction was written through a white, patriarchal lens where issues of race and ethnicity were frequently overlooked or elided with other interlocking systems of oppression, those of gender, class and sexuality. Isiah Lavender has acknowledged this, arguing that 'for most of its history sf has considered itself a "colorblind" genre'. He adjudges that conventionally, science fiction

blithely portrays a future free from racial struggle (not seeming to notice
that this harmony is accomplished by eliminating non-white people)
or else projecting racial anxieties on to the body of the alien without
seeming to notice that the humanity united against this external threat is
suspiciously monochrome. (185)

It is clear that much of early science fiction in general paid scant consideration to issues of 'race' and ethnicity with some writers of the genre significantly either ignoring 'the racial issue' altogether or who saw the matter of race as somehow unimportant. In many cases criticism of the genre easily succumbed to the idea that possible future worlds did not need to dwell on race topics as, it was implied, racism had somehow 'burned itself out' in the future. According to Mark Bould, however, the problem with this way of thinking is that:

> rather than putting aside trivial and earthly things, it validates and normalises very specific ideological and material perspectives, enabling discussions of race and prejudice on a level of abstraction while stifling a more important discussion about real, material conditions, both historical and contemporary. And by presenting racism as an insanity that burned itself out, or as the obvious folly of the ignorant and impoverished who would be left behind by the genre's brave new futures, sf avoids confronting the structures of racism and its own complicity in them. (180)

If Utopian thinking seems to imply that distinctions based on race will become invalid in future worlds, then conversely anti-Utopian and dystopian writers imagine cultures that are affected by what is recognized as the 'imperial process' of colonization. Colonialism and its effects are represented in science fiction by narratives that explore possible worlds where colonized 'others' are shown to lack agency. These show how power relations between the colonizer and the colonized are revealed and enforced. According to Homi Bhabha an important feature of colonial discourse is its dependence on the concept of 'fixity' in the ideological construction of otherness. He argues that '[f]ixity, as the sign of cultural/historical/racial difference in the discourse of colonialism, is a paradoxical mode of representation: it connotes rigidity and an unchanging order as well as disorder, degeneracy and daemonic repetition' (66). Significantly, within colonial discourses 'otherness' has been predominantly historicized by emphasizing the repercussions of subjugation on other races. In this way the 'otherness' which according to Bhabha is both an 'object of desire and derision' becomes an articulation of difference contained within the 'fantasy' of origin and identity. He argues that 'once those boundaries are revealed it enables a transgression of these limits from the space of that otherness' (67). For science fiction writers race, along with gender and sexuality, are interlocking systems of oppression that can be transgressed by the creation of other worlds where historical and political constructions of 'otherness' can be unfixed. Science fiction's potential to explore race and ethnicity is virtually limitless and as such it provides fertile ground for writers to interrogate theories regarding race in their work.

'Try the Oankali Way. Embrace Difference'

Although George Schuyler's *Black No More: Being an Account of the Strange and Wonderful Workings of Science in the Land of the Free, AD 1933–1940* (1931) is seen as one of the earliest works of science fiction by a writer of colour, Delany's *Babel-17* (1966) and *The Einstein Intersection* (1967) are among the first novels to garner accolades for exploring issues of race and ethnicity. *The Einstein Intersection* is set on a post-apocalyptic Earth sometime in the future. The novel (winner of the Nebula prize) is a finely nuanced narrative of 'otherness', drawing on myth and legend to debate among other things issues of race and racial stereotyping. In later works such as the hugely influential *Dhalgren* (1975) and *Trouble on Triton* (1976) Delany explores interracial relations, sexualities and cross gendered relationships. For Delany, it is the traditional science fiction frame of the future that generates the possibility for a 'new panoply of possible fictional incidents' that have the potential to generate an 'entirely new set of rhetorical stances' (287). He draws on his own reading of Robert Heinlein's *Starship Troopers* (1959) as an example of the genre's ability to produce new expectations. He says that Heinlein:

> by a description of a mirror reflection and the mention of an ancestor's nationality, in the midst of a strophe on male makeup, generates the data that the first-person narrator with whom we have been travelling now through two hundred and fifty-odd pages (of a three hundred and fifty-page book), is black .... What remains with me, nearly ten years after I first read the book, is the knowledge that I have experienced a world in which the *placement* of the information about a narrator's face is *proof* that in such a world the 'race problem', at least, has dissolved (287, emphasis in original)

For Delany, the book became a symbol of a world that only science fiction can provide, a world where the 'race problem' no longer exists. For other writers such as Octavia Butler and Nalo Hopkinson (among others) race can be reconstructed within a range of powerfully imagined worlds and communities.

Octavia Butler's work sees the potentiality of genetically altered bodies and the hybridity that is the result of multi-species couplings as a means to unfix racist attitudes. In Butler's *Xenogenesis* trilogy (1987–9) the alien Oankali ensure their survival by mixing their genetic material with other species, evolving into a species that embrace diversity. In *Adulthood Rites* (1988), Lilith tells us, 'Oankali crave difference. Humans persecute their different ones, yet they need them to give themselves definition and status. Oankali seek difference and collect it. They need it to keep themselves from stagnation and overspecialisation. If you don't understand this, you will [...]. When you feel a conflict, try the Oankali way. Embrace difference' (80). Throughout the trilogy Butler criticizes the tendency of human beings to abhor diversity they do not understand. The symbiotic relationships between species that she foregrounds in many of her novels suggests we can no longer rely on the contemporary constructs of superiority and inferiority that are rather dubiously attached to racial identities.

Nalo Hopkinson's *Brown Girl in the Ring* (1998) is set in a future Ontario where the society is powerfully evoked by drawing on (among other things) the legacy of Afro-Caribbean mysticism and spirituality. The protagonist Ti-Jeanne must connect with the past and draw on ancient powers in order to survive in the new world. Her grandmother Mami tells her: 'The African powers, child. The spirits. The loas. The orishas. The oldest ancestors. You will hear people from Haiti and Cuba and Brazil and so call them different names .... Them is the ones who carry we prayers to God father' (126). The old beliefs of walking between two worlds, this world and the next, are played out against a system of oppression and fear. The inability to 'own' one's body, even in death is a central trope in both aspect of Hopkinson's narrative. In the voodoo tradition spirits are called on to inhabit the living and state legislation decrees that 'biomaterial' belongs to the state and they harvest it at will from people who are near death and kept alive by 'CP bypass machines'. Mami's heart is transplanted into the state's Premier and 'white blood cells from her bone marrow' are supposed to take over the 'foreign organ' and 'vice versa', a 'chimerism that would trick the immune system into accepting a foreign organ so that body and heart could coexist peacefully' (167–8). The hybridi-sation of the body and state is an obvious metaphor here, where the Premier eventually gains control over the wayward transplanted heart and becomes 'a new woman', complete with a social conscience that will find new ways of promoting 'enlightened self-interest .... Integration of body parts for all but no one will be forced to be a potential donor. Anyone can sign the opt-out card ... But most people won't bother ... one donor cadaver can benefit fifty people' (239). In this chimerical new world Hopkinson offers a glimpse of rejuvenation with the past inscribed on the present and the beginning of new ways of being.

Other works of note include Nicola Griffith's *Ammonite* (1992), while both Maureen F. McHugh's *China Mountain Zhang* (1992) and Neal Stephenson's *The Diamond Age* (1995) debate new 'tribal' allegiances with China. Maggie Gee's *Ice People* (1998) has a protagonist whose mixed-race heritage allows him the potential to escape a society in the throes of a new Ice Age to live in Africa, and Andrea Hurston's *Mindscape* (2006) contains a future world divided in three zones, one of which is a racist state. Jewell Parker Rhodes reworks the voodoo legacy in novels such as *Voodoo Dreams* (1993) and *Yellow Moon* (2008) to examine a history of slavery and racism. In much of the writing discussed race relations are likely to be theorized as symbolic cultural differences that are constructed out of mutually meaningful notions of 'otherness'. Identity then becomes the relationship between one society, one culture or one group of people that can be transcended by mutually beneficial engagements with alien 'others'. In 'Futurist Fiction & Fantasy: The "Racial" Establishment' Godfrey Rutledge lists a number of African American writers who he claims mark 'the beginning of a new world of autonomy created out of the desire to scrap 500 years of intellectual imperialism' (236–52). Among those he cites, Steven Barnes's novels *Streetlethal* (1983), *Firedance* (1993) and *Blood Brothers* (1996) are perhaps the best known. Derrick Bell's *Afrolantica Legacies* (1997) reflects on notions of racial exclusion and subordination based on colour in American society. The president of the United States is forced to speak on racial matters at the moment when an island called 'Afrolantica' emerges from the ocean. The island will only accept African Americans and is hostile to any other race of people that approaches it. The sociopolitical aspect of Bell's writing is evident here in the President's speech:

> Unfortunately, the conditions of racial exclusion and subordination based on color that prompted the initial emigration movement have not improved significantly and, in many areas, have grown worse. Many Americans point to the large, black middle class, the outstanding achievements members of the group have made in many fields, their presence in neighborhoods, work areas, even television commercials, as proof that there are no barriers for blacks who are talented and qualified, and that racism is no more. These assessments wrongly dismiss the major gaps between blacks and whites in matters of employment, income, education and health care. They ignore the polls that show far larger numbers of blacks than whites who report that racism remains a pervasive presence in their lives. (3–4)

The president's narrative continues with an apology for ignoring the lack of agency and the continuing burden of race discrimination that still predominates. The notion that those in power should 'do more' is potentially a call to arms for the government, although it might be argued that Bell's rather heavy-handed attempt to surmount cultural and racial differences merely continues to essentialize race. Rutledge's selection of writers encompasses two writers who have made that border crossing into science fiction. He sees LeVar Burton's *Aftermath* (1997) and Walter Mosley's *Blue Light* (1998) as most significant in that respect, as he believes they may provide 'greater legitimacy among the African- and European-American lay and academic communities' for futuristic fictions. Although written at the turn of the twenty-first century Rutledge believed that 'diasporic African arts and letters [are] going where no person has gone before'. Whether that has been the case in the intervening decade remains to be seen. However, Sheree Thomas's edited collection of stories and essays, *Dark Matter: A Century of Speculative Fiction from the African Diaspora* (2000) certainly points the way forward in terms of innovation and debate.

While considerable attention is given to African American writers, recent study has taken into account the broad range of science fiction and futuristic writers whose work contains tropes of colonialism and neocoloniasm. The latter years of the twentieth century saw a range of writers draw on their experiences to reconstruct and reconnect to colonization. Zainab Amadahy's *The Moons of Palmares* (1997) is set in a future world where slavery and bondage echoes the subaltern experience and Bharati Mukherjee's *The Holder of the World* (1993) puts Asia at the heart of the colonization of America. Japanese-American writer Cynthia Kadohata sets her novel *In the Heart of the Valley of Love* (1997) in a future segregated world where the white people live in exclusive gated communities and the slums are where everyone else lives in a battle for survival. More recently a number Latin-American science fiction writers have come to the fore including Bernado Fernndez Brigado, Ricardo Guzmán Wolffer and Pepe Rojo Sotís. The growing recognition of this work is critically examined in Darrell Lockhart's *Latin American Science Fiction Writers* (2004) and Rachel Haywood Ferreira's *The Emergence of Latin American Science Fiction* (2011). According to Lockhart these writers are producing 'highly motivated vehicles for communicating trenchant social commentary' (xi) and recognized as part of science fiction's legacy discourses of protest.

Case Study: Yesterday is Within Us: Adventures in Time Travel

As noted above a number of writers have produced fictions that are thematically preoccupied with race. Apart from Octavia Butler's *Kindred* (1979) which has already been discussed in this book, Ward Moore's *Bring the Juville* (1953) is an earlier time-travel narrative complete with time paradoxes and anachronisms that also (among other things) addresses the rigidity and the frequently unchanging order of racist beliefs. Moore's early novel is set in an alternative history where the Confederate South won its independence in the Civil War, named here as 'The War of Southron Independence.' In the alternative world the United States consists of 26 states that function as backwards-looking agrarian societies while The Confederacy includes the rest of states, parts of Central and South America and is a world power. As the 'real' history of the United States of America is bound up in the movement from an agrarian society to an urban, capitalist society, Moore positions his story at the heart of this change. After Emancipation up to the beginning of the twentieth century a great proportion of the agrarian population (both black and white) continued to be bound by a system of debt peonage, serfdom and slavery. This is a point Octavia Butler returns to in *Parable of the Sower* (1993) and *Parable of the Talents* (1998) where she draws on the collective memory of slavery and what Allen describes as 'debt servitude' (1353–65). As with other time-travel science fiction narratives, in *Bring the Jubilee* Moore explores socio-political themes entwining past and present through changes and slippages in historical knowledge. His protagonist, Hodge Backmaker, lives in a world where men had lost the ability to work for wages that would support a family and where the only alternative is a system of indenture and to sell oneself to a company. His grandfather had fought for independence and made speeches, 'Advocating equal rights for Negroes or protesting mass lynchings so popular in the North, in contrast to the humane treatment accorded these non-citizens in the Confederacy' (4), even though in the independent state that followed it was believed he had been proved wrong. Moore draws attention to the attendant discontent and provincialized ideas that flourished in the United States at the time. When Hodge leaves home to make his fortune in New York he comes across a young black boy fleeing from his master, who

> was barefoot and wore a jute sack as a shirt with holes cut for his arms and ragged pants. His face was little browner than my own had often been at the end of a summer's work under the burning sun. He came to the end of indecision and stated across the highway, legs pumping high, head turned watchfully. A splendid tawny stallion cleared the wall in a soaring jump his rider bellowing, 'There you are you damned black coon'. (14)

Moore's conceptual refiguring of racist language embraces the cultural and historical positioning of the boy as 'other'. However, this is bound up with notions of shame on the part of Hodge who tries to analyze his reaction to the event. At first he had tentatively tried to grasp the reins on the horse but he found himself drawing back. The novel written on the cusp of civil rights activism engages in a powerful debate about racism at a time when high visibility of the black population demonstrated the need for a greater under-standing of the legacy of slavery. More invites readers to question whether you stand back and passively observe and justify what is happening to a race of peoples or whether you actively participate and try to change matters. In doing nothing, Hodge feels only shame: 'I had been immobilized by the fear of asserting my sympathies, my presumptions, against events …. I could have wept with mortification' (15). Later Hodge tries to excuse his actions:

> The fugitive might have been a trespasser or a servant; his fault might have been slowness, rudeness, theft or attempted murder. Whatever

it was, any retaliation the white man chose could be inflicted with impunity. He would not be punished or even tried for it. Popular opinion was unanimous for Negro emigration to Africa, voluntary or forced; those who went westward to join the unconquered Sioux or Nez Perce were looked on as depraved. Any Negro who didn't embark for Liberia or Sierra Leone, regardless of whether he had the fare or not, deserved anything that happened to him in the United States. (15)

Writers such as Moore reinscribe history (and fiction) with the experiences of black peoples, a history and treatment that was based on denial. His protagonist Hodge spends a considerable amount of time with a member of the 'Grand Army', a fictional organization that takes a similar stance to the Ku Klux Klan in the Southern states after Reconstruction. Moore was writing some 20 years before The Bill of Rights was revived to include the renego-tiation of identity that demanded an agreement that *all* Americans should be seen as free and equal and his examination of race relations draws on an historical legacy of racism and slavery. Hodge who becomes an historian by profession eventually joins a commune in Pennsylvania where intellectuals, quasi-scientists and other scholars live together. Here he comes across the inventor of a time machine in which he travels back through time to witness the great battle of 'Southron Independence'. Hodge inadvertently changes the events that caused the Southern states to win. History is played out before him as we know it and the North triumphs. He becomes stuck in time and witnesses the world as changed:

What was brutal never got the upper hand ... The Negro is free, black legislatures pass advanced laws in South Caroline, black congressmen comport themselves with dignity in Washington [...] immigrants pour in to a welcoming country to make it strong and wealthy; no one suggests they should be shut out or hindered. (193)

While Moore's novel plays around with other weighty historical matters, it seems that the engagement with racial issues successfully integrates past and present themes of the outsider status that was part of the historical legacy of enslavement. Indeed Hodge the time traveller becomes an alienated other, an outsider in a narrative that blurs the past and present of 1950s America.

The contradiction that Moore explores grows out of the historical condi-tions of slavery and out of the way racial identity is constructed. Novels and short stories that engage with issues of race and ethnicity show how in science fiction's ever-evolving forms it is, as Isiah Lavender argues, excep-tionally well suited for the critical study of race because of its postcolonial depiction of subordinate positions, as well as its imagination of alternate histories where cultural memories of past events can be both engaged with and potentially changed.

Conclusion: Aliens, Others and Destabilised Identities

The diversity of science fiction where identity and difference is linked to subjectivity is uniquely suited for the exploration of peripheral/liminal spaces where identities can be tested and contested. Science fiction narratives are frequently informed by radical politics that both reveal and explore destabilized identities with self-conscious explorations of otherness, outsider status and different sexualities. The science fiction writers discussed here engage in the deconstruction of textual meaning and the conflict inherent in gender, sexual and racial constraints that are both subordinate to and conflict with socially constructed barriers. Science fiction writers create a space where they can defiantly transpose and challenge barriers from outside and inside the human body and gesture towards new ways of being.

Works Cited

Allen, Marlene (2009). 'Octavia Butler's *Parable* Novels and the "Boomerang" of African American History'. *Callaloo*. 32. 4. 1353–65.

Amadahy, Zainab (1997). *The Moons of Palmares*. Toronto, ON: Sister Vision.

Attebery, Brian (2002). *Decoding Gender in Science Fiction*. New York & London: Routledge.

Barnes, Steven (1983). *Streetlethal*. London: Penguin.

—(1993). *Firedance*. London: Tor Books.

—(1996). *Blood Brothers*. London: Tor Books.

Bell, Derrick (1997). *The Afrolantica Legacies*. Available online http://www.nytimes.com/books/first/b/bell-legacies.html

Bhabha, Homi (1994). *The Location of Culture*. London: Routledge.

Bould, Mark (2007). 'Ships Landed Long Ago: Afrofuturism and Black SF'. *Science Fiction Studies*. 34: 2. 177–86.

Burdekin, Katharine (1985) [1937]. *Swastika Night*. New York: CUNY Feminist Press.

Burton, LeVar (1997). *Aftermath*. London: Vista.

Butler, Judith (1990). 'Gender Trouble, Feminist Theory, and Psychoanalytic Discourse'. *Feminism/Postmodernism*. Linda Nicholson (ed.). New York and London: Routledge. 324–40.

—(1990). *Gender Trouble: Feminism and the Subversion of Identity*. New York: Routledge.

Butler, Octavia (1988) [1979]. *Kindred*. London: The Women's Press.

—(1987). *Dawn*. New York: Warner Books.

—(1988). *Adulthood Rites*. New York: Warner Books.

—(1993). *Parable of the Sower*. London: The Women's Press.

—(1998). *Parable of the Talents*. London: The Women's Press.

Cadigan, Pat (1998). *Tea from an Empty Cup*. London: Harper Collins.

Carter, Angela (1977). *The Passion of New Eve*. London: Gollancz.

Cranny-Francis, Ann (2000). 'The Erotics of the CyBorg: Authority and Gender in the Sociocultural Imaginary'. *Future Females, The Next Generation: New Voices and Velocities in Feminist Science Fiction Criticism*. Marleen Barr (ed.). New York and Oxford: Rowman and Littlefield Publishers Inc. 145–64.

Delany, Samuel R. (1975). *Dhalgren*. New York: Bantam.

—(1987) [1966]. *Babel-17*. London: Gollancz.

—(1992) [1967]. *The Einstein Intersection*. London: Grafton.

—(1996) [1976]. 'From The *Triton* Journal'. *Trouble on Triton*. Hanover: Wesleyan University Press. 279–91.

De Witt Kilgore, Douglas (2010). 'Difference Engine: Aliens, Robots, and Other Racial Matters in the History of Science Fiction'. *Science Fiction Studies*. 37. 16–22.

Dodderidge, Esme (1988). *The New Gulliver*. London: The Women's Press.

DuBois, W. E. D. (2007) [1903]. *The Souls of Black Folk*. Oxford: Oxford University Press.

Duncker, Patricia (1992). *Sisters and Strangers: An Introduction to Contemporary Feminist Fiction*. Oxford: Blackwell.

Editorial Preface (1989). 'The Past Before Us: Twenty Years of Feminism'. *Feminist Review*. 31. 55–65.

Elgin, Suzette (1984). *Native Tongue*. London: The Women's Press.

—(1987). *The Judas Rose*. London: The Women's Press.

Emschwiller, Carol (1988). *Carmen Dog*. Northampton, MA: Peapod Classics.

Farmer, Nancy (2004). *Sea of Trolls*. New York: Simon and Schuster

Ferreira, Rachel Haywood (2011). *The Emergence of Latin American Science Fiction*. Hanover: Wesleyan University Press.

Gearhart, Sally (1980). *The Wanderground*. London: The Women's Press.

Gee, Maggie (1998). *The Ice People*. London: Richard Choen.

Gibson, William (1984). *Neuromancer*. London: Harper Collins.

Gilman, Carolyn Ives (1998). *Halfway Human*. Rockville, MD: Phoenix Pick.

Gilman, Charlotte Perkins (1979) [1915]. *Herland*. London: The Women's Press.

Griffith, Nicola (1992). *Ammonite*. New York: Ballantine.

Hairston, Andrea (2006). *Mindscape*. Seattle, WA: Aqueduct Press.

Halberstam, Judith (2005). *In a Queer Time and Place: Transgender Bodies, Subcultural Lives*. New York: New York University Press.

Hall, Sandi (1982). *The Godmothers*. London: The Women's Press.

Heinlein, Robert (1997) [1959]. *Starship Troopers*. London: Titan.

Hopkinson, Nalo (1988). *Brown Girl in the Ring*. New York: Warner Books.

Ives Gilman, Carolyn (2010) [1998]. *Halfway Human*. Avon, 1998. Rockville: Arc Manor.

Kadohata, Cynthia (1997). *In the Heart of the Valley of Love*. London: Secker & Warburg.

235

Lauret, Maria (1989). 'Seizing Time and Making New: Feminist Criticism, Politics and Contemporary Feminist Fiction'. *Feminist Review*. 31. 95–101.

Lavender III, Isiah (2009). 'Critical Race Theory'. *The Routledge Companion to Science Fiction*. Mark Bould et al. (eds.) London: Routledge. 185–193.

Le Fanu, Sarah (1988). *In the Chinks of the World Machine*. London: The Women's Press.

Le Guin, Ursula (1982) [1969]. *The Left Hand of Darkness*. London: Orbit.

—(1982). *The Language of the Night: Essays on Fantasy and Science Fiction*. New York: Berkeley.

Leroux, Lise (1998). *One Hand Clapping*. London: Viking.

Lockhart, Darrell (2004). *Latin American Science Fiction Writers*. Westport: Greenwood Press.

McHugh, Maureen F. (1998). *Mission Child*. London: Orbit.

—(1992). *China Mountain Zhang*. London: Orbit.

McKee Charmas, Suzy (1978). *Motherlines*. London: Gollancz.

—(1999). *The Conqueror's Child*. London: Tor Books

McMaster Bujold, Lois (1999). *A Civil Campaign*. Riverdale, NY: Baen Books.

Melzer, Patricia (2006). *Alien Constructions: Science Fiction and Feminist Thought*. Austin, TX: University of Texas Press.

Mitchison, Naomi (1985) [1962]. *Memoirs of a Spacewoman*. London: The Women's Press.

Moore, C. L. (1977) [1944]. *No Woman Born. The Best of C.L. Moore*. C. L. Lester del Rey (ed.). New York: Taplinger Publications

Moore, Ward (2001) [1953]. *Bring the Jubilee*. London: Gollancz.

Mosley, Walter (1998). *Blue Light*. London: Serpent's Tail.

Mukherjee, Bharati (1993). *The Holder of the World*. London: Chatto & Windus.

Pearson, Wendy Gay (2003). 'Science Fiction and Queer Theory'. *The Cambridge Companion to Science Fiction*. Farah Mendlesohn and Edward James (eds). Cambridge: Cambridge University Press. 149–60.

—(2008). 'Alien Cryptographies: The View from Queer'. *Queer Universes: Sexualities in Science Fiction*. Wendy Gay Pearson, Veronica Hollinger and Joan Gordon (eds). Liverpool: Liverpool University Press. 14–38.

Piercy, Marge (2001) [1976]. *Woman on the Edge of Time*. London: The Women's Press.

Plant, Sadie (1996). 'On the Matrix: Cyberfeminist Simulations'. *Cultures of Internet: Virtual Spaces, Real Histories, Living Bodies*. Rob Shields (ed.). London: Sage.

du Plessis, Michael (1996). 'Blatantly Bisexual; or, Unthinking Queer Theory'. *RePresenting Bisexualities: Subjects and Cultures of Fluid Desire*. Donal E. Hall and Maria Pramaggiore (eds). New York & London: New York University Press. 19–54.

Rhodes, Jewell Parker (1993). *Voodoo Dream*. London: Headline.

—(2008) *Yellow Moon*. New York: Washington Square Press.

Rosinsky, Natalie M. (1984). *Feminist Futures: Contemporary Women's Speculative Fiction*. Ann Arbor Michigan: University of Michigan Press.

Russ, Joanna (1968). *Picnic on Paradise*. New York: Ace Books.

—(1975). *The Female Man*. Boston, MA: Beacon Press.

—(1982). 'The Mystery of the Young Gentleman'. *Worlds Apart: An Anthology of Lesbian and Gay Science Fiction and Fantasy*. Lyn Paleo, Camilla Decamin, Eric Garber (eds). New York: Alyson Publications. 164–92.

—(1995). *To Write Like a Woman: Essays in Feminism and Science Fiction*. Bloomington and Indianapolis: Indiana University Press.

Rutledge, Gregory E. (2001). 'Futurist Fiction & Fantasy: The "Racial" Establishment'. *Callaloo*. 24. 1 (Winter). 236–52.

Ryman, Geoff (1999) [1989]. *The Child Garden*. London: Voyager.

Sage, Lorna (1992). *Women in the House of Fiction*. London: Macmillan.

Schuyler, George (1971) [1931]. *Black No More: Being an Account of the Strange and Wonderful Workings of Science in the Land of the Free, AD 1933–1940*. New York: Collier Books.

Scott, Melissa (1995). *Shadow Man*. Maple Shade, NJ: Lethe Press.

Sedgwick, Eve Kosofsky (1991). *The Epistemology of the Closet*. Berkeley, LA: University of California Press.

—(1996). 'Gosh Boy George, You Must Be Awfully Secure In Your Masculinity!'. *Constructing Masculinity*. Maurice Berger, Brian Wallis and Simon Watson (eds). New York: Routledge. 11–20

—(1997). 'Paranoid Reading and Reparative Reading; or, You're So Paranoid You Probably Think This Introduction Is About You'. *Novel Gazing: Queer Readings in Fiction*. Eve Kosofsky Sedgwick (ed.). Durham: Duke University Press. 2–3.

Stephenson, Neale. (1995). *The Diamond Age*. London: Roc.

Stone, Sandy (1991). 'The Empire Strikes Back: A Post Transsexual Manifesto'. *Body Guards: The Cultural Politics of Gender*. Julia Epstein and Kristeva Straub (eds). London: Routledge, 280–304.

Thomas, Sheree R. (ed.) (2000). *Dark Matter: A Century of Speculative Fiction from the African Diaspora*. New York: Warner Books.

Vonarburg, Elisabeth (1988). *The Silent City*. London: The Women's Press.

Wheeler, Pat (2009). '"Gender", "Transgender", "Transexuality"'. *Women in Science Fiction and Fantasy*. Robin Reid (ed.). Westport: Greenwood Press.

Wolmark, Jenny (1994). *Aliens and Others: Science Fiction, Feminism and Postmodernism*. New York and London: Harvester Wheatsheaf.

Worthington, Kim (1996). *Self as Narrative: Subjectivity and Community in Contemporary Fiction*. Oxford: Clarendon Press.

Mapping the Current Critical Landscape

Sherryl Vint

The academic study of science fiction thrives in the twenty-first century: courses and graduate degrees are frequently on SF at universities in North America and in the UK; three library collections are devoted to genre materials (the Merril Collection in Canada, the Eaton Collection the US, the Foundation Collection in the UK); the genre has its own academic conferences, including that of the Science Fiction Research Association; and journals publish exclusively on genre materials, such as *Extrapolation, Science Fiction Studies, Foundation, The Journal for the Fantastic in the Arts* and *Science Fiction Film and Television*. This is a considerable change from both the early days of the pulps, when critical commentary existed only in the letters pages and fanzines, and from the early days of academic attention in the 1950s, during which scholars quietly worked on SF projects in the interstices between their more canonical work. Much has changed about both the genre and the academic study of culture in general that explains SF's move from the margins to the centre of humanities scholarship. Indeed, as we shall see, some of the central motifs and themes of SF have become so relevant to our current moment that at times SF seems to be disappearing as a distinct genre and thus as the object of a distinct kind of scholarly attention.

Two key events are central to this journey. First is the 'linguistic turn' of humanities scholarship in the late 1960s and early 1970s when the concepts of French post-structuralism began to circulate in English translation. The greater attention to language as an ideological practice of cultural production (rather than as a neutral medium of reflective representation) radically shifted work being done in a number of disciplines toward an interrogation of the premises underlying so-called reality and an attentiveness to the discursive production of 'truth'. Similarly, Foucault's genealogies opened up the past and present to a new way of thinking about complex relationships among institutions, discourses of truth and the production of humans as specific kinds of subjects. One of the consequences of these insights was that the techniques of SF – world building, estranging the 'natural', narrating from the outsider perspective – began to converge with the interests of literary culture more generally.

In part as a result of these shifts, contemporary literary culture adopted the styles and motifs we now label postmodern: metafiction, play with surfaces, rhizomatic narrative structures, irony and indeterminacy, intertextuality. Such literature strove to cope with the displacements and uncertainties of a postmodernity characterized by rapid change, competing viewpoints and loss of faith in totalizing narratives as grounds for meaning and truth. Not only did this literature converge with the tools and perspectives already dominant in SF, but a parallel shift in SF cultures – influenced by New Wave writers and Judith Merril's rubric of 'speculative fiction' – meant SF writers were also embracing aesthetic virtuosity. As SF writers borrowed techniques of postmodern fiction, and postmodern fiction embraced the settings, themes and motifs once solely the province of SF, distinctions between genre and mainstream or – in Delany's words – 'mundane' fiction (Delany, *Shorter Views*) became difficult to make. Bruce Sterling coined the term 'slipstream' in 1989 to describe an emergent type of ambiguously positioned fiction, drawing attention to writers such as Kathy Acker, William Burroughs, Robert Coover, Angela Carter, Thomas Pynchon, Ishmael Reed and David Foster Wallace. The increasing convergence between SF and postmodern fiction, as well as the erosion of the high/low boundary in scholarship, ushered SF into the academic acceptance it now enjoys.

In 1991, *Science Fiction Studies* editor Istvan Csicsery-Ronay Jr published 'The SF of Theory: Baudrillard and Haraway' which pointed to a new fusion between the genre and contemporary critical theory that found its most succinct expression in these two theorists. Highlighting Baudrillard's 'Simulation and Science Fiction' (1991) and Haraway's 'A Manifesto for Cyborgs' (1985), Csicsery-Ronay Jr demonstrated how contemporary critical theory was not only analyzing SF but, more importantly, *was* SF in its inter-rogation of the logic of the contemporary reality and its use of speculative and estranging techniques to provoke readers to see that world otherwise. That same year, Larry McCaffery published the influential volume *Storming the Reality Studio* that combined works of fiction, criticism and theory that made manifest Fredric Jameson's contention in *Postmodernism* (1991) that cyberpunk was 'the supreme *literary* expression if not of postmodernism, then of late capitalism itself' (419). Cyberpunk's evident pertinence to pressing topics of emergent information capitalism and shifting social relations made possible by personal computing catalyzed academic interest in the sub-genre; although scholarship in the 1980s and into the 1990s focused almost exclusively on this narrow segment of SF, the ubiquity of cyberpunk scholarship in this moment drew the genre and its critical potential to the attention of a broad academic audience.

The current critical landscape is thus informed by the multiple sites of intersection between the motifs of SF and the fascinations of critical theory. Indeed, in 2000 Carl Freedman wrote *Critical Theory and Science Fiction* premised on precisely this link, which he deemed 'not fortuitous but fundamental' (23). Building on the dominant Suvinian definition of the genre as the literature of cognitive estrangement, Freedman argues that 'science fiction, like critical theory, insists upon historical mutability, material reducibility, and utopian possibility' and that its key quality is that the 'science-fictional world is not only one different in time or place from our own, but one whose chief interest is precisely the difference that such difference makes' (xvi). Freedman, Suvin and Jameson all work in a Marxist tradition, and until relatively recently much of the critical work on the genre has emphasized the genre's continuities with Utopian and dystopian social critique. Writers and critics have embraced the genre's abilities to comment also on gender and racial orders, and the feminist tradition of SF that rose to prominence in the 1970s made palpable its capacity for such critique.

A number of the most important works published in the past ten years have built upon this Suvinian estrangement of the reader from dominant perceptions, and on the affinity of both SF and theoretical modes of enquiry to ask questions about ideologies embedded in the genre. Such work has helped us to see that SF is always and simultaneously both a mode of resistance to dominant contemporary ideological structures and a reflection of these same structures. In short, such criticism asks about and incorporates SF's blind spots and embedded assumptions. An important book in this vein is Brian Attebery's *Decoding Gender in Science Fiction* (2002); it treats 'both gender and science fiction as sign systems' (2) and looks at the ways these two systems intersect and overlap to produce particular understandings and experiences of the social world. The innovation in Attebery's work is that he reads gender itself as a kind of SF, a constructed and artificial code that functions as a technology for 'assigning social and psychological meaning to sexual difference, insofar as that difference is perceived in form, appearance, sexual function, and expressive behavior' (2). Both SF and gender are 'cultural systems that allow us to generate forms of expression and assign meanings to them' (2). Attebery builds on an established tradition of feminist SF scholarship, including a number of important essays by *Science Fiction Studies* editor Veronica Hollinger, critical works by SF writer and scholar Joanna Russ and Sarah Lefanu's important overview *In the Chinks of the World Machine* (1988).

Looking at the gender politics of SF from its early days in the pulps to contemporary postmodern examples, Attebery provides a systematic overview of the ways that gender has permeated the genre's themes and forms, paying attention to multiple sites of engagement: the limited roles for women in technocratic SF of the golden age; the forgotten women's contributions to the genre; the overlapping and at times contradictory discourses of gender experienced by early pulp readers who encountered SF stories embedded with advertisements; the self-consciously revisionist feminist SF of the 1970s; and the theoretically inflected SF of the 1990s, written by both men and women, that understands, with Attebery, that gender is a sign system. Attebery does not read SF for its representations of gender alone, but argues that 'gender is not merely a theme in SF ... it is an integral part of the genre's intellectual and aesthetic structure' (10). His approach is consistent with the Suvinian emphasis on political engagement and reflects also the postmodern interest in semiotics that is rooted in a conviction that 'if we change the signs, the world might follow' (15). Thus, SF not only reflects and comments on our gender arrangements, but might also be a tool for revising them.

Other recent feminist scholarship has challenged the idea that SF was almost exclusively a male endeavour until the explosion of feminist SF in the 1970s. Lisa Yaszek's *Galactic Suburbia* (2008) has been crucial to establishing the presence of women writers in earlier decades and to analyzing their distinctive contributions as to the field. Yaszek points out that the earliest and most wide-ranging changes produced by technoculture occurred in the domestic, 'feminine' space of the home in the new daily routines inaugurated by 'modern plumbing, gas, electricity, and prefabricated household goods' (9). Yaszek convincingly demonstrates through a close reading of 1950s texts by female authors that such works explored themes similar to those found in contemporary SF written by men – critiques of consumerism, anxiety about nuclear war, depiction of the rising military-industrial complex – but informed by women's unique perspective as those excluded from the power structures of the time. Helen Merrick's *The Secret Feminist Cabal* (2009) also recovers a lost history of women's contributions to SF, expanding her framework to include editors and fans as well as authors. Merrick connects her analysis of feminist themes in SF to feminist critiques of science itself in the work of science studies scholars. Taken together, Yaszek's and Merrick's work prompts us to reconsider the genre by regarding women's contributions as central to its development rather than as footnotes to a predominantly male enterprise.

Similarly, Hollinger, Wendy Gay Pearson and Joan Gordon's collection *Queer Universes* (2008) demonstrates that questions of sexuality beyond gender have always been fundamental to the genre, despite its overt prudishness about such matters through most of its history. In 'Alien Cryptographies' (1999) a Pioneer award-winning essay reprinted in this collection, Pearson productively reads John W. Campbell's celebrated 'Who Goes There?' (1938) to reveal the homophobic anxiety so central to its definition of the human. Similarly in 'Something Like a Fiction', Hollinger reads C. L. Moore's 'No Woman Born' (1944) as a story infused by assumptions about gender and sexuality through its representation of the mechanical Deirdre as not a 'real' woman because she 'is no longer a sexually available body' (147). This ground-breaking collection lays bare the degree to which SF has repeatedly reproduced heteronormativity as it produces the figure of the human.

Douglas DeWitt Kilgore looks back at the genre from the point of view of race, coining the term 'astrofuturism' to denote the ways that a historically nuanced understanding of the dreams of space travel encapsulated in SF is integrally related to fantasies of transcending the limitations of human cultures, including racial difference. In Kilgore's analysis, much SF can be defined by an 'astro' attitude toward the future. This kind of SF is 'self-consciously didactic literature unapologetically aiming to produce readers who understand the mechanics of science and technology, are able to defend their rationale, and take pleasure in their dramatization in particular exotic regions' (2). Although such hard SF is often thought to be the opposite of politically engaged SF, Kilgore reveals that dreams of space exploration can also be fuelled by dissatisfaction with the status quo and an investment in the new societies made possible by technoscientific achievements. While at its most conservative astrofuturism can be 'an eternal extension of contemporary political and economic arrangements, albeit stripped of unpleasant resonances and rendered innocent', it has also the potential to narrate 'space frontiers predicated on experimental arrangements and the production of relationships uncommon or unknown in the old world' (4).

Kilgore's work is what we might call a cultural materialist study of the genre: alongside the fiction, he reads the work of science popularizers, advocates of spaceflight and radio interviews and television appearances of people such as Wernher von Braun, Carl Sagan and Gerard K. O'Neill. Here SF becomes one among many discourses making science visible to the public and shaping popular attitudes toward research agendas, and we begin to see a new way of conceptualizing the genre that emphasizes the convergence of SF visions and everyday life and thus understands SF as a response to an increasingly technoscientific world. Just as Attebery posited gender codes as integral to the genre's structure, Kilgore calls attention to racial codes as 'a wellspring' of the astrofuturist agenda, noting that 'while the technophilic, masculine, and white space future hero anchors astrofuturism's representations of the good or perfectible society, authors commonly appeal to a space frontier that is pioneered "for all mankind" and populated by a racially and ethnically diverse constituency of both sexes' (10). Thus, race, whether as threat or promise, must be considered central rather than peripheral to SF. Kilgore's title, of course, also echoes the discourse of afrofuturism, a contemporary aesthetic mode combining elements of SF with those drawn from magic realism to articulate a different future, one that is specifically the product of non-Western, non-white cultures. Until relatively recently the term has been most strongly associated with music, emerging from Sun-Ra's space-themed work such as the albums *We Travel the Spaceways* (recorded 1956–60; released 1967) and *The Futuristic Sounds of Sun Ra* (1961), and the film *Space is the Place* (1974), and taken up further by George Clinton in the bands Parliament and Funkadelic and in his Starchild persona in the album *Mothership Connection* (1975). Such cultural productions deconstruct a logic, also interrogated by Kilgore, in which black people and space seem incongruous, and offer new visions of how non-white cultures have their own technological traditions.

Afrofuturism came to critical attention outside the field of SF, predominantly in the collection *Technicolour* (2001), one of whose editors, Alondra Nelson, also edited a special issue of the journal *Social Text* on the topic in 2002. In 'Hidden Circuits', the collection's introduction, editors Alicia Headlam Hines, Nelson and Thuy Linh N. Tu question both pronouncements of a colour-blind future and jeremiads which envision non-white people as only and inevitably the victims of technology. Their project is threefold: to query the digital divide and its implications for race and technology, to broaden the definition of technology so that it moves beyond computers to include other technologies of everyday life and to highlight the work of non-white artists using technology as both method and theme. SF criticism has only recently begun to pay sufficient attention to matters of race and look at its own history from a similar point of view. Sheree R. Thomas's collections *Dark Matter* (2000) and *Dark Matter: Reading the Bones* (2005) drew critical attention to a long and mainly neglected tradition of African American speculative fiction. *Science Fiction Studies* published its own special issue on afrofuturism in 2007, edited by Mark Bould and Rone Shavers, which provided readings within postcolonial and critical race theory frameworks. Two recent anthologies have further drawn attention to postcolonial themes and alternative perspectives in the genre, *So Long Been Dreaming* (2004), a collection of postcolonial SF and fantasy in English edited by Nalo Hopkinson and Uppinder Mehan, and *Cosmos Latinos* (2003), edited by Andrea R. Bell and Yolanda Molina-Gavilan, which provides English translations of a number of Spanish and Latin American SF works.

The distinctive Latin American perspective on colonialism and technology, topics crucial to SF's history, has been taken up in recent scholarship. Both M. Elizabeth Ginway's *Brazilian Science Fiction* (2004) and Rachel Haywood

Ferreira's *The Emergence of Latin American Science Fiction* (2011) offer detailed readings of SF works not widely known in Anglo SF criticism, and through this work help us to understand the genre's role in various kinds of nation building. Although this work on postcolonial and world SF is only in its very early stages, it promises to be an important part of genre criticism into the twenty-first century as more translations and other pioneering studies make such traditions available for analysis within Anglo SF scholarship. One of the most influential critical works recently published is John Rieder's *Colonialism and the Emergence of Science Fiction* (2008), which argues that

> many of the repetitive motifs that coalesced into the genre of SF represent
> ideological ways of grasping the social consequences of colonialism,
> including the fantastic appropriation and rationalization of unevenly
> distributed colonial wealth in the homeland and in the colonies, the racist
> ideologies that enabled colonialist exploitation, and the cognitive impact
> of radical cultural differences on the home culture. (20–1)

Early SF, Rieder suggests, cannot be understood without reference to the colonial adventure fiction that preceded it and acknowledgement of the degree to which some of its assumptions were translated, unreconstructed, into SF scenarios. Through a close reading of a number of pulp magazine stories, scientific romances and disaster narratives, Rieder demonstrates that such work 'articulates the structures of knowledge and power provided by colonialism' (97).

If the heritage of Suvin and a more widely cast net of SF politics is one of the main influences on the contemporary critical landscape, the other is the ongoing synthesis of critical theory and SF first embodied in the postmodern work of Haraway and Baudrillard. Indeed, a phrase from 'A Manifesto for Cyborgs' – 'the boundary between science fiction and social reality is an optical illusion' (149) – might be taken as a key to the contemporary critical landscape. In that crucial essay, Haraway provocatively sketches out topics that continue to shape recent work: theorising the posthuman by interrogating the intersections among humans, animals and machines; thinking about shifts in subjectivity and governance concomitant with a changed technological mode of production; rewriting myths of origin and teleology to refuse purity, wholeness and innocence; taking responsibility for our acts of world making, while simultaneously recognizing them as partial and fragmented; and taking seriously science as a discourse that might be used as a tool of revolution.

New critical perspectives now central to scholarship in the humanities and social sciences – posthumanism, animal studies, science studies, biopolitics – reveal ongoing affinities between SF and critical theory. Their interest in examining the boundaries of the human, our relationships with figures of alterity, our modes of social and political organisation and the limits of our knowledge of the physical world are all recognizable motifs of SF. These critical paradigms are embraced both by scholars working within a tradition of SF scholarship and increasingly by those for whom SF occupies no special place, either celebratory or segregated. Posthumanism is undoubtedly the most significant of these perspectives and one of its most important contemporary critics is N. Katherine Hayles. She reads SF through information and second-order systems theories to understand the centrality of cybernetics to our current understanding of subjectivity. *How We Became Posthuman* (1999) is an extended critique of contemporary fantasies of artificial intelligence and transcendence of embodiment found in the work of futurists such as Hans Moravec and Ray Kurzweill, who imagine the fusion of humans and machines. Returning to Claude Shannon's information theory, Hayles cogently critiques the technophilia that informs such fantasies of disembodiment, demonstrates how information relies on material instantiation to be meaningful, and offers a vision of another kind of posthumanism – rooted in post-structuralist theory, AI research, and cognitive science – that rethinks the human from the point of view of fragmented, distributed processes interacting to produce complex, emergent phenomena such as consciousness. The 'post' to posthuman, then, is a 'post' to the limitations of a liberal humanist conception of self, a model best superseded given its heritage of gender, race and class exclusion.

Hayles predominantly uses SF examples in *How We Became Posthuman*, but ultimately it is a work of posthumanist theory rather than work of literary criticism. One of her contentions is that the fiction itself is a kind of theorization and intervention into constructions of hegemony. SF, she contends, often has the effect of 'shifting the emphasis from technological determinism to competing, contingent, embodied narratives about the scientific developments' and she suggests that critical work such as hers 'is one way to liberate the resources of narrative so that they work against the grain of abstraction running through the teleology of disembodiment' (22). In *My Mother was a Computer* (2005), Hayles builds on this work and her interest in electronic literature to theorize changes in our reading practices pertaining to the distinction between language and code that are pushed by SF texts that explore AI themes. Arguing that we have moved beyond a paradigm of disembodied information/embodied human lifeworlds, Hayles suggests that we now inhabit a Computational Universe, a model that simultaneously 'enables deeper insight and new intuitions into certain aspects of reality' and 'obscures other aspects of reality, including constructions of subjectivity that have traditionally found expression in the humanities and social sciences' (3). Texts, she suggests, are evolving and changing alongside humans in a reciprocal and mutually constitutive relationship, and she considers speech and writing as the first prosthetic technologies that changed our relationship to nature and moved us into the realm of technoculture.

More recent work on posthumanism has shifted the focus away from defining the human in opposition to the intelligent machine and has looked simultaneously at the boundaries among humans, machines and animals. Cary Wolfe's *What is Posthumanism?* (2009) argues that we must go beyond the figure of the posthuman body and embrace posthuman thought. Using second-order systems theory, which understands cybernetic feedback in conjunction with chaos theory so that each closed system is simultaneously open through its interactions with multiple and overlapping systems, Wolfe argues that we need a mode of thought that can encompass both patterns of meaning and processes that can never be reduced to codes. Wolfe argues, we need to recognize that 'the human is, at its core and in its very constitution, radically ahuman and constitutively prosthetic' (xxvi). Wolfe's posthumanism does not frequently draw on SF examples; it understands the posthuman as something that is simultaneously before and after the human, both a return to being before the artificial constraints of the category 'human', and simultaneously something new that repudiates the boundedness of the 'human'.

Dominic Pettman theorizes this 'new' posthumanism through what he calls the cybernetic triangle in *Human Error* (2011), 'the unholy trinity of human, animal, and machine, including the various ways in which they have been figured, and reconfigured, conceptually over time: sometimes spliced together, other times branching off into different directions' (5). Written against the discourse of human exceptionalism, Pettman's work reads like an example of SF criticism, although he mentions SF texts only in passing and concentrates on the human/animal boundary. His work questions whether 'the much-celebrated human capacity for compassion [is] a genuine empathy with other (nonhuman) beings, or ... merely *use[s]* these others as a screen on which to project reassuringly narcissistic images of our own finer sensibilities and sensitivities?' (60), a framework that might usefully be deployed to read SF depictions of the alien. Pettman's work is also informed by the recent rethinking of agency in object-oriented ontology, by theorists such as Bernard Stigler, which conceives humanity through 'toolness' in ways that suggests promising connections with SF's capacity to estrange our relationship to particular modes of technological being. 'To be German or Han Chinese or Iroquois', Pettman writes, 'means to be ontologically oriented by the tertiary retentions enabled by tools, techniques, and technologies that weave a particular world and a particular relationship to time and space' (152). He concludes with the very science fictional observation that '[t]he human certainly "exists". But it does not belong (exclusively) to humanity' (196).

In contemporary works of cultural studies such as Pettman's, we see how the preoccupations of recent critical theory converge with territory long of interest to scholars of SF. The process of charting these connections is only just beginning, but this pioneering critical theory suggests new avenues for future SF scholarship. *Science Fiction Studies* published a special issue on Animals and Science Fiction in 2008 that drew on the field of animal studies, and my book *Animal Alterity* (2010) provides an overview of the various ways that animals have been conceptualized in the genre using the insights of animal studies theory. Further work remains to be done in thinking through productive sites of intersection among posthumanist philosophy, theorizations of technics and SF.

The field of science studies is another area where more critical work is needed, building on the important cultural histories of science and technology by Roger Luckhurst. His *The Invention of Telepathy* (2002) positions this phenomenon at the moment of transformation between the gentleman-scholar science of the nineteenth and earlier centuries and the corporate-institutional science of the twentieth century and beyond. Tracing telepathy's path from science to spiritualism, Luckhurst offers a view of SF as one participant in a complex nexus of intellectual exchanges. Similarly, his *The Trauma Question* (2008) links the SF imagination with other paradigms for explaining the shock of rapid social and technological change. *Science Fiction Studies* special issue on Technoculture and Science Fiction (2006), edited by Luckhurst, introduced the work of science studies scholars such as Bruno Latour, Friedrich Kittler and Manuel Castells to SF scholarship, tracing a number of ways that cultural studies of science share insights and critiques with the study of SF.

Castells's work on the social implications of the digital age and its political and economic exclusions has since been taken up in recent scholarship on cyberpunk and singularity fiction, but more work remains to be done on establishing other productive connections between the fields. For example, Karen Barad's *Meeting the Universe Halfway* (2007) uses quantum theory to challenge the distinctions among ontology, epistemology and ethics. Drawing on a detailed understanding of particle physics, Barad argues that we should theorize the world not from the point of view of objects but from that of phenomena, which are continually produced through intra-actions and have no inherent boundaries or properties. In her understanding, 'reality is therefore not a fixed essence. *Reality is an ongoing dynamic of intra activity*' (206); technoscientific practices – which implicate the observer in the observed, and distribute agency across all components – are 'about making different worldly entanglements[;] and ethics is about accounting for our part of the entangled webs we weave' (384). This is science studies theory that reads like SF, just as the work of Baudrillard and Haraway was a kind of SF semiotics for its cultural moment.

Barad offers another kind of new posthumanism which argues that we must think about 'socialnatural practices in a performative rather than representationalist mode' (88) and offers a theory of what she calls 'agential realism', in which we recognize that our practices of knowing and representing the world are also, materially, practices of making it at the quantum level. Thus, she concludes, intellectual activity needs to move beyond representing the world and embrace changing it by 'taking responsibility for the fact that our practices matter; the world is materialized different through different practices' (89). Barad's work has much in common with Deleuze and Guattari's metaphysics of 'becoming' (on ongoing process of never-stable ontology rather than the fixed existence they associated with 'being'), but she reaches her conclusions through a framework of quantum theory, making it of particular interest to scholars of SF. Such work, and that of feminist and anti-racist scholars of science such as Sandra Harding and Kavita Phillips, points to productive ways that ongoing interest in hard SF might be theorized through frameworks that embrace rather than deny the entwinement of science and the political world of social power.

The human is also being rethought in recent biopolitical theory, which builds on Foucault's biopower to theorize contemporary governance as that of bodies and populations. In his most recent work, Foucault analyzed a shift from sovereign power expressed in the right to 'make die' or 'let live' toward a power of security expressed through the right to 'make live' or 'let die'. There are many affinities between biopolitical theory and the visions embodied in SF and they are only beginning to be explored in recent scholarship. Our contemporary moment is infused with apocalyptic sensibilities and experiences: global warming, a mass extinction event, the looming peak-oil crisis, recent pandemic outbreaks of zoonoses, a tipping point of environmental damage, frequent 'natural' catastrophes that are symptoms of the damage we have done to the Earth and more. Biopolitical theory offers one way to think about how popular culture, including SF, reflects, articulates and interrogates these anxieties and realities.

Two recent works examine SF's contributions to understanding this present moment. Evan Calder Williams's *Combined and Uneven Apocalypse* (2010) offers a practice he calls salvagepunk as a way of responding to ongoing crisis. Williams differentiates this practice from both cyberpunk – which he suggests 'wrote the fantasies of a post-state corporate global order ... with a canny awareness of the gap between the illusions of free-market ideology and the real need for states to act as support systems for corporate extension into recolonised spaces, material or virtual' (17) – and steampunk – which he dismisses as a 'romanticised do-over, a setting of the clock back to a time of craftsmanship and real (fetishised) objects' (19). In contrast, salvagepunk is 'the post-apocalyptic vision of a broken and dead world, strewn with both the dream residues and real junk of the world that was, and shot through with the hard work of salvaging, repurposing, détourning, and scrapping'

(1920). Drawing on examples from the *Mad Max* franchise (1979–85) to the reinvention of zombies, Evan Calder Williams suggests SF can help us to see that 'the world is already apocalyptic. Just not all at the same time' (149). Peter Paik's *From Utopia to Apocalypse* (2010) similarly strives to convey how apocalyptic images in SF help us understand political problems. In readings of Alan Moore's *Watchmen* (1986–7) and *V for Vendetta* (1982–5), and the films *Nausicaa of the Valley of the Wind* (1984) and *Save the Green Planet* (2003), Paik reveals how the Utopian energy of SF has been invested in explorations of apocalypse and renewal, prompting us toward 'profound and probing insights into the principal dilemmas of political life' (1).

As this recent work demonstrates, SF is perhaps uniquely positioned to help us understand contemporary reality. Increasingly the boundary between scholarly work addressed to a field of SF studies, and scholarly work whose critical methods and intellectual questions are simply inherently science fictional, is becoming diffuse. Concurrently, the boundaries of the genre also appear to be in flux, and much recent scholarship has focused on this matter of taxonomy. John Rieder's Pioneer Award-winning essay, 'On Defining SF, or Not' (2010), provides a solid overview of competing definitions and interrogates what is at stake in these struggles to define and delimit the genre. New critical terms that have recently sprung up to describe the hybrid qualities of some fiction – interstitial, the New Weird, mythic – speak also to this sense that genre fiction is transforming, blurring the boundaries of what had until recently been perceived as distinct genres. This change encompasses both the distinctions among the speculative genres of SF, fantasy and horror, and the boundary between SF and so-called mainstream literature. In *Evaporating Genres* (2011), Gary Wolfe suggests that the pulp period, with its firm marketing divisions, was an aberration and that the speculative texts now emerging as hybrid more accurately reflect the genres' potential. Wolfe uses the term 'evaporation' to capture the dynamic through which these genres are not 'disappearing altogether' but instead are 'growing more diffuse, leaching out into the air around [them], imparting a strange smell to the literary atmosphere' (3).

The most ambitious work of recent taxonomy is Istvan Csicsery-Ronay Jr's *The Seven Beauties of Science Fiction* (2008). It seeks to understand the specific way SF techniques and tropes grasp the world through identifying seven distinct features of the genre: fictive neology, fictive novum, future history, imaginary science, SF sublime, SF grotesque and the technologiade. Csicsery-Ronay Jr frames his project by noting the contemporary 'widespread normalization of what is essentially a style of estrangement and dislocation' which has 'stimulated the development of science-fictional habits of mind, so that we no longer treat SF as purely a genre-engine producing formulaic effects, but rather as a kind of awareness we might call *science-fictionality*' (2).

Csicsery-Ronay Jr's deep and wide knowledge of the field enables him to chart the connections between the science-fictionality of the current landscape and the genre's long history of theorizing, testing, revising and reproducing certain tropes and themes. He organizes his analyses around two gaps explored by SF texts: between imaginative ideals of 'technoscientific transformation of the world' and possibilities for realizing such transformations, that is, issues of plausibility; and between 'belief in the immanent possibility (perhaps even the inexorability) of those transformations' and reflection on their consequences, that is, issues of ethics (4). He concludes that, just as the bourgeois novel encapsulated the contradictions and preoccupations of the nineteenth-century cultures from which it emerged, so has SF become 'a central mediating literary institution for this imaginary empire of technoscience' (245) which dominated the twentieth century.

SF scholarship at the dawn of the twenty-first century is a vibrant and fertile field of enquiry. Many of its themes and images embody concepts at the intellectual centre of contemporary scholarship, and it is a mode well positioned to help us work through the challenges of a postmodern world of ubiquitous simulation in cultures thoroughly saturated by technoculture. Although historically criticism in the field has focused almost exclusively on Anglo-American and print texts, recent histories of the genre have stressed its many media (film, television, radio, comic books) and traditions beyond those of the US and the UK. Work that explores SF's relationship to new theories of posthumanism emerging from animal studies and second-order systems theory, to biopolitics and to science studies is only in its early stages, and the coming decades promise a flourishing field of enquiry as SF scholarship continues to, in Haraway's words, help us discover 'a way out of the maze of dualisms in which we have explained our bodies and our tools to ourselves' (181).

Works Cited

Attebery, Brian (2002). *Decoding Gender in Science Fiction*. New York: Routledge.

Barad, Karen (2007). *Meeting the Universe Halfway: Quantum Physics and the Entanglement of Matter and Meaning*. Durham: Duke University Press.

Baudrillard, Jean (1991). 'Simulacra and Science Fiction'. Trans. Arthur B. Evans. *Science Fiction Studies*. 18. 309–13.

Bell, Andrea R. and Yolanda Molina-Gavilan (eds) (2003). *Cosmos Latinos*. Middletown, CT: Wesleyan University Press.

Bould, Mark and Rone Shavers (eds) (2007). 'Afrofuturism Special Issue'. *Science Fiction Studies*. 34. 2.

Campbell, John W. (1938). 'Who Goes There?' *Astounding Science-Fiction*. 21. 6 (August). 60–98.

Clinton, George (1975). *Mothership Connection*. Los Angeles: Casablanca Records.

Coney, John (dir.) (1974). *Space is the Place*. USA: North American Star System.

Csicsery-Ronay, Jr, Istvan (1991). 'The SF of Theory: Baudrillard and Haraway'. *Science Fiction Studies* 18: 387–403.

—(2008). *The Seven Beauties of Science Fiction*. Middleton: Wesleyan University Press.

Delany, Samuel R. (1999). *Shorter Views: Queer Thoughts & the Politics of the Paraliterary*. Hanover: Wesleyan University Press.

Ferreira, Rachel Haywood (2011). *The Emergence of Latin American Science Fiction*. Hanover: Wesleyan University Press.

Freedman, Carl (2000). *Critical Theory and Science Fiction*. Middleton: Wesleyan University Press.

Ginway, M. Elizabeth (2004). *Brazilian Science Fiction: Cultural Myths and Nationhood in the Land of the Future*. Cranbury, NJ: Rosemont.

Haraway, Donna (1991). 'A Cyborg Manifesto: Science Technology, and Socialist-Feminism in the Late Twentieth Century'. *Simians, Cyborgs and Women: The Reinvention of Nature*. New York: Routledge. 149–81.

Harding, Sandra (1986). *The Science Question in Feminism*. Ithaca, NY: Cornell University Press.

—(1998). *Is Science Multicultural: Postcolonialisms, Feminisms and Epistemologies*. Bloomington, IN: Indiana University Press.

Hayles, N. Katherine (1999). *How We Became Posthuman: Virtual Bodies in Cybernetics, Literature, and Informatics*. Chicago: University of Chicago Press.

—(2005). *My Mother was a Computer: Digital Subjects and Literary Texts*. Chicago: University of Chicago Press.

Hines, Alicia Headlam, Alondra Nelson and Thuy Linh N. Tu (eds) (2002). 'Hidden Circuits'. *Social Text* special issue.

Hollinger, Veronica (1990). 'Feminist Science Fiction: Breaking Up the Subject'. *Extrapolation*. 31. 3. 229–39.

—(1992). 'Cybernetic Deconstructions: Cyberpunk and Postmodernism'. *Storming the Reality Studio: A Casebook of Cyberpunk and Postmodernism*. Larry McCaffery (ed.). Durham: Duke University Press. 203–18.

—(1998). 'The Vampire and the Alien: Variations on the Outsider'. *Science Fiction Studies* 16. 2. 145–60.

—(1999). 'Rereading Queerly: Science Fiction, Feminism and the Defamiliarization of Gender'. *Science Fiction Studies*. 26. 1. 23–40.

—(2008). '"Something like a fiction": Speculative Intersections of Sexuality and Technology'. *Queer Universes: Sexualities in Science Fiction*. Veronica Hollinger, Wendy Gay Pearson, and Joan Gordon (eds). Liverpool: Liverpool University Press. 140–60.

Hollinger, Veronica, Wendy Gay Pearson and Joan Gordon (eds) (2008). *Queer Universes: Sexualities in Science Fiction*. Liverpool: Liverpool University Press.

Hopkinson, Nalo and Uppinder Mehan (eds) (2004). *So Long Been Dreaming: Postcolonial Science Fiction and Fantasy*. Vancouver: Arsenal.

Jameson, Fredric (1990). *Postmodernism, or the Cultural Logic of Late Capitalism*. Durham, Duke University Press.

Jang, Joon-Hwan (dir.) (2003). *Save the Green Planet*. South Korea: Sidus Pictures.

Kilgore, Douglas De Witt (2003). *Astrofuturism: Science, Race and Visions of Utopia in Space*. Pittsburgh: University of Pennsylvania Press.

Lefanu, Sarah (1988). *In the Chinks of the World Machine*. London: The Women's Press.

Luckhurst, Roger (2002). *The Invention of Telepathy*. Oxford: Oxford University Press.

—(2008). *The Trauma Question*. London: Routledge.

Luckhurst, Roger and Partington, Gill. (eds) (2006). *Science Fiction Studies: Special issue on Technoculture and Science Fiction*. 33. 1.

McCaffery, Larry (ed.) (1991). *Storming the Reality Studio: A Casebook of Cyberpunk and Postmodernist Fiction*. Durham: Duke University Press.

Merrick, Helen (2009). *The Secret Feminist Cabal: A Secret History of Science Fiction Feminisms*. Seattle, WA: Aqueduct Press.

Merril, Judith (1968). *England Swings SF*. New York: Doubleday.

Miyazaki, Hayao (dir.) (1984). *Nausicaa of the Valley of the Wind*. Japan: Hakuhodo, Nibariki, Tokuma Shoten.

Moore, Alan. (1988) [1986–7]. *Watchmen*. New York: DC Comics.

—(1990) [1982–8]. *V for Vendetta*. New York: Vertigo.

Moore, C. L. (1977) [1944]. *No Woman Born. The Best of C.L. Moore*. C. L. Lester del Rey (ed.). New York: Taplinger Publications

Nelson, Alondra, Thuy Linh N. Tu, and Alicia Hedlam Hines (eds) (2001). *Technicolor: Race, Technology and Everyday Life*. New York: New York University Press.

Paik, Peter Y. (2010). *From Utopia to Apocalypse: Science Fiction and the Politics of Catastrophe*. Minneapolis: University of Minnesota Press.

Pearson, Wendy Gay (2008). 'Alien Cryptographies: The View from Queer'. *Queer Universes: Sexualities in Science Fiction*. Wendy Gay Pearson, Veronica Hollinger, and Joan Gordon (eds). Liverpool: Liverpool University Press. 14–38.

Pettman, Dominic (2011). *Human Error: Species-Being and Media Machines*. Minneapolis: University of Minnesota Press.

Phillips, Kavita (2003). *Civilizing Natures: Race, Resources and Modernity in Colonia South India*. Piscataway, NJ: Rutgers University Press.

Rieder, John (2008). *Colonialism and the Emergence of Science Fiction*. Middleton: Wesleyan University Press.

—(2010). 'On Defining SF, or Not'. *Science Fiction Studies*. 37. 2. 191–209.

Russ, Joanna (1983). *How to Suppress Women's Writing*. Austin, TX: University of Texas Press.

—(1995). *To Write Like a Woman: Essays in Feminism and Science Fiction*. Bloomington, IN: Indiana University Press.

Sterling, Bruce (1989). 'Slipstream'. *Science Fiction Eye*. 5. 1 (July). 77–80.

Sun-Ra. (1967). *We Travel the Spaceways*. Chicago: Saturn.

—(1961). *The Futuristic Sounds of Sun Ra*. Newark, NJ: Savoy Records.

Thomas, Sheree R. (ed.) (2000). *Dark Matter: A Century of Speculative Fiction from the African Diaspora*. New York: Warner Books

—(2005). *Dark Matter: Reading the Bones*. New York: Warner Books.

Vint, Sherryl. (2010). *Animal Alterity: Science Fiction and the Question of the Animal.* Liverpool: Liverpool University Press.

—(ed.) (2008). *Science Fiction Studies: Special issue Animals and Science Fiction.* 35. 2.

Williams, Evan Calder (2010). *Combined and Uneven Apocalypse.* Park Lane: Zero Books.

Wolfe, Cary (2009). *What is Posthumanism?* Minneapolis: University of Minnesota Press.

Wolfe, Gary K. (2011). *Evaporating Genres: Essays on Fantastic Literature.* Middletown, CT: Wesleyan University Press.

Yaszek, Lisa (2008). *Galactic Suburbia: Recovering Women's Science Fiction.* Columbus: Ohio State University Press.

Index

Page references in bold denotes principal entry on the topic